An official portrait of General Norstad as SACEUR.

Also by Robert S. Jordan

ALLIANCE STRATEGY AND NAVIES: The Evolution and Scope of NATO's Maritime Dimension

DAG HAMMARSKJÖLD REVISITED: The UN Secretary-General as a Force in World Politics (*editor*)

EUROPE AND THE SUPERPOWERS: Essays in European International Politics (*editor*)

EUROPE IN THE BALANCE: The Changing Context of European International Politics

GENERALS IN INTERNATIONAL POLITICS: NATO's Supreme Allied Commander Europe (*editor*)

INTERNATIONAL ADMINISTRATION: Its Evolution and Contemporary Applications (*editor*)

INTERNATIONAL ORGANIZATIONS: An Institutional Approach to Governance in a Global Society

MARITIME STRATEGY AND THE BALANCE OF POWER: Britain and America in the 20th Century (*co-editor*)

POLITICAL LEADERSHIP IN NATO: A Study in Multinational Diplomacy

THE NATO INTERNATIONAL STAFF/SECRETARIAT, 1952–57: A Study in International Administration

Norstad: Cold War NATO Supreme Commander
Airman, Strategist, Diplomat

Robert S. Jordan
Research Professor of International Institutions
University of New Orleans
New Orleans
Louisiana

Foreword by Robert O'Neill

Afterword by Robert E. Hunter

First published in Great Britain 2000 by
MACMILLAN PRESS LTD
Houndmills, Basingstoke, Hampshire RG21 6XS and London
Companies and representatives throughout the world

A catalogue record for this book is available from the British Library.

ISBN 0-333-49085-1

 First published in the United States of America 2000 by
ST. MARTIN'S PRESS, INC.,
Scholarly and Reference Division,
175 Fifth Avenue, New York, N.Y. 10010

ISBN 0-312-22670-5

Library of Congress Cataloging-in-Publication Data
Jordan, Robert S., 1929–
Norstad : Cold War NATO supreme commander : airman, strategist, diplomat / Robert S. Jordan.
p. cm.
Includes bibliographical references and index.
ISBN 0-312-22670-5 (cloth)
1. Norstad, Lauris, 1907–1988.   2.United States. Air Force-
–Generals Biography.   3. North Atlantic Treaty Organization
Biography.   I. Title.
UG626.2.N67J67   1999
355'.031'091821092—dc21
[B]   99-37877
                                                                      CIP

© Robert S. Jordan 2000
Foreword © Robert O'Neill 2000
Afterword © Robert E. Hunter 2000

All rights reserved. No reproduction, copy or transmission of this publication may be made without written permission.

No paragraph of this publication may be reproduced, copied or transmitted save with written permission or in accordance with the provisions of the Copyright, Designs and Patents Act 1988, or under the terms of any licence permitting limited copying issued by the Copyright Licensing Agency, 90 Tottenham Court Road, London W1P 0LP.

Any person who does any unauthorized act in relation to this publication may be liable to criminal prosecution and civil claims for damages.

The author has asserted his right to be identified as the author of this work in accordance with the Copyright, Designs and Patents Act 1988.

This book is printed on paper suitable for recycling and made from fully managed and sustained forest sources.

10 9   8   7   6   5   4   3   2   1
09 08 07 06 05 04 03 02 01 00

Printed and bound in Great Britain by
Antony Rowe Ltd, Chippenham, Wiltshire

Dedicated to the memories of

Dr Norman H. Gibbs
Chichele Professor of the History of War
All Souls College, Oxford University

A Gifted Teacher and Scholar

and

Evan Luard
Member of Parliament (Labour)
and Supernumerary Fellow
St Antony's College, Oxford University

A Scholar and Practitioner of Multilateral Diplomacy

Contents

Frontispiece: General Lauris Norstad, Supreme Allied Commander, Europe

List of Charts   ix

List of Plates   x

Foreword: Dr. Robert O'Neill, Chichele Professor of the History of War, All Souls College, Oxford University   xi

Acknowledgments   xv

List of Abbreviations   xviii

PART I   ON BECOMING SACEUR

1 The End and the Beginning   3
    I. The End of a Career   3
    II. Laying the Foundation   13

2 Applying Planning and Operational Skills in North Africa and the Pacific   21
    I. His First Great Opportunity   21
    II. The North African Experience   27
    III. The Twentieth Air Force and Washington   38

3 The Battles for Unification and for Berlin   45
    I. Separating the Army Air Force from the Army   45
    II. Unifying the Armed Forces   50
    III. Berlin: A Testing Ground for the West   66

4 Norstad and the "Grand Strategy" for the Cold War   73
    I. Contingency planning for Europe   73
    II. NATO and the Eisenhower Administration's "New Look"   84
    III. Norstad Becomes SACEUR   96

PART II   ON BEING SACEUR

5 Nuclear Weapons for Europe's Defense: Norstad and the Eisenhower Administration   103
    I. The Introduction of Atomic Warheads into NATO   103

	II. Norstad's Attempt to Make NATO a "Fourth Nuclear Power"	110
	III. France, De Gaulle, and Norstad	118
6	**The 1958–59 Crisis Over Berlin: Putting the Consultative Machinery in Place**	**133**
	I. Origins of the Crisis and the Initial Response	133
	II. Norstad's Attempts at Coordinated Planning	141
7	**The Berlin Crisis Intensifies**	**148**
	I. Berlin Contingency Planning and Execution	148
	II. Issues of Command and Control	155
8	**The 1961–62 Berlin Crisis: The Unraveling of a Relationship**	**167**
	I. A Change in Presidents and a Change in Policy and Strategy	167
	II. The Erection of the Wall Provides New "Opportunities"	172
	III. Organizational and Policy Responses to the Wall	181
9	**The End Nears**	**194**
	I. The Strains Persist and Intensify	194
	II. Relationships Improve in Spite of Provocation	203
	III. A New Doctrine for NATO	208
	Conclusions	**213**
	I. Norstad as a Man of His Generation	213
	II. Norstad's Leadership	216
	Appendix: A New Career as Corporate Executive	**224**
	Afterword: Some Thoughts on NATO's Future Leadership Challenges: former US Ambassador to NATO, Robert E. Hunter	228
	Notes	239
	Source Material	292
	Index	309

List of Charts

2.1	Twelfth Air Force Command Structure, October 1942	29
2.2	TORCH Central Task Force Landing in Oran, November, 1942	30
2.3	Northwest African Air Forces (NAAF), March 1943	34
2.4	Mediterranean Allied Air Forces (MAAF), January–June 1944	37
3.1	Organization of the Army Air Forces (AAF), Post WWII (as of March 21, 1946)	46
3.2	US Armed Forces, 1947	62
3.3	The Air Staff, Headquarters, USAF, October 1947	64
3.4	US Armed Forces, 1949	66
4.1	Norstad as CINCUSAFE and CINCAAFCE, April 1951	82
4.2	Norstad as Air Deputy, July 1953	90
6.1	USCINCEUR Chain of Command, 1959	145
7.1	LIVE OAK Structure, March 1959	150
7.2	Norstad's Three "Hats" as of March 1959 (in August 1961 the FRG joined political discussions and LIVE OAK)	160
8.1	The Berlin Wall and Crossing Points, August 1961	173
8.2	Operational Command Channels for Berlin, 1961–62 (in August 1961, the FRG joins political discussions and LIVE OAK)	178
8.3	Access Routs to Berlin, 1961–62	191
	European newspaper cartoons: public attitude	174

List of Plates

An official portrait of General Norstad as SACEUR
Dinner honoring General Norstad
A standing ovation for General Norstad
Norstad's record at the Air Corps Advanced Flying School
Norstad with General LeMay in the Pacific
Norstad at the Potsdam Conference 17 July to 2 August 1945,
  seated between General Eisenhower and General Arnold
Norstad with his mentors – General Arnold and General Marshall
Norstad at the signing of the proclamation establishing
  8 January 1947 as Air Force Day
SHAPE commanders meeting in Paris, 19 June 1952
Norstad with Isabelle and their cocker-spanial, Mugsy
Norstad with Isabelle and Marshal of the RAF, Lord Tedder, at the
  service of commemoration in honor of American World War II
  dead, 4 July 1952, at St Paul's Cathedral, London
View of the grounds of the villa St. Pierre at Marnes la Coquette,
  near Paris
Life cover photograph of Lt-General Norstad, AF Deputy Chief of Staff,
  Operations, 1 November 1948
Newsweek cover photograph of General Norstad, 17 December 1956
Kristin, Isabelle and General Norstad at a garden party, villa St. Pierre,
  10 July 1957
General Norstad with Secretary of Defense McNamara, accompanied
  by Assistant Secretary of Defense for International Security Affairs,
  Paul H. Nitze and JCS chairman General Lyman L. Lemnitzer,
  23 July 1961
General Norstad with former President Eisenhower
General Norstad being awarded the French Grand Cross of the
  Legion of Honor by President Charles de Gaulle, 20 December 1962
Invitation issued by the Registrar of Oxford University to award
  General Norstad a doctorate of civil law, *Honoris Causa*, 26 June
  1963
General Norstad on becoming an executive with Owens-Corning
  Fiberglas Corporation

Foreword

This study of Lauris Norstad, his professional development and his effectiveness in senior command appointments, is particularly timely. There is a natural tendency on the part of many of us who are concerned professionally with defence issues to see the Cold War as a bygone era. We hope this is true. It is, with regard to the monolithic power that resided in the Warsaw Pact and the massive conventional force superiority which that structure enjoyed over the forces of the North Atlantic Alliance. It is almost certainly not true if we take the optimistic view to apply to major interstate conflict as a whole and the need to maintain complex alliances linking democratic states. Such coalitions remain essential for the maintenance of respect for the rule of law in the international community. General Norstad's life is full of rich experiences from which we can learn much relating to the maintenance of peace and security in the post-Cold War world.

The military profession is demanding and requires from those who wish to follow it a long apprenticeship. Dedication is needed to weather the periods when an individual's personal star does not seem to be rising, or when he or she is put into an apparently frustrating job, at the disposal of superiors whose competence is open to question. In the decade before World War II Norstad showed that he had the qualities necessary to survive a proving period of junior leadership, when financial circumstances were extraordinarily straitened, both for the armed services as a whole and for their members personally. He faced danger as an aviator in the primitive aircraft of those times, flown in accordance with safety procedures that would never be countenanced today. After but a few years of service he was no stranger to the deaths of those close to him. He faced many other tests of professional competence and leadership. There was no doubt in the minds of those who knew Norstad at the outbreak of World War II as to his fitness for major command and staff appointments. And he had the confidence and cutting edge which followed naturally from this period of learning his profession.

From 1941 onwards Norstad's career developed rapidly, both in response to the tremendous need for military professionals which was felt in the United States after Pearl Harbor and as a result of his proficiency as a planner, analyser and implementer of policy. He saw the long period of weakness which resulted from the very low base from which the United States armed forces had to build their strength. He knew, and shared, the attendant personal risks which came from operating against more experienced and better equipped enemies in the Mediterranean and the Pacific during that period of weakness. He saw how easy it was to throw the valuable lives of men away in operations which did little to crimp the strategic power of the enemy, and he became sharply focused on the need for rigorous assessment of effectiveness and hence operational priorities. As an airman he felt at the leading edge of a new way of conducting war – strategic bombardment – and worked hard to free strategic air power in the United States from Army control. This struggle for independence left him with a clear concept of strategic warfare and weaponry which suited him well to continue his rise in the coming atomic era.

He also learned in Operation TORCH of the baffling complexities of inter-Allied relationships, particularly when one of those Allies, France, was internally torn, weak, yet proud, wanting to play a leading role yet unable to do it convincingly. As his experience of the war widened, he came to see more of the problems of coalition leadership through working more closely with the British. In the light of Eisenhower's excellent example of security in personality and leadership, Norstad could see that the challenges facing the commander of an alliance of parliamentary democracies were formidable and exciting. He also acknowledged that these challenges could not be met without patience and tolerance. He had the luck to be in a good place for his talents to be noticed, not least by Eisenhower, and from the mid part of World War II onwards his career followed a favoured trajectory, positioning him splendidly to take positions of high responsibility in the late 1940s.

As East–West tensions built up during the Berlin Blockade and the first year of the Korean War, Norstad was in no doubt as to how to respond. He had helped to shape President Truman's policy on containment, and he understood the weaknesses of the Soviet Union in terms of withstanding strategic attack. Norstad was a strong believer in the use of nuclear weapons, not only for deterrence but more particularly for war-fighting purposes. Unlike others in his service Norstad did not allow this belief to lead him into unrestrained public advocacy of nuclear warfare. He had a multi-dimensional approach to the problems of achieving security, and he could see that the political objections to the early use of nuclear weapons in conflict were formidable. He placed his effectiveness as an alliance leader above his faith in this one approach to the conduct of war and helped to develop an enduring structure of defence – one whose sound political foundations enabled it to outlast its rival, the Warsaw Pact.

Norstad endured the four years of intense frustration which attended the efforts of those who attempted to found the European Defence Community. From our current perspective this failure is not to be taken so seriously: NATO has been a better structure than the EDC would have been; and we are no longer surprised that the Europeans are unable to agree on anything which appears to diminish their national sovereignty. But for Alliance leaders in the early 1950s this was a profoundly depressing episode in which the West seemed to have failed an important test. This perspective was relieved by the wisdom and determination of Chancellor Konrad Adenauer in bringing the Federal Republic of Germany solidly into a defensive partnership with the West in NATO. It was only natural that Norstad's respect for the Germans as allies should have increased rapidly during the early and mid 1950s, giving him an unusual capacity to interpret their desires and policies and to work smoothly with them, without provoking many of the problems which seemed to erupt when anything touched French sensitivities.

Norstad was thus extremely well equipped by his military and political understanding of the Atlantic Alliance to weather the long crisis which attended Nikita Khrushchev's attempts to change the status of Berlin between 1958 and 1961. None the less Norstad found it taxing, and despite his cultivation of his side of the political military relationship, it was a period of trial from which he was glad to escape. But the lesson of this culminating phase of his professional life is clear: Alliance leadership demands a very deep understanding of the constituent governments, their policies, their basic motivation, and their political strength. Norstad had the necessary intelligence and personal skills in relating to people to enable him to keep the Alliance working together. Other military leaders in similar situations – Douglas MacArthur comes most immediately to mind – have proved severely inadequate. Norstad's intrinsic political strengths had to be nurtured by long experience and many crises before the consummate alliance leader was created. His life serves as a very apposite series of case studies in the political and military aspects of alliance leadership through a long period of tension, from which we can learn much today.

I warmly commend to readers Robert Jordan's analysis of General Norstad's career, whether they are studying it to learn more about the historical record or to gain deeper insights into the nature of military leadership at the highest levels. This is a fine work, produced on the basis of careful research of an extensive resource base, over many years. Its insights are the richer for Dr Jordan's earlier work on leadership at the political and military levels. This book will, I am sure be a catalyst for further studies in alliance leadership, and will help to keep our minds focused on the great complexities which face all who have to work in, comprehend, or teach in this field.

ROBERT O'NEILL
Chichele Professor of the History of War
All Souls College, Oxford

Acknowledgments

This study would not have been possible without the support and personal encouragement of many persons and institutions, stretching over a period of nearly ten years. Not the least of these persons was General Norstad himself. During his final years he persisted in encouraging me to undertake this study and provided me with free and complete access to his papers and other more personal sources. His wife Isabelle and daughter Kristin were equally supportive.

The list of other persons is a long one, but even at the risk of offending some who may feel entitled to be included, I feel constrained to mention only a few key persons without whose support the book would have been an impossible task. The first to come to mind is Martin Teasley, the Assistant Director of the Eisenhower Library, where the Norstad Papers were deposited and put in proper archival order. David Haight of the staff of the Library assumed most of the burden for accomplishing this all-important task, and was attentive to my every research need during my stays at the Library. In this connection, I am grateful for research travel grants provided by the Eisenhower World Affairs Institute and the Graduate School of the University of New Orleans, that enabled me to go to Abilene, Kansas on several occasions. The Dean of the College of Liberal Arts, Dr. Philip B. Coulter, assisted me both by providing computer equipment and by encouragement.

I am also grateful to the United States Educational Commission in the United Kingdom (Fullbright Commission), for recommending me for a Visiting Professorship at the University of Lancaster, and to the Commission's Director, John Franklin, for maximizing the financial support provided to me by the Commission. The grants enabled me to draw extensively on the newspaper clipping collection of the University's Centre for the Study of Arms Control and International Security to fill in important details of General Norstad's career at NATO. I should also thank the Centre's Director, Professor Ian Bellany, for providing institutional and personal hospitality, and the Centre's secretary, Ms. Susan Parkinson, for her unfailing technical and administrative support. My graduate research assistant at both the University of New Orleans and at the University of Lancaster, Paul Sanchez-Navarro, effectively kept track of documents and clippings, as did another former University of New Orleans graduate student, Thomas

M. Sisk, when he accompanied me to the Eisenhower Library and to the Air Force Historical Research Agency. He also provided a thorough editorial assessment of the manuscript in its penultimate form, as did Marshal A Zeringue of the White Burkett Miller Centre of Public Affairs at the University of Virginia. Five other University of New Orleans graduate students contributed their time in useful ways as the work progressed over several years: Mark Armstrong, Allen Bostick, Martin Kofler (also of the University of Innsbruck), Edward J. Mikulenka III (especially in preparing the Appendix), and Mark Ziegler. Brett Rasmussen assisted me in the sorting out of General Norstad's official papers at the National Archives and at the National Security Archive, and he also designed the graphics. Robert Hatch Jordan was instrumental in enabling me to learn how to use computers in research and writing.

The Air Force Historical Research Agency, located at Maxwell Air Force Base, Alabama, generously provided me with travel funds to visit the Agency's archives on two occasions. While I was a Visiting Professor of International Relations at the Air War College, the Chairman of the Department of National Security Studies, Colonel Gary Schneider, and my former colleague, Dr. David Sorenson, encouraged me to obtain two travel grants from the Air University Foundation. Also providing encouragement, in this respect, was General John A. Shaud, USAF (Ret.) and Richard Steeves, Executive Director of the Foundation.

Donations for research expenses were provided through the efforts of Mr. Robert Knight, of the legal firm of Shearman and Sterling, New York, and of Mr. William W. Boeschenstein of Owens-Corning Fiberglas Corporation, along with the Corning Glass Works Foundation and the Houghton Foundation. Major General Richard Yudkin, USAF (Ret.), who had been associated with General Norstad in SHAPE and then later at Owens-Corning Fiberglas, took a lively interest in the project, as did Axel Holm.

Intellectual encouragement came from many sources, including Dr. Stephen Ambrose, Emeritus Boyd Professor of History, University of New Orleans; the late Lord Beloff, formerly of All Souls College, Oxford University; Professor Barton Bernstein of Stanford University; Andrew Erdmann, John M. Olin Institute, Harvard University, Dr. John B. Hattendorf, Ernest J. King Professor of Maritime History at the US Naval War College; the Hon. Martin Hillenbrand, former US Ambassador to the Federal Republic of Germany; Dr. Lawrence S. Kaplan, Emeritus University Professor of History, Kent State University;

Dr. Douglas Kinnard, Brig. Gen., USA, (Ret.), former Chief of Military History, US Army; Dr. Richard H. Kohn, former Chief of the Office of Air Force History; Dr. Thomas Langston, Associate Professor of Political Science, Tulane University; Dr. Eduard Mark, Historian, Air Force History Support Office; Dr. J. Kenneth McDonald, former Chief Historian, Central Intelligence Agency; Colonel (and Dr.) Philip S. Meilinger, USAF, former Dean of the School of Advanced Airpower Studies, Air University and currently Professor of Strategy at the US Naval War College; Dr. Daniel R. Mortensen, Historian, Office of Air Force History; Dr. Gregory Pedlow, Chief, Historical Office, Supreme Headquarters Allied Powers Europe (SHAPE); Warren Treat, Retired Senior Airforce Historian; The Hon. George Vest, US Department of State; Dr. Robert Wampler of the National Security Archive; Dr Michael Wheeler, Science Applications International Corporation; and Herman S. Wolk, Senior Historian, Air Force History Support Office. When cardiac problems threatened to derail this project, this group provided encouragement to me to continue my efforts.

My wife, Jane, was both longsuffering and supportive as the years went by, as was my editor, Keith Povey, and indexer, Tony Howard.

Responsibility for the use of all these valuable personal and material resources rests, of course, with the author. As agreed to beforehand, material obtained from personal interviews are unattributed. Instead, material, so obtained is used only if corroborated by other sources. Where applicable every effort has been made to contact copyrightholders, but if any have been inadvertently omitted the publisher will be pleased to made the necessary arrangement at the earliest opportunity.

Covington, Louisiana ROBERT S. JORDAN
September 1999

List of Abbreviations

AAF	Army Air Forces (US)
AAFCE	Allied Air Forces, Central Europe (NATO)
ACC	Allied Control Council (Berlin)
ACE	Allied Command Europe (NATO)
ACLANT	Allied Command Atlantic
ADC	Air Defense Command (US)
AFCC	Air Force Combat Command (US)
AFHRA	Air Force Historical Research Agency
AFMED	Allied Forces Mediterranean (NATO)
AFSC	Air Force Service Command (US)
AFSOUTH	Allied Forces Southern Europe (NATO)
ANF	Atlantic Nuclear Force (NATO)
APC	Armored Personnel Carrier
ATAF	Allied Tactical Air Forces (NATO)
ATL	Associated Television Limited
AWPD	Air War Plan D (US)
BASC	Berlin Air Safety Center (Quadripartite)
BATSC	Berlin Air Traffic Safety Center
BEA	British European Airways
CAF	Continental Air Force (US)
CATF	Combined Airlift Task Force
CEO	Chief Executive Officer
CFSP	Common Foreign and Security Policy (EU)
CG	Commanding General
CINC	Commander-in-Chief
CINCAAFCE	Commander-in-Chief, Allied Air Forces, Central Europe (NATO)
CINCAFCENT	Commander-in-Chief, Air Forces Central Europe (NATO)
CINCAIRCENT	Allied Air Commander-in-Chief Central Europe (NATO)
CINCBAOR	Commander-in-Chief British Army of the Rhine
CINCENT	Commander-in-Chief Allied Forces Central Europe (NATO)
CINCEUCOM	Commander-in-Chief, European Command (US)
CINCEUR	Commander-in-Chief, European Command (US)

CINCFFG	Commander-in-Chief French Forces Germany
CINCLANT	Commander-in-Chief, Atlantic (US)
CINCNELM	Commander-in-Chief, US Naval Forces, Eastern Atlantic and Mediterranean (NATO)
CINCPAC	Commander-in-Chief Pacific (US)
CINCSAC	Commanding General, Strategic Air Command (US)
CINCSOUTH	Allied Commander-in-Chief, Southern Europe (NATO)
CINCUSAFE	Commander-in-Chief, US Air Forces in Europe
CINCUSAREUR	Commander-in-Chief, US Army Europe
CNO	Chief of Naval Operations
COMSFOR	Commander, Stabilization Force (NATO)
CONAC	Continental Air Command (US)
COS	Chief of Staff
CSA	Chief of Staff, US Army
CSCE	Conference on Security and Cooperation in Europe
DOD	Department of Defense (US)
EDC	European Defence Community
EDP	Emergency Defense Plan
ESDI	European Security and Defense Identity (EU)
ETO	European Theatre of Operations
EWP	Emergency War Plan
FEAF	Far East Air Forces (US)
FRG	Federal Republic of Germany
GDR	German Democratic Republic
ICBMs	Intercontinental Ballistic Missiles
IFOR	Implementation Force (NATO)
INS	International News Service
INTAF	Interim Air Force (US)
IRBMs	Intermediate Range Ballistic Missiles
JCS	Joint Chiefs of Staff (US)
JPS	Joint Plans Staff or Joint Staff Planners (US)
JSCP	Joint Capabilities Plans (US)
JSPC	Joint Strategic Plans Committee (US)
JSP	Joint Staff Planners (US)
JSSC	Joint Strategic Survey Committee (US)
JSPG	Joint Strategic Plans Group (US)
JTG	Joint Target Group (US)
JWPC	Joint War Plans Committee (US)
MAAF	Mediterranean Allied Air Forces (NATO)
MATS	Military Air Transport Service (US)

MEDOC	Western Mediterranean Area (NATO)
MLF	Multilateral Force (NATO)
MRBM	Medium Range Ballistic Missile
MSP	Mutual Security Program (US)
MWDP	Mutual Weapons Development Program (US)
NAC	North Atlantic Council (NATO)
NACAF	Northwest African Coastal Air Force (US-UK)
NASAF	Northwest African Tactical Air Force (US-UK)
NATAF	Northwest African Tactical Air Force (US-UK)
NGO	Non-governmental Organization(s)
NATO	North Atlantic Treaty Organization
NMR	National Military Representative (NATO)
NOFORN	No Distribution to Foreign Nationals (US)
NSAM	National Security Action Memorandum (US)
NSC	National Security Council (US)
NWAAF	Northwest African Air Forces (US-UK)
OCF	Owens-Corning Fiberglas Corporation
OJCS	Office of the Joint Chiefs of Staff (US)
OSCE	Organization for Security and Cooperation in Europe
OSD	Office of the Secretary of Defense (US)
PCC	Partnership Coordination Cell (NATO)
PIC	Peace Implementation Conference (NATO)
QBAL	Quadripartite Berlin Airlift Plan
RAF	Royal Air Force (UK)
ROE	Rules of Engagement
SAC	Strategic Air Command (US)
SACEUR	Supreme Allied Commander, Europe (NATO)
SACLANT	Supreme Allied Commander, Atlantic (NATO)
SBS	Strategic Bombing Survey (US)
SFOR	Stabilization Force (NATO)
SHAEF	Supreme Headquarters Allied Expeditionary Force
SHAPE	Supreme Headquarters Allied Powers Europe (NATO)
STRAC	Strategic Reserve Army Corps (US)
TAC	Tactical Air Command (US)
UK COS	UK Chief of Staff
UK	United Kingdom
UN	United Nations
UNPROFOR	United Nations Protection Force
USAREUR	US Army Europe

USEUCOM	US European Command
USAAF	US Army Air Forces
USAF	United States Air Force
USAFE	US Air Force Europe
USBER	US Diplomatic Mission, Berlin
USCINCEUR	US Commander-in-Chief Europe
USCOB	US Commander Berlin
USRO	US Regional Office
USSR	Union of Soviet Socialist Republics
VOPOS	GDR Police
WEU	Western European Union

Part I
On Becoming SACEUR

1
The End and the Beginning

> There is within the military mind a deep and abiding need for order arising out of the very chaos of warfare. The continuing need to make predictions about matters so volatile by their nature requires a steady frame of reference. Weapons, then, tend to be viewed in a manner which makes their effects most calculable.[1]

I. The end of a career

This is the story of a Supreme Commander and the institutions for which he served. These institutions doubtless contributed to the making of General Lauris Norstad. They certainly provided the opportunities that propelled his spectacular rise from very modest beginnings to become one of the leaders of the "Free World" at the height of the Cold War. In the course of this rise, his sharp and disciplined intellect and physical bearing brought him to the attention of powerful sponsors – General Henry H. "Hap" Arnold, the architect of the US Air force (USAF), and General Dwight D. "Ike" Eisenhower, the hero of World War II and a defining figure in the formation of the North Atlantic Treaty Organization (NATO).

Norstad aspired to be a seminal shaper of the course of post-World War II European affairs on the order of Charles de Gaulle, that master of the not-so-diplomatic *"non"*. In pursuing that goal, he was not unaware of the model of Douglas MacArthur, that master of the drama of war. Norstad certainly displayed attributes of both of these "heroic" figures in the manner in which he conducted his affairs. But the two institutions that provided him with the opportunities to participate in the making of history also withheld from him that aura of power possessed by de Gaulle and MacArthur. Try as he might, he could not transcend, only shape, his USAF and NATO roots. In the final analysis, for all three men, the nature of the international political system, based as it is on the primacy of the national State, exposed the fruitlessness of their aspirations. Just as de Gaulle was essentially a secondary figure in a political-military universe dominated by the two Superpowers, MacArthur was essentially a military officer who served at the pleasure of his President and Commander-in-Chief. Norstad, on his part, was essentially a "servant" of his government and of the North Atlantic Council (NAC), and ultimately neither were willing to share their prerogatives with the Supreme Commander. In other words, as was true for de Gaulle and MacArthur, Norstad's reach threatened to exceed his grasp.

Nonetheless, no one can deny that Norstad was at the center of the great and defining episodes of World War II and the Cold War. There could be no more dramatic exercises in the use of power than the atomic bombing of Hiroshima and Nagasaki, the planning for which was his responsibility under Arnold's aegis. Nor could there have been more high drama during the Cold War than the doctrinal debates and diplomatic fencing within the US government and NATO over how and whether to use nuclear weapons against the Soviet Union. Finally, ranking alongside the relatively brief high drama of the Cuban Missile Crisis was the seemingly endless crisis over the control of Berlin and by extension the continuing struggle over the control of Germany.

It is ironic and perhaps a little unfair that, even though Norstad was at the heart of these events, the fame and glory often went to others. There was Curtis LeMay who emerged as the "hero" of the air war against Japan and then became the embodiment of the Strategic Air Command (SAC); along with "Hap" Arnold and "Tooey" Spaatz, there was Hoyt Vandenberg who emerged as "founding fathers" of an independent Air Force; there were Chancellor Konrad Adenauer, President de Gaulle, Secretary of State John Foster Dulles, and NATO Secretary-General Paul-Henri Spaak who dominated the politics of NATO. Finally, there were the leaders of the Soviet Union, who would have cared little about the career and aspirations of an American four-star general, albeit the youngest in the history of the Air Force.

Partly for these reasons, after having served in Europe for nearly a decade, Norstad hinted in January 1962 that he might retire in about a year. He was still extraordinarily young – he was only 56 at the time – and was "slim and boyish, his hair ash-blonde, his handsome face unlined, his shoulders almost frail for the burden of those four stars. His uniforms, Italian-made, are so immaculate he could wear them at an operating table. So crisp they seem made of parchment."[2] But there were good reasons, besides anything personal, that prompted the

Supreme Allied Commander Europe (SACEUR) to muse about his future. Having reached the apex of a distinguished career and with the withdrawal of President Eisenhower from public life and a younger President taking office, a new – and wrenching – political-military situation faced the General.

The change was to become all too evident, as Norstad had unwittingly foretold in his letter of farewell to Eisenhower:

> I am forced to an awareness of what to me is a sad fact: that your departure from office will sever an official relationship between us which has continued almost unbroken for nearly twenty years ... My particular reaction towards service with you is that I have enjoyed it – that it has been fun. Not every problem has been solved nor has every effort been successful, but just trying has brought great satisfaction ... [3]

The pleasure and satisfaction that he experienced working with Eisenhower was not to be enjoyed for very much longer because he was soon seen as passé by the new generation of political and military leaders who had come to Washington in the wake of the Kennedy electoral victory of 1960.[4]

There was a new Secretary of Defense, Robert S. McNamara, who had suspicions about the "military" in general.[5] McNamara had little or no professional or political ties that would have identified him with the senior officer corps, including Norstad.[6] Furthermore, with the mutuality of total nuclear destruction that had become the hallmark of the Cold War after *Sputnik*, the likelihood of nuclear war was the predominant concern of the New Frontier's civilian planners, as it had been for their Republican predecessors. They were especially concerned about control over the overseas deployment of nuclear-tipped medium range ballistic missiles (MRBMs), which were Norstad's responsibility under both of his "hats" as SACEUR and as Commander-in-Chief, US European Command (USCINCEUR). Norstad wanted multilateral NATO control, partly to provide a disincentive to any West German aspirations to "go nuclear". The Kennedy Administration wanted to "renationalize" American control over these weapons.

Norstad had given the appearance that he wanted to build up his authority as SACEUR by advocating that NATO should become a "fourth nuclear power." He also had expressed publicly his unease that the Kennedy Administration's version of the concept of "flexible response" – whereby large conventional forces would be built up in

Europe that could credibly deflect a Soviet thrust, thus delaying the introduction of nuclear weapons and thus lessening the risk of nuclear escalation that would involve directly the continental United States. Norstad had viewed conventional forces, which the European Allies had been reluctant to build up to officially-declared force levels, as simply a "tripwire" that would set in motion an escalatory process that almost inevitably would result in a strategic nuclear exchange.

Furthermore, "flexible response" was neither politically satisfactory nor militarily realistic to the European Allies. This Kennedy/McNamara concept looked suspiciously like an attempt on the part of the US to confine to Europe proper, war between the two blocs. For this reason, they were very much opposed to it. They believed, as did Norstad and the JCS, that the true and only deterrent had to be the American strategic deterrent. They did not want a lengthy "pause"; they wanted only just enough of a "pause" to know that all-out nuclear war would be intensified. To them, this was the credible deterrent both to the Americans and to the Soviets.

Given these differing concepts of what the appropriate deterrent and warfighting strategy for NATO should be, it is not surprising that McNamara's civilian managers "had doubts about Norstad's and the Joint Chiefs' attitude toward the role of conventional forces in Europe."[7]

For so much of the Cold War maneuvering in Europe, the role of Germany – both East and West – was central. This was true not only in regard to nuclear weapons, but also in regard to the seemingly never-ending series of Soviet-provoked crises over Berlin, and especially Western access rights. Again, there was disagreement between Norstad and the Kennedy Administration over who had command and control to respond to these provocations: NATO in the person of Norstad as SACEUR/USCINCEUR, who clearly was responsible for contingency planning, or the US and its Tripartite British and French partners, utilizing shifting and at times confusing command and consultative channels.

Consequently, in the face of this policy impasse, in the Spring of 1962 Kennedy began sending up trial balloons about Norstad's retirement. In what appears to have been a leak to the *Washington News*, on April 24, 1962 the paper published an article by Henry J. Taylor on "Norstad's Fine Job," which after praising him, contained the statement that Norstad was "scheduled to retire later this year."[9] At about the same time the British Ambassador, who was a close friend of Kennedy's, reported that McNamara might persuade Kennedy to discuss with Prime Minister

Harold Macmillan during his forthcoming visit to Washington "the problem of a successor to General Norstad as SACEUR." The reporter commented that "this is the first we have heard that General Norstad might be leaving SHAPE [Supreme Headquarters Allied Powers Europe]. I am not aware that he himself wants to go." Believing that Norstad had Kennedy's confidence, as well as that of the other NATO heads of government, the surmise was that the only possible reason for Norstad's departure would be that Kennedy wanted him for some other high position, such as Chairman of the Joint Chiefs of Staff (JCS).[10] As will be seen, this was, of course, out of the question.

When Macmillan met with McNamara, Macmillan expressed high regard for Norstad and hoped that he would stay on as SACEUR for as long as possible. Norstad already was the longest-serving SACEUR since NATO's inception. McNamara replied that his high opinion was shared by the Administration, which was why Kennedy had asked Norstad to continue in office even though (presumably) he wanted to retire. McNamara added that Norstad: "had suffered a heart attack, and the long period during which he had held his post had no doubt had a general effect on his health."[11] This observation ignored the fact that Norstad had apparently recovered fully from his heart attack, which had occurred two years earlier.[12] He always had been very careful about his physical well-being, drinking moderately, eating carefully, and playing golf regularly.

In fact, since the days in Hawaii where they met, both Isabelle and Lauris Norstad enjoyed outdoor sports – including fly-fishing for him and swimming for her. Lauris was from Minnesota, where fishing and hunting were normal boyhood pastimes. Isabelle was from the Hawaiian Islands. As she said: "We spent so much time on the water and in the water, all the time I was growing up, I was on the beach, one way or another."[13] In other words, reasons of health or fitness concerning either of the Norstads were weak reeds on which to hang a reason for replacing Norstad.

Nonetheless, turning away from this issue, the discussion then turned to Norstad's possible successor, and Macmillan inquired if Lemnitzer would be retiring in the near future. McNamara replied that Lemnitzer's normal tour of duty would indeed expire soon and "he might perhaps be a possibility to succeed General Norstad."[14]

The final crisis seems to have been precipitated by McNamara's May 1962 speech in Athens, Greece on the subject of the control of nuclear forces to the annual ministerial meeting of NATO defense and foreign ministers. In the speech, he appeared to ignore all the efforts that his predecessors – along with Norstad – had made to reassure the NATO Allies that NATO's nuclear defense, or deterrent, was credible. He stated boldly, if not baldly:

> More than XXX* [US] weapons are scheduled against SACEUR's nuclear threat list. SACEUR plans to assure the destruction of XXX targets on the list with his forces alone. Approximately XXX targets are scheduled for attack and destruction solely with external [US] forces. SACEUR schedules sorties against another XXX more targets with his own forces, but the assurance he will be able to destroy them is not enough to warrant reliance on his attacks alone.[15]
> [* X indicates classified material]

McNamara went on to exhort the Allies to build up their conventional forces in order to avoid the horrendous human as well as material losses that *any* form of nuclear engagement would incur. Further, to avoid nuclear war occurring under circumstances that would escape US control, he maintained that: "There must not be competing and conflicting strategies in the conduct of nuclear war ... [W]eak nuclear capabilities, operating independently, are expensive, prone to obsolescence, and lacking in credibility as a deterrent."[16]

On June 16, McNamara reiterated his views in a very public speech at the University of Michigan in Ann Arbor, which received widespread press attention. De Gaulle, in particular, was incensed, since the speech appeared to discredit France's attempts at obtaining an independent but complementary nuclear capability. For Norstad, the impending demise of his efforts at making NATO a "fourth nuclear power" was all too plain: "McNamara's blunt insistence on central control flew in the face of General Norstad's plan for an MRBM force for Europe, about which Norstad had been acting like 'a proconsul in Outer Gaul ... .'"[17]

This was not just political talk; Norstad at this time did indeed feel that he had sufficient political influence in Washington to persist in his views. As he observed: "I had the NATO votes, and they knew that. At that time, I had very strong congressional support."[18] Reflecting later, Norstad observed: "I *think* initially it was a matter of my being too well established in a position of importance to them, and I can understand that. It wasn't comfortable for them."[19]

In a meeting Norstad had with Secretary of State Dean Rusk and McNamara in June 1962, according to Norstad, they wanted him to do something that he considered wrong, and he informed them that:

"Even if it weren't wrong, I couldn't and wouldn't do it because I have obligations. I've been around here for ten years and in the course of time these governments have done things because I've asked them to do it. And many times they've done it solely because I asked them to do it. And every time I've done that I've taken on an obligation, and I know it and I respect the obligation."[20]

Ignoring indications to the contrary, Norstad felt that his problem with the Kennedy Administration was not with the President himself: "Most of the problem came from the fact that too often they expected me to be the one who would carry out an American decision independently of the NATO countries. And I couldn't and I wouldn't do that."[21] When it was put to him bluntly at the June meeting – "that's the question we have – just to whom do you have an obligation?" – Norstad felt that McNamara was:

> challenging my loyalty. My first instinct was to hit him and I thought that wouldn't be very dignified, so I didn't do that. I just stood there and I tried to smile and cool off a bit and I gave him a short explanation of what NATO meant and what the supreme commander meant in that whole cloth, whole picture. And I said, "Well, gentlemen, I think this ends this meeting." Whereupon I walked in [my office] and slammed the door. Went back and called my senior staff together and said, "Gentlemen, we aren't going to be together very much longer. If they can't put up with me after this, and I can't put up with them – so one way or another it's going to come to an end."[22]

According to French General Pierre Gallois, McNamara had told Norstad during this confrontation that he was "sorry that your health problems are going to force you to retire," and brushed aside Norstad's protests that he felt fine and would like to continue in his post. Norstad then met with Kennedy in Washington and heard the same regrets that health problems would make it necessary for him to retire.

When he returned to Paris, Norstad told Gallois: "Peter, I've been fired."[23] By early July, there was speculation that General Maxwell D. Taylor had been offered the post of SACEUR, and had turned it down.[24] In any event, there inevitably were some expressions of relief that the conflict between Norstad and Washington on NATO policy was coming to a head.[25]

Not long afterward, the expected summons arrived, and on July 15, 1962 Norstad flew to Washington, arriving on the morning of the

16th. After meeting briefly with the JCS, he saw McNamara. It was quite clear what was afoot. As Norstad recounted:

> Then [McNamara] admitted as to how they were talking about Lem's coming over, and I remember saying, "Now if you go through with this, I want to be helpful. I have put a lot of time and effort in that position and so have others, and I will do nothing to attack it. I want this to be done in a dignified manner … . Do you people have a date in mind – apparently you do." He gave me a date which was within 30 or 60 days, something like that. I said, "Well, that is not acceptable."
> This was a shocker to them. He said, "Why not?" I said, "I *cannot* disengage with dignity in that time. I am *not* going to end my military career by being a party to something that is disorderly, particularly at this level".[26]

And then: "The president gave a final audience to Norstad. Then the distinguished general, one of the most famous Americans in Europe at the time, crossed the Potomac to see McNamara. McNamara asked him, 'Well, Lauris, what are your plans? … An era was ending.' "[27]

Norstad arrived back in Paris on the evening of July 17. The next day at SHAPE he met with his Chief of Staff, General Cortlandt van Rennssaler Schuyler, and his Political Adviser, Ray Thurston. He reported to them:

> Here's what happened. Gentlemen, I must acquaint you with a conclusion I have now reached, that we must tidy up everything we are working on because the situation is becoming unsatisfactory from my standpoint. It is obviously unsatisfactory, for some reason, from the standpoint of the United States Government. It is bad when the Government loses confidence in an individual official. It's much worse when that individual loses confidence in his own Government. I must tell you sadly that I have reached that point. I am not going to be effective much longer, and I am not going to be around here if I am not effective.[28]

Then he called on Secretary-General-Dirk U. Stikker and Belgian Ambassador André de Staerke (the *doyen* of the NATO diplomatic corps) at NATO headquarters, in observance of diplomatic protocol.

In his letter of resignation to Kennedy, Norstad stated that during their meeting the previous January, he [Norstad] had mentioned his desire to retire during the coming winter. The letter was vague about why he wished to retire but mentioned that he had been in his post longer than usual. The desired date was November 1.²⁹ One sentence in Kennedy's letter of acknowledgement and acceptance stands out, and perhaps epitomized Norstad's success in his NATO "hat": "During that period you have become a living symbol of the US commitment to the alliance and of the strength of the alliance itself."³⁰

To the outside observer, it seemed apparent that, with a new Administration, and a new professional military leadership in Washington symbolized by Taylor, who became Chairman of the JCS when Lemnitzer was nominated as Norstad's replacement, Norstad should have been prepared to step aside rather than be pushed.³¹ It obviously did Norstad little good, for example, to have been seen as a *protégé* of Eisenhower and therefore presumed to be close to the Republicans.³² But Norstad firmly believed that within NATO, the SACEUR needed to represent the European member-states to Washington, as well as the other way around.³³ *Reflecting* their views was one thing; *advocating* policies that appeared to the new leadership to favor the security needs of the Europeans over the perceived security needs of his own government was quite another.

Reinforcing this situation, at this time Stikker was seen by the NATO Allies as being too pro-American, which doubtless contributed to Norstad's determination to "stand up" to Washington.³⁴ Norstad's success in some quarters and his failure in others can be summed up thus: "With respect to the need to maintain allied cohesion, national governments have failed in at least two areas. They have failed in many instances in their task to inform their electorates adequately about the reality of the international situation and the dilemmas of allied security. They have equally failed in their understanding of the psychology of mutual confidence in allied relations."³⁵

Norstad's attempt to make up for these two failures made him one of the most influential as well as one of the most controversial of the US's Cold War generals. One reason why Norstad let matters unfold as they did could, perhaps, be attributed to his personality, for as he observed to his wife Isabelle when he was in North Africa in 1942: "This is a serious game to me and one which permits little time or thought for anything else. Although I realize full well my modest contribution is not going to end the war, I still find it hard not to take things as seriously as if it were. That is perhaps my most glaring weakness."³⁶

Overall European sentiment toward Norstad was probably best expressed by Admiral Lord Louis Mountbatten, who is reported to have had doubts about "this young airman" who was appointed SACEUR. He later saw that he was mistaken. Although Mountbatten thought that Norstad was misguided on tactical nuclear weapons, he believed that, in general, Norstad did an almost impossible job with exemplary skill.[37]

Norstad's contemporary, General Thomas D. "Tommy" White, who had recently been Air Force Chief of Staff, wrote in *Newsweek*: "Norstad had the brilliance and intimate grasp of the situation to represent NATO and America, together with the moral stamina and nerve to stand up to both, whatever his convictions so dictated."[38]

Even de Gaulle paid him a sincere compliment when he awarded him the Grand Cross of the Legion of Honor:

> When I say that you are detaching yourself, I am of course referring only as regards the duties which were yours here. For insofar as your work is concerned, it exists and will remain. No doubt, as the strategist you are, you have sometimes seen your plans, in turn, somewhat complicated by the soldier. The fact remains that, in six years, you have done everything that could and should be done on behalf of the Atlantic Alliance. I wish to render you my very sincere recognition of this.[39]

Another graceful note was struck by the three Allied Commanders who had worked with him during the protracted Berlin crisis: "We, the three Allied Commandants in Berlin, speaking on behalf of the Allied Garrisons in the City, wish to express to you our great appreciation of the deep interest, sympathy and understanding of our problems which you have shown over the last six years. We are unanimous in feeling that it has been the greatest honour and pleasure to have been associated with you and we all wish you much happiness and every good fortune in your retirement."[40]

As an interesting sidelight, in August 1962, when it had become known that Norstad was leaving, Adenauer awarded him the FRG's Grand Cross of Merit, which was a customary formality given to distinguished personages. Nonetheless, it was reported that the award was a subtle rebuff to Kennedy because Adenauer suspected that Kennedy had eased Norstad out over their disagreement on the future nuclear strategy of NATO. This was, of course, indeed the case. As it was reported: "Mr. Adenauer is known to think highly of General Norstad, especially since the general endorsed West Germany's call for making

NATO a nuclear power, independent of the United States."⁴¹ But it was more than that: "Informants said the fear of some European NATO partners that the United States might be reluctant to use nuclear weapons in the defense of Europe was increased with the retirement of General Norstad and the appointment of Gen. Maxwell D. Taylor as chairman of the Joint Chiefs of Staff."⁴²

A Joint Resolution was passed by the Senate and the House of Representatives on October 4, 1962:

> Resolved by the Senate and House of Representatives of the United States of America in Congress assembled, That the President is authorized to present to General Lauris Norstad a gold medal of suitable design in recognition of his outstanding service as chief of the armed forces of the North Atlantic Treaty Organization. General Norstad's firmness and steadfastness of purpose, implemented by his consummate tact and diplomacy, have made a vital contribution to the free world's defense in a most critical period of history.⁴³

The way was now clear for the Kennedy Administration to persuade the NATO Allies that their security was guarded better by the doctrine of flexible response, which although developed initially by the Eisenhower Administration, was adopted by the Kennedy Administration. As Kennedy, somewhat inaccurately, given the intermediate role of tactical nuclear weapons in the strategy of flexible response, had put it: "Under every military budget submitted by the [Eisenhower] administration, we have been preparing primarily to fight the one kind of war we least want to fight and are least likely to fight. We have been driving ourselves into a corner where the only choice is all or nothing at all, world devastation or submission – a choice that necessarily causes us to hesitate on the brink and leaves the initiative in the hands of our enemies."⁴⁴

Tactical nuclear weapons, if applied locally, in Kennedy's view: "can't necessarily be confined locally. [The] Russians would think it a prelude to strategic bombing of their industrial centers. They would retaliate – and a local use would become a world war."⁴⁵ In a nutshell, this fundamental policy change, rejecting the premise of one of Norstad's major efforts as SACEUR, dictated a change in the Alliance's chief military policy-maker. It is, in a way, a tribute to Norstad's great prestige, that the change was so long in coming. How did this illustrious career begin?

II. Laying the foundation

In examining Norstad's military career, stretching from the 1930s to the 1960s, it is apparent that the cadré of officers that emerged as air leaders in World War II and thereafter were drawn from an extraordinarily small pool. This was partly because of the fact that between the two world wars, the US purposely restricted the size and composition of its armed forces, which were entirely composed of professional soldiers, sailors, and airmen, and there was great reluctance on the part of Congress to expand the military budget. Consequently, not only were the forces small and relatively unimpressive when compared with the rearming dictatorships, they were also under-equipped. But these professionals' commitment to their careers was strong.

It was in the years between the two great wars of this century that the debate over air power raged among the potential allies and enemies as they searched for the best means to provide for their own defense needs.[46] As it was said about the most famous US airman of this period:

> one of Billy Mitchell's most significant achievements was the inculcation among his followers of the feeling that they were different. The brash, self-confident personalities of Mitchell, [Henry H. "Hap"] Arnold, [Carl A. "Tooey"] Spaatz, [James H. "Jimmy"] Doolittle, [George C.] Kenney; [Claire] Chennault, and [Hoyt S. "Van"] Vandenberg were not atypical in the Air Corps; they were expected, perhaps even cultivated … .one first and foremost had to be technically able; he had to be a good pilot … . That was the way respect was won.[47]

The country was only too familiar with the travails of Billy Mitchell as he enthusiastically asserted that air power was not only coequal, but in fact, was the dominant means of projecting military power in warfare among industrialized states.[48]

Norstad had been an attentive observer of these men from the time he entered West Point in 1926, from which he graduated in 1930 as a second lieutenant of cavalry.[49] He had come to West Point from Red Wing, Minnesota, the product of an upper Mid-West small-town upbringing. The reaction in Red Wing to Norstad's appointment was probably similar to those of towns from which his contemporaries came: "It was the thing to do. Everybody wanted to go, and when they knew I was appointed, for instance, everybody, including the people in the town, would rally around and make it a point of building this up to a great event ... . It was a special event, not only for me, but for the town and for the school."⁵⁰ Small-town patriotism was an important ingredient in the community life of those times.

As was true for many serious middle-class young men of his generation, he conscientiously kept in touch with his family back home while away getting an education. For example, on October 13, 1927, Norstad wrote to his aunt, Miss Helen K. Johnson of Red Wing:

Dear Aunt Helen:

You will have to excuse my tardiness in answering your letter, but my academic work has kept me so busy that I have little time to devote to correspondence.

I am mighty glad to hear that you are feeling so much better. It is certainly more than we dared hope for when you had your last siege of sickness. You seem to be staying at a good place to regain your health. I imagine that the quiet is almost oppressive after staying with the family. The "little boys" with their noise don't offer the best conditions under which to recuperate.

The family seems to be enjoying life in Minneapolis. Marie's letters are always full of big times she is having. I would like to get back for Christmas but I'm afraid that is impossible. I'll have to wait until my furlough next June.

It looks to me as though yearling year will prove to be the hardest of my course. We have to take a regular engineering mathematics course besides the studies which are supposed to give us our cultural education. I rank very near the top in English and quite far down in math so it is quite obvious that I will not be an engineer. My leanings are still toward law – Oxford if I can make it financially possible.

Peg Beckmark arrived in New York last week. I hope to see her in the next few days. I'm looking forward to seeing her at New Haven for the Yale-Army game a week from next Saturday.

Hope you continue to get better.

Love, Lolly.

P.S. I can stand the sweets. We get very little of them around here. Thanks.⁵¹

In some respects, the setting for the 1992 movie starring Robert Redford, *A River Runs Through It* could be applied to Norstad's boyhood and early manhood. His father was a Lutheran minister, who had what was a large family for those times – four boys and one girl. One of his brothers became a Lutheran clergyman; the other two engaged in various types of business activity. His sister married a chemist who worked in large corporations. The family's central sense of "home" was Red Wing, where his mother's parents, Swedish immigrants, settled, and where various members of the Norstad family lived at various times.

One of the formative figures in Lauris's life was his grandfather Norstad, a farmer. He never forgot his grandfather's advice as he dealt with the vicissitudes of increasingly higher command: "Be a believer. Critics are useful in their places, but no one can point to a critic who created a great idea or a new idea or wrote a piece of music or a great book. Believers do things. Furthermore, if one is to be a leader – and I hope that someday you will be – people follow believers, and unless you believe, no one is going to follow you."[52]

Norstad's first introduction to military life came when his father was called in World War I to be a "camp pastor." The family was living at the time in Jewell, Iowa, and to provide him with some company, Lauris's father invited him to stay with him in Manhattan, Kansas, where Camp Funston was located, adjacent to Fort Riley. While there during the Fall of 1917 and Spring of 1918, young Lauris came into contact with many soldiers, Camp Funston at the time being an induction center for about 100 000 men. As he recounted: "General Wood [Maj Gen Leonard] was in command there, and he used to go around that post a great deal, so I would see him. He always had three or four officers, second lieutenants, traipsing along with him. They were different from the rest of them, a different breed. I asked my father one time, 'Why are they different?' He said, 'Well, that's easy, they are West Pointers.' From that time on West Point had a special meaning to me. From that age on, I always wanted to go to West Point."[53]

One of the attractions of the Army was its tradition of horses and horsemanship. In those days "[r]iding and fencing were military accomplishments."[54] Earlier, while at West Point, he had written home: "My class is working hard at riding. It is during 'yearling' year that we first seriously take up equitation. Yesterday we went over jumps for the first time. It was quite a thrill. I have some hopes of making the polo squad – a lifetime ambition of mine."[55]

He was stationed at Schofield Barracks – more precisely, Wheeler Field – in Hawaii as a young captain, serving as commander of the 18th Pursuit Group, when he met Isabelle Jenkins at a prenuptial party on May 30, 1932. He was a groomsman and Isabelle was a bridesmaid. After going to the University of Oregon for a year and a half, Isabelle was back home enjoying dating young and promising officers from both the Army and the Navy. By then, Norstad had indeed become a dashing polo player, and it was not long before they were thinking of marriage, which took place in Honolulu on April 27, 1935.[56] Not long thereafter they sailed to New York via San Francisco and the Panama Canal. Norstad had been assigned to Mitchel Field, Long Island, where he was the Adjutant of the 9th Bombardment Group from 1936–39.[57]

Having transferred to the Air Corps in 1931, Norstad became an active participant in the rapidly-evolving circle of officers who were convinced, even at this comparatively early period, that a separate and independent "Air Force" was required to exploit fully this new, highly technological, and "scientific" dimension of modern warfare. Thus, as will be seen, he became one of those men who were chiefly responsible for developing the US's air strategy and implementing it after World War II.[58] Norstad played a key role in planning and organizing the postwar Air Force and in negotiating the unification legislation that led to the National Security Act of 1947, which created an independent air force.

Few of these men kept personal diaries and only a minority of them left collections of personal papers. But from these sources and from oral histories and official records we can learn something about them. While some of the air leaders had influential family connections in their local communities, collectively they could hardly be said to have sprung from the country's social, political or financial elite.

It is true that Vandenberg, who became the second Air Force Chief of Staff, was a nephew of Senator Arthur M. Vandenberg of Michigan, and that Nathan Farraghut "Nate" Twining, who became the third Air Force Chief of Staff and then Chairman of the Joint Chiefs of Staff (JCS), came from a family of naval officers. But Doolittle, leader of the first US bombing raid against the Japanese homeland, was the son of an itinerant carpenter. Curtis E. "Curt" LeMay, who was the second commander of the Strategic Air Command (SAC) and then became Air Force Chief of Staff, grew up in a lower-middle-class suburb. The father of Carl A. "Tooey" Spaatz, the first Chief of Staff of an independent Air Force, published a rural weekly newspaper. The father of the Commanding General of the US Army Air Forces (AAF) in World War II, Henry H. "Hap" Arnold practiced medicine. Haywood S. "Possum" Hansell, Jr., one of the chief planners of the air war in World War II, was the son of an army surgeon. Barney M. "Bennie" Giles grew up on a farm. The father of Thomas D. "Tommy" White, who became the fourth Air Force Chief of Staff, was an Episcopal bishop. Elwood A.

"Pete" Quesada, who left the Service to become a leader in the airline industry, came from an Irish-Spanish heritage.[59]

Although almost all these officers were born in the US, their geographical origins within the country were diverse, but mostly mid-Western. Vandenberg and Twining were born in Wisconsin; Spaatz and Arnold came from Pennsylvania; Eaker and Giles from Texas; Norstad and White from Minnesota; LeMay from Ohio; Quesada from Washington, DC.[60] In comparison with the leadership of both the Navy and the rest of the Army, there was a very small number from the South and Southeast.[61]

The small group that composed the senior air leadership of World War II had, professionally speaking, grown up together during these interwar years. As Haywood Hansell put it: "In a way, the men of General Arnold's new staff were particularly fortunate. Few were unknown to each other. In the days of struggle for the Air Corps, their paths had crossed many times ... . Already tested in a hundred different ways, virtually every man on the staff knew the dedication, skill and potential of the men with whom he would be working."[62]

Thus, the younger officers, among them Norstad, had already caught the notice of these senior officers – especially Arnold and Spaatz – by the time the war had begun. For example, immediately after Pearl Harbor Spaatz, on behalf of Arnold, looked around for able young officers to help in sorting out the confusion following Pearl Harbor, and his eye fell on Major Norstad, stationed nearby at Bolling Field.[63] Norstad was at the time assigned to Air Force Combat Command Headquarters. As the officer in charge of intelligence, he had reported to his superior that he was picking up garbled accounts of a Japanese attack on the Hawaiian Islands but he thought it must be a hoax.[64] Fortunately for him, Spaatz must have ignored this error in judgement.

Norstad defined quite accurately the role that he and his generation of officers was to perform in the crisis-laden days, weeks and months that lay ahead:

> If we are to understand the events, great events and great men, one should also know something of the lesser events and the lesser men who formed the context in which great things are done by great people. I am quoting from the book now, "I am one of the lesser who formed the context. It was my privilege to help people do important things in war and in peace." We had that experience because my generation was really the senior staff generation during the war, which meant that the policies were first written by us and

given to our bosses. That was the basis of discussion, what we thought became the basis for their consideration.[65]

But it was not until 1941 that an Air Staff separate from the Army was authorized. In March 1942 the air arm was given coordinate status with the Army and the Navy, and "Hap" Arnold became Commanding General of the Army Air Forces (AAF). Arnold and his subordinates formed a strong emotional bond deriving from those years of working together as flyers, administrators, instructors and members of a branch that considered itself possessed of a "mission": "Though its top leaders were in most cases West Point graduates, their long identification with the Air Corps, which had regarded itself as the victim of an entrenched conservatism in the [Army] General Staff, encouraged a view of themselves as advocates of new approaches to military problems."[66] Because of the small size of the officer corps, promotion was rapid and younger men were given responsibilities which in the ground army went to more senior soldiers. Even so, there were only 1600 Air Corps officers in 1938, so that the business and professional world was tapped to fill special administrative and service skills.[67] For example: "There was ... no military model or parallel for the development of a world-wide system of air transport, but the experience of the civilian airlines constituted a source of talent that was drawn upon heavily."[68] These young officers were given ranks appropriate to their function.

In fact, the ties between industry and the Air Corps were deep-rooted even before the war. The imperatives of the rapidly-changing technology had dictated it.[69] In November 1941 Arnold had asked the Wallace Clark management consultant firm to advise him on to how to create an effective air force system of administration. Arnold wanted to apply business's organizational and managerial skills to the formidable challenge which confronted him of running a rapidly expanding air force engaged in combat. A Directorate of Management Control was established in October 1943 under Harvard Law Professor (and Reserve Air Corps Colonel) W. Barton Leach in recognition of the fact that "[e]very mission in hitherto uncharted field of warfare ... was in greater or lesser degree an experimental venture to which the techniques of quantitative analysis could make a well-nigh indispensable contribution."[70] The Directorate's purpose was to make a rational assessment of the ongoing and unfolding experience of air warfare.[71] Out of this came the Air Force's preoccupation with what came to be known as "operational analysis", or, operations research based on techniques of statistical analysis.

Thus, the entire field of operations research had become very familiar to Norstad as he moved during the early wartime years from Washington to London, and then to the Mediterranean, and finally back to Washington. He was very much a product of his generation of career airmen who were imbued with the notion that, just as the technological wizardry of better and better aircraft could bring more effective destruction against the enemy's forces, this destruction could be measured statistically and interpreted to assess human will and perserverance.[72] For Norstad, these measurements should have been seen as tools for effective decision-making, not as ends in themselves.

2
Applying Planning and Operational Skills in North Africa and the Pacific

> A leader should look for ways to increase the velocity of innovation.[1]

I. His first great opportunity

In an effort not to lose sight of the long-term perspective while dealing with short-term problems, Arnold decided to create his own informal group of advisors to help him in long-range thinking. He had found that he was swamped with short-term problem-solving – or putting out brushfires. As he described it:

> My office organization in Washington contained an Advisory Council, a group of young men, the brightest I could get, who sat in an office close to me, and whose instructions were: "Don't get mixed up with any routine business. What I want you to do is sit down and think. Think of the problems confronting us. Think of the solutions to those problems. Bring in new ideas. If you bring in one new idea every two or three days I will be satisfied. But don't get mixed up with the routine operations of this office. Think! Think of the future of the Air Force!"
>
> That Advisory Council, made up changeably of anywhere from three to five officers, was invaluable to me. They brought me new ideas; kept me up-to-date, and best of all, made certain that I was very seldom caught off base by higher authority with any new problem before I had been able to give some thought to it.[2]

In mid-February 1942, he called Norstad and Charles Pearre Cabell into his office and told them: "You two boys ... will be my advisory council.

I need a small office that reports directly to me and can help me with my problems. What I want you two boys to do is to do my thinking for me – my long-range, blue-sky thinking. I don't want you to get into daily operations. As a matter of fact, if I ever catch you mixing in with daily operations, I'm going to fire you both."[3] Cabell and Norstad were called, at various times, "the twins," "the Gestapo," "the kibitzers," "the kids." Norstad said he and Cabell were referred to as the "heavenly twins," because they didn't work through channels, and reported directly to "God."[4]

General Jacob Smart, who joined the Advisory Council in June, summarized the Council's duties:

> Their primary purpose for existing was to think, to evaluate the matters that were being presented or should be presented to him as Commanding General, US Army Air Corps, to him as a member of the American Joint Chiefs of Staff, and as a member of the Combined Chiefs of Staff. We had a fourth mission and that was to measure the matters that he was being confronted with in light of his special relationships with General Marshall.[5]

Norstad and Cabell kept putting up memoranda to Arnold with which he would often disagree. He was indeed a hard taskmaster. As one observer put it: "Arnold had a ruthless impatience with failure, slackness, and incompetence coupled with a furious, sometimes uncontrolled, temper. Above all, he relentlessly drove himself and those around him to succeed at their tasks."[6]

One example of Norstad's and Cabell's attempts to influence Arnold's thinking was their unsuccessful recommendation that Arnold should oppose legislation being considered in Congress that would have established the grade of Flight Officer, and instead to support the retention of the existing policy of commissioning aviation cadets upon graduation from flight school.[7] Another example was a memorandum on plane-borne rockets, in which Cabell and Norstad informed Arnold: "Tests to date have been limited to fighter aircraft but are designed to establish a common basis for the future development of rockets for all types of aircraft. The application to bombardment is expected to entail some additional problems, the seriousness of which have not yet been determined."[8]

Apparently, however, the bulk of the Council's work had to do with the planning activities of the US Joint Chiefs of Staff and the Anglo-American Combined Chiefs of Staff Committee.[9] From this point forward, Norstad was to meet many of the men on both sides of the Atlantic with whom he had to work when NATO was formed and especially when SHAPE was created. This was Norstad's great career opportunity, for it enabled him to demonstrate his extraordinary skills at planning and negotiating to key wartime figures who were to go on to play equally important postwar roles. These skills were to prove essential as he rose in rank and responsibilities.[11] Not the least of these was Churchill's wartime chief aide, General Lord Ismay, who subsequently became the first Secretary-General of NATO.[10]

During and after the war, talented fast-rising officers who shared Norstad's skills – such as Laurence Kuter and Cabell – inevitably formed close relationships as they won the confidence of their superiors. These men, as well as the more famous "fighters" such as Quesada, LeMay and Vandenberg, were equally vigorous and relatively young. Their average age was a little over 42 when the Japanese attacked Pearl Harbor. Arnold was the oldest at 55, Norstad, at 34, the youngest. After the war, when Spaatz succeeded Arnold as Commanding General of the AAF, and then became the first Chief of Staff of the Air Force, this group of younger officers moved into the key positions. Quesada became for a short time Assistant Chief of Staff for Intelligence and then Commander of the Tactical Air Force, Norstad became Assistant Chief of Staff for Plans, and Vandenberg was at first Assistant Chief of Staff for Operations, and then later Spaatz's Chief of Staff. As Norstad put it: "This was a 'new look' Air Force, the young Air Force."[12]

Perhaps the most important tie that all of them shared was their common relationship with death. In the formative years of their military lives, the men who were to run the AAF and then the USAF had lived constantly with death. Even in peacetime, fatalities from aircraft crashes were common, and those who did not survive were often close friends and colleagues. Norstad recalled: "It seems to me that a part of [flying school] routine was going to funerals of people who had been killed, many times classmates, in airplane accidents ... . Certainly, every week of my last year at West Point, it was reported that someone we knew of from a previous class or previous two or three classes had been killed in an airplane accident." Norstad was perhaps reflecting the attitude of his contemporaries when he went on to comment: "That didn't diminish our interest; it enhanced our interest."[13]

Nonetheless, the possibility was ever-present that, on any given day, one or more of their fellow flyers would die. And there was always the possibility of one's own death. This constant presence of lethal danger had its effect on the young air officers. Besides intensifying their fraternal bonds, it tended to engender among them a sense of fatalism, or a belief in fate as a determining aspect of their lives. It also shaped the way they felt about the deaths of those who served under them. Eaker believed it made army flyers more "realistic" about losses before combat actually began: "I won't say you get callous ... but you get realistic."[14] He thought air commanders were more inured to loss than most land or naval commanders. It was once observed about Vandenberg: "Vandenberg had many acquaintances but few close friends. He preferred to keep people at arm's length. Perhaps all the friends he had lost in peace and war ... had hardened him."[15] But this did not mean that they were indifferent to losses, partly because every aviator brought with him very expensive and specialized training as well as a spirit that enabled him to contemplate severe risks.

As it was put: "The special training of officers like Eaker, Arnold, and LeMay, their professional experience, and their common humanity all conditioned the way they reacted to moral issues that arose in their work. What made those reactions so important in the revolution of military morality was the way the attitudes of air leaders were linked to the changes in military technology and theory, which placed civilians, cities, and the treasures of humanity in the battlefield."[16] Norstad was also an heir to this legacy.

This generation also had come to believe in "strategic" bombing as the most desirable primary mission for the Army's air arm. The strategic air power doctrine was worked out in the 1920s at the Air Corps Tactical School, then located at Langley Field, Virginia, just when Norstad was becoming a professional airman.[17] The principles were:

1. Modern great powers rely on major industrial and economic systems for production of weapons and supplies for their armed forces, and for manufacture of products and provisions of services to sustain life in a highly industrialized society. Disruption or paralysis of these systems undermines both the enemy's *capability* and *will* to fight.
2. Such major systems contain critical points whose destruction will break down these systems, and bombs can be delivered with adequate accuracy to do this.
3. Massed air strike forces can penetrate air defenses without unacceptable losses and destroy selected targets.
4. Proper selection of vital targets in the industrial/economic/social structure of a modern industrialized nation, and their subsequent

destruction by air attack, can lead to fatal weakening of an industrialized enemy nation and to victory through air power.
5. If enemy resistance still persists after successful paralysis of selected target systems, it may be necessary as a last resort to apply direct force upon the sources of enemy national will by attacking cities. In this event, it is preferable to render the cities untenable rather than indiscriminately to destroy structures and people.[18]

The constant presence of death was bound to affect the way these airmen felt about decimating populations and destroying the infrastructure of enemy nations. Following the tenets above, many of them came to accept civilian casualties as an inevitable consequence of their work. By the closing years of World War II, *ipso facto*, civilian casualties themselves had become a strategic goal. As it was put: "Mass terror bombing was a whirlwind … . Taking innocent life on a massive scale was being judged acceptable, even unremarkable."[19] From the earliest years of the debate between the efficacy of mass as against precision aerial bombardment there was also always the debate over the scale and the kind of damage to be wrought. Norstad, as his career progressed, was very much involved in this debate.

The special technical training of officers like Norstad, their subsequent professional experience, and overall their shared experience of confronting death almost daily conditioned the way they reacted to the moral issues that arose as they advanced in their command and staff assignments. What made those reactions so important was the way their attitudes were linked to the revolutionary changes that were taking place in military technology and its accompanying theory. They had a tendency to want to see what the new technology would do before they had developed a governing strategic rationale for its use in combat. And they either were unaware of, or uninterested in, the moral implications involved. As one observer said: "the emotional mechanisms airmen used to cope with danger necessarily diminished their sensitivity to combat and destruction. They might become, commented air force psychiatrists, 'effective, careful fighting men, quiet and cool on the ground and in the air' but 'drained of most feelings other than those having to do with combat.'"[20] In this sense, they were the ultimate pragmatists and therefore much in tune with the temper of their times. As General J.F.C. Fuller said as early as 1919: "Tools, or weapons, if only the right ones can be found, are ninety-nine per cent of victory."[21]

LeMay reflected this attitude when considering low-altitude firebombing of Tokyo. He did not have permission from Arnold to change from high-level to low-level bombing with the B-29s, but he heard clearly from Norstad that, in effect: "You go ahead and get results with the B-29. If you don't get results, you'll be fired. If you don't get results, also, there'll never be any Strategic Air Forces of the Pacific – after the battle is finally won in Europe, and those ETO [European Theatre of Operations] forces can be deployed here. If you don't get results it will mean eventually a mass amphibious invasion of Japan, to cost probably half a million more American lives."[22] LeMay also recalled: "Norstad didn't have an idea what I was thinking about, but he did opine that he thought General Arnold was all for going in and getting the war won."[23]

Many of the persons involved in developing and employing the atomic bomb, such as Leslie R. Groves, saw it as a "weapon of opportunity" which must therefore be used.[24] Some of the civilian scientists who had fashioned these lethal instruments – including napalm, the V-2 rockets, the B-29 Superfortress, and the atom bomb – wondered whether mankind would end up in an apocalyptic disaster. When civilians, cities, and the "treasures of humanity" became the battlefield for both combatants, was warfare still an honorable and noble (to say nothing of profitable) profession?[25] Questions such as these were only just beginning to be addressed when Norstad was assuming more and more responsibility, not only in planning large-scale air operations, but also in conducting them.

His first opportunity came early in 1942, when Arnold asked Spaatz to form the Eighth Air Force. Spaatz immediately started preparations for a bombing campaign against Germany.[26] Then later Arnold asked Eaker to go to England to form the Eighth Air Force Bomber Command. As Arnold put it: "'Understudy the British and work out the plans. Then I'll get you some bombers and some crews. You'll be in charge of the Eighth Air Force Bomber Command.' 'Bombers!' Eaker exclaimed. 'But I've been in fighters all my life!.' 'That's why I'm giving you this job,' Arnold said. 'I want you to put some fight into the bombers.'"[27]

Eaker went to England in February with a staff of three career officers and three "converted civilians," to help shape the future conduct of the air war.[28] Later that year, Norstad was assigned to this group. As Norstad recounted:

> I was called down again in the morning ... "You are going to Europe ... you are going to England." Of course, my hope was that I would

get the hell out of there sometime. I didn't want to be caught there for the war. I knew this relationship had been too useful for [Arnold] to give it up easily. I said, "For how long, sir?" He banged the desk and flushed, and his eyes flashed, and he said, "How in the hell do I know how long this war is going to go on?"[29]

Then later: "When I went over, there was no firm decision on either [Europe or Africa]. I can remember we did some work on the areas where we might make a cross-channel landing and what forces would be required, *et cetera*, and on a time-phase basis. We worked more on that than on Africa for awhile. Then the shift was to Africa."[30]

This period in England saw changes in his domestic situation as well. For one thing, Isabelle was left to find a house in wartime by herself, and additionally, she got their daughter Kristin started in school. As with any concerned parent, Norstad had plenty of advice to offer from afar: "I don't believe it would hurt her to learn to read now and I am sure she would get a lot of pleasure out of writing her own name. She has reached a point where she is a little bored with just playing."[31] His sense of idealism concerning the war also was conveyed to his wife and small daughter:

> I think that any estimate of what price we must pay for victory is pure conjecture at this time but it is certainly true that we must pay it willingly no matter what it costs. I also argue that no one in America whose family has not been broken up can talk much about sacrificing. Even in those cases it is more a case of discharging an obligation than of sacrifice. There is always too damn' much loose and sentimental talk about aches and pains that are never felt. You can't realize what a luxurious existence Americans live even in wartime until you see other nations'. Next to us, this country [Britain] has perhaps the best life, but the contrast is a marked one.[32]

II. The North African experience

The Twelfth Air Force, scheduled for North Africa, was activated in England with "Jimmy" Doolittle designated as commander. He formally assumed command on September 23, 1942, thus becoming chief air commander for Operation TORCH working directly under Eisenhower, who had been made Commander in Chief, Allied Forces.[33] Eisenhower at first was reluctant to have Doolittle, but Arnold persisted, and in the end the choice turned out to have been a good one.[34] Arnold personally chose Brigadier General Vandenberg as Doolittle's Chief of Staff, and Colonel Norstad as Assistant Chief of Staff for Plans and Operations. Doolittle was pleased: "Both were superior individuals."[35]

Norstad said: "the planning for the air participation in that [North African] landing was my responsibility, my office."[36] This was when Norstad and Vandenberg became close friends. As it was later described: "This was the first close contact between 'Van and Larry,' and soon the two became close personal and professional friends whose careers were intertwined thereafter."[37] As Norstad wrote to Isabelle from North Africa in January 1942: "I moved about ten days ago to a nicer place where Van and I now live with three other chaps. This has the advantage of giving us coffee and orange juice in the morning and relieves the lonesomeness when one or the other of us happens to be away for a few days. All in all it is a very satisfactory setup. Each of us has his own room and Van and I even have private baths. Of course, you must realize that hot water is usually produced only after heating it in buckets over a fire."[38] Vandenberg's son, Major General Hoyt S. Vandenberg, Jr. confirmed this relationship in a letter to Isabelle written at the time of Norstad's death: "I was aware at an early age that my own father considered General Norstad the absolutely top officer in the Air Force."[39]

In order to assemble the aircraft for the Twelfth Air Force, Arnold stripped the England-based Eighth Air Force of fighter, light bomber, and even some heavy bomber squadrons. These and additional units from the US – often inadequately trained – became three functional Twelfth Air Force components: XII Bomber Command, XII Fighter Command, and XII Air Support Command.[40]

In common with Royal Air Force (RAF) units, the Twelfth Air Force employed both tactical and strategic elements.[41] By "strategic elements" Eisenhower meant bombing units that could destroy distant military targets, such as air bases, shipping, ports, and communications centers. The XII Fighter and XII Bomber Commands – indeed all Allied air resources – would be available to support TORCH ground forces as determined by Eisenhower. Major General George S. Patton, Jr., sailing directly from the US, commanded the Western Task Force that invaded Morocco. Brigadier General John K. "Uncle Joe" Cannon commanded the XII Air Support Command, also formed in the US.

The Central Task Force, which was to land at Oran, and commanded by Major General Lloyd Fredendall, was assembling in Scotland. This was Norstad's unit, having been put in charge of portions of the XII Fighter and XII Bomber Commands.[42] So Norstad personally brought

Applying Planning and Operational Skills in North Africa and the Pacific 29

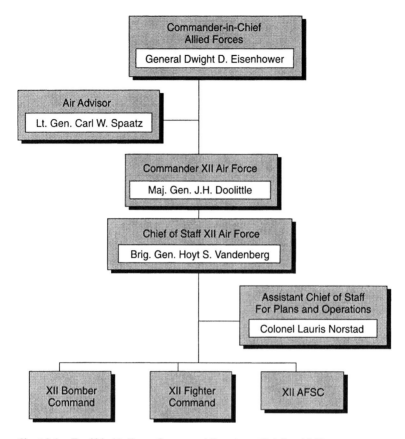

Chart 2.1 Twelfth Air Force Command Structure, October 1942

the air plan from London to Fredendall. As he recalled: "I got into the train ... and put [the plans] on the floor right next to my head, but before I went to sleep, I began to worry about that. I thought, 'My God, somebody could unlock that door and come in here and take that, and I might not know it ... .' I threw out the pillow and I put it under my head. It was just like sleeping on ... marble."[43] It was Norstad's job, during the TORCH landings, to locate the airfield for the Spitfires to land. Their mission was to provide air cover for the Allied invading forces. As he recounts, after having been dropped off on a sandy beach in about two feet of water: "I walked up to where this colonel was. He was someone I knew pretty well in this armored division. 'What can I do for you?' I explained that my duty was to go in. I said, 'I want to go

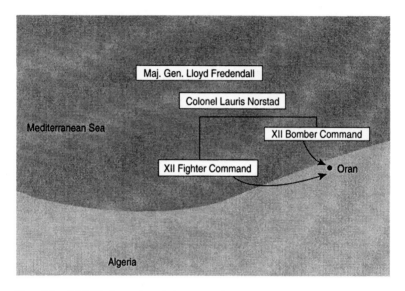

Chart 2.2 TORCH Central Task Force Landing in Oran, November 8, 1942

to Tafaraoui.' This was one of the two or three airfields in the plan that we thought would be captured by this time. 'My job is to get there and send word back to Gibraltar to bring in the fighters so that we have got some cover in the morning.'"[44]

In fact, Norstad was the first air officer to land at Oran. He was the commander on the ground, while Doolittle and Vandenberg remained with Eisenhower on Gibraltar. As Norstad observed: "It was a pretty shaky operation [providing close air support and air cover] because of communications. There was no air–ground communication. We had no system, we had no equipment for that. So the only thing we could do was get some communications technicians who were with us to jimmy up some equipment existing for other reasons, other purposes."[45] Matters went well: "French Dewoitine fighter planes did duel British Seafires and American Navy aircraft over the beaches, but by the afternoon of the first day the airfield at Tafaraoui, near Oran, was in American hands, and Doolittle ordered the 31st Fighter Squadron to depart Gibraltar South."[46]

After Norstad had arranged a local cease-fire with the Vichy French forces, he wanted to encourage positive relations with them.[47] As he recounted it: "I had taken over this little administration building of this base. There were two flagpoles, one on each side of it, a little sort of tower. We had gotten a French flag, and I had arranged that we would have a flag-raising – American flag on the right and a French on the left. I invited the senior French officials in that region to come and participate in this. They came down, and I made a little speech ... ."[48]

Norstad apparently had won the approval of his superiors in his activities around Oran. Doolittle, Norstad's immediate superior, reported to Arnold: "Larry Norstad went to Oran on the Command ship and was in charge of all Twelfth Air Force operations until I arrived. He did an excellent job. He proved himself to be not only a fine planner but an outstanding operator. I intend to recommend Larry ... for promotion ... ."[49] Arnold replied: "I was not surprised to hear of the good work done by Cannon, Hawkins, Norstad, Williams, Allard and Kane. They, as well as many others in your Command, have been well trained to take care of the type of emergencies they are bound to run into."[50]

Throughout this time overseas, Norstad wrote regularly home. His letters were not particularly specific about his official duties, probably due as much to wartime censoring as to inclination. But they did reflect the private emotions that most of his colleagues – commissioned or non-commissioned – were experiencing:

North Africa 15 March 43
My dear Isabelle:
I meant to write to you last night but conferenced until my eyes would no longer stay open. It was my birthday and, once I was reminded of the fact, my thoughts stole back home frequently during a busy day. My only purpose in wanting to write last night was, as usual, to tell you of my love for you and Kristin.

It has been very springlike today. The temperature must have been about that of the middle of May at home and the sun was quite hot. The sun here seems to be much stronger than we normally know it because just a few minutes of it will burn you. My nose is a nice cherry color although the rest of my face seems to be tanning. Perhaps it is still the three months in UK that make me so conscious of sunshine. They were certainly gray and dull enough.

How are your exercises getting along? Don't forget about the danger of my popping in on you. Your walking in California must have been very good for you and I strongly recommend that you continue doing it even if it isn't as convenient in Oak Park [Illinois]. I have always been of the opinion that no amount of the setting up type of exercise can take the place of such thing as walking or swimming. This is a most serious matter.

You mentioned in your last letter that you had received the first three money orders. There are a total of eighteen and they are numbered consecutively. Please keep me informed on their arrival because I was a little worried about sending them by mail.

I am going to take a day off next week and visit the ruins of a large Roman city quite near by. All of this area is full of such things and their state of preservation is most remarkable. So far I have seen only the walls, viaducts, and bridges that you can't escape when driving in a car. My history must have been faulty because I don't recall having known of the great extent to which the Romans developed and lived here. Some of the ruins antedate the Romans and were originally built by the Phoenicians. In fact, where I am at present was a great trading center for the Phoenicians, or so I am informed. It is all most interesting and I will tell you more about it later and also try to get some pictures to send back.

I hope you see some of the pictures of our operations here so that you can learn from them what I am unable to tell you. Many have gone back and I suppose some find their way into the newspapers and magazines.

I am getting sleepy so will give you our goodnight kiss and we will both go to sleep. I love you more than ever and share every wish and thought and hope that you may have, even those little thoughts that cannot be expressed but only felt to exist. Give the family my love and Kristin a big kiss from her wandering daddy who misses her very much.

Goodnight, sugar pie. Larry.[51]

After the ground forces that had landed at Oran and Casablanca had achieved their objectives, they were consolidated into the Fifth Army. A dispute then arose between Doolittle and the two commanders of the ground forces – Patton and Fredendall – over how best to use their air resources. In a report to Patton, Doolittle, while agreeing that ground warfare continued to be the main focus of the theater's operations, also maintained that the first priority was air superiority, with supporting ground action taking second priority.[52]

This priority caused some consternation in Fredendall's case, because he did not want his air cover to be used for anything other than to protect his headquarters from attack. This bothered Spaatz when he learned about it. Norstad recalled: "We [Spaatz and Norstad] went down to Fredendall's forward command post and talked to Fredendall and his staff about the waste of air power. It was utterly useless having it fly around. The only thing to do was put it on Air Force-type missions. They looked blank on that ... . Spaatz talked to Eisenhower. Spaatz gradually took more and more direct control until we finally had direct [command] control."[53] Eisenhower supported Spaatz's view, gained from the experience of TORCH, that overall control of the air battle should be kept separate from the land battle. Even British General Bernard L. Montgomery supported this view: "The greatest asset of airpower is its flexibility, and this enables it to be switched quickly from one objective to another in the theater of operations. So long as this is realized, then the *whole weight* of the available airpower can be used in the selected areas in turn; this concentrated use of the air striking force is a battle-winning factor of the first importance ... . Such air resources will be in support of his army, and not under his command ... ."[54]

Norstad, after the war, observed:

> from November, 1942 to February, 1943 ... Our task force there took that long to learn a great, if rather costly, lesson ... . What, then was responsible for our failures in the winter of 1942–43? The answer, quite simply, is faulty organization. RAF and AAF units were both responsible to Headquarters, Allied Air Support Command, which was under the control and virtual command of the First Army's ground officers. This was in line with the then current American concept of "Support Aviation" and the RAF units were forced to go along with it.
>
> "Support Aviation", as the term implies, shackled air power to the immediate movement and requirements of the ground forces – a hangover from the fairly recent World War I but in effect as outmoded as the Macedonian phalanx. Our American high command had not yet learned the necessity of having an airman run the air war while, independently but always in coordination, the ground officer runs his own campaign. The results of this lag in military science were not disastrous but they might have been; as it was, the enemy hit us hard in Northwest Africa.[55]

The result of the experience being gained in North Africa was the publication on July 21, 1943 of Field Manual 100–20, "Command and Employment of Air Power." This manual was, in a way, a tribute to the British airmen's capacity to learn how to utilize airpower under combat conditions. To many senior Air Force and Army officers, this manual was seen as the AAF's "Declaration of Independence," because it

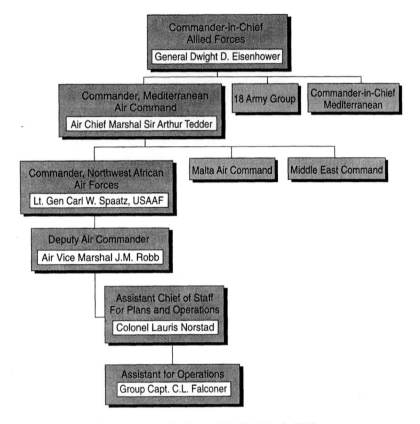

Chart 2.3 Northwest African Air Forces (NAAF), March 1943

established the doctrine for a tactical air force along the lines outlined above by Montgomery.[56] The manual: "stated unequivocally that land power and air power were coequal and that the gaining of air superiority was the first requirement for the success of any major land operation."[57]

After much shuffling of command arrangements, Eisenhower was made theater commander in the Mediterranean, thus separating the European Theater from the Mediterranean Theater.[58] As it was put: "Since the British form of organization was used in the theater, Eisenhower and his successors had coequal land, sea and air leaders under them."[59] The "Mediterranean Air Command," formed under Air Marshal Arthur Tedder, consisted of three units, the most important of which was the Northwest African Air Forces (NAAF), put under

Spaatz.⁶⁰ As Norstad commented: "At the Casablanca Conference [in January 1943], a reorganization was ordered, placing all the air forces in the Mediterranean Theatre under the *command* of Air Chief Marshal Tedder, and the Northwest African Air Forces under the *command* of General Spaatz."⁶¹ Norstad also had this to say about Eisenhower: "I may be somewhat prejudiced on the point since I was there at the time but I think history will support my own feeling that this action of Eisenhower early in 1943 created the US Air Force in fact, if not in name."⁶² He assisted in the formation of the NAAF, which had two components, one being the Northwest African Coastal Air Force (NACAF). The major component, the Northwest African Strategic Air Force (NASAF), under Doolittle, was composed of medium and heavy bombers – B-17s, B-25s and B-26s – which Doolittle used to disrupt enemy rear-area activities.⁶³

Norstad loved bombers so much that he violated the rules and flew missions when he (and Doolittle and Vandenberg) had been ordered not to. The bad example was set by the more senior Doolittle. As it was recounted: "Eisenhower called Doolittle into his office and told him bluntly that he could either be a major general and command NASAF, or he could be a lieutenant and fly airplanes. Which did he prefer?"⁶⁴ Norstad recalled: "Jimmy, Van and I used to sneak out ... . Spaatz not only took my shirt off, he took half my skin off when he caught us at it!"⁶⁵ They were privy to the information received from the top-secret *Ultra* intercepts, and if they had been shot down and captured, there could have been serious consequences for the further prosecution of the war. As Norstad confessed: "I was getting the product of it several times a day. We had a little unit in the attic of the little building where we had the headquarters, with Group Captain Humphreys [R.H.], who is mentioned in the book *Ultra* as one of the original people. He was the guy who briefed me many times a day."⁶⁶ So Spaatz's concern was well-placed.

Norstad wrote to Isabelle explaining to her why he felt detailed reports of his work were neither useful nor desirable:

> You were concerned over the fact that I seem miserly in sending you news of our activities here after they have become accomplished and well publicized facts. One of my recent letters explained that or at least tried to. The answer is the fact that the press reports are quite accurate, very prompt and far more complete than anything that would be said by an individual. You really have the news far better than I could give it. Also, it is sometimes hard to separate

past, present and future when one is familiar with all and all are closely related. There is another reason which you will perhaps think silly. I like to think of these letters of ours as very personal discussions of subjects of personal interest to us. If I were to write about work, it would spoil that atmosphere.⁶⁷

As the North African campaign drew to a successful conclusion, the NASAF turned its attention to Sicily, Sardinia, and Italy.⁶⁸ By January 1943, the priority targets assigned to the NASAF were: the eviction of Axis forces from Africa; strikes on Axis air and naval forces in the Mediterranean; direct support of the Sicilian landings; and destruction of oil refineries at Ploesti, Rumania.⁶⁹ In other words, the focus was shifting from the Mediterranean to the "soft underbelly." Practice for the Ploesti raid took place at Benghazi, and so it was inevitable that Norstad knew of this significant example of early low-level mass bombing.⁷⁰

An indication of the high regard in which he was held at that time, is the Letter of Commendation given Norstad by Spaatz, who was then commanding the Northwest African Air Forces:

> The careful and scientific preliminary planning for and the final execution of air operations against the Island of Pantelleria resulted in its surrender with practically no loss of life to our forces. This outstanding air offensive has demonstrated the results which can be expected of properly planned air operations.
>
> I cannot commend you too highly, as the General Officer in charge of operations, for your splendid and untiring efforts which have resulted in obtaining such notable success for the Northwest African Air Forces and I desire that a copy of this letter be placed in your official record.⁷¹

At the time of his promotion to Brigadier General in March 1943, he wrote to Isabelle: "I am not quite sure it is true yet, having heard only of the nomination, but yesterday 'T' [Tedder] pinned the stars on me, and told me I would wear them even before we heard of the final confirmation. So I am wearing them. It would be far less than honest to say that I am not thrilled. It would also be dishonest to accept this recognition as something which I had earned without the assistance of others. So many people have contributed so much to my life, and luck has also played its part."⁷²

Norstad became Director of Operations and Intelligence of the Mediterranean Allied Air Forces (MAAF), which had formerly been

Applying Planning and Operational Skills in North Africa and the Pacific

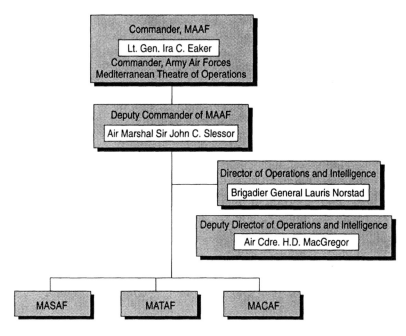

Chart 2.4   Mediterranean Allied Air Forces (MAAF), January–June 1944

the Mediterranean Air Command under Tedder, but now was under the command of Eaker.[73] In this capacity, he helped plan bombing missions aimed at destroying Axis oil installations and interdicting highways in the Balkans and in Italy.[74] The association with bombers underscored Norstad's essential commitment to bombers rather than fighters. As he commented early in the war: "it was clear to me that the fundamentals of air power were around bombers."[75] With an eye on the political aspects of military operations, he advocated a strategy aimed at blocking the Russians from Germany by an Allied push into Austria and Hungary through Yugoslavia's Ljubljana Gap, and then through eastern Germany and western Poland.

Norstad later reflected on the experience of the AAF in North Africa and the Mediterranean: "Here the classic pattern of victorious air power in World War II began to take shape: (1) Eliminate the enemy's air force. (2) Carve out a battle area of your own choosing and cut all enemy supply lines into that area. (3) Cooperate in the attack of your advancing ground troops."[76] A noted British scholar on air doctrine explained why the air war in North Africa was so much a mater of trial and error: "Above all the instability of air doctrine lay in the fact that air forces were compelled to make guesses about how aircraft would be used once war had actually broken out ... much air doctrine was an act of faith that the guesses of one particular air force were the right ones."[77]

III. The Twentieth Air Force and Washington

Norstad was reassigned to Washington in mid-1944 to succeed Haywood Hansell as Chief of Staff of the newly-formed Twentieth Air Force.[78] He was, of course, excited at the prospect. As he wrote to Isabelle in July: "There won't be many more letters from here since in only about a week begins my long trek to the rainbow's end."[79] He later observed wryly: "I came back in the fall of 1944, but in the fall of 1945 and early 1946, we had the return of the young, victorious heroes. I was never a young, victorious hero. I was young, but I was never a victorious hero because I came back too soon."[80]

But just being reunited with his family – as was true for so many of the airmen, soldiers and sailors with whom he had been working and living – seemed an impossible dream. For example, he observed, remembering Kristin's sixth birthday, which fell on March 16, 1944:

> Kristin has given us a great deal of pleasure in the six years she has been with us. I am sure that she will always do so. The time and care you are putting in toward this end will be rewarded in the years to come when we see her grown from a lovely child to a fine young woman. As you know, among my several regrets is the fact that I must be away during such a large and interesting part of her young life. My paternal obligations are a pleasure I hate to miss. The fact that you are doing so well in caring for her is a great consolation.[81]

The Twentieth had been placed directly under Arnold by the JCS. They decided on the kinds of targets to be attacked and left it to Arnold to see that the operations were carried out.[82] This arrangement meant that, in addition to his demanding duties as head of the AAF and member of the JCS, Arnold was commanding a bomber force in combat operations.[83] The unit was independent of theater or area commanders, though the latter were responsible for providing logistical support and base defenses. The theater commanders could, however, utilize the B-29s for their own operations in an emergency.

When Hansell was assigned to command the XX Bomber Command, he wanted to employ sustained precision bombing by large formations of heavy bombers operating at high altitudes. Not obtaining the results Arnold wanted quick enough he was relieved of his command in January 1945, and replaced by LeMay. Norstad was ordered to break the news personally to Hansell in a special trip from Washington.[84] Here we had: "Three young generals – Hansell, the eldest, was forty-one – were arranging for a turnover in what was the most coveted operational command job in the AAF. Norstad was Hansell's friend, had worked with him in the same office, and had succeeded him as Chief of Staff in England in 1943."[85]

LeMay was a stocky, pipe-smoking and cigar-chewing mid-Westerner, only 39 years old. He was naturally shy, which made him uncomfortable in one-to-one situations, and he did not help matters any by speaking in a low tone of voice. His manner approached being taciturn, if compared with his fellow senior officers.[86] Nonetheless, LeMay was to become the symbol of US air might for nearly a generation to both the American people and to the world.

In sharp contrast, Norstad was a tall, slim, graceful – almost elegant – man, who possessed an intensely analytical mind yet who kept his inner thoughts to himself. He was a forceful participant in committee meetings, having a clear, almost loud speaking voice, but he was not verbose. It is difficult to imagine that Norstad and LeMay could be very comfortable with each other, given their diverse social and military backgrounds and temperaments.

Vandenberg became the Air Force's most popular symbol of the glamour of air power. He was the prototypical ever-youthful flyer. General Omar Bradley, who was to serve as Chairman of the JCS when Vandenberg was Air Force Chief of Staff, observed: "Van was as handsome as a movie star and cool as a cucumber."[87] Both Vandenberg and Norstad were more similar to each other than either was to LeMay. Norstad explained it this way: "Van and I, as one looks over the record, so frequently came up with exactly the same position. How could two men think so much alike … . Because we saw so much of each other and we were working together so many hours a day and night, we were always talking about almost every subject … . We talked about everything, and anything he had in his mind he would raise, and anything I had in my mind I would always raise."[88] Unfortunately, Vandenberg died in 1953 of cancer.

Initially, LeMay, after the handover of the command from Hansell, was also frustrated with weather and logistics problems and was obtaining results not dissimilar to Hansell's. On March 9–10, 1945, having shifted, at LeMay's initiative but with the tacit support of Arnold and Norstad, from explosives to low-level mass incendiary firebombing, the Twentieth's B-29s reduced to rubble and ashes most of the congested residential areas, nearby factories, and transportation centers of Tokyo.[89] In talking with Norstad before the raid, LeMay wanted Tokyo "burned down – wiped right off the map."[90] He almost got his wish. General Thomas Power, who took aerial photographs of the city, recalled: "True there is no room for emotions in war. But the destruction I witnessed that night over Tokyo was so overwhelming that it left a tremendous and lasting impression on me."[91] When the 314th Wing returned to Guam, LeMay was there to greet it with Norstad at his side. LeMay told his flyers that if they had shortened the war by "only one day or one hour," they had "served a high purpose."[92] Arnold wired him: "Congratulations. This mission shows your crews have got the guts for anything."[93] Power later called the Tokyo raid: "The greatest single disaster incurred by any enemy in military history ... . There were more casualties than in any other military action in the history of the world."[94] The historian Ronald Spector concurred: "It was the most destructive single bombing raid in history ... ."[95]

These "saturation" bombing raids subsequently became the object of intense inquiry. Norstad had expected that morale bombing would cause Japan to capitulate rather than resist invasion. Earlier, in November 1944, Norstad had proposed to Arnold that Pearl Harbor should be commemorated with a massive air attack against the Emperor's palace as a way to diminish the Emperor's prestige, thereby weakening the Japanese faith in him.[96] Arnold had replied: "Not at this time. Our position – bombing factories, docks, etc. is sound. Later destroy the whole city."[97] Further, when one of the conclusions of the postwar Strategic Bombing Survey (SBS) suggested that saturation bombing increased morale, Norstad remarked that he was "astonished."[98] In any event Norstad was not alone in this assessment concerning area bombing and morale because after the war, Japanese officials agreed that the B-29 attacks did indeed kill morale.[99] LeMay went even further than Norstad in his expectations when he told Norstad that the air war against Japan had provided the opportunity to show that strategic bombardment could win wars.[100]

The exigencies of winning the war seemed to justify employing the most awesome airborne weapons ever devised up to that time – the B-29 Superfortress and then the atom bomb.[101] At Potsdam, where President Truman decided to use the atomic bomb (then little more than a clumsy "device"), Arnold reluctantly gave his assent. As it was reported (but not documented) by Margaret Truman:

The following day [July 22] my father convened a conference of his chief advisers in the little White House at Babelsberg [near Potsdam] to make the final decision about the use of the bomb. More than two months of thought by the best available minds was at his fingertips. Once more [since the White House meeting of June 18] he polled the men in the room. Only one man had changed his mind. Commander of the Army Air Force General Hap Arnold now thought Japan could be bombed into submission with conventional weapons ... but none of the other military men – especially General Marshall – concurred with General Arnold.[102]

Whether or not, in fact, Arnold did or did not concur with the decision to use the bomb, either before or after the decision had been made, he was convinced that the B-29 could be the instrument to bring the Japanese to sue for peace. This, in turn, would bring a public relations dividend to the AAF in its constant desire to shape the course of the air war to reinforce Arnold's desire for independence. He had invested enormous energy and prestige in bringing the B-29 on line, overcoming financial, technological, and political obstacles. As LeMay had put it to Norstad the previous April: "I am influenced by the conviction that the present stage of the development of the air war against Japan presents the AAF for the first time with the opportunity of proving the power of the strategic air arm ... . I feel that the destruction of Japan's ability to wage war lies within the capability of this command."[103] Norstad had commented also that LeMay's XXI Bomber Command could make the Japanese "lose their taste for more war."[104] Norstad was part of Arnold's staff, thereby participating first-hand in Arnold's last significant military act. Arnold retired early in 1946 after having suffered yet another in a series of heart attacks in November 1945.[105]

For most of his professional life, Norstad believed that massive air power, inflicting if necessary indiscriminate destruction, would ultimately – almost inevitably – lead to victory and peace. It might also be said that air power was a useful concept to support the argument that "operational necessity" governed decisions to escalate the violence.[106]

The top civilian and military leaders of the US war effort shared the goal of defeating the Axis as efficiently and rapidly as possible, and the methods of air warfare they utilized were all aimed at that objective. Yet none of these men, including Norstad, acted simply on the basis of rational calculation in determining the course of the air war. Like everyone involved in the conflict, from combat troops to heads of state, the people responsible for the air attacks felt the stress of warfare and developed mental protections against it. The pressure to be tough, or at least not to appear soft and idealistic, was present in military organizations at all levels. Scientists felt this pressure too, and so did other civilians who worked with military people and who needed to retain their confidence. For instance, Spaatz was almost convinced that Sir Solly Zuckerman's "very coldly analytical and precisely applied method ... almost persuaded him that in modern war the best general was a 'mathematical genius.'"[110] Even Eugene Rabinowitch, one of the committee members of the Strategic Bombing Survey, commented: "We were all deeply moved by moral considerations, but we did not think that in the necessarily a-moral climate in which wartime decisions have to be made these would be effective."[111]

This fusion of science and military strategy, with an avoidance of the moral or amoral implications in order to defeat absolutely absolute dictatorship, was to continue into the Cold War. As Zuckerman observed: "if all-out nuclear warfare really does mean mutual suicide, and if it were ever to break out, those who survive, or their descendants – such as they might be – might well judge that technical developments of the 1940s had led to somewhat disastrous national and military policies and strategies. This, rather bluntly, is what I mean by the danger of technological developments forming strategies which may be incompatible with presumed national interests."[112]

Whatever cautious men such as Zuckerman may have had in mind, the advent of the atom bomb as the supreme instrument of warfare also coincided with the emergence of a suitable enemy – or "threat" – that would justify its use. In a study that Norstad conducted in September 1945, in which he made the first working estimate of the number of atomic bombs the US should stockpile during the years 1945–1955, Norstad assumed that the Soviet Union and the US would be deadly rivals. Therefore, the US should plan to destroy the Russian capability to wage war against the US and its allies, and this should be the basis for estimating atomic bomb requirements.[113] Destroying Russia's capability to wage war would have, inevitably, destroyed the fabric of Russian society as well.

When World War II was over, changes inevitably took place in the military leadership in Washington. One of the greatest beneficiaries of these changes was Norstad. Having worked closely with Arnold and Spaatz, he found himself being promoted to Major General and assigned as the Assistant Chief of Staff for Plans and Operations to the new Army Chief of Staff, Dwight D. Eisenhower. As Norstad observed: "He wanted an Air Force guy in Plans and Operations, which was the key job. That was really the center of the staff, the War Department General Staff."[107]

In Norstad's opinion, the Cold War began in December 1946. It had to do with the Soviet Union's threatening Turkey over access to the Dardanelles – or Turkish – Straits. Norstad, for the Army, was part of a group convened by the Secretary of War, Robert Patterson, and the Acting Secretary of State, Dean Acheson, to consider what the US should do. Vice Admiral Forrest G. Sherman represented the Navy. This was the beginning of what came to be a very significant collaborative relationship between Norstad and Sherman. When the group had arrived at a consensus, Truman asked them to join him in the White House. As Norstad recalled, Truman said to them:

> "Gentlemen, I have asked the Secretary of State to bring you over here because this is a critical development. This could be a turning point in history. Up to this time, we have all hoped that, based on our experience in World War II, we could get along and work together in the future, but this presents a difficulty in that respect. This could be, not only a turning point in US history, but it could be a turning point in world history." He said, "For that reason, I have asked you all to come over, and I want to hear from each of you why you believe this is the position that must be taken." He went down the line, and each of us had to say that we believed we should tell the Turks to say no to the Russians, and in order to do that, we would have to promise to back the Turks. We each had to give our reasons for believing that. When we got all through, the President said, "Gentlemen, this is now the policy of the United States."[108]

The US rivalry with the Soviet Union was the platform from which Norstad's talents as planner, commander, and negotiator took him to the pinnacle of multinational military leadership. The logical conclusion of the interwar and wartime concept of strategic "air power" was the Cold War doctrine of "massive retaliation." Norstad came to the belief that retaliating massively with weapons of mass destruction was essential, first, to deter and then, if deterrence failed, to destroy the Soviet Union. He came to that belief naturally. For him, it did not require a leap of faith to justify using the "ultimate weapon" for an ultimate purpose; in fact, it would have required a leap of faith for him *not* to have believed in deterrence through massive retaliation. As Zuckerman observed: "Having lived and worked with [Norstad] in North Africa in 1943, I felt that I knew him well enough to realize that he meant what he said when he declared that he would not hesitate to initiate a nuclear attack .... The result would be a devastated Europe covered in radioactive rubble and dust, not a Europe that had been saved."[109]

At this time, Arnold asked Spaatz to head a committee of three to assess the meaning of the atomic bomb for the AAF, and by extension, for the US. Specifically, they were to assess: "the effect of the atomic bomb on the size, organization, composition, and employment of postwar Air Forces." The other two members were Norstad and Vandenberg; thus Norstad was kept at the center of nuclear affairs in the evolution of the US's postwar military planning. In their report, submitted in October 1945, the so-called Spaatz Board assumed: that the secret of atomic bombs could not be preserved; that other nations would soon have delivery systems comparable to those of the US; that no one would risk war with the US unless they possessed an equal or greater number of weapons; that the US should find overseas bases for its planes; that the heavy bomber would continue as the main delivery vehicle for ten years or so; that a stockpile of nuclear weapons would be available for war; and that there would be no time for mobilization after the onset of future wars. Although some of these assumptions proved invalid, essentially the Board reaffirmed the validity of the air doctrine developed in the battle against Germany and then applied against Japan. It also affirmed that the atom bomb "only enhances the validity of the strategic bombing doctrine."[114] It did not replace it with a new "strategic" doctrine – at least not yet.[115]

To keep abreast of the new technologies, which had been developed in the secrecy of the Manhattan Project, the Spaatz Board recommended setting up a new position of Deputy Chief of Air Staff for Research and Development. LeMay was given the assignment. He proposed that the US should begin to think of a first-strike strategy of defense, assuming that the prospective enemy's capacity to inflict early and devastating damage would preclude the "lead time" for mobilization that the US had enjoyed in World Wars I and II. Thus was born the doctrine of deterrence, based upon a threat of a preemptive "first strike" that would be so damaging to the enemy that the enemy would be deterred from itself launching a first strike.[116]

3
The Battles for Unification and for Berlin

> Let us give the people of the United States the best, the most efficient, the most modernly equipped armed forces possible ...[1]

I. Separating the Army Air Force from the Army

Throughout the war, Arnold had been very sensitive to the public's perception of the uses of air power. He wanted public opinion to assist him to move quickly, as soon as the hostilities ceased, to establish the Air Force as a separate and coequal Service with the Army and the Navy. This is one reason for his focus on "strategic" bombing as the central concept of Air Power doctrine, rather than on the use of air power in support of the land (or naval) battle. As he had written to Eaker in June 1943, when Eaker was Commanding General of the Eighth Air Force:

> It is also very important, for whole-hearted public and official support of our Air Forces in their operations, that the people understand thoroughly our Air Forces precepts, principles, and purposes ... it is important for the people to understand that our prime purpose is destruction of the enemy's ability to wage war, by our planned persistent bombing and sapping of his vital industries, his transportation, and his whole supply system ... . In short, we want the people to understand and have faith *in our way of making war*.[2]

In December 1943, Major General Barney M. "Bennie" Giles, Arnold's Chief of Staff, wrote: "We are devoting a great deal of thought to plans for the organization and composition of a postwar Air Force. At the present time, a preliminary outline only has been completed, but it is contemplated that the Air Force will be identified separately and equally with the Army and Navy."³ In May 1945, when Arnold made Norstad Assistant Chief of Staff for Plans on the Air Staff, he made it clear to him that in this critical position Norstad should take the lead in planning for the postwar Air Force. As it was observed: "With the uncanny eye for talent that characterized him, Arnold now turned to another rising young two-star, Major General Lauris Norstad, who took over [Laurence] Kuter's post as Assistant Chief of Air Staff, Plans. Norstad had been a top planner and combat air commander in England, North Africa, and Italy and had been promoted to the rank of brigadier general at thirty-six."⁴

Although Norstad worked closely with Eaker, who had become Deputy Commander, AAF, by the end of the Summer Norstad had, by and large, assumed the major role in shaping the postwar Air Force. When asked how the Army felt about this, Norstad replied: "I must say I think they were reluctant to see it because it took something away from them. It is understandable. So they saw this as giving the Air Force independence at the expense of taking something very vital away

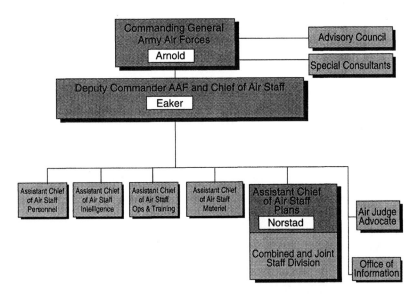

Chart 3.1   Organization of the Army Air Forces (AAF), Post WWII (as of March 21, 1946)

from them."⁶ He recounted how Eisenhower, when he became Army Chief of Staff in 1947, handled this sentiment:

> Eisenhower came back as Chief of Staff of the Army. He asked Tooey before he arrived to meet with the Air Staff and the senior officers of the Air Force first. That was his first meeting. At the second meeting he asked to meet with the Army equivalents. He invited me to both meetings. Of course, I would go to the Air Force meeting by virtue of position, but he invited me to the Army meeting. He came into the Air Force meeting and told us about what he thought of the Air Force performance in the war and the contribution to the war effort. I knew this well because I had served with him during the war. But he made it clear, and said not only had the Air Force come of age, but it should be independent and operate itself. It was clear that it had to be independent if we were to get the greatest effectiveness out of it.⁷

In November, 1945, anticipating retirement, Arnold directed that Spaatz, his tipped successor, should oversee Norstad's work, and "render the policy decisions which will govern the Air Forces' objectives, aims and methods."⁸ At the same time, Arnold specified that Norstad should take the lead in coordinating the work of the entire Air Staff as it pertained to unification matters.⁹

The Division was headed by Colonel Reuben C. Moffat, and had by the end of the war completed a draft bill to establish an independent Air Force. Further, with Norstad monitoring his work, in November and December 1945, the Air Judge Advocate suggested for the sake of discussion three alternatives: a separate Air Force coequal with the Army and Navy with a Secretary of the Air Force of cabinet rank; a completely unified Department of Defense; and *the status quo*.⁵ It goes without saying which Norstad preferred.

Norstad was dealing with two major organizational questions. The first was the broad issue of the command relationship between the AAF and the War Department, and the second was the postwar organization of the AAF. Since budgets can control both the functions and the composition of all the Services, it obviously was not going to be easy shaping a postwar Air Force while at the same time agitating for the creation of an independent air arm that would inevitably become a competitor for scarce funds. The Army was not only concerned about the Air Force's seeming preoccupation with strategic bombing rather than close air support; it was also concerned that vital logistical support resources would be diverted to this new – and presumably expanding – Service. In fact, as early as 1944 the Air Force had recommended a 105-Group postwar Air Force to Marshall, who responded that this would be impossible because of economics.[10] Norstad agreed: "the 105 [figure] really never had any position. It was never accepted as a position. The first really firm Air Force position was a 70-Group program, and that was later cut down for practical reasons, largely budget ... ."[11]

Norstad's planning staff also inherited tentative planning assumptions made by Brigadier General F. Trubee Davison's Special Projects Office. In July 1945, Davison had drawn up a so-called "V-J Plan," to be activated upon Japan's surrender. This plan was similar to the notion of an Interim Air Force which Eaker had approved in May 1945. Immediately following the dropping of the two atomic bombs on Japan in August 1945, and with surrender imminent, Norstad decided to move ahead with planning for a postwar Strategic Air Force along the lines of the Twentieth Air Force to include all "very heavy" bomb units. The Twentieth thus became the harbinger of the Strategic Air Command (SAC) as a specified JCS command.[12]

Norstad noted at that time: "Greater consideration should be given to a more smooth transition from the Air Force of this period to the ultimate peacetime Air Force."[18] Prior to Arnold's official retirement in February 1946, Norstad held long conversations with him about this. One key element of this consideration was not to ignore the unique command arrangement that had worked so well for the Twentieth. As Arnold put it:

> The average military man accepts certain principles of war as fundamental. Yet, these principles were violated, or would have been violated, time and time again, had we of the Air Force not fought against dispersion ... against scattering our airplanes all over the world. It required constant attention and vigilance to assure that such diversions were not made ... . Even as late as January, 1944, we still had to resist a pressure that would have weakened our bomber operations in the Pacific, destroying the genuine air power that comes only from mass formations of bombers.[19]

Most important would be the precedent of the Twentieth operating directly under Arnold and out of the control of theater commanders. Arnold had made it quite clear why he had run the Twentieth in this way: "while everybody wondered why I kept personal command of the Twentieth Air Force – the B-29s – there was nothing else I could do, with no unity of command in the Pacific. I could find no one out there who wanted unity of command, seemingly, unless he himself was made Supreme Commander."[13]

Then, in late August 1945, based upon the War Department's guidance, Eaker asked Norstad to prepare another Interim Air Force plan which would be in effect until July 1948. The plan was completed by mid-September. Both of Norstad's plans called for an Air Force consisting of 78 Groups and 32 separate Squadrons. The "Interim Air Force" – that is, bridging the period between the end of World War II and the creation of an independent Air Force – was charged to furnish occupation forces in Europe and Asia; to provide a long-range striking force; to include a strategic reserve; to provide an Air Transport Service; and to maintain training and research facilities in order "to insure the ability to engage in total warfare in a minimum of time." The interim force would level off to 550 000 by July 1948.[14] The Air Force would operate all land-based military aircraft "with the exception of liaison aircraft which are included in ground force elements as part of their unit equipment and with the exception of certain types of land-based aircraft organic to the Navy."[15] The object here, of course, was to build an effective postwar Air Force from what air leaders knew would be the shambles of demobilization.[16]

Spaatz, Eaker, and Norstad moved to establish a "Committee on Reorganization of the Army Air Forces," which would formulate the AAF's objectives. The Committee had initially proposed that four "air forces" – one strategic, one tactical, and two air defense – be established under the Continental Air Forces. But Spaatz and Norstad wanted to form only two commands: a Continental Air Force and a strategic bomber force. As mentioned earlier, based on the strategic bombing experience during the war, Norstad and the top leadership of the AAF were determined to create a strategic force separate from the tactical and air defense forces. He and his colleagues were convinced that strategic bombing was inseparable from the drive for an independent Service. By establishing a Continental Air Force (CAF) and a separate strategic force, they figured that the CAF would be coordinate with the Army Ground Forces, and that the Air Staff would be coordinate with the War Department General Staff. Finally, the Committee on Reorganization recommended that an "Air Force Combat Command" (AFCC) should be created immediately, thereby placing the Army Air Forces on an equal line with the Army Ground Forces. AFCC would consist of a strategic, a tactical, and two geographical air defense organizations, separated by the Mississippi River. This proposal was approved by Spaatz in early January 1946.[17]

As these command relationships were being worked out, Eisenhower, was under pressure from General Jacob L. Devers, the Commanding General of the Army Ground Forces, to designate a tactical air command to support the ground forces. The question of what to do with the strategic air component was not Devers's concern.

In response, in March 1946, immediately after succeeding Arnold as AAF Chief of Staff, Spaatz created three major combat air commands. Spaatz first fulfilled his obligation to match the ground Army's continental US structure by creating the Air Defense Command (ADC) at Mitchel Field under Lieutenant General George E. Stratemeyer. Six air forces would be assigned to ADC, aligned geographically to coincide with the six army areas. Spaatz then formed the Strategic Air Command (SAC) at Bolling Field under General George C. Kenney. Last but not least, he created Tactical Air Command at Langley Field under Lieutenant General Elwood A. Quesada, thus meeting the Army's desire for a tactical entity to support the ground forces.[20]

Probably most important for Norstad out of all of this planning, with Arnold now in retirement, was the opportunity of working so closely with Eisenhower, and fortunately for Norstad, they had achieved a fine *rapport*. As Norstad observed, quite correctly: "the friend I had was Eisenhower because by that time Eisenhower had long since accepted me as one of his principal advisors ... . [This is something that] has to be built up, and without it, you are powerless. In official life you are powerless unless you have the Eisenhowers or somebody like an Eisenhower behind you. The big stick in the United States in those days was Eisenhower ... . He had the prestige with the public, with the Congress, with the press, and with the President."[21]

Eisenhower had made clear to Norstad his support for a separate Air Force, the need for economy in military administration, and the necessity for unified command. It was evident that they shared certain fundamental principles of modern command which were not necessarily shared to the same degree by many of their contemporaries.[22]

II. Unifying the Armed Forces

Enjoying Eisenhower's confidence, Norstad became the point man on the Army team formed to draw up a unification bill that both the Army and the Navy could accept. Secretary of War Robert P. Patterson and Assistant Secretary of War for Air Stuart Symington provided the political support which was vital if the Air Force was to achieve its goal. But the Navy took a harder position on eventual unification than had the Army under Marshall's and then Eisenhower's leadership.[23] For example, in the Spring of 1945 Secretary of the Navy James V. Forrestal had sought to counter their argument that a single department would foster economy and efficiency. It was a fallacy, Forrestal emphasized, "to assume that the difficulties and over-lapping inherent in administering two large operations ... can be resolved by the act of merging them." The history of large business organizations showed that there was "a course inherent in the fact of bigness itself – a law of diminishing efficiency."[24] Forrestal and the Navy stressed administration through coordination. They pointed out that at the highest military policy-making level, unity and coordination had been achieved successfully through the mechanism of the JCS. They also worried publicly about the effect unification would have on *l'esprit de corps*, the "high state of morale which causes a man to believe that the organization to which he belongs is better than anything else."[25]

The Navy's most senior admirals – Nimitz, Leahy, and King – opposed the majority recommendation of the JCS Special Committee on Reorganization (Richardson Committee) that favored a single Department of National Defense and a separate Air Force. Their counter-argument was that the creation of three separate Services could result in even more duplication in procurement. Nimitz stressed that the AAF should continue to be part of the War Department. King claimed that placing four Services – Army, Navy, Air Force, and Marine Corps – within a single department would further divide them because it would breed friction. The Navy feared that unification could well result in its losing naval aviation as well as losing the Marine Corps.[26]

Persisting in his opposition, Forrestal even turned down the recommendations of a report that an old friend of his prepared. Testifying in October 1945 before the Senate Committee on Military Affairs, Forestall emphasized that he did not accept the recommendations of the so-called Eberstadt Report, even though, while proposing three separate departments, Eberstadt had opposed creating a single Department of National Defense. As he had concluded in his testimony: "It seems highly doubtful that one civilian Secretary, with limited tenure of office, could successfully administer the huge and complex structure resulting from a unification of our military services." Instead, the three coordinate departments would be connected by committees under the JCS. Coordination remained the key for Forrestal, as opposed to centralized administration.[27]

With this firm opposition coming from the Navy, Eisenhower's testimony became critical. Whereas Arnold was expected to advocate before the Committee independence based on the overwhelming success, as he saw it, of the air forces during the war, Eisenhower was expected to speak from the experience of the wartime Supreme Commander who came to his task from a career in the ground Army. Moreover, given the manner in which Eisenhower had handled difficult issues and personalities as Supreme Commander, most of the Senators viewed Eisenhower as a true military statesman. They expected from him an objective and reasoned presentation in the midst of all the Service partisanship that was taking place. Eisenhower emphasized unity of command as opposed to joint command. He stated flatly that unity of command had been absolutely necessary for victory in World War II; without it no system of joint command could have worked. "Separation at the top," he noted, "necessarily fosters separation all along the line." In this connection, Eisenhower informed the Military Affairs Committee that plans for the Normandy invasion had been

> based on a deep-seated faith in the power of the Air Forces in overwhelming numbers to intervene in the land battle, *i.e.*, that the Air Forces by their action could have the effect on the ground of making it possible for a small force of land troops to invade a continent ... without that Air Force, without its independent power, entirely aside from its ability to sweep the enemy air forces out of the sky, without its power to intervene in the ground battle, that invasion would have been fantastic. Unless we had faith in air power as a fighting arm to intervene and make safe that landing, it would have been more than fantastic, it would have been criminal.[28]

Eisenhower fervently believed in what he called the principle of "the three-legged stool." Each Service had to be mutually dependent upon the other, since in peacetime no one Service would be able to be budgetarily as well as functionally self-sufficient. It was no longer feasible, he emphasized, "to arrive at the size and composition of each arm without simultaneously considering the others. Each arm supplements the other and no single service can be independently considered." So long as the War and Navy departments existed "we will continue to be harnessed with the needless extravagance of double administration, overlapping duplications, differing standards, and competitive procurement."[29] "Competition," he reminded the Congress, "is like some of the habits we have – in small amounts they are very, very desirable; carried too far they are ruinous."[30]

Eisenhower's belief that a single department buys more security for less money found a most receptive audience in Congress. Furthermore, his view was fully reinforced by Truman, who had become a strong supporter of the principle of unified command. The disaster at Pearl Harbor, in Truman's mind, was as much "the result of the inadequate military system which provided for no unified command, either in the field or in Washington, as it was any personal failure of Army or Navy commanders."[31] He wanted a system which would respond more effectively to national emergencies.

Influential newspapers and journalists supported Eisenhower's and Truman's position. *The New York Times*, for example, editorialized that a unified department would "simplify and speed up procedure, eliminate rivalry and assure the same kind of coordination in peace which necessity compelled in war."[32]

Well aware of fundamental disagreement over roles and missions between the Navy and the War Department, on December 19, 1945 Truman delivered to the Congress a special message on defense reorganization. He stated bluntly that the coordination of strategic planning by committees of the JCS would no longer suffice. The unified direction of land, sea, and air forces was mandatory. As he put it: "any extended military effort required overall coordinated control in order to get the most out of the three armed forces. Had we not early in the war adopted this principle of unified command for operations, our efforts, no matter how heroic, might have failed."[33]

Truman recommended the creation of a Department of National Defense headed by a civilian "Secretary of National Defense." Based on the wartime experience, he proposed a separate Air Force, coequal to the Army and Navy: "Air power has been developed to a point where its responsibilities are equal to those of land and sea power, and its contribution to our strategic planning is as great. In operation, air power receives its separate assignment in the execution of the over-all plan. These facts were finally recognized in this war in the organizational parity which was granted to air power within our principal unified commands."[34]

Truman emphasized that much work remained to be accomplished. It was not simply a matter of organization: "It [unification] will require new viewpoints, new doctrine, and new habits of thinking throughout the departmental structure."[35] The President's message sent a clear signal: In the wake of the failure of the Senate Military Affairs Committee to report a bill, he wanted action. It was now up to the Congress and the two competing Services to produce one. Truman's speech to Congress broke loose the conflicting Navy and Army positions on this matter.

With Truman, Eisenhower, and Arnold lined up behind the concept of reorganization, the Navy found itself in the difficult and tenuous position of opposing what seemed to be, in Norstad's words, "An idea whose time had come."[36] The Navy however, led by Forestall, continued to firmly oppose the idea.

In response, Senator Elbert D. Thomas, Chairman of the Senate Military Affairs Committee, formed a subcommittee, including Senators Warren R. Austin and Joseph Lister Hill, to write unification legislation. This subcommittee asked Norstad and Vice Admiral Arthur W. Radford, Deputy Chief of Naval Operations (Air) to advise them. "I was intensely interested in this," Norstad recalled, "and I got an extra office in the Pentagon, and I put up paragraph by paragraph, or subject by subject, all of the proposals that had been made on every one of the pertinent subjects, on organizational relationships. I could sit there at a desk and see all of the proposals that had been made and compare them ... ." This "did not require a hell of a lot of staff work. It required a little leg and arm work."[37]

During the early months of 1946, Norstad and Radford sat in on the meetings of the subcommittee that was writing the bill. After much deliberating, rewriting, and refining, the subcommittee reported a bill (S.2044) in April 1946 to the Military Affairs Committee. The Common Defense Act of 1946 called for a single Department of Common Defense, three coequal Services, and a "Chief of Staff of Common Defense" as military advisor to the President. Norstad was generally encouraged with this bill, although he was aware that the Navy continued to mount stiff opposition.[38]

This notion of a chief of staff to a Secretary of Defense was popular in military circles. For example, Norstad stated in a memorandum for the record at this time that "my view on the necessity for a Chief of Staff had not changed in two years and reiterated my opinion that the National Military Establishment could not get on a sound basis until it had a strong military man to advise the Secretary, to carry into effect policy matters which required implementation by the Services."[39]

Forestall remained deeply suspicious about creating a Secretary of Common Defense and an independent Air Force. He and the naval leaders still feared that eventually the naval air arm and perhaps the Marine Corps would be lost. They also convinced themselves that an overall Secretary would likely make decisions that would adversely affect the Navy.

Truman, meanwhile, desired action. He made clear to Patterson and Forestall that he expected them to resolve these contentious issues – and quickly. He directed the Service Secretaries to present him with a satisfactory solution by the end of May 1946.[40]

Norstad and Symington went to work, checking with Patterson and meeting with Forrestal, Eberstadt, and Radford. Norstad enjoyed a close working relationship with Symington: "we really could work as one and it was a splendid experience." He recalled that when it came to trust, Symington had emphasized: "I have put my heart and my lungs in your hands." For Norstad, speaking of Symington and Vandenberg: "There was a long time when we had reason to believe perhaps the only people we could really trust were each other."[41] Another, perhaps more pro-Navy, version had it: "Another air force general who was coolly skeptical of Symington was Lauris Norstad, a West Pointer of exceptional ability. A rational air-power advocate, he took a much broader view than most of his fellow air force officers and strongly supported Eisenhower's vision of truly integrated forces."[42] In any event, Symington has gone down in history as a vigorous advocate of a strong and independent Air Force, both as the first Secretary of the Air Force and later as a Senator from Missouri.[43]

The May meetings resulted in agreement on eight points, primarily the creation of various agencies in the overall national security establishment, but they failed to resolve the questions of the single department, a separate Air Force, the future of land-based aviation, and the status of the Marine Corps. The Navy continued to harbor the suspicion that a civilian Secretary of National Defense might make decisions prejudicial to its interests. Norstad, on his part, continued to make the point that unification worked in war and was needed in peace; he also noticed that naval leaders seemed to be easily offended when criticism was directed their way.[44]

Truman welcomed the agreement on the eight points, although he was perturbed that the four outstanding issues were obviously the crucial ones. He met with Patterson, Forrestal, Norstad, and Radford, and spelled out what he wanted: a Department of National Defense that was headed by a civilian; each of the three Services would be run by a civilian secretary; the Navy would keep the Marines and aircraft essential for naval operations. The Services, Truman told Patterson and

Forrestal "should perform their separate functions under the unifying direction, authority and control of the Secretary of National Defense. The internal administration of the three services should be preserved in order that the high morale and *esprit de corps* of each service can be retained."[45]

To speed matters along, Forrestal asked Vice Admiral Forrest Sherman to represent the Navy Department, replacing Radford in the unification negotiations with Norstad. Because Radford was viewed as a "hard liner" even in the Navy, Forrestall and the Chief of Naval Operations, Admiral Nimitz, had decided that Sherman, who supported a balanced fleet and the establishment of an independent Air Force, could negotiate more effectively with Norstad and the Army. He was an aviator, as was Radford, but Sherman was considered "a centrist" rather than a zealot. Radford subsequently noted that Sherman and Norstad had "removed the impasse between the services."[46] In July, the JCS formally named Norstad, now Director of Plans and Operations for the War Department General Staff, and Sherman to write a unification plan which would satisfy both the Army and the Navy. This represented a turning point in the struggle to find a compromise.

Norstad's move from AAF Headquarters to the War Department gave him more leverage in the unification talks and a clear mandate to represent the views of Patterson and Eisenhower.[47] Norstad was pleased, of course, that Eisenhower had specifically requested him, but no one was more delighted than Spaatz. The assignment was not received with unalloyed enthusiasm in some Air Force circles, however. As one Air Force consultant put it: "I must say that I have received with some alarm the news of your assignment to the General Staff. In my opinion it is flattering to the Air Forces but by no means in their best interests."[48]

Norstad and Sherman structured their work into three parts: organization of unified commands; national security organization; and functions of the Services. The question of overseas unified commands bore some immediacy and had already been under discussion for several months. Under an overall unified commander the component commanders from the Services would be supported by a joint staff drawn from the various components. Unified command had been put into practice in Europe during World War II under Eisenhower, but not in the Pacific. Divided command had prevailed between MacArthur, commanding the Southwest Pacific Area, and Nimitz, commanding the Central Pacific.[49]

Led by Eisenhower and other prominent Army and AAF commanders, the War Department and the AAF wanted unity of command based on functions, whereas the Navy favored establishment of commands according to geographic areas. Eisenhower was convinced that his system of unity rather than joint command had made victory possible.[50] Later, when SHAPE was set up, Eisenhower and Norstad applied the same principles of organization to NATO's international command.

The going was not easy. As Norstad commented to a friend in mid-1946: "Some of the Naval Affairs Committee testimony on the Unification Bill used to raise my blood pressure. Recent reports however, if correct, appear too ludicrous to get excited about."[51] But he remained optimistic, telling friends and colleagues throughout this period of negotiations that he thought that the merits of Truman's desire for unification would prevail. He reported to his former mentor, Arnold, at one point:

> Of course, we are all impatient because of the delay in getting action on the Floor of Congress, but at the same time we believe that the Bill has a good chance. You are more familiar than I with the various means by which delay can be introduced into Congressional action. I think we would under-estimate the Navy if we thought for a moment that they wouldn't take advantage of every possible means of stalling off final action. This may not, however, work entirely to their advantage since it is becoming evident in many quarters that the more the subject is discussed, and the more clearly understood the general framework of a Single Department becomes, the greater is the willingness to accept it as a necessary forward step.[52]

Norstad was very much involved with countering any adverse editorial opinion that appeared in the major newspapers and in the columns of the syndicated political journalists. In fact, he had been dealing with the press for some time, having been designated by Arnold to be the Air Force spokesman. For example, he read with great care Hanson Baldwin's column in *The New York Times*. Norstad wrote to an Air Force political consultant after one of Baldwin's articles had appeared to favor the Navy: "I would like to discuss with you the subject of an answer to Hanson Baldwin's article in the *New York Times* on June 21st. We certainly should prepare something in general rebuttal, but the release must be carefully timed with the status of legislation."[53] In 1947, Norstad and Sherman felt it necessary to approach Baldwin directly about one of his columns: "I am sure that neither the Navy nor the Army wish to interfere in any way with honest, objective reporting, but I feel that in this instance there may be at least a tinge of misunderstanding."[54] Norstad's civilian boss, Symington, was more blunt about Baldwin. As it was recounted: "One evening [General Elwood] 'Pete' Quesada was having cocktails with Baldwin at the Mayflower Hotel, when Symington walked into the bar and saw them together. The next day he called Quesada to his office and said: 'You don't pick your drinking companions very carefully, do you?'"[55]

Norstad claimed that Baldwin was not a thorn in his side, which probably was true, but also it appears that Norstad favored more his relationship with Arthur Krock, another influential *New York Times* journalist. He said: "Arthur Krock was a great friend of mine, and I admired him tremendously. I spent, it is fair to say, hours a week with Arthur .... Krock had, of course, better than any journalist that I have known in my lifetime, a political understanding, and he had an understanding of the role of the military in political matters and in power."[56]

Certainly a source of power for Norstad was his affiliation with the Krock and the Joseph Alsop groups. Both men staged dinner parties where conversation was the main menu item, and there would be a core set of invitees, of which Norstad was one. For example, in a letter to Isabelle and Kristin in July 1948, when they were away from Washington's oppressive summer heat, he mentioned: "Joe Alsop stopped in night before last to chat about a Post article he is writing. He came in shorts and we sat around until about eleven. It was very interesting."[57] Candidly, Norstad observed about his efforts to cultivate what today we would call "the media": "believe me, this helped me a great deal in my work."[58]

Because of the high visibility that the Norstads had achieved at this point in their Washington experience, Isabelle now had the opportunity to observe first-hand from such experienced and famous hostesses as Gwen Cafritz and Pearl Mesta, how to organize large and gracious dinner parties whose purpose was essentially business although appearing as social occasions.

In fact, the Norstads' "reach" of highly-placed friends and acquaintances extended beyond Washington. In a personal vein, for example, Norstad wrote to Mrs. Cornelius Vanderbilt Whitney: "I am flattered that you remembered me in connection with CV's birthday gift. I am getting off this afternoon a pair of small stars, to which I'm afraid I cannot attach any very significant occasion. Their period may be established by the fact that I wore them at the Potsdam Conference in the summer of 1945."[59] On a more official level, Norstad wrote quite candidly to Whitelaw Reid of *The New York Herald-Tribune*, referring to an editorial that appeared to be slanted toward the Navy: "Frankly, I thought it was below the standards of the paper and, of course, would like to see your paper on our side of this subject. However, I think that reasonable and constructive opposition is good for any cause as long as it fairly represents an honest difference of opinion."[60] David Lawrence, of U.S. News & World Report fame, whose column was carried in influential New York and Washington papers, expressed alarm and dismay over the battle of words that was taking place: "President Truman may urge and Congress may even some day legislate a merger of the armed services, but it will be a useless move unless some way is found to remove the bitterness which apparently is increasing as between the Army Air Forces and the United States Navy in certain important segments of personnel."[61]

In their effort to defuse the situation, the Norstad–Sherman approach asked: "What is the problem? What are we trying to do?"[62] Norstad had already answered the question in his Congressional testimony in which he had recommended that the roles and missions debate be kept outside the passage of the unification legislation, and agreement had been obtained for the two negotiators to do this. As he put it: "Even if now we do have a favorable decision by the President on this subject [roles and missions], the injection of this subject into legislation is still unsound and I am convinced that the fight that would result would successfully sabotage any attempt at getting something through this year."[63] Norstad and Sherman aimed to create a system of unified command in all theaters, with the theater commander responsible to the JCS. Each theater commander would have a joint staff and three Service commanders under him. They solved the problem in the Pacific by recommending the formation of two commands, the Far East Command and the Pacific Command. A total of seven unified commands were created under their Outline Command Plan. Norstad reported to Arnold the final stages of this legislative Odyssey:

> Having worked with the Subcommittee for almost four months, I accompanied them when the Bill was presented to the President. We were there for almost an hour, during which the draft of the law was gone over paragraph by paragraph. The President appeared to be satisfied with it and expressed general approval. It would be unfair to state that he approved S. 2044 at that time since he hadn't personally read it and, also, I understand that there is some protocol governing the President's expressing a too definite opinion on specific legislation which is in the process of consideration by the Congress.[64]

It was approved by the JCS, and signed by Truman on December 14, 1946. The JCS approved establishing the following unified commands: Far East Command; Pacific Command; Alaskan Command; Northeast

Command; Atlantic Fleet; Caribbean Command; and European Command. The JCS also recognized the existence of the Strategic Air Command (SAC) as an AAF Command composed of strategic air forces not otherwise assigned and not usually based overseas. SAC had already been formed as an AAF major combat command in March 1946, but the JCS did not formally assign a mission to SAC until April 1948 and it was not formally reorganized as a JCS specified command until 1951. This evolution was entirely consistent with Norstad's earlier concept for SAC.

Truman's approval of this system of unified theater command set the stage for the further changes in the command structure that have taken place since. Service component forces hereafter would be commanded by the unified commander acting under the direction of the JCS through an executive agent. The JCS would determine operational assignments. The three Service Departments under the Department of Defense were given roles restricted primarily to organizing, training, and equipping the forces for operational employment within the unified command structure. The Norstad–Sherman discussions thus resulted in a landmark command reorganization, flowing from the lessons of World War II.

Following the approval of the Unified Command Plan, Norstad and Sherman worked with the Senate Military Affairs Committee to craft legislation for the new national security organization. Their strategy called for them always to appear together before the Committee. "We agreed," Norstad recalled, "that if one of us was called ... one would notify the other and would also suggest to the committee that they call the other member ... . Sherman and I were invited every time ... . It was clear that there were differences between us, certainly in degree, but they never really split us on the principles."[65] Norstad emphasized: "It was characteristic of our relationship, due more to him than to me perhaps, that we never wasted time rearguing established differences between the services. We outlined the issues."[66] Working with the Committee, they were able to agree generally on Service functions and on a draft organizational setup. This was presented to Patterson and Forestall, who insisted that the individual military departments retain their administrative autonomy.

In January 1947, they forwarded a joint letter to Truman with a draft organization that included a provision for a Secretary of National Defense and departments of the Army, Navy, and Air Force, each headed by a civilian Secretary. Roles and missions would be promulgated by a Presidential executive order to be issued concurrently with Truman's approval of the legislation.[67]

In late February, Truman sent Congress a draft of the National Security Act of 1947 which was introduced into the Senate as S.758 (H.R. 2319 in the House). A Secretary of National Defense would head the National Military Establishment consisting of departments of the Army, Navy, and Air Force. A separate position of Chairman of the JCS was added in the 1949 Amendment to the Act.[68] The Marine Corps would be kept intact as part of the Navy Department and naval aviation would be responsible for naval reconnaissance, anti-submarine warfare, and protection of shipping.

This bill was certainly a compromise. On the one hand, Truman, Eisenhower, and Spaatz had succeeded in creating an independent Air Force, but on the other hand the Navy had won its point on having a weak Secretary of National Defense who would basically be a coordinator. As Symington put it, this amounted to a good first chapter, but hardly a book. The Senate and the House approved the bill in July by voice vote. On July 26, 1947 Truman approved the legislation known as the National Security Act of 1947 and on the same day he also signed Executive Order 9877 which spelled out the functions of the armed forces. Norstad and Sherman could take justifiable pride in their accomplishment.

The Navy had wanted roles and missions, or functions, written into the Act, detailing and protecting missions of land-based reconnaissance and anti-submarine warfare. Eisenhower, Spaatz and Norstad opposed the Navy's view, arguing that roles and missions should be approved by the executive branch as a function of the Commander-in-Chief. Norstad and Eisenhower emphasized that the issue of roles and missions could not be resolved through a statement attempting to spell out in detail each Service's responsibilities. The major objective of this legislation should be to chart fundamental principles.[69] Executive Order 9877 specified the Navy's air functions as naval reconnaissance, anti-submarine warfare, and the protection of shipping. Specific Air Force functions included gaining general air supremacy; establishing air superiority; operating the strategic air forces; air support to land and naval forces; air transport except that provided by the Navy; and coordination of air defense among the Services.[70]

Executive Order 9877 further prescribed the function and role of the newly-created Air Force:

1. To organize, train, and equip air forces for:
   a. Air operations including joint operations.
   b. Gaining and maintaining general air supremacy.

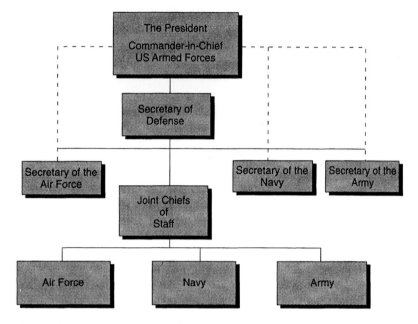

Chart 3.2 US Armed Forces, 1947 (As Cabinet Members, the Service Secretaries had direct access to the President)

    c. Establishing local air superiority where and as required.
    d. The strategic air force of the United States and strategic air reconnaissance.
    e. Air lift and support for airborne operations.
    f. Air support to land forces and naval forces, including support of occupation forces.
    g. Air transport for the armed forces, except as provided by the Navy in accordance with paragraph 1f of Section III.
2. To develop weapons, tactics, technique, organization and equipment of Air Force combat and service elements, coordinating with the Army and Navy on all aspects of joint concern, including those which pertain to amphibious and airborne operations.
3. To provide as directed by proper authority, such missions and detachments for service in foreign countries as may be required to support the national policies and interests of the United States.
4. To provide the means for coordination of air defense among all services.

5. To assist the Army and Navy in accomplishment of their missions, including the provision of common services and supplies as determined by proper authority.[71]

Not unexpectedly, Norstad's and Sherman's accomplishment was resented in some quarters in both the Air Force and the Navy. According to Norstad: "We were both suspect" and Sherman's role "was deeply resented" by admirals who continued to oppose the establishment of a separate Air Force. "I ... think," recalled Norstad, "that he could have cared less."[72] In the AAF, those who felt let down by Norstad thought that he had given in to the Navy on land-based air, and as Norstad himself put it: "I had not diminished the naval air service." The fact remained that Norstad thought that there was a role for naval aviation because it retained "some very special missions which are quite separate and distinct and the Marine Corps has some."[73]

Even Arnold, Norstad's mentor, had some feelings of disapproval. Norstad recalled that after Arnold retired he had returned to Washington from California to attend a reception. But at the reception, as Norstad went to the group surrounding Arnold: "I could tell from the look in his eyes that he was going to make a pronouncement so I braced myself. He said, in the presence of these people, including some Air Force people, 'You have sold us down the river!' That was a blow. With that, I turned – I didn't say a word – I just turned and I walked out of the reception and went home. I was sick."[74] Not long after however, Arnold again returned to Washington, and this time Arnold embraced him in a group of people "and that was the end of that problem."[75]

Despite the negative feelings and the backstabbing both in the Navy and the Air Force, Norstad and Sherman succeeded because the officials who really counted retained unwavering confidence in them. Forrestal and Nimitz had replaced Radford, the hard-liner, with the moderate Sherman because they knew that Sherman could work well with Norstad and yet not surrender too much. Spaatz, Eisenhower, Patterson, and Symington appreciated Norstad's acumen, and all in some way had groomed him for this culminating role. During negotiations and appearances before committees, Norstad regularly reported to Patterson and Eisenhower. He did not, however, have to clear anything with either of them; they let Norstad represent them and the War Department. Norstad of course knew their views and precisely how far he could go. "Ike" and "Tooey" thought like Patterson: "you pick a

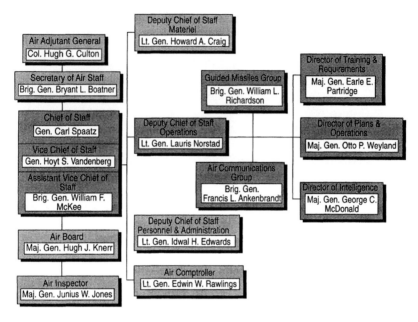

Chart 3.3   The Air Staff, Headquarters USAF, October 1947

man to negotiate, in whose judgement you have confidence and who you feel understands the objective you have in mind, then you back him and you support him. You don't tie him down in little details."[76] Buttressed by these personal relationships of long standing, Norstad could engage with confidence in the give-and-take with Sherman and the politicians.

Despite this strong support and understanding, even after passage of the Act, the antipathy to Norstad within the AAF persisted. Recognizing that this was the situation, Norstad asked Spaatz for a transfer out of Washington, possibly with a reduction in grade, or if he remained in headquarters that he not be promoted in grade or position.[77] Spaatz and Symington ignored his suggestion, and instead, to his undoubted satisfaction, in October 1947, Norstad was appointed Deputy Chief of Staff for Operations in the new Headquarters, USAF. His career was far from over, and soon was to take on more significance than he could ever have imagined. But this was one reason why, when Norstad's name was mentioned in the speculation over who would succeed Vandenberg as Chief of Staff in 1954, there was never any serious possibility that this would happen. A bona fide "flyer," rather than what was unfairly seen by many Air Force officers and their civilian supporters as a compromising negotiator, was preferred.[78]

Overall, there were expressions of appreciation for Norstad's having completed a difficult task. For example, the Chairman of the Atomic Energy Commission, David E. Lilienthal, wrote to him: "Your work in the development of the Unification Plan is something in which you should take great satisfaction. Plans and reports are all very well but it is the fellow who can translate them into actuality, as you and your associates have done in respect to the unification of the services, that is the kind of accomplishment that most appeals to me."[79] An influential Member of Congress extolled him:

> Now that the tumult and the shouting have subsided, I cannot resist the urge to express to you my gratitude and admiration for the work you did in connection with the so-called Unification Bill. Of all the persons engaged in building this structure you, I am convinced, laid the most important foundation stones ... . It was a structure that the country *had to have* and you contributed mightily to its erection. And I may add that I derive great satisfaction and advantage from the help which you gave me in reaching a better understanding of the intricacies of the task and in clarifying my own conception of it. I am grateful to you and wish you continued success in the service of our country.[80]

Norstad and Sherman continued to maintain a very cordial relationship. For example, in one exchange, Norstad commented: "I feel that I owe you the utmost frankness since that has been the basis of our association in the past ... . One further preface – you have been sorely missed by at least one person in Washington. I am sure that my work has doubled and that frustration at times has at least quadrupled because of the lack of someone in your department with whom I could at least disagree on a logical and reasonable basis."[81]

Sherman responded: "I hope that I can achieve the point of view that [Eisenhower] had in mind. It is easier to achieve it in the calm surroundings of a flagship afloat than it would be to maintain it in Washington ... . Of course I may never again be involved in the higher command organization in Washington. If I ever am, I hope you will be on hand as before to lighten the load."[82] Sherman went on to become Chief of Naval Operations (CNO), but regretfully he died unexpectedly before he had time to complete his tour of duty.

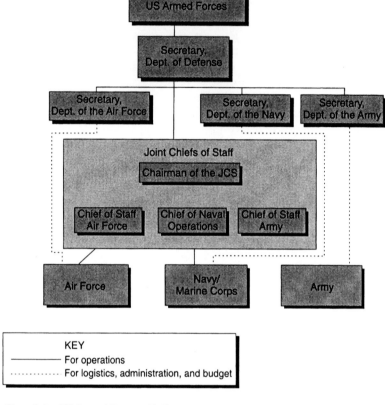

Chart 3.4 US Armed Forces, 1949

III. Berlin: a testing ground for the West

While Norstad was negotiating armed forces unification – essentially at this stage a matter of internal military politics – the international situation turned more threatening to the US's interests in Europe. On March 20, 1948, the Soviet Representative walked out of the Allied Control Council (ACC), which had been formed to provide quadripartite governance for the city. The arrangement had been agreed upon at the Potsdam Conference, which Norstad attended to assist Arnold.[83]

Then, on March 31, the Soviet Deputy Military Governor informed the US governor that beginning on April 1, all US personnel passing through the Soviet zone would be asked for their identification, and they would inspect all freight shipments and other baggage except personal. The US Military Governor, General Lucius Clay, rejected these conditions. Nonetheless, trains were stopped at the interzonal border in order to prevent their continuing on if the train commanders refused to submit to inspection. Finally, between April 1 and July 1, Soviet troops sealed off all highway, rail, and river traffic into and out of Berlin. "Technical difficulties" were offered as the explanation.

The Soviet argument was that the US had never possessed a legal right to be in Berlin; later, this argument was changed to assert that even if the US possessed a legal right, that right had been forfeited.[84] The immediate argument was that in February the three Western Occupying Powers – the US, Britain, and France – had combined their three zones into "Trizonia" and in June had extended the arrangement to the Western sectors of Berlin. One of the primary purposes for these actions was to revalue the mark in order to bring about economic revival in their zones. It was this currency reform that the Soviets found threatening because this step was an important stage in the *de facto* partitioning of Germany as a whole, and which had its reflection in the *de facto* partitioning of Berlin. The Soviet's intentions were to forestall the creation of a West German government and this appeared to be the next logical step that the US and its two occupying partners would take.[85]

It was difficult to prove the matter of "rights" one way or the other because the arrangements had been made by the generals on the scene at the time of the collapse of the Nazi regime. Clay, who had been the US participant, later confessed that he should have insisted on a written confirmation of the agreement.[86] But the real issue was, as Truman put it flatly: "What was at stake in Berlin was not a contest over legal rights ..., but a struggle over Germany and, in a larger sense, over Europe."[87] The Chairman of the JCS, General Omar Bradley, said that Clay's first cable sent on March 5, reporting on the changed situation in Berlin: "lifted me right out of my chair."[88] Clay had asserted: "For many months based on logical analysis, I have felt and held that war was unlikely for at least ten years. Within the last few weeks I have felt a subtle change in Soviet attitude which I cannot define but which now gives me a feeling that it may come with dramatic suddenness."[89]

One of the consequences of this challenge was that the Air Force scored a dramatic public relations *coup* in the budgetary and roles and missions politics then going on in Washington. More important, perhaps, the actions of the Air Force – with the noteworthy cooperation of Britain's RAF – was to score an even more dramatic political–military victory over the Soviet Union in the struggle to control the future of Europe. As Air Force Deputy Chief of Staff for Operations, Norstad was at the heart of the planning and execution of the famed airlift that was instituted to "run" the land blockade that had been imposed.

Clay, and his State Department Political Advisor, Robert Murphy, had advocated using armed convoys to break through the barriers that had been erected to control land access, but the JCS opposed this idea.[90] Norstad agreed with the JCS. As he put it: "Some of us felt at the time that the worst thing we could do would be to do some blustering and shed some blood and when we got the reaction, strong reaction, just back off."[91] When Clay sent a train across the Soviet zone border, the Soviets shunted it to a siding where it stood along with other trains that had been deprived of their engines. After a few days, Clay ordered the train to return to the Western zone. His "shoot our way in" policy had been rejected in Washington. What Clay wanted was the movement of convoys with troop protection, either on the highways or by rail. From April to June the Soviets steadily tightened a noose around Berlin through enforcement of measures of harassment and intimidation concerning the access routes and political appeals directly to the citizenry of Berlin to oppose the currency reforms. Initially these efforts were successful, but then matters turned against them.

According to Dean Acheson, the month of June was the turning point that led to the final break with the Soviet Union over Germany. He listed these events:

June 7   London [currency reform] recommendations announced.
June 11 Soviet Union stops rail traffic between Berlin and West for two days.
June 12 Soviets stop traffic on a highway bridge for "repairs."
June 16 Soviet representative leaves *Commandatura* (four-power military control in Berlin).
June 18 Western powers announce currency reform in West Germany.
June 23 Soviet Union imposes full blockade on Berlin. Western powers stop freight from combined zones to Soviet zone.[92]

Also, in June, the matter had been referred to the United Nations as being a "threat to the peace." The debates proved unproductive, but eventually it was through this channel that the crisis was resolved.[93] Philip Jessup, the Deputy US. Representative who was put in charge of US diplomacy in the Security Council, is credited with keeping this diplomatic channel open.

Then, on June 27, Forrestal, Royall, Lovett, Bradley, and Norstad met to determine what to do. They visualized three possibilities: to withdraw from Berlin before September 1, when a constituent assembly for a west German government would have met; to retain the Allied position in Berlin by all means; try for a diplomatic solution while staying firm, thus postponing an ultimate decision.[94] They also considered sending the B-29s to Europe as a show of force – noting that the symbolism of atomic weapons associated with the B-29 would not be lost on either the Europeans or the Soviets. As Spaatz overstated it, given the paucity of actual bombs in place: "[the B-29s had a capability] comparable to a fleet of 79,200 fully loaded B-17s carrying TNT ... and these demonstrations have not been lost on the rest of the world, including Soviet Russia."[95] The following day, at a meeting with Truman, Truman simply stated that there would be no discussion on that point, because "we were in Berlin by terms of an agreement and ... the Russians had no right to get us out by either direct or indirect pressure."[96] Truman also authorized sending the B-29s, which were in actuality non-nuclear equipped, to Germany and to England.

This represented a substantial increase in the US's air "presence" in Europe, which imposed severe financial strains on Britain.[97] As Norstad reported to Vandenberg in February 1949: "The British are having difficulty maintaining, from an aircraft standpoint, their part of the Berlin airlift." The notion was to loan twenty-four C-54s to the British, and also to assist in providing construction funds for the four new bases to be built to accommodate the B-29s that were being sent.[98]

Clay, who was a logistics and construction engineering specialist, and LeMay, who was at the time the Air Force theater commander, possessed extensive World War II experience in staging airlifts and utilizing large air fleets.[99] They advanced the idea of a temporary airlift to bring food and supplies into Berlin. The air routes had not been challenged, and were therefore not vulnerable to the "legalisms" of the ground access routes. LeMay was opposed to a permanent airlift because the transport had been earmarked for war mobilization and evacuation, not for hauling food and coal. Vandenberg also had misgivings.[100]

"Operation Vittles" was created on June 22, 1948, when LeMay was ordered to "utilize the maximum number of airplanes to transport supplies to Tempelhof Air Drome, Berlin ... Strict adherence to existing air corridors will be maintained."[101] When LeMay outlined what he thought was necessary to carry out this order, Norstad promptly authorized the following:

> Approximately 39 C-54 skymasters, passenger and cargo carrying acft [aircraft], from the Alaskan, Caribbean and Tactical Air Commands of the USAF have been ordered to the Frankfurt area of Germany at the request of the Theater Commander, Gen. Lucius [D.] Clay, for increased air facilities to supply Berlin. When they arrive in Germany the airplanes will be under the operational control of Lt. Gen. Curtis LeMay, CG [Commanding General] of the USAF in Europe. The airplanes will begin leaving their bases within 24 hours, singly or otherwise as they become operationally ready for the mission.[102]

On July 9, LeMay informed Norstad that the Russian element at the Berlin Air Traffic Safety Center had filed notice that the Soviet Air Force would, on that day, undertake an indefinite period of instrument training in specified areas within the Frankfurt–Berlin Corridor at altitudes as high as 11 500 feet. Fortunately, no engagements between Soviet and US planes ensued.[103] In the Berlin air corridor crises a decade later, Norstad was to experience similar forms of harassment at Soviet hands.

When, inevitably, the airlift began to take on more than an improvisational quality, Vandenberg continued to express concern that it was taking up too much of the Air Force's resources in aircraft and personnel, thus drawing down against commitments needed elsewhere.[104] At a meeting on July 22 of the NSC, after Vandenberg had reiterated his reservations, Clay assured him that another airfield (Tegel) would be built to handle the increased traffic in and out of Berlin.[105] Then Truman "directed the Air Force to furnish the fullest support possible to the problem of supplying Berlin."[106] There was no more hesitation after that about making a strong effort to test the notion that Berlin could be supplied entirely by air.

A special organization, the Combined Airlift Task Force (CATF), was created within USAFE on July 26, 1948, and was placed under the command of Air Force Major General William H. Tunner, who was Deputy Commander of the Military Air Transport Service (MATS). He formally took command on July 31, 1948.[107] Tunner had made his reputation during World War II organizing resupply operations over the famous "Hump," into China.[108] Nine MATS squadrons totaling eighty-one C-54 four-engine transports were sent to Germany. The transport planes were mobilized from wherever they could be found.

During the Fall of 1948, the Air Force did indeed find itself dangerously over-stretched. Because of Soviet buzzing of the Berlin air corridors, placing of barrage balloons at various points, and occasional ground firing, fighter escort also had to be requisitioned. Morale in the Air force was low, and evacuation plans to Britain were revived. As General John K. Cannon (who had replaced LeMay when LeMay assumed command of SAC) reported to Vandenberg: "he could evacuate, but he could not fight."[109] Fortunately, the Soviets did not want war; if they had, they could have jammed the radio-guidance mechanisms that would have made flying at night and in bad weather virtually impossible, thus crippling the airlift.[110]

Through "Operation Vittles," the Air Force was able to move some 5600 tons of food and fuel a day, which was sufficient to maintain the Berliners (and the West's troops) on 1880 calories per day. The result was that some of those involved considered the airlift to be the greatest success of the Cold War. From June to September, the Berliners rallied against the Soviets and toward the US.[111] On April 16, 1949, almost 1400 aircraft had landed in Berlin and the average daily deliveries at this time were well over 8000 tons, including more than 5000 tons of coal. The USAF was responsible for about two-thirds of this achievement, with the RAF providing the remaining one-third.[112] This laid the foundation for a solid West German ally in the heart of Europe, which was considered the "flashpoint of the Cold War."

The beginning of the resolution of the crisis had come at the end of January, when, in reply to a letter sent him by Kingsbury Smith, the European manager of International News Service (INS), Stalin failed to mention the currency reform as the reason for the blockade. On February 15, when Jessup queried Jacob Malik about this lapse, the Soviet representative to the United Nations replied that he would find out the significance of the omission. On March 15, Jessup received word from Malik that the omission had been intentional and by May an agreement had been worked out to end the blockade.[113] The barriers over the land routes were lifted at midnight on May 11.

The airlift had been a spectacular success, not only in logistical terms, but probably equally important, in raising the spirits and the confidence of the West that the Soviets could be successfully challenged in Europe. The purpose of the entire exercise was to avoid a war with the Soviet Union, but not at the expense of having the invaluable resources of Western Europe – and Germany in particular – sacrificed. This attitude was to prevail throughout the remainder of Norstad's career, and was to provide the foundation-stone for him as he rose to become the West's foremost symbol of determination to "face down" Soviet provocations and intimidations in its gigantic struggle with the US over Europe.

During this entire period, the JCS worked without any specific guidance from either the NSC or from Truman. As Bradley said: "During the critical phase of the Berlin Blockade, when we were nose to nose with massive Soviet military power, the JCS were so poorly advised that we could not draw contingency war plans. Our exposure was enormous."[114] Forrestal, however, claimed that the paralysis was due precisely to the roles and missions debate then going on. In fact, at a meeting on March 11–14 Forrestal had convened at Key West, in which Norstad was a participant, to devise a statement of Service functions, Berlin was also discussed.[115] Perhaps significantly for Norstad's future, the Berlin crisis was the catalyst that brought about the signing in April 1949 of the North Atlantic Treaty and the subsequent creation of the military dimension of NATO. It is noteworthy that the first meeting of the Seven-Power Ambassadors' Committee to frame the Treaty took place on July 6, 1948 against the backdrop of the crisis over Berlin. This whole process was not without its fits and starts as the US moved gingerly toward entering into an "entangling alliance" in peacetime – or what came to seen as the militarization of the Cold War.[116]

Later, when Norstad was acting as the lynchpin for the Berlin crises of the late 1950s, he constructed a system of US national and NATO multinational planning operations that permitted extensive contingency planning to go forward continuously as the crises unfolded. But also, as will be discussed later, the channels for decision-making had become much more complicated, thanks in part to the need to consult NATO Allies.

4
Norstad and the "Grand Strategy" for the Cold War

> Alliance command is fundamentally different from national command and its legitimacy depends on the authority of national leaders.[1]

I. Contingency planning for Europe

By January 1950 Norstad expected to leave his assignment as Air Force Deputy Chief of Staff for Operations, to replace Twining as Commander in Chief of the Alaska Command.[2] But, as he said to Barton Leach: "I wouldn't bet even money on it at this time."[3] Planning had been going rapidly forward as to how the US should confront the Soviet Union in Europe.[4] It was becoming increasingly apparent that the loose structure created after the signing of the North Atlantic Treaty in April 1949 did not provide enough political reassurance as well as military security.[5]

This was due, of course, to national budgetary politics as well as to the exigencies of military planning. In this pre-Korea period, the overall armed forces were being reduced to bring them into line with the budgetary cuts that Truman and his second Secretary of Defense, Louis Johnson, had decreed. It was therefore vital that the Air Force fight hard on the Washington political battlefield in support of its budget requests. In this inter-Service competition for budgetary favor, Norstad had been an effective "player." This situation and the assignment he held suited Norstad's temperament perfectly.[6]

One method to justify the budget was by devising a supporting rationale based on contingency plans – and planning, of course, was Norstad's *forté*. The immediate postwar period contingency plans had been developed by the Joint War Plans Committee (JWPC) for the Joint Staff Planners (JSP), who in turn shared their work with the Joint Strategic

Survey Committee (JSSC). The JWPC had assumed, in a concept of operations prepared in March 1946, that although the Soviet Union did not seek a war with the United States, the possibility of clashing territorial interests could result in conflict. This would more likely break out in the area of Turkey and Iran than in Europe itself, but could spread rapidly. Therefore it was necessary to acquire the forward bases and lines of communication from which the United States could strike at the Soviet Union's military-industrial installations.[7] By April 1946 this concept of operations had acquired the designation of PINCHER, and remained the basis of further war planning.[8]

Even then, however, official thinking was very cautious rather than bellicose. For example, in October 1946, Norstad, as Assistant Chief of Air Staff for Plans, had observed to Truman: "There are ... several factors which would tend to indicate that resort to force of arms by the Soviets is not imminent."[9] Norstad gave as his reasons for this conclusion that: "the Soviet Union had a depleted war potential; an incomplete assimilation of the satellite nations; lack of a strategic Air Force or an effective defense against such a force; and our possession of the atomic bomb."[10]

A JPS document of February 1947 stated:

> The outline plan has been prepared on the conservative assumption that weapons of mass destruction, such as the atomic bomb, will not be used by the United States and its allies, even though it appears almost certain that these could be made available in considerable quantities initially and an additional number produced over the three year period covered by this guidance.[11]

Not long afterward, however, the JCS, and particularly Army Chief of Staff Eisenhower, concluded that it was virtually inevitable that atomic weapons would be used and that planning should take this reality into account. It should be noted, however, that for a brief time Truman entertained some hope that a system of international control of atomic weapons could be devised through the United Nations, and that this colored the military planners' conclusions. In fact, there had been established an "Ad Hoc Committee" to ensure the collaboration of the State, War and Navy Departments in regard to the Security Council functions of the United Nations. For the War and Navy Departments, the JSSC provided their representation. In any event, Norstad was reserved, if not skeptical, about the utility of the United Nations: "this is one step – and a good one – but that it takes some working out before we can count on it being anything more than a good effort."[12] As it turned out, the Cold War prevented the internationalization of the atom from ever reaching the level of a "good effort."

Once the United Nations prospect dimmed, then the planning could include both conventional high-explosive weapons and atomic weapons. The "special weapons" – the official euphemism for atomic weapons – planning component eventually resulted in a SAC Operation Plan, dubbed OPLAN 14-47. LeMay, serving as Deputy Chief of Air Staff for Research and Development, was intimately involved in these activities, which were to continue when he assumed command of SAC in October 1948.[13]

The Air Force had already developed an Emergency War Plan (EWP) code-named MAKEFAST. It was more of a targeting plan modeled after the wartime strategic bombing goals of World War II – that is, focusing on petroleum refineries. By August 1947, the JWPC was instructed to prepare a joint war plan against the Soviet Union that would cover the following three years. By November 1947, the Joint Strategic Plans Group (JSPG), which had replaced the JWPC, had completed "Joint Outline War Plan BROILER." The JSP had also been reconstituted as the Joint Strategic Plans Committee (JSPC). BROILER foresaw that the Soviet Union would overrun Western Europe and consequently the United States and its allies would need to defend the Western Hemisphere, Britain, and the Cairo-Suez area. In order to do this they would need to undertake a strategic air offensive utilizing both conventional and atomic bombs against "vital elements of Soviet warmaking capacity."[14]

As US–Soviet relations continued to deteriorate, planning continued apace. For example, in April 1948, planners from Britain and Canada met in Washington with their American counterparts to produce the EWP HALFMOON, which was an abbreviated version of BROILER.[15] The plan assumed that there would be a Soviet sweep to the English Channel in 60 days or less, and within 200 days most of Turkey, Iraq and Iran would be overrun. A British-inspired plan, DOUBLEQUICK, had provided that if Soviet troops were to invade through the plains of Central Europe, the US and Britain would withdraw their ground and air forces from the Continent in order to regroup in preparation for another Normandy-type operation.[16] In later versions of the various plans, the Pyrenees to the south-west would be the line, thus giving the Western Allies at least a foothold on the continent.[17] As can be imagined: "Any plan that is predicated on the evacuation of troops to strongholds across the Pyrenees or at the Channel would inevitably excite more hostile attention from continental Europeans than from Americans, Canadians or British."[18]

Nonetheless, the main US Joint EWP which governed all the actions of the three Services in the event of war with the Soviet Union was HALFMOON, which contemplated that the US would strike "massively" at the Soviet Union, and this gave the main task of HALFMOON to the Air Force.[19] The plan envisioned a SAC air offensive at D+15 from bases in Britain, Cairo-Suez, and Okinawa. General Omar Bradley, Chairman of the JCS at the time, observed: "This [HALFMOON] was the first formal and comprehensive enunciation of what later became known as a strategy of nuclear 'massive retaliation'."[20] Later, in December 1948, with the Berlin crisis blowing very hot, a revised Joint EWP was devised, called TROJAN, which was approved by the JCS in January 1949. It called for both primary atomic strikes and secondary conventional strikes on Soviet industrial-urban areas.[21]

All of this planning activity could be summarized thus:

> the development of post-Second World War command organization was the consequence of several factors. The need to create a detailed joint US–British strategic concept (Broiler/Doublequick) to defend against the Soviet Union in response to a comprehensive threat estimate (Pincher) produced a formal command organization for implementation in the event of such an immediate war. This organization was based on World War II experiences and arrangements. Simultaneously, a European command organization for the defense of Western Europe, the Western Union Chiefs of Staff, was created independent of US-British arrangements. Its structure was similar to that of SHAEF in the Second World War. With the shift in US political orientation toward Europe during the Berlin blockade, a new joint US, British, and Canadian strategic concept, Doublestar/ Speedway/Bullmoose, was developed from Broiler/ Doublequick; this concept was more comprehensive and attempted to include the Western Union Defense Organization in its command arrangements.[22]

Finally, TROJAN was replaced with OFFTACKLE, approved by the JCS in December 1949. It also called for a strategic offensive in Europe, built around ever-more atomic bombs hitting ever-more Soviet targets. During this phase of Norstad's career, he had obviously been in the thick of the planning for these massive "strategic" retaliatory strikes utilizing atomic weapons against the Soviet heartland. As it was described: "OFFTACKLE posited the use of 292 atomic bombs (220 plus a re-attack reserve of 72) and 17 610 tons of conventional high-explosive bombs against these target systems during the first three months."[23] But OFFTACKLE had some real drawbacks. It contemplated overthrowing the Soviet government by the atomic assault of 104 cities, which would cause around seven million casualties and would dislocate some 28 million more. As George Baer observed: "No one could say what would be left."[24] It also engendered the opposition of the European NATO Allies, and in fact underscored the difference in outlook between the US and, in particular, France and Germany.[25]

The shift from a World War II Normandy-type strategy to a "hold the line" or retardation strategy occurred with the replacement of OFFTACKLE with CROSSPIECE/GALLOPER, which was NATO MC/14. As it was put:

> Although its objectives and basic undertakings were the same as those of previous plans, CROSSPIECE/GALLOPER planned for the defense of the Rhine River–Italian Alps line in Europe and made active provisions to impede the Soviet advance ... . A fighting withdrawal was to be staged and a substantial bridgehead area in Western Europe held to facilitate later offensive action. If these conditions could not be met, a base area in North Africa would be developed from which an offensive could be mounted.[26]

Initially, this meant making a stand at the Rhine, or the Franco-German border, but later, with the creation of the Federal Republic of Germany (FRG), the defensive line had to be moved farther east to the Elbe. Bases in Britain would also come under Soviet air attack, and later the southern flank (Greece, Turkey, Suez) would also be vulnerable. No longer would a plan of Continental withdrawal and then "liberation" by means of a cross-Channel invasion – or invasion of any sort – be politically acceptable.

Clearly, however, during this pre-SHAPE period of Norstad's career "[e]ach of the services was refashioning itself in a nuclear mold ... . But the air force had captured the dominant strategic role. It had the B-36 strategic bomber, the most potent weapons system the world had seen ... . The air force also deployed nuclear-capable medium-range bombers and fighter aircraft."[27] But the Air Force was looking forward to another generation of intercontinental bombers – the B-50. In fact, it fell to Norstad (now a Lt. General), as Deputy Chief of Staff for Operations to send a memorandum on April 24, 1948 to his counterpart, Lt. General H. A. Craig, Deputy Chief of Staff for Materiel, suggesting terminating B-36 construction at 61 aircraft.[28] They would be used for training and transition purposes, and as tankers. But the B-36, in its various forms, survived for several more years as the Navy and the Air Force struggled to seize control over the role and the mission of atomic weapons. Arnold's B-29 Superfortresses were now relegated to "medium" status, but played a key role in the Korean conflict.

Norstad's goal of a "minimum of seventy first-line group" air force was still the Air Force's official estimate of what was needed. But Truman and Johnson had recommended for fiscal year 1949 only 55 "limited strength" Groups plus 15 "skeleton" Groups.

During this period, the Air Force did a considerable amount of aggressive lobbying with Congress. As Truman remarked: "The air boys are for glamor ... I want a sensible defense for which the country can pay."[29] There were no more "glamorous" senior officers than Vandenberg and Norstad, and they knew how to lobby. For example, the cover story of *Life* Magazine for November 1, 1948 featured a photograph of Norstad. It was titled: "US Air Force's Top Planner, Lieut. Gen. Lauris Norstad," and had showed a stern-visaged, boyishly handsome officer who probably seemed to the general public the embodiment of the increasingly-popular Air Force. On the following page, an equally stern-visaged all-American type photograph of Vandenberg looked out at the reader, over the title: "The Air Force's New Command Team: Handsome group of colorful but earnest young career officers have replaced the old 'baling wire' boys."[30] There was some consternation around the Pentagon and in the Norstad household that having Norstad's picture on the cover and the new four-star Chief of Staff, Vandenberg, on the inside was not too politic. The other members of this new team were: General Muir S. Fairchild (age 54), Vice Chief of Staff; Lt. General Elwood R. Quesada (age 44), Commander of Tactical Air Command (TAC); Lt. General Edwin W. Rawlings (age 44), the Air Comptroller; and Lt. General Curtis E. LeMay (age 41), Commander of the Strategic Air Command. Fairchild died suddenly from a heart attack in early 1950, so Norstad became Acting Vice Chief of Staff. The top group's average age was 47.

Life reported:

> It is a Washington canard that the new Air Force is currently being run by a group of flashy, high-blue-yonder extroverts who cannot speak without gestures and who speak only to themselves because no one else can understand their jargon ... Lieut. General Lauris

Norstad, the Air Force's Deputy Chief of Staff for Operations, likes to say that he is "representative of a generation in the Air Force." This deprecatory self-analysis is true in that Larry Norstad, like other young air officers, has practically grown up with the airman's point of view ... apart from a faith in the strategic mission of air power that is common to his generation, Norstad is an extraordinary phenomenon.

Physically, the 41-year-old Norstad looks like the character in a college play who has sprinkled white powder on his temples to indicate a lapse of 20 years between Acts 2 and 3. The son of a Norwegian Lutheran minister, he often talks as if he were mulling over a homely sermon. Where other airmen speak in terms of groups, wings and advance bases, Norstad adds spiritual dimensions to his military theory. Modern wars, he observes, are not fought over boundary lines or economics, but over philosophical issues ... the only weapon against an idea is a better idea ... . His theory is that you can't think straight unless you "renew your intellectual capital from time to time."[31]

Rumors of his being reassigned persisted. As he wrote in March 1950 to British Air Chief Marshal Sir John Slessor: "After having served here for a longer continuous stretch than any living man, there is little use in trying to add to that record. I think that Van will let me out of here in the early summer, but as yet he has not decided where I am to go. There is a possibility that I may go to Europe when Joe Cannon's tour is over, but that is only one of several alternatives."[32]

One of the goals of the Air Force was to establish a four-star position in Europe, coequal to the Army's Commander-in-Chief, European Command (CINCEUR) and the Commander-in-Chief, US Naval Forces, Eastern Atlantic and Mediterranean (CINCNELM).[33] As Norstad wrote to LeMay: "we propose to create a Commander-in-Chief, US Air Forces in Europe, the United Kingdom, and the Mediterranean (CINCUSAFE), with headquarters in London."[34] Norstad explained: "The world situation and the increased strength to which the Air Force is now building have necessitated some major organization changes ... . It is planned to establish CINCUSAFE ... completely free from CINCEUR ... I am anxious that this be done as early as practicable so that we may have a going concern by the time a [NATO] Supreme Commander is established."[35] Shortly thereafter Norstad was named CINCUSAFE, with the Air Force recommending that he be promoted to full General.[36]

The scope of USAFE was described thus:

> USAFE's strength grew steadily as it assumed responsibilities for providing tactical air forces for NATO and for a host of other duties stemming from American rearmament. These duties included direction of the Berlin Airlift in 1948–49; ferrying large numbers of aircraft to countries receiving mutual aid assistance; training pilots and maintenance men for these countries; and furnishing support to SAC units on training missions to Europe and North Africa. The command eventually stretched from the big depot at Burtonwood in the west of England to the air-conditioned base at Dhaharan, in the Saudi Arabian desert.[37]

Understandably, the outbreak of the Korean War in June 1950 had created a mood of uncertainty in NATO. As it was put: "From the point of view of many European officials, the American commitment to the defense of Western Europe against the USSR in 1949 was of value primarily because it placed Europe under the protection of US strategic weapons ... at the time [of the outbreak of Korean hostilities] it seemed clear that a Soviet-sponsored military action had not been deterred by the United States. Could it be assumed that the deterrent would be more successful elsewhere?"[38]

Throughout the Summer of 1950, the Administration had debated what the commitment of the US should be toward Europe. As late as August, Truman was asking: "Are we prepared to commit additional United States forces to the defense of Europe; Are we prepared to support, and in what manner, the concept of a European defense force, including German participation on other than a national basis; Are we prepared to look forward to the eventuality of a Supreme Commander for the European defense forces; Are we prepared to consider full United States participation in European defense organs ... ."[39] The imperatives of facilitating rapid rearmament by NATO's European Allies pretty much dictated what the answers to these questions would be.

NATO's "forward strategy" was to establish "forces-in-being" in Europe, under a Supreme Allied Commander, Europe (SACEUR) and a Supreme Headquarters Allied Powers, Europe (SHAPE) as soon as possible. Eisenhower, as SACEUR, was needed desperately to reinvigorate Western Europe and to restore morale – a task that he could do *par excellence*.[40] Aside from the force of his personality, one key element was his serving as a living symbol of the US's reassurance to come to the aid of the Allies if war with the Soviet Union were to occur.

The Air Force assumed that if war were to occur, it would be a very destructive war of indefinite duration and uncertain outcome. Norstad, in this respect, would become the symbol of the commitment of US air power to Europe's defense. Coming from the highest command circles of the Air Force, he was *very* credible. In fact, when he arrived in Europe in January 1951, his first major responsibility was to re-establish the Third and Twelfth Air Forces.[41] Then, on March 29, 1951, he became SHAPE's Commander-in-Chief, Allied Air Forces, Central Europe (CINCAAFCE), which was located at Fontainebleau, in addition to being CINCUSAFE.[42] Norstad's role, working with Eisenhower but at this time not assigned directly under him because Eisenhower was not yet an American commander, was to ensure that nuclear weapons would continue to provide the assurance that SHAPE would indeed be a "going concern." It was his responsibility, in his two "hats," to prepare an atomic weapons plan for Eisenhower and SHAPE.[43] As a result, by 1952 there was an Atomic Weapons Annex to SACEUR's EWP.

But the need was for Eisenhower to have the authority, as well as the means, to provide reassurance to friend and foe alike that the US would "stand and fight" if unequivocally provoked. As he put it: "The employment of atomic weapons constitutes one of the most significant means which SACEUR can utilize in fulfilling his mission. [So] it is important that he has all necessary authority in the planning and control of atomic operations in his area."[44] Otherwise the Allies would not be convinced that they should embark on rearmament programs in support of a "forward strategy."

Norstad led the effort to coordinate SAC's mission with the SACEUR's plans, so that Eisenhower would have command authority over atomic planning and operations in the NATO area. Eisenhower, Norstad and General Alfred A. Gruenther (Eisenhower's Chief of Staff) met with SAC commander LeMay in December 1951 to arrange the coordination of LeMay's "retardation operations" with Eisenhower's plans. The agreement was:

- SACEUR would determine the military significance and priority of retardation targets;
- LeMay and SAC would judge the technical and operational suitability of targets and select the weapons;
- SACEUR would be responsible for obtaining the necessary approval of his recommended retardation objectives and for weapons expenditures;

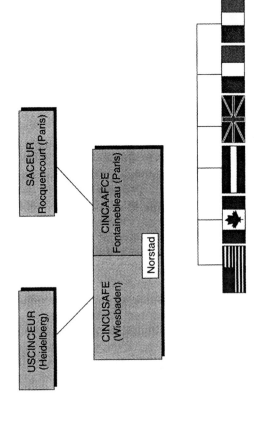

Chart 4.1 Norstad as CINCUSAFE and CINCAAFCE, April 1951

- Acting, in effect, as a staff officer for SACEUR and independently of CINCAAFCE, Norstad would coordinate the details of the necessary arrangements with SAC, which in turn would establish a command element – HQ-SAC (ZEBRA) – to draw up a plan to formalize the procedures for conducting support operations. SAC would work only with Norstad and designated US officers on a NOFORN (no dissemination to foreign nationals) basis.[45]

There was also an intense interest in how the Air Force should handle the base network that was being put into place for SAC in North Africa and in England. One major decision, in which Norstad participated, was to draw a distinction between SAC's "reach" and the other uses to which these bases might be put. As Norstad told LeMay: "if we were to accept your concept of the command relationships that should exist in North Africa, you would find yourself burdened with a multitude of operational and planning responsibilities that have no direct bearing on the conduct of the strategic air offensive."[46]

On the political level, Lord Ismay, NATO's first Secretary-General, shared Eisenhower's concern that clear lines of authority should be established. He was also concerned that there were no provisions whereby the North Atlantic Council (NAC) could control the SACEUR in this area: "It became normal for the Council to refer (and defer) to the most important military figure who was on the spot, more particularly because he was also the personal embodiment of the United States' commitment to the alliance and upon whose nuclear power almost total reliance for deterrence was then placed."[47] By inaction, the responsibility of decision was left to the national authorities, which meant the US. As Ismay observed: "Everyone realizes that the use of the A-bomb is a political decision. No commander could take it without consulting his government."[48]

Eisenhower, being at this time only an international and not a US national commander, as pointed out above, had to rely on US national planners in addition to a JCS representative located in Europe to develop the annexes for both his US and NATO forces. To overcome this problem, in late 1951, Secretary of Defense Robert A. Lovett asked Eisenhower if it would be a good idea for him to become "two-hatted." Eisenhower appointed an *ad hoc* committee in February 1952 to study the feasibility of establishing a unified Army-Air Force Command in Europe over which he would become Commander-in-Chief. On 1 August 1952, the Headquarters, US European Command (USEUCOM), was created at Frankfurt, and Eisenhower's successor as SACEUR, General Matthew B. Ridgway, was given the national command "hat" of USCINCEUR.⁴⁹

II. NATO and the Eisenhower administration's "new look"

At the NAC meeting at Lisbon, in February, 1952, the NATO Allies had agreed to a military plan that relied heavily on major contributions of conventional forces by the member-states. The NAC set the most ambitious goals in NATO's history – 50 divisions, 4000 aircraft, and 704 combat vessels by 1952; 75 divisions and 6500 aircraft by 1953, with 35–40 divisions to be ready for combat at all times. There were also to be 12 divisions from the Federal Republic of Germany (FRG) within an all-European army.⁵⁰

Ridgway, having succeeded Eisenhower as SACEUR in May 1952, recognized immediately that these so-called "Lisbon goals" were unrealizable.⁵¹ Acting accordingly, he initiated a study of NATO's force requirements because, as one observer noted: "The honeymoon was over. [Ridgway's] job was to collect on the promises that had been made to Ike."⁵² Ridgway's study concluded that NATO's conventional forces would continue to be inadequate to meet the threat, and so he recommended additional ground attack fighters to exploit Allied atomic counterstrikes. The study also concluded that to be effective, Ridgway must have advance authority to launch his atomic counter-offensive immediately upon the outbreak of war. Furthermore, setting the stage for one of Norstad's major efforts as SACEUR, Ridgway felt that he needed the authority to stockpile atomic weapons.⁵³

A review of the basic strategy of the US after the Eisenhower Administration took office resulted in the conclusion that if the European Allies would not, or could not, live up to these NATO goals, then the US would have to reassess its own capability economically. Eisenhower believed strongly that the Cold War with the Soviet Union could be lost on the economic front as well as on the battlefield. He was also keenly aware that one reason the Republicans had won the Presidency was because of the sharp rise in inflation resulting from the high defense budgets accompanied by deficit spending brought on by the long-term needs of European rearmament, as well as by the short-term needs of the Korean War.⁵⁴ As it was put: "Given Eisenhower's strategic views and the domestic and international constraints he perceived, his problem was to blend those views into a credible strategy that could be implemented at a relatively low cost and be sold to both the American public and American allies."⁵⁵

There was some speculation at this time that Norstad would be the next Chief of Staff of the Air Force. Vandenberg, afflicted with cancer, was planning to retire. It was reported, erroneously:

> The next head of the Air Force will be Lt. Gen. Lauris Norstad, commander of the NATO Air Force in Europe.
> His selection has been approved by Gen. Eisenhower. Norstad worked closely with the Republican presidential candidate when he was organizing the NATO military structure. Eisenhower expressed his approval of the choice of Norstad in response to an inquiry from the Joint Chiefs of Staff. Reason for their unannounced action was that Gen. Hoyt Vandenberg, ailing Air Chief of Staff, will retire next January. He will resume his duties in the Pentagon on August 1, but on a limited basis. Norstad's appointment will be made in December by President Truman, before he retires from the White House. Behind the selection of 45-year-old Norstad was a backstage tussle over Gen. Curtis LeMay, 46-year-old, dynamic bomber commander. Air Secretary Thomas Finletter strongly favored LeMay as successor to Vandenberg. But the Joint Chiefs considered Norstad better fitted for the job in temperament and staff experience. They finally persuaded Finletter to their view and President Truman approved the choice of Norstad.[56]

Walter Winchell also included this line in his nationally syndicated column: "Lt. Gen. Norstad our next Air Force boss?"[57] Given the ways of Washington's military politics, these were probably "trial balloon" stories, planted to see what the reaction would bring in Congress as well as around the Pentagon and the White House. After his years in Washington, Norstad was well known. He was considered "serious" in the sense that the French use the term, to signify a person who could rise above the day-to-day hurly-burly of politics and public life to discern larger trends and significances. This reputation set him apart from many of his military contemporaries, who at times seemed to speak before they had considered the consequences of their speech. Norstad was not one to make this mistake. As a result, he had established close and lasting friendships with such important newspapermen as C.L. "Punch" Sulzberger of *The New York Times*, and the influential political columnists, Joseph and Stewart Alsop, and Arthur Krock.[58]

Norstad, as CINCUSAFE, and General Otto P. Weyland, as Commanding General, Far East Air Forces (FEAF), received Senate confirmation in July 1952 for their promotions, which were signed by President Truman on July 5.[59] Norstad received his fourth star at age 45, thus becoming the youngest four-star general in the US armed forces. A brief ceremony on July 9 was held in Fontainebleau, and Col. Tim Dolan, Judge Advocate, pinned the four stars on him.[60] Not long after he moved his headquarters from the 500-year-old chateau of Henri IV to a new two-story miniature Pentagon in the heart of Avon forest, two miles away. The headquarters was equipped with the latest communications, radar, and electronics control equipment. At the opening ceremonies of the new headquarters "Twenty-one jet planes thundered overhead. Several windows were broken by the vibration. The flags of the six NATO nations represented here were hauled aloft to the strains of the Marseillaise."[61]

This reference to Allied flags was to Norstad's NATO "hat" as CINCAAFCE.[62] Units were assigned to him from the US, Britain, France, Belgium, the Netherlands, and Canada.[63] Eisenhower at this time had a British Air Deputy, but SHAPE was not an "operational" headquarters – this was the purpose of the three regional commands. Each of the three air forces in the north, center and south had their own air commanders (COMAIRNORTH and COMAIRSOUTH), with the north and south reporting respectively to a British and a US "CINC."[64] With his promotion, the way was cleared for a consolidation of the three subordinate NATO air forces into a single NATO tactical air arm.

Norstad had concluded that local air planning in each of the three commands was sufficiently developed to merge them into a single, centrally-controlled, tactical arm for the SACEUR. Norstad was a firm exponent of centralized air defense, making the point that there can be no "frontiers" in air warfare – a lesson he had learned while in North Africa, helping to work out command and operational arrangements between both different Services and different national forces.[65]

The build up of NATO air power was nearing nearly 11 000 combat aircraft, and Norstad recognized that this size force, while it had to be commanded in local areas by tactical commanders, had to be used as a "single weapon" to protect the long Allied front from North Norway to the eastern border of Turkey.[66] One advantage for Norstad, in making his argument, was that there was not yet enough aircraft overall in NATO to afford restricting them to only one region; during hostilities they would have to be allocated rapidly in and out of the three regions. Another advantage would be that NATO's tactical air power could be coordinated more effectively with the US's SAC.

After the November 1952 US elections, speculation persisted that President-elect Eisenhower would tap his NATO colleagues for his new military leadership team. This meant that Gruenther might become Army Chief of Staff, Admiral Robert B. Carney (CINCSOUTH) might become Chief of Naval Operations, and Norstad Air Force Chief of Staff. In fact, Eisenhower had wanted Gruenther to succeed him at SHAPE, but he had been overruled by the Chairman of the JCS, General Omar Bradley.[67] The speculation went along these lines:

> Gen. Norstad has been often tipped to succeed Gen. Hoyt S. Vandenberg, whose tour of duty as USAF Chief of Staff expires on June 30 [1953]. If he held that post for a few years and then retired he could probably take his pick of many highly-paid jobs in American commercial life. Regulations, however, require American generals to complete 30 years' service before retiring. This Norstad will not do until June 12, 1960 ... . If Gen. Norstad does succeed Gen. Vandenberg he could complete his service as chairman of the US Joint Chiefs of Staff, the post now held by Gen. Bradley.[68]

Doubtless one serious consideration for the younger candidates was this problem that early promotions during the war could result in retirements at a very early age during the 1950s. As it was observed: "The astoundingly youthful looking airman [Norstad] who was a general at 36, would be all washed-up at 50, if he is given Van's job and holds it for four years." LeMay would be required to retire at age 51.[69] This point was raised again the following March, when the speculation had broadened to include both Thomas D. White and Nathan F. Twining as possible successors to Vandenberg.

The speculation by a noted Washington correspondent about Twining, proved to be the most accurate: "Twining is 55 and a choice of the greybeards of the air world. He has completed 30 years of service and is eligible now for retirement. Though he is now not believed to be the number one political choice as Vandenberg's successor, Twining's range of experience far outdistances that of rivals for the job."[70] As it turned out, General Nathan "Nate" Twining became Chief of Staff, and then later Chairman of the JCS. When Norstad retired in 1962, his official certificate of retirement was issued and signed by his longtime Air Force colleague and sometime rival, LeMay, who had by then become Chief of Staff.

By the time that Eisenhower became President, Norstad could point to considerable achievements in bringing the Alliance's air arm to a high state of readiness:

1. In the first Central European air maneuver in late April, 1951, there were 500 planes operating from 10 airfields. In an exercise

MC 48

88 *Norstad: Cold War Supreme Commander*

in June, 1952, there were 1400 aircraft flying from 45 bases. In the latest exercise 44 of the 54 air squadrons participating were jets. The number of planes is increasing monthly. The goal is 2500 aircraft by the end of 1952.
2. The number of airfields with runways of 8000 feet, which are capable of handling all types of aircraft, was increased in a ratio of 3 to 1.
3. Taxiways permitting better parking of aircraft and faster takeoffs after an alert have been expanded greatly.
4. A radar screen from Northern Germany to the Alps is in operation several hours a day. It is hoped to have the equipment and personnel for 24-hour-a-day operations by the end of this year.
5. A new headquarters, dispersed over 100 acres of a former royal hunting reserve near Fontainebleau, is in operation.
6. Morale has soared.[71]

These achievements must have pleased Eisenhower as he moved forward in developing a "grand strategy" for his Administration. This did not mean, however, that Eisenhower favored an indefinite American military commitment in Europe; the problem was that he could not find a way to get around the necessity for nuclear weapons as an integral part of NATO's planning for Europe's defense. This requirement inevitably led to more, rather than less, of a perception on the part of the Europeans that they could rely on the US to keep the Soviet Union at bay with nuclear weapons. As it was put: "The Europeans accepted the strategy [of MC/48]. In so doing, they were transferring to the American president, and in some cases even to American military commanders, the power to start a war – a power which in extreme cases might have to be exercised without even consulting them."[72] Thus, using atomic weapons as part of a retardation strategy meant "blunting" the attack by "paralyzing" the enemy through a pre-emptive strike against its strategic offensive capability. This was an awesome responsibility for Norstad.

To make the point further, it should be recalled that to compensate for his emphasis on budgetary restraint, Eisenhower concluded that "the major deterrent to aggression against Western Europe is the manifest determination of the US to use its atomic capability and massive retaliatory striking power if the area is attacked."[73] Norstad would probably have strongly supported this contention. He had said in January 1953 that NATO's air power was far short of the military requirements. I believe, however, that the forces we now have in process of organization and equipment represent a significant factor in the overall balance. We are reaching about this time a level where in the sad event of war we could take a toll and exact a price. We cannot, of course, achieve our full military mission by any means. But I think we have become at least a small deterrent factor.[74]

This "small deterrent factor" was to blossom in just a few years into the most important initiative Norstad was to take during the period of what came to be known as the "High Cold War." But his search for a NATO tactical nuclear deterrent capability when he became SACEUR finally came up against the reality of political costs versus military effectiveness. The cost of "nuclearizing" Central Europe multilaterally ran up against the Kennedy Administration's conviction that a local nuclear exchange would inexorably lead to the destruction of the US itself, and, therefore, this NATO strategy exacted too high a domestic political price. Kennedy was persuaded that a NATO "flexible response" strategy that emphasized strong conventional forces was more sensible, even if more expensive.[75]

In March 1953, popular speculation about Norstad's future intensified:

He looks like the Hollywood war hero – a nonchalant hunk of man with his 12st. [stone] of sinew impressively draped round a 6ft. 2in. frame. Here are the squared shoulders under the firm jaw, the casually immaculate look – fair hair impeccably groomed, the trimmed fingernails and the heavy wedding ring. But there is nothing synthetic about General Lauris Norstad. He is no celluloid hero. As boss of Allied Air Forces in Central Europe, at forty-five he is America's youngest four-star General, the wonder-boy of World War II who has zoomed to stardom, and is still going places at jet speed.[76]

He was, indeed, still "going places" when, in July 1953, Norstad's role in NATO was strengthened when he went to SHAPE as Ridgway's Air Deputy. Gruenther reported to Eisenhower: "Matt [Ridgway] submitted to the Standing Group a few days ago that [Marshal Alphonse] Juin should be made Commander-in-Chief of the Central Region with Land, Air and Naval subordinate commanders. He also in the same letter recommended that the functions of the Air Deputy be expanded to include coordination of the overall air effort. The Air Commander in

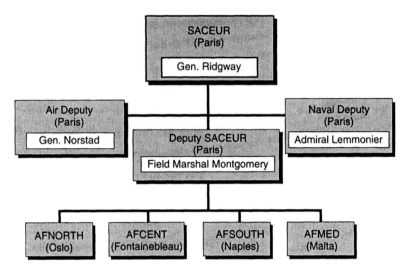

Chart 4.2   Norstad as Air Deputy, July 1953

the Center would be a British officer, while the Air Deputy would be an American."[77] It was reported: "In addition to widening the responsibilities of the job to gain greater centralization of control over the growing Western European air forces, Gen. Norstad will also have general responsibility at SHAPE for atomic weapons and their tactical use by the European armies and air forces."[78]

As early as the previous February, speculation had it that these changes were afoot.[79] The explanation was: "One of the main reasons behind the proposed change, it is understood, is the continuance of the US law that top secrets of American atomic warfare must be kept strictly in American hands ... . The new air deputy would therefore probably have considerably wider terms of reference than the existing British holder of that post."[80] As "air generalissimo" for SHAPE, Norstad's authority enabled him to shift squadrons and air units from one area to another.[81]

The JCS, in October 1953, supported a set of guidelines, which came to be known as NSC 162/2, that linked economic strength with overall military strategy. Its main conclusions were: the perceived threat from the Communist world to the US and its Allies was defined as a tenacious and lasting one; the US military should adopt the concept of the "long haul," thereby abandoning the idea of predicting a specific year of maximum danger; American troop commitments worldwide must be substantially cut back and the nation's defenses must be secured without jeopardizing its economic stability; the US should rely more on nuclear power to deter Communist aggression and be prepared if necessary to use its nuclear arsenal to eliminate the enemy; the US should rely more on collective security.[82] In response, in April 1954 the NAC officially accepted the notion of the "long haul" for NATO.

Clearly, however, concern over the potential usefulness of atomic (then nuclear) weapons did not originate with the Eisenhower Administration. As Truman recalled: "By the spring of 1949 we had to think [sic] of atomic weapons on a different scale. We now had a stockpile, but I wanted to know whether the weapons we had on hand and those that were planned were adequate in number and whether we were keeping up with technological progress."[83] Eisenhower recalled in a long letter he wrote in October 1953 to Gruenther: "From the very beginning, some of our troop dispositions were visualized as temporary or emergency measures. I think none of us has ever believed for an instant the United States could, over the long term (several decades), build a sort of Roman Wall with its own troops and so protect the world ... ."[84] He was reacting to press reports at the time that his administration was contemplating sharp troop cuts.

When Gruenther became SACEUR in 1954, he specifically linked the long-anticipated contribution of West German conventional military forces – thus strengthening collective security in NATO – with the use of atomic weapons. He saw these two dimensions of military strength as comprising the dual cornerstones of NATO's credible deterrent. He stated in March 1955: "we will be able to defend Europe when we have two conditions, an effective German contribution and the ability to use atomic weapons. Last September we presented a study concerning this question to the North Atlantic Council through the Standing Group. The NATO nations met in Paris and took a very momentous decision. They said that we should make plans on the basis that atomic weapons would be used."[85]

Gruenther had summed up the new policy in an address to the English-Speaking Union in London in June, 1954: "We are working on a philosophy to have a force in being that is the smallest possible, and to depend on reserve forces. That shield must be able to hold long enough for those reserves to mobilize. We feel it will not hold that long unless we have atomic power to support it."[86] He anticipated that a shield, consisting of "highly trained covering land forces," should provide a "cushion of time" following the failure of deterrence to allow for the mobilization of reserves that would be "brought into action immediately after the outbreak of hostilities." "Hard-hitting air forces" would provide tactical support and Allied long-range air forces would conduct powerful retaliatory attacks deep into enemy territory against industrial and other vital targets. As Gruenther said: "In our thinking, we visualize the use of atomic bombs in the support of our ground troops. We also visualize the use of atomic bombs on targets in enemy territory."[87] Not long thereafter, however, it became apparent that the anticipated reserves would not be forthcoming, so that instead, greater reliance was placed on low-yield battlefield atomic weapons, which would remain in peacetime under US custody and control. This was affirmed in the December 1955 NAC meeting.[88]

The assumption was that NATO would need to win a war in Central Europe within thirty days of the outbreak of hostilities. How would SACEUR/USCINCEUR plan to meet such a situation? Gruenther raised this with the Chairman of the JCS, Admiral Arthur Radford. The immediate matter concerned the USEUCOM Joint Capabilities Plan I-55, in which Norstad would have played a large role in developing:

> You will note that the concept of operations for action subsequent to the initial phase of a general war is strictly in accordance with the strategy outlined in US JCS. Joint Strategic Capabilities Plan, 1 July 1955–1 July 1956. However, I have followed such an approach with certain misgivings. I find that the concept of a large-scale more or less conventional penetration to the heartland of Russia in a war extending over some two or more years is open to serious questions from an economic as well as a military standpoint. Further, I would anticipate serious difficulty on an international basis in obtaining the support of other NATO countries for such a concept. As indicated previously in the covering letter forwarding the "CINCEUR/ SACEUR 958 Atomic Weapons Requirement Study," I, as SACEUR, continue to define my objective as a limited advance to protect and recapture NATO territory pending further guidance as to the role of SACEUR's force in concluding a general war. In my capacity as US CINCEUR, I find it difficult to plan further major counter-offensive operations on a unilateral basis.
>
> It appears to me that a most important factor in the consideration of the strategy for continued operations in the event of a general war is an analysis of the situation that will exist at the completion of the initial atomic exchange. In an attempt to evaluate the effects of such atomic campaigns, a select group of the SHAPE Staff has been studying this problem for some time. The initial and incom-

plete results of this analysis are such that I hesitate to pursue this study further on a NATO basis because of the dearth of information which can be used internationally and because of possible undesirable morale and political repercussions. Unfortunately, even working on a "US only" basis, my staff is faced with the prospect of being unable to evaluate the immediate effects that the atomic campaigns of such external forces as CINCSAC and SACLANT would have in the area of direct concern to my forces.

This question is so essential to the development of a practical strategy for continuation of a general war in the European area that I now feel I must ask for some assistance in this regard. Therefore, I request that the Joint Chiefs of Staff provide guidance concerning the strategic concept and objectives which would establish the pattern of operations for general war subsequent to the initial phase, reflecting their estimate of the effects of the initial atomic exchange on the situation in Allied Command Europe.[89]

In his response, Radford reaffirmed that Gruenther would *not* be able to obtain authority to use atomic means in advance of hostilities:

The problem expressed is one of continuing concern to all planning agencies. In selecting the possible causes of action contained in the JSCP the Joint Chiefs of Staff recognized that unforeseeable political, economic, and military developments as well as an evaluation of the outcome of the initial atomic exchange would determine the ultimate strategy to be adopted, the extent to which any given task would be pursued, and the scope of operations to be undertaken. These qualifications and conditions are set forth in appropriate portions of the current JSCP. The concept in JSCP is considered sound and represents the best judgement of the Joint Chiefs of Staff as a means of assuring final victory.

With regard to the difficulty you anticipate in obtaining international approval of this concept, it was not intended that such approval be obtained at this time. It is realized that these operations will include Allied forces and, that in the final analysis international approval will be required. However, until such time as there is an internationally approved concept which provides for the final defeat of the USSR and the successful conclusion of a general war with the Soviet Bloc, this planning must be accomplished on a unilateral basis.[90]

This concept relied heavily on a strong NATO resupply and reinforcement capacity, and so had to depend on its air defense capability, which was Norstad's responsibility. As Gruenther reported: "In [1951–1953] the number of NATO airfields has increased from 20 to 120 – a truly remarkable achievement .... We at SHAPE have given first priority to the development of our air forces."[91] This fact made it almost inevitable – aside from Norstad's personal standing with Eisenhower – that Norstad would be the frontrunner to succeed Gruenther. Gruenther helped to keep Norstad in Eisenhower's eye. For example, he said in one of his many very personal "Dear Boss" handwritten notes to Eisenhower: "Larry Norstad will be in Washington .... I hope you will have a chance to say hello to him. As always, he is doing a fine job here."[92]

At the December 1956 ministerial meeting of NATO, the NAC reaffirmed its earlier commitment that MC/48 was the official NATO strategic statement. This enhanced Norstad's position even further. This document placed major reliance on atomic weapons for the defense of Western Europe. As it was put: "the Council approved a directive for future military plans, taking into account the continued rise in Soviet capabilities and the various types of new weapons available for NATO defense. The concept of forward defence in NATO strategy will be maintained."[93] At the time, Secretary of State Dulles made three points, which reiterated the Eisenhower Administration's overall policy: it was financially impossible to maintain two strategies, atomic and non-atomic; only atomic weapons could provide a forward defense; and therefore MC/48, which represented the advice of the military to the NAC, should be approved. With this decision, atomic weapons were introduced into the NATO European area itself to compensate for NATO's inability to assemble sufficient conventional ground and air forces.[94]

Talk in Washington and in NATO of "predelegation" to SACEUR to decide when and where to use these weapons persisted, uncomfortable as it was to all concerned. As it was put: "With the MC 48 strategy, the United States was essentially asking the allies to put their fate in American hands – indeed, largely in the hands of an American general."[95]

These tactical atomic weapons were coupled with the strategic striking forces of the US that would "strike massively" against the Soviet heartland. Eisenhower had, perhaps disingenuously, protested to Gruenther at that time that "the considerations I have outlined are not dependent upon the advent or effectiveness of 'new weapons.'"[96]

Yet the NAC announced that future military plans would take into account "the various types of new weapons available for NATO defence." But it was not until the December 1957 NAC meeting that the Ministers actually mentioned nuclear weapons: "NATO has decided to establish stocks of nuclear warheads, which will be readily available for the defence of the Alliance in case of need."[97]

This action came out of the "Minimum Forces Study" which Norstad undertook upon becoming SACEUR. Its main point was that, as Norstad put it: "the Shield forces can no longer be considered as 'conventional forces,' ... although they retain a conventional capability, their minimum size requires that they be equipped with the most modern weapons, including nuclear weapons, deployed and available on a wide basis throughout the NATO forces ... . A NATO Atomic Stockpile system is being established, which will permit atomic warheads to be released to appropriate Allied Commanders when necessary for defense against attack."[98]

Norstad, having been responsible for establishing the air defenses of NATO, and then for planning for the introduction of these "new weapons," inevitably became known as the "nuclear SACEUR" as well as the "Cold War SACEUR." During Norstad's time as SACEUR, he presided over SHAPE during a crucial period of the Cold War in which the superpower adversaries were still working out how to use their respective – and expanding – nuclear weapons without actually triggering war. It was necessary for Norstad to devise strategies and doctrines that would be acceptable to the US's NATO Allies, including two Allies in possession of nuclear weapons and aspirations of their own (France and Britain). There was also one (the FRG) which no one wanted to see come into possession of the weapons. Obtaining trust and confidence in his capacity to be even-handed in his dealings with friends and enemies alike on such a sensitive subject was one of the SACEUR's greatest challenges. Eisenhower also wanted the NATO Allies "to act with the United States in crises and thus give the United States greater freedom of action to use atomic weapons as required."[99]

Another challenge for Norstad was to engage actively in "public diplomacy," without overshadowing NATO's chief political figure, the Secretary-General, or perhaps more importantly, the heads of the various member-states. Public diplomacy was necessary to help mobilize public opinion in favor of supporting the Western coalition both economically and militarily. This was not easy because domestic and electoral politics have a powerful influence on the external relations of democracies, and voting citizens resist paying high taxes everywhere, even for worthy causes. As already noted, even before he became SACEUR Norstad had been spectacularly successful in this respect. Both he and his family had become well-known figures in Paris. They were an exceptionally photogenic family. For example, the Swiss magazine, *Illustré* ran an article, "Un Amércain à Paris," with a picture of Norstad with his wife Isabelle and daughter Kristin on the cover of its issue of June 28, 1956.[100]

In September 1956, when the time drew near for Norstad to succeed Gruenther as SACEUR, the news magazines displayed feature stories on both him and his family. The photo magazine *Jours de France* described him as a "philosophe en uniforme." It also showed Norstad playing golf with Ben Hogan, presumably to humanize him. *Newsweek* had him on its December 1956 cover; inside, the feature story talked about the "unusual new commander in Europe." Norstad was described thus: "Most associates consider the shy, modest-spoken Norstad a highly complex individual whose main characteristics are brains, vast curiosity, tremendous will power, uncanny memory, and brains again. One SHAPE officer reported: 'you seldom meet Air Force generals who are such experts, and yet so uncompromisingly intellectual.' One astonished Frenchman said: 'I didn't know they made such Americans.'"[101] Margaret Biddle, a close friend of the Norstads, wrote an article for *Realities* in which she included this observation: "[Norstad] is a man who has his own personality and his own way of looking at things … . He has great ability to get to the bottom of problems and the capacity of finding ways to solve them. He always thinks before answering a question. Any reply of Norstad's is always a thought-out reply."[102]

III. Norstad becomes SACEUR

Eisenhower had nominated Norstad on April 3, 1956 to replace Gruenther. The NAC promptly approved the nomination, to take effect later in the year, and the announcement was made.[103] Eisenhower stated: "General Norstad is an officer of outstanding ability. He has the special qualification of long years of experience in Europe, culminating in almost three years of devoted service as Air Deputy to SACEUR. The confidence placed in him by the member nations has been amply demonstrated."[104] After his appointment Norstad wrote Eisenhower: "I must tell you how really greatly moved I am by the responsibility you have given me. I will be supported by your confidence, by my own devotion to this Cause [sic], and by my feeling that at least I think I understand what you set out to accomplish when you first organized SHAPE."[105]

The following analysis sums up the popular impression of Norstad:

> Circumstances have pushed Gen. Lauris Norstad out of his long-followed career – that of being an efficient No. 2 man ... . Tall, lithe, with the look of an airman about him ... . A quite deep voice ... the easy manners of a diplomat and the cold, precise mind of a strategist ... . A long memory for facts and faces ... . Like the man he is succeeding ... Gen. Norstad is looked upon in the military as a "brain," a thinker and planner ... . He also has a reputation as a persuader, in American military circles and abroad, among men over there whose interests are not always identical ... . Sometimes, among the men in the trade, there is discussion of whether Gen. Norstad and Gen. Curtis E. LeMay, chief of the Strategic Air Command, see eye to eye on all facets of air power. Gen. Norstad's exponents' reply is to look back into papers carrying Gen. Norstad's name, drafted in World War II and setting forth the plans and theories of strategic air power.[106]

The appointment brought a flood of congratulatory notes and messages from throughout NATO and the US. One that must have been highly appreciated by Norstad came from Bernard Baruch: "One time Jim Forrestal asked me to come in to his office because he wanted me to size up a young man of whom he thought very highly. That was the first time I met you, and when you had left, I said, 'That is a good man, Jim. He will go a long distance.' It is pleasing to have one's judgment confirmed. And so it is that I am congratulating you upon your appointment to be the head of NATO."[107]

Certainly another note, from his old friend Lt. General Charles P. Cabell, would have been deeply appreciated, since Norstad's tie with Cabell can be traced at least from their days together as members of Arnold's Advisory Council: "Congratulations! We're proud of you for having established yourself and the Air Force in a position worthy of carrying the responsibility of SACEUR. Of course, no one knows better than I the worthiness of both you and the Air Force."[108]

A direct reflection of the sense that the Cold War was indeed "hot" during those days, is contained in then-Secretary of the Air Force Donald Quarles's, congratulatory letter:

> I now hasten to tell you how very pleased I am with the President's nomination and the NATO Council's confirmation of you to succeed Al as Supreme Commander. This is splendid recognition of

your own outstanding ability and, I am sure, very gratifying evidence of the readiness of the other NATO nations to accept your leadership. It is, of course, also tacit recognition of the increasingly important role that air power must play in this free world versus Communist world situation, and this makes all of your associates in the United States Air Force not only proud of you but pleased that the realities of the situation are so clearly seen.[109]

Probably most to the point was this note: "It has been a long ladder from the early 1942 days in the Munitions Building, and you certainly have run up it and skipped unnecessary rungs to reach the top successfully."[110]

There were many expressions of Air Force pride in seeing one of their own occupy what had theretofore been an Army appointment – and as it was to be continuously thereafter. Everyone from Air Force Chief of Staff General Nathan Twining through virtually all of the major commanders expressed their pride and satisfaction to Norstad. Major General Wiley D. Ganey wrote from his assignment at the National War College: "This is not only an outstanding personal achievement, but a real 'feather in the cap' of the Air Force. All of us are very proud of this well deserved recognition and honor which you have received."[111] Major General Donald W. Hutchinson, Deputy for Operations of Tactical Air Command was even more effusive: "The news of your appointment as Supreme Allied Commander in Europe was a tremendous boost to all in the blue uniform. The task of getting an airman into such an important assignment appeared far more difficult for the Air Force than breaking the sound barrier."[112]

Probably the most thoughtful appraisal of Norstad's new situation was given by a former high NATO official:

> Allow me to offer you my very best congratulations upon your splendid appointment as Supreme Allied Commander Europe. You know the work and the difficulties of Shape so well, that you will not expect your new assignment to lead you only over rose-strewn paths. However, as our French friends say, *le jeu vaut la chandelle*, or in other words the Atlantic Alliance is too all-important to all of us that one puts up with a lot of things, which would be unbearable in other circumstances.
>
> As a European I am delighted that the new Saceur has as intimate a knowledge of the Old World as his very distinguished predecessor. This fact will undoubtedly be of great help to you in dealing with

countries that do not yet fully realise that they represent not more than counties in this air-atomic age. But then we have all learned that the power of inertia is all too frequently the dominant force in this world.[113]

When it came to appraising himself, Norstad was quite candid: "I realise quite well the magnitude of my new task and I am completely dedicated to its successful performance."[114] Given his years working with his predecessors as SACEUR stemming from World War II, it would be surprising if Norstad had not by then acquired confidence in his ability to lead an organization ostensibly military, but in reality political in nature.

It was in this comforting and familiar environment that Norstad moved steadily forward to the pinnacle of his career. He was a dedicated airman, but during World War II he had also become a brilliant planner in a time when such talents were not only in short supply, but, as far as general American political opinion went, were not necessarily needed until a crisis proved otherwise. He had also proven himself a shrewd "political general" in the turbulent military politics of postwar Washington.[115] Norstad had become a skilled practitioner of public relations, reflecting the Air Force's longstanding sensitivity to the importance of good publicity in advancing or defending its causes. He well understood that the SACEUR had a constant "selling" job with friend and foe alike. As it was put by Burke Wilkinson, one of his public relations aides: "Norstad had a keen sense of public relations. When he hired me he explained that he was not looking for someone to grind out press releases, but that I was to share in every part of the policy-making process. He encouraged Milton Caniff, Steve Canyon's creator, to create an episode at SHAPE. Later he urged me to write a suspense novel about the command. In the novel, *Night of the Short Knives*, he figures as the nameless Supreme Commander. I deliberately gave him no name, for he is seen in the story as a kind of nimbus, an almost mystical force and symbol. That was the way many of us had come to see him."[116]

Finally, he had moved onto the multinational stage at a time when the US had committed itself to the most powerful peacetime coalition in American – or, for that matter, in any nation's – history.

Part II
On Being SACEUR

5
Nuclear Weapons for Europe's Defense: Norstad and the Eisenhower Administration

> Our requirements are all on a minimum basis, designed to meet conditions of a general war which would involve major Soviet participation.[1]

I. The introduction of atomic warheads into NATO

Having come to Europe as Commander-in-Chief, US Air Forces, Europe (CINCUSAFE), Norstad was all too familiar with the problems and possibilities of creating an effective "nuclear umbrella" for NATO. Even though, as pointed out earlier, nuclear weapons played no formal part in the early planning of NATO, Norstad had emphasized that NATO could not just ignore them. He was convinced that a way must be found to give the European Allies a sense of sharing in the formulation of the doctrine for their employment and, if deterrence were to fail, their possible use. The issue, in a nutshell, was whether NATO nuclear proliferation should be unilateral or multilateral. In this respect, he had to work closely with the Federal Republic of Germany (FRG) as well as with France and Britain. As it was put:

> The relationship between the nuclearization of NATO and the settlement with the Federal Republic is not totally clear, but I suspect that there was an important link: nuclearization meant that the Americans, who controlled the most important forces and who in effect operated the strategy, would have to stay in Europe for a very considerable period of time, and as long as the Americans were in the French and many of the other allies could be relatively relaxed about a buildup of German power. Any possible German threat would be contained in a structure dominated by American power.[2]

But Norstad had to deal with the constraints imposed on him by US nuclear policy. Eisenhower had also chafed under the legal restrictions set by Congress. "The matter of nuclear strength and possible deployment was troublesome from the beginning," Eisenhower said. He was referring to the McMahon Act 1946, which controlled the production of fissionable materials, the manufacture and storage of nuclear weapons, and the transfer of such weapons to other states. As he said, the Act "prevented us from making any workable agreements with our partners in NATO respecting nuclear weapons – indeed it was difficult and embarrassing, because of the restriction imposed upon us, even to discuss the matter intelligently and thoroughly." In spite of these hindrances, discussions took place at SHAPE during Eisenhower's tenure concerning the implications of battlefield nuclear weapons for European defense; and Eisenhower confessed that "the effect of the nuclear deterrent was taken in account in all our joint planning."[3]

Fortunately for Norstad, the Atomic Energy Act of 1954 revised the McMahon Act. It "permitted the use on an allied basis of more atomic information than had been allowed previously." At the same time, Norstad noted that "... the restrictions imposed by that act still prevent NATO forces from training on a fully realistic basis or developing the operational capability and readiness status required, particularly in view of the many types of modern atomic-weapons systems which are now becoming available." To improve further the situation, he endorsed subsequent changes in the Act which would "provide greater latitude for the dissemination of essential information within this Allied Command."[4] An important reason for this concern over secrecy as noted previously, was that both Norstad and his predecessor Gruenther had been lobbying during this period for the creation of a "NATO atomic stockpile."

Norstad had advocated publicly that "mid-range ballistic missiles, land and sea based, and with great mobility, should be made available to NATO as a part of the weapons modernization program, to meet the presently assigned functions of this command."[5] His desire to introduce land-based Intermediate-Range Ballistic Missiles (IRBMs) into the NATO area was prompted by the persistent imbalance of NATO's conventional forces *vis-à-vis* the Warsaw Pact. There were two options available to do this: through bilateral assurances that the US would stockpile nuclear warheads but would keep them in US custody except in wartime, or that the warheads would be stockpiled with NATO, restrictive US legislation permitting.[6] Secretary of State Dulles saw some real advantages in the latter option:

If we were to give this as much of a NATO flavor as possible, subject to the limitations of present legislation, we might obtain large political benefits therefrom while, at the same time, not sacrificing any of the aspects of US control which the present situation now affords. Such a formula appropriately portrayed as a NATO stockpile might be of assistance to us with respect to the Fourth Country problem, the problem of obtaining nuclear storage rights for our own forces, and, should the situation so require, the British desire for an assurance of nuclear weapons material in the event the Soviets should accept our disarmament proposal for cut-off of nuclear weapons production.[7]

The main immediate argument for sharing was to sidetrack French unilateralism – France was the only NATO member-state that could embark on such a program any time soon. Norstad recognized that a pledge of French "abstinence" would have to be accompanied by the US's willingness to place nuclear weapons under French control or as the French put: "integrated NATO atomic capability." Otherwise, motivated both by prestige and by a desire to become less dependent upon the US in times when the US might be reluctant to use nuclear weapons, France would move rapidly to develop its own nuclear capacity.

At the NAC Heads-of-Government meeting of December 1957, doubtless to Norstad's satisfaction, he was authorized to go ahead:

NATO has decided to establish stocks of nuclear warheads, which will be readily available for the defence of the Alliance in case of need. In view of the present Soviet policies in the field of new weapons, the Council has also decided that intermediate range ballistic missiles will have to be put at the disposal of the Supreme Allied Commander Europe.

The deployment of these stocks and missiles and arrangements for their use will accordingly be decided in conformity with NATO defence plans and in agreement with the states directly concerned. The NATO military authorities have been requested to submit to the Council at an early date their recommendations on the introduction of these weapons in the common defence. The Council in permanent session will consider the various questions involved.[8]

The NAC suggested that Norstad, as SACEUR, should develop military requirements for nuclear warheads for Allied Command Europe (ACE) and also for the British forces in Britain proper. These requirements should take into account the degree of readiness of the various NATO forces to use nuclear warheads if necessary. Norstad should then forward these requirements to US military authorities through his USCINCEUR "hat".

Although the stockpile of the warheads for the nuclear-capable delivery systems would be located in sites in the various member-states, they would altogether comprise a single NATO stockpile under the control of Norstad as SACEUR. In other words, they would not be reserved or earmarked for the forces of any particular NATO member-state. The US would place the warheads in locations requested by Norstad as SACEUR for the ready use of those NATO forces able to use them, but the warheads would remain the property of the US and would remain in USCINCEUR's custody. The weapons could be transferred from Norstad as USCINCEUR to the national military authorities only with the agreement of the NAC or in the event that sudden hostilities in ACE or Britain would require action prior to the decision of the NAC. Since the NAC can act only by unanimity, thus requiring the consent of the US, and since SACEUR/USCINCEUR would be a US officer, the US could retain national control even while deploying the weapons multilaterally.[9]

The US would train Allied military personnel in the use of the vehicles, and would help to develop a supply system for them.[10] The initial concept provided that the personnel guarding the weapons in each site would be US personnel under Norstad's command as USCINCEUR, and the release of the weapons to national forces in the event of hostilities could only be authorized by the personal order of Norstad in his dual SACEUR/USCINCEUR capacities.

Even though the concept of a NATO stockpile of atomic warheads had been developed by Norstad and obviously protected US national concerns, the JCS initially had opposed the idea. They wanted bilateral storage arrangements worked out between the US and individual NATO member-states, patterned after the US arrangements with Britain in connection with the Canberra and V-bomber programs.[11] The disagreement between Norstad and the JCS centered around the following points:

1. General Norstad uses the term "NATO atomic stockpile", which the JCS thinks is dangerous terminology for the United States. 2. General Norstad states that only multilateral arrangements could be consistent with NATO procedures, while the JCS feel that bilateral

arrangements are necessary to retain US freedom of action ... 4. The JCS do not subscribe to the NATO "common atomic stockpile concept", and have told the Secretary of Defense that they would prepare procedures for "providing US atomic weapons for the common defense of the NATO area." This document would be introduced through the Standing Group and the North Atlantic Military Committee, to the North Atlantic Council and thus would be a NATO document, which would outline on a uniform and impartial basis the terms of reference for the necessary bilateral agreements for storage sites."[12]

To Norstad's gratification, on January 13 1958, the JCS were persuaded otherwise, and stated clearly that all IRBMs based in the NATO member-states in Europe, to include those in the US, should be under the operational control of SACEUR in both peace and war. In practice, this meant that the weapons under Norstad would contribute directly to the overall deterrent capacity of both NATO and the US (along with the smaller British strategic force). Such a deployment would also demonstrate that NATO was determined to build up a firm defense, which incidentally, in the not-too-distant future, made the West's – and thus Norstad's – position on the emerging crisis over Berlin more credible.[13]

But the root of the credibility problem for Norstad was the 1953 Eisenhower "New Look" concept. Would the threat of massive nuclear retaliation by the US from bases in Europe and the US against the Soviet Union deter *any* Soviet military intervention in Western Europe? It was the uncertainty that surrounded the answer to this question that impelled Chancellor Adenauer, after the admission of the FRG into NATO by 1955, to feel that he should have a strong voice in the discussion of NATO nuclear affairs. A very germane fact in all of this was Norstad's estimation that the NATO conventional defense "shield" in Central Europe would need about thirty divisions, a goal that could only – and then with difficulty – be met with West German troops.

Because the IRBMs in NATO, with their atomic warheads, could reach to the Soviet heartland and thus could serve as a compensatory regional deterrent, the Allies could claim this as a *quid pro quo* in return for their willingness to allow the stationing of these lethal weapons on their territory. Norstad wanted them deployed by the end of the year. One of the difficulties for Norstad, in his "atomic diplomacy," was that the IRBMs were seen as a "holding operation" by the US pending the development and deployment of its own strategic ICBM force.[14] In response to a question that continually bedeviled the Alliance about whether the situation would remain the same after the US possessed ICBMs, Norstad said:

> Our retaliatory forces, our principal deterrent forces, as they exist today, are quite capable of carrying out their mission. The introduction of intermediate range ballistic missiles and intercontinental missiles is for the purpose of keeping this force modernized and keeping it capable of carrying out its deterrent mission. An extension and development of our weapons system was created and maintained for this purpose – for a deterrent purpose – for the purpose of preserving the peace.
>
> ... unless a political and military foundation has been laid which would virtually eliminate the dangers of a war, then any agreement not to station tactical weapons with atomic capability in Central Europe would not only jeopardize our strategic concept, but I must in all honesty say would leave us defenseless.
>
> ... it is our considered opinion that the introduction of these new weapons of great destructive power, and these accurate and effective reliable delivery means, makes the shield force – the Army, the Navy and the Air forces – in the forward line for the purposes of protecting NATO, even more important than in the past.[15]

Because of the success of *Sputnik* in 1957, the Soviet capacity to strike with intercontinental ballistic missiles (ICBMs) directly against the continental US had become a real and frightening possibility. This new reality threatened to transform the unilateral US nuclear strategic deterrence into a mutual US–Soviet nuclear standoff that might leave Europe exposed to Soviet "salami" tactics. On April 12 1957 the US had announced that it would make available to certain Allies, including the FRG, advanced battlefield weapons – the HONEST JOHN, MATADOR, and NIKE short-range missiles.[16] Norstad made the case for equipping the FRG with these weapons in a television interview he gave in West Germany in February 1958. He put it thus:

> Q: Many people believe that the atomic arming of the German forces would increase the tension between East and West. The American forces in Germany have tactical nuclear weapons. Do the German troops also require them, in your opinion?
> NORSTAD: So long as the over-all situation does not change, defensive atomic weapons are absolutely indispensable for the

strengthening of the defensive power of the *Bundeswehr* – for the protection of the Federal Republic and all NATO nations; that is the purely military standpoint.

Now, however, for the German standpoint: a comprehensive defense contribution by the Federal Republic is coming into being. It is wholly unthinkable that these forces should be condemned to a second-class function, in which they would be practically useless for defense.

We cannot give the German forces inadequate arms; the German nation cannot allow its soldiers to be armed with weapons long since obsolete.[17]

He had always considered one of his foremost diplomatic priorities to be how to respond to Adenauer's concern that the FRG would be considered a second-class citizen in NATO. As he put it: "From the German standpoint, if I were a German – and in my capacity I must look upon myself as being at least partly German – we must consider the very real fact that we will have a substantial contribution of forces from the Federal Republic. And it is absolutely unthinkable that these forces should be condemned to a second-class function – a function that might make them really useless for their purpose of defense … . The German people must have these forces equipped with the means that are necessary for them to carry out their mission."[18] Although the US might have had a "special" nuclear relationship with the British, based in part on ties that reached back into World War II, Norstad was in full agreement with Eisenhower that without the West Germans – and this would include the West Berliners – NATO's *raison d'être* would be considerably weakened, if not rendered irrelevant.

Norstad was undoubtedly pleased when, in December 1958, agreement was reached in NATO to extend the NATO atomic capability to the military forces of the FRG under the same arrangements as applied to the forces of the other NATO member-states, which really meant Britain. The British agreement stipulated that US forces would retain custody of the atomic warheads at all times prior to their expenditure; that British forces would not be given any functions not in keeping with the US Atomic Energy Act of 1954, as amended; and that such US custody would be retained until expenditure orders were given by SACEUR/USCINCEUR, which meant that the US was obligated to follow SACEUR's orders only if Norstad, as USCINCEUR, acted with authority from the President or other appropriate US superiors.[19]

Obviously, Norstad's proposals for a NATO nuclear force could forestall the development of a drive by the FRG to attain an independent nuclear capability. Norstad and Adenauer had discussed the issue as early as 1957. Norstad recalled that:

> The Chancellor was the first to raise with me, in 1957, two questions which he said had been raised in the Federal Republic as well as in other countries in Europe. One was: If all these countries organized their defense on a foundation of nuclear weapons, was it not reasonable for the European countries to ask that a certain number of weapons be firmly committed on the basis that they would not be withdrawn by unilateral decision of the United States? The other was: should not NATO have some degree of influence, perhaps even control, over the conditions under which the weapons would be used? No one said at the time that they wanted control, they just said due influence ... .
>
> I sought to provide a specific answer to the questions. My proposal was that we establish an Executive Committee within NATO consisting of the United States, Great Britain, and France. The Secretary General would be chairman and Germany would have a special relationship to this group which would have some control over any nuclear weapons deployed in Europe.[20]

The dilemma for Norstad was not only what to do about the FRG. He also had to deal with the fact that the US treated Britain and France very differently in regard to nuclear affairs. One of Norstad's first priorities had been to obtain French consent to accept IRBMs and to permit the stockpiling of the atomic warheads at sites in France. France, instead, decided to embark on building its own *force de frappe*, as will be seen shortly.

II. Norstad's attempt to make NATO a "fourth nuclear power"

Norstad wanted to keep the atomic stockpile issue separate from the IRBM issue because in his view their political problems were dissimilar. Furthermore, Norstad was dead set against the European NATO member-states diverting resources in order to develop their own nuclear weapons. He made it clear that those that attempted to do so could not look to the US for financial aid for their conventional forces. At this time, there was some talk of a joint West German–French–Italian agreement on the research, development and production of nuclear weapons. As Norstad put it: "If the concept of inter-dependence, etc., is going to mean anything, this is one place to emphasize it."[21]

Obviously, the process of placing IRBMs in NATO Europe was proving difficult. To overcome some of these obstacles, Norstad favored a piecemeal, or step-by-step, approach, thus keeping various intra-NATO national political pressures to a minimum. To Norstad's frustration, even though the NAC had adopted a deployment program in December 1957, for various reasons no actual deployment had yet taken place by the following October. He wanted to keep the numbers of THOR and JUPITER liquid-fueled missiles to a minimum because an improved version – or second generation – IRBM which would utilize solid propellants was shortly to be made available to NATO.

In addition to the four IRBM squadrons that had already been committed to the British, Norstad had proposed that three squadrons be earmarked for France and three for the Mediterranean area, making a total of ten.[22] Although Turkey was the best located geographically to reach deep strategic targets in the Soviet Union, Nostad favored putting France first in line to receive the squadrons because, as he put it: "[The] Turks would be too warlike," given the state of instability in the Middle East at that time. In a meeting held in Washington between Norstad and Deputy Secretary of Defense Donald Quarles, it was noted that "the fact that JCS recommend Turkey and then France, while Gen. Norstad recommends France and then Turkey, doesn't seem to raise any conflict in [Quarles'] mind. We do France first because of political reasons. We should leave politics and such obstacles for Gen. Norstad to surmount."[23] For similar reasons, Norstad favored Italy as an alternative to France, rather than Turkey. Both the US and Norstad maintained firmly that all IRBMs deployed on the Continent should be assigned to him.

Implementation of Norstad's IRBM program moved slowly partly because the French insisted on a primary role in the control of nuclear weapons stationed in France. Put simply, there would be no assignment of any IRBMs in France to Norstad.[24] Under these circumstances, the US decided to delay embarking on IRBM production and training activities beyond the eight squadrons already committed to Norstad, with the other two going to such locations as Alaska and Okinawa. The decision was made without fanfare, and the NAC was so informed.[25]

One important reason for the delay was that the projected "second generation" solid-propellant IRBM program was arousing some anxiety and hesitation because the US desired that the equipment should be produced in Europe and paid for by the Allies. What the US wanted was some relief from the seemingly formidable costs of providing NATO with an IRBM capability, and saw that one way to do this was for the Europeans to produce a European solid propellant IRBM for themselves. Because of the enormous complexity and cost of a second generation IRBM program, Norstad understood that it was unlikely that NATO Europe could succeed in such a project without active US leadership and substantial US financial assistance, as well as technical aid.

Nonetheless, Norstad remained a firm advocate of moving ahead to the second generation. He believed that there was a high priority requirement for the deployment by 1963 of hard-based and/or mobile IRBMs with their very fast reaction time. He recommended that this be accomplished by the US providing solid-fuel POLARIS-type missiles on a grant basis, with the Europeans being asked to produce the ground support equipment – reportedly as costly as the missiles.[26]

Because the issues were of transcendent importance to the nuclear future of NATO, the opposing arguments are worth summarizing:

> A primary consideration underlying the USRO-Norstad recommendation is the importance of ensuring maximum NATO control of strategic as well as tactical capabilities in Europe and of preventing the increase of independent national nuclear-capable forces. They believe that the only possibility of accomplishing this lies in a US offer of Polaris missiles to Europe with the understanding that they would be assigned to SACEUR. Such an offer should, of course, have a great financial appeal to the Europeans since it would save them a great deal of the enormous costs involved in IRBM development and production. This would be particularly significant in the case of Britain if it led to the cancellation of the UK's Blue Streak program which should free substantial resources for improvement of UK conventional capabilities. Thus, it is possible, although perhaps unlikely, that a US offer of Polaris would persuade France and the UK to accept some form of NATO framework or control for second generation IRBM's.
>
> The converse of the USRO-Norstad position is that the US should not assist in accelerating the creation of diverse and uncoordinated national centers of strategic weapons. This would mean that any US assistance (including technical information) to a European IRBM program should be strictly conditioned on NATO control of the finished weapons. It is almost a foregone conclusion, of course, that the French and British would insist on independent national

control over a strategic weapon produced entirely in Europe. Therefore, such a US position would prevent a NATO IRBM production program from getting under way, although it would not preclude eventual European production outside the NATO framework.[27]

The British were not too interested because they wanted to continue to develop their BLUE STREAK missile with US financial assistance unless the US could assure them that they could have independent control over the IRBMs placed in their custody. This was what the French also wanted.[28] In any event, the British had little interest in the role of SACEUR so far as IRBM deployment in Britain was concerned; instead, they continued to persist in developing a totally independent IRBM.

A careful estimate of the consequences of providing the solid-fuel POLARIS to NATO and the motives of the various major parties was undertaken at this juncture by the State and Defense Departments. A major US consideration was whether a given amount of US resources devoted to increased striking power subject to Alliance control would be preferable to using these resources to augment the strategic forces under exclusive US control.[29] It was assumed, for example, that the French and the British were determined to have their own IRBMs and warheads free of NATO or the US control. The French were more interested in getting the "know-how" and in launching an indigenous IRBM program than they were in achieving an early operational capability. What they wanted was a missile of about the same size and range as the British BLUE STREAK – 2000 nautical mile range.[30] The expectation was that the first squadrons of POLARIS missiles produced would have a range of 500–1200 nautical miles, with this range gradually increasing thereafter to about 2000 nautical miles by 1963–1964.

As one observer at these meetings put it: "The February 6 discussion between Mr. Quarles, General Norstad, Mr. Murphy and Mr. Holaday on this subject was fascinating ... I believe that the issues are being given a healthy airing and we may come to grips with them in the near future."[31] To Norstad's relief, the US decided to provide POLARIS missiles, together with technical assistance for European production of the ground support equipment, conditioned upon NATO control. This option made it possible to meet Norstad's goal of having an operational IRBM capacity in NATO by 1962 or 1963.[32] He believed that a US offer to provide POLARIS missiles would help greatly to solve the problem of control of the missiles because he would insist on firm commitments from the Europeans on all aspects of the program, including their own financial contributions, acceptance of the missiles, control, etc., before the US should agree to provide the missiles.[33] Furthermore, Norstad, as SACEUR, had the right to establish the numbers of warheads located in any given member-state at any given time, and to remove or to shift the stocks of weapons.[34]

As the time drew near for a public announcement of the agreements, not only with the FRG but also with Greece, Turkey, and the Netherlands, the Soviet Union became openly concerned. Norstad wanted to go ahead, even over a Soviet protest, "provided this can be accomplished without indicating great anxiety, feverish haste or extraordinary pressures."[35] The point was to make the announcement before the May 1959 meeting of the foreign ministers of the US, Britain, France and the Soviet Union in Geneva. Khrushchev wanted this meeting to set the stage for a Four-Power Summit, for which he had been angling for some time. As the Soviet Note claimed:

> At the present moment, when the Governments of the United States of America, England and France and also the Government of the Federal Republic of Germany, have expressed agreement to discuss in forthcoming negotiations the question about a peace treaty with Germany, it would be impossible to evaluate measures for the atomic armament of the Federal Republic of Germany otherwise than as an attempt beforehand to torpedo these negotiations. It is impossible not to come to the conclusion that the measures being prepared for the atomic armament with nuclear and rocket weapons of the Federal Republic of Germany, Greece, Turkey, and certain other state-participants of the North Atlantic bloc and the plans for the stationing on the territories of these countries of American sites for launching rockets are in contradiction with those tasks which stand before the Conference of Ministers of Foreign Affairs and the Summit Conference.[36]

The delays and frustrations that Norstad encountered lay partly in the fact that within the publics of the member-states involved, there was very little informed discussion on these issues, which in any event seemed arcane to the average citizen. The debates were mostly taking place in government ministries. Within a democratic political framework, there was little incentive for elected legislators to respond to Norstad's proposals because the entire issue seemed beyond the public's understanding.

So, on November 21, 1959 Norstad, going public, told the NATO Parliamentarians' Conference that "consideration should be given to guaranteeing to the Alliance the availability of a basic pool of atomic weapons, those essential to the direct defense of Europe, and to give all nations of the Alliance an essentially equal voice in the control of these particular weapons."[37]

In addressing these problems of nuclear sharing and control, Norstad was speaking of tactical and not strategic weapons, making the point in various fora that, although a nuclear weapons stockpile was being put in place, still lacking was "a satisfactory procedure in terms of the Alliance exercising its authority, and this is something which the United States does not dictate." To augment NATO's authority, he believed that machinery should be established which could authorize the use of the US's nuclear weapons even though custody of the bombs or warheads might remain under US control. "Let's keep our own custody," he said, 'but let's let them collectively participate in the decision by which a limited number of weapons would be used in the NATO context, and, if possible, when they should be used." The decision-making procedure should be such that there would "be a certain minimum number of weapons which will be available even if the US, which is most unlikely, would positively dissent from the decision and not commit its own forces."[38] Matters had come a long way since Dulles's expectation that the Europeans – or for that matter, Norstad – would be satisfied with the "flavor" of integration and sharing.

To accomplish this, he renewed his earlier proposal that there be created a primary decision-making body – the Executive Committee – which would consist of the Heads of Government of the US, Britain, France, and the FRG, plus some others, who would establish a permanent subordinate group of "people who would live with the subject, actually live with the subject, in whom the Prime Minister or President or Chancellor had great confidence and to whom he had direct access."[39] Norstad asserted that the creation of this group would only formalize existing custom. "This proposal for a Heads of State group was not pulled out of the air," he said. "This is confirming practice, at least practice during my time. These are the people with whom I maintained the contact. These are the people whom, when I got into difficulty, I called on the telephone or I went to see, or they called me on the telephone."[40] In a curious way, Norstad's Executive Committee notion for NATO was not dissimilar to de Gaulle's "directorate" concept for tripartite Western globalism, discussed later in this chapter.[41]

Furthermore, on the question of how to share in the command and control of nuclear weapons, Norstad had some sympathy with the Gaullist view that the American nuclear deterrent had, by 1958 and *Sputnik*, lost some of its credibility. In particular, de Gaulle had argued that although he found no fault with American intentions to defend Europe, he was not convinced that the US could be expected to live up to its commitments in all possible crisis situations. This was not a uniquely American weakness, he pointed out, it was a fact of international life that no state would likely invite its own destruction in order to defend others.

In this kind of nuclear situation the "others" must be armed with nuclear weapons so that if the nuclear umbrella failed to operate, the small Allies would still have an independent means of deterring possible moves against *their* vital interests. It would be, in other words, in order to cover the 5 percent of hypothetical cases when the US might *not* retaliate that Europe should have its own nuclear weapons.[42] From Norstad's perspective, which was shared by other states in NATO besides France, this 5 percent needed to be taken seriously and plans should be made to demonstrate how to meet this concern.[43] For Norstad, there was a practical reason why he – or any other SACEUR – would be greatly concerned. As one scholar put it: "An alliance in which each nation is independently drafting plans to fight *its* political objectives is an alliance bound to lack coordination and common purpose."[44]

Secretary-General Spaak summed up the appeal, both specific and general, which the so-called Norstad Plan might have. The possibility that NATO might become "the fourth atomic Power in the world," said Spaak, would be "a new milestone for the Alliance... . It constitutes a valid and lasting answer to the problem of the atomic armament of Germany. It is also an answer to the queries and the anxieties of France. It may put an end to the dangerous controversies now developing in the United Kingdom. It constitutes for the Alliance as a whole, and more particularly for Europe, a tremendous increase in its power."[45]

Before Eisenhower left office in 1961, he decided to take an active interest in another "Norstad Plan" – the establishment of a control and inspection regime in Central Europe. To Norstad, this could be seen as being a complementary form of de-escalation to the perception held by the Soviet Union that putting IRBMs in NATO/Europe was escalatory. In fact, Eisenhower had discussed this with Adenauer when Adenauer came to Washington in March 1960.[46] Adenauer thought the area involved should be all of the Communist bloc and all of NATO. It was important to Adenauer politically for the area to embrace more of NATO than just the FRG.

Eisenhower had also raised it with de Gaulle when they met in Paris that April. But de Gaulle responded that he felt that an inspection zone should apply on a world-wide basis, covering the means of delivery to include aircraft and missiles, of nuclear weapons. Nothing more came of the idea, although Eisenhower had made the point that it might be of more value to propose a more limited project which could test the good faith of the Soviets, as well as the practical possibility of achieving effective inspection.[47] The notion had the support of the British, who in general had favored schemes of disengagement in Central Europe.

From a military standpoint, Norstad thought a system of control and inspection could be instituted covering a portion of West and Central Europe. The minimum area for such a project, in Norstad's view, would include Poland, Czechoslovakia, the GDR and the FRG, Belgium, the Netherlands, and Denmark. Joint inspection teams could be formed with the Soviets, with each party having the right to go anywhere in the area, upon notification. Norstad even envisioned that perhaps Alaska and Siberia could be included – even perhaps some of the Northwestern US.

This would utilize mobile inspection groups with total personnel coming to something like 1500 troops. The techniques would parallel Eisenhower's Open Skies proposal, using advanced photography. Also there could be overlapping radar nets, with Western radars located as far east as Poland, and Communist radars located in the FRG. It would be necessary to designate a specific geographic area to which these techniques could be applied. Norstad thought that these radar nets could provide effective inspection which would let both sides know what may be taking place where that might have appreciable military significance. One very positive benefit would be substantial relief from the danger of surprise surface attack that preoccupied the Europeans, and especially the West Germans; tensions could be reduced without any loss of security. Then, after some twelve to eighteen months of experience, consideration could be given to some thinning out of the respective alliance forces.[48] But Norstad did not want any consideration of reducing forces in Central Europe to affect the resolute image of the West while the standoff over Berlin persisted.

One of the most pleasant times of Norstad's period as SACEUR, as the Eisenhower Administration was drawing to a close, were the two occasions when he attended luncheons at the magnificent villa at Menaggio on Lake Como of Dirk Stikker, the Netherlands Permanent Representative to NATO and soon to be Spaak's successor as Secretary-General. Adenauer was accustomed to vacationing in the summer at a villa nearby, which provided opportunities for informal conversations with weekend visitors. On the second such occasion, on September 9, 1960, Norstad, Adenauer, Spaak, Ambassador André de Staercke (the Belgian Permanent Representative and *Doyen* of the NAC), and Ambassador Wilhelm Blankenhorn (the West German Permanent Representative) were gathered together for a long and leisurely lunch. They were all aware that all of the issues that had engaged Norstad so intensely since he had become SACEUR centered on the question of the role and function of nuclear weapons in Europe. As Adenauer put it: "Europe must have something" in the atomic field. He wanted to know from Norstad what the character of US leadership would be if there were a change at the top. Norstad expressed the belief that in his view the American people would not turn over atomic weapons to any country for its independent use, and he agreed with this view. Hence it did not matter, in this respect, who the leaders of the government in Washington were.

But Adenauer persisted, wondering how the West Europeans could organize their defense around atomic weapons when the US government had a monopoly over them and could take them away if it wished. This gave Norstad an opportunity to remind Adenauer of his notion of making NATO a fourth atomic Power, which Adenauer favored. There was an air of optimism at the luncheon which undoubtedly pleased Norstad.[49] But then Spaak raised the question of "who in NATO" would control these transferred weapons? Norstad cleverly pointed out in response that NATO had made much progress without answering unanswerable questions of exactly how the Alliance would go to war. He thought that still further progress could be achieved without doing so. Unfortunately for Norstad, one leading figure who claimed to be a friendly ally did not agree with him.

III. France, De Gaulle, and Norstad

Norstad opened formal discussions with France early in 1958 for the purpose of obtaining agreement for the installation of IRBM sites on French territory.[50] He wanted the US to give him the authority, as USCINCEUR, to release to SHAPE and, as deemed appropriate, to French staff officers, such information as: personnel requirements; training information and plans; site selection criteria; and extracts from documents used by USAF in recent negotiations with the British. It was quite clear at this time that Norstad wanted to treat France as a co-equal with Britain as far as IRBMs were concerned.[51] The French, on their part, were anxious to have IRBMs partly because they were quite aware that IRBM sites were already being selected and developed in Britain.

In a meeting on February 1, 1958 with General Paul Ely, Chairman of the French Chiefs-of-Staff, Norstad reported: "[Ely] referred to need for 'National Equality' in determining the use or control of weapons and to French interests in achieving a preferred status by obtaining special information and financial help for the production of IRBMs." Norstad pointed out that the creation of IRBM units was a matter entirely separate from the production aspect, which would have to come within the NATO framework, and which France had wanted to avoid. But Norstad made it quite clear where the US considered its interests were: "high US authorities were not rpt not necessarily inclined to accord France the highest priority [a deal exchanging sites for technical production information], such a priority being of greater interest and importance to France than it was to the United States, although it obviously was of importance to both."[52]

Much to Norstad's relief, the French did not object to placing the IRBM units under his operational control as SACEUR. But the French preferred that the IRBM units would be under a French officer responsible to Norstad, and preferred that the British arrangement be similar. In other words, France wanted the British to have no IRBM control outside the NATO command. As to who would pull the trigger, it was made clear to Norstad that if the British could act independently, then the French would want the same authority.

As the negotiations went forward – and this meant for Norstad with the various relevant parts of the US government as well as with the French – matters became more complicated. As it was put: "the French proposal deviated from the concept recommended at the Heads of Government meeting by repeatedly emphasizing French requirements for French forces and American requirements for American forces rather than SACEUR requirements for NATO forces."[53] In other words, Norstad felt that the French were overemphasizing the bilateral aspects of atomic stockpiling. Norstad wanted *all* IRBMs in Europe – including those for US forces – to be part of the NATO stockpiles. He was pushing for multilateral sharing rather than bilateral for he felt that only in this way would the FRG be satisfied not to want its own independently-controlled stockpile.

The late Professor Edgar S. Furniss of Princeton University, in a working paper for a Council on Foreign Relations Study Group, posited that prestige and numbers are the two most compelling reasons for France's desire to remain a major military presence. As Furniss put it: "As status and inter-Allied relations come to be measured by nuclear stockpiles of varying power for varying purposes, so must France have its own nuclear weapons as quickly as it can. If at all possible, it must be *the* Fourth Country in the so-called 'Fourth Country' problem so seriously and seemingly so fruitlessly being debated by Americans."[54]

On March 19 Norstad, in his capacity as SACEUR, sent to the French government the draft text of an IRBM agreement regarding the deployment of JUPITER IRBM squadrons to France. The main provisions were:

1. The Government of the United States shall supply to the Government of France an agreed number of intermediate range ballistic missiles and their related specialized equipment and make available training assistance in order to facilitate the deployment by the Government of France of the said missiles. The missiles shall be located only in France at sites and under such conditions as are determined by the two Governments in agreement with SACEUR.
2. The French Government shall provide the sites and supporting facilities required for the deployment of the missiles.
3. Ownership of the missiles and related equipment shall pass to the French Government under established United States Mutual Assistance Program procedures as soon as the French Government is in a position to man and operate the missiles.
4. The missiles will be manned and operated by French personnel, who will be trained by the United States Government for the purpose of this project at the earliest feasible date.
5. For the purposes of this agreement, training involving firing of missiles will take place on United States instrumental ranges.
6. Material, equipment, and training provided by the United States Government to the French Government pursuant to the arrangements recorded herein will be furnished pursuant to the United States Mutual Security Act of 1954, as amended, act amendatory or supplementary thereto, appropriation acts thereunder or any other applicable United States legislative provisions.

7. The French military formations equipped with intermediate range ballistic missiles will be under the operational control of SACEUR in peace and war (as defined in Section 2, Paragraph 9A3, MC/57).
8. The decision to launch these missiles would be taken by SACEUR only in agreement with the two Governments. The agreement of the two Governments will be given in the light of the circumstances at the time and having regard to the undertaking they have assumed in Article 5 of the North Atlantic Treaty.
9. References to intermediate range ballistic missiles in this agreement do not include the nuclear warheads for such missiles. The nuclear warheads for such missiles will be provided from the stocks, which, pursuant to the decision of the North Atlantic Council, are to be established as to be readily available for the defense of the Alliance in case of need. All nuclear warheads provided by the United States to these stocks shall remain in full United States ownership, custody and control in accordance with United States law ... .[55]

Then, on April 18, Ely proposed to Norstad that paragraph 7 of the text be amended to read: "The French military units equipped with IRBMs under the command of a French general officer, will be assigned to SACEUR in peace and war under the conditions stipulated in the NATO documents presently in effect." Because at that time French politics were in the turmoil that a month later would result in General Charles de Gaulle's returning to power, Norstad did not respond to this proposal. For one thing, it was not clear whether Ely himself would survive politically. Nonetheless, Norstad was prepared to accept this amendment with the *proviso* that the text would be terminated after the word "war" and that in place of the last clause, separate classified letters of understanding would be exchanged clarifying his requirements for "operational control" over IRBM units.[56]

The whole enterprise came to naught in the July conversations between Dulles and de Gaulle, and with it came the end of making French territory the cornerstone of Norstad's design for creating a European-based IRBM capability. Eisenhower and Dulles agreed to let Norstad, as SACEUR, handle any further contacts with de Gaulle.

Norstad informed the French leader that de Gaulle had to meet a deadline in securing France's agreement to accept IRBMs, and that if this "absolute deadline" were not met, he would be forced to make other arrangements for the three squadrons originally scheduled for

France. The "other arrangements" meant that Italy, Greece or Turkey would immediately be approached by Norstad. However, as a fallback option Norstad let it be known that if de Gaulle so desired, other IRBM units could be made available in a year or so.⁵⁷ As to the question of an atomic NATO stockpile in France, the US reiterated that the overall program providing a nuclear deterrent for NATO, including missiles and warheads, must be placed at Norstad's disposal as SACEUR. This would not be possible if de Gaulle were to insist on a bilateral stockpile arrangement with the US.

A dramatic event occurred in September when de Gaulle asked Norstad to discuss details of the deployment of NATO forces in France. As it was recounted:

> Norstad agreed, and made an extremely brilliant exposition, with his interallied staff in attendance. After congratulating him, the head of the French government asked the American general for a precise account of the deployment of nuclear weapons in France and of the targets assigned to them. Norstad: "Sir, I can answer only if we are alone." "So be it," said de Gaulle. The two staffs withdrew. "So then?" "Then, sir, I cannot reply to your questions, to my very great regret ... ." And de Gaulle in conclusion: "General, that is the last time, and make yourself understand it, that a responsible French leader will allow such an answer to be made."⁵⁸

Later, after talking to President Kennedy on the same subject, de Gaulle recounted: "But in answer to the specific questions I put to [Kennedy], he was unable to tell me at what point and against what targets, far or near, strategic or tactical, inside or outside Russia itself, the missiles would in fact be launched. 'I am not surprised,' I told him. 'General Norstad, the Allied Commander-in-Chief, whom I hold in the highest esteem and who has shown me every confidence, has never been able to enlighten me on these points, which are vital to my country.'"⁵⁹

What de Gaulle was after at this time, however, was something entirely different. He felt that, as the three Western Powers with global responsibilities, primary emphasis should be given to the co-ordination of world-wide strategy among the US, Britain and France. On September 17, 1958, de Gaulle had proposed to Eisenhower in a confidential memorandum his famous notion of a three-Power "Directorate" to supplant what he saw as the Anglo-American "special relationship."⁶⁰ De Gaulle also passed to Norstad privately a copy of the memorandum, although it was addressed only to Eisenhower and to British Prime Minister Harold Macmillan. Understandably, Eisenhower chose not to reply. As he explained: "I believed that any attempt to organize a coalition of the 'Big Three' NATO nations would be resented by all the others to the point that NATO itself might disintegrate ... . What we should be seeking ... was the substance and benefits of coordination, not the façade of self-assumed authority among three great nations."⁶¹

Whatever the justifications, de Gaulle felt that Eisenhower had not responded adequately. Norstad felt that de Gaulle was interested primarily in "global atomic strategy" – that de Gaulle had taken the position that he wanted to discuss situations anywhere that might lead to war. Norstad felt that neither the US nor NATO should get into a situation where the military representatives of the US, Britain and France were "sitting down and planning on a global basis."⁶² As discussed earlier, Norstad had enough problems protecting his command "turf" from such USAF rivals as LeMay and SAC.

Obviously, de Gaulle felt very strongly that he could not agree to NATO arrangements regarding the use of nuclear weapons that would permit NATO member-states without global responsibilities to veto the use of nuclear weapons. In other words, he wanted maximum freedom in the use of nuclear weapons and, to have this, France must possess them. By the same token, de Gaulle opposed *any* agreement which put the storage of warheads in France under NATO, preferring a bilateral agreement with the US.⁶³ One of his actions, in this respect, was to veto the US plan for meeting the costs of the new missile sites through the collective NATO infrastructure budget.

De Gaulle also wanted national, rather than NATO, control of atomic weapons extended to the FRG because France shared responsibility on a trilateral basis. After some deliberation, Chancellor Adenauer responded to de Gaulle's proposals by reaffirming to Eisenhower that, while following a tactful path with the French, his government would continue to accord the higher priority to its relationship with the US Adenauer interpreted de Gaulle's motives as reflecting an underlying animosity toward the "Anglo-Saxon" Powers, coupled with a desire to line up the FRG and Italy as counterweights to his perception of the Anglo-American dominance in NATO.⁶⁴

In a radio interview in London commemorating the tenth anniversary of the signing of the North Atlantic Treaty, Norstad suggested that there was perhaps a grain of truth in de Gaulle's assertion:

CLARK: General, with the experience of the past ten years behind you, what changes and improvements would you like to see in the North Atlantic Treaty Organisation in the next ten years?

NORSTAD: Speaking from my own position, I would of course like to see in the next year or two the completion of the military programmes which will give us the strength that is required to provide for the defence of NATO Europe. I would like to see, on a longer-term basis, those forces equipped with the modern weapons which would give them the greatest possible effectiveness.

CLARK: That means nuclear weapons, does it?

NORSTAD: That includes nuclear weapons ...

CLARK: General Norstad – there's a certain feeling, a growing feeling, that NATO has rather outgrown its usefulness in the ten years since it was founded to protect Western Europe. After all, President Eisenhower said the other day that in the Berlin matter we would never think of fighting a war in Europe on the ground, because it was one we couldn't win. Doesn't that really mean that Europe is protected by the American nuclear bombs and not by NATO at all? ...

NORSTAD: American atomic bombs? Yes, we are depending upon atomic weapons; but atomic weapons used in conjunction with the shield forces ... and that involves not only the forces, but also the equipment, the weapons – including atomic weapons.

CLARK: Wouldn't it then be militarily tidier and perhaps more effective to put the nuclear bombs, the deterrent, directly under NATO's command?

NORSTAD: I'm glad you raised that question. I'm glad you used the word "deterrent" in that sense. Because too frequently we continue to use deterrent to mean only the retaliatory forces ... . Now, the striking force, or the atomic force, that relates to the shield ... does come under our command and control. And as new weapons come into being – those that related to the task of NATO directly – it is planned that they will come under, they are coming under at the present time, NATO direction. I am personally very strongly in favour of that. I think that there are great advantages, from military and other standpoints, in having these weapons, these new weapons, brought under the control of NATO authority.

CLARK: But at the moment Britain and America are the two countries with the nuclear weapons at their disposal. Doesn't this special Anglo-American relationship rather tend to throw a strain on the rest of the alliance?[65]

In response to this question, Norstad fell back on references to the wartime ties between the US and Britain, and then maintained that this relationship was the "rock" on which NATO was built. Very perceptively, Norstad went on to point out that this "pattern of relationship" had been broadened through the formation of NATO's political organs and the creation of the integrated military staffs, and that this was a strength.[66]

With France's military relationship to NATO thus very unclear, on January 2, 1959, Norstad informed the Greek and Turkish National Military Representatives (NMRs) at SHAPE that he was ready to start discussions so that he could press ahead with deployment.[67] However, in his desire to open formal discussions with the Greek and Turkish governments, Norstad was running ahead of his policy counterparts in the State and Defense Departments, who wanted to wait for a joint State–Defense study on the technical military, political and funding questions that had been raised regarding the IRBM program.[68] Some of those questions had to do with a fear that, over time, physical control of the weapons might pass to the host country, and therefore their use might become hostage to the unstable domestic politics of either Greece or Turkey.[69] Also, locating them so close to the Soviet Union might increase tensions in that area, thus perhaps weakening rather than strengthening deterrence. The same argument was made concerning locating IRBMs in the FRG.

In June, 1959, going a step further down the road of unilateralism, de Gaulle officially refused to allow the US to stockpile nuclear warheads on French soil unless France could participate fully in the decision to use them. This created a serious situation that "forbade any precaution being overlooked."[70] Norstad reported on this development to the NAC on June 11, and although the official word was that no decision had been taken, in actuality Norstad had already concluded that without this issue being resolved in NATO's favor, the future of stationing US tactical fighter planes armed with atomic warheads in France was seriously in doubt.[71] Without the nuclear warheads being retained under US control, the problem of a possible West German desire to possess them could well arise, thus complicating the desire of the US to restrict as narrowly as possible the decision-making authority over nuclear weapons. This possibility could not be ignored because, by 1959, for the first time the FRG was making a larger military contribution to NATO than was France.[72]

After an unsatisfactory meeting between Dulles and de Gaulle in July 1959, Norstad and his staff conducted a very comprehensive review of the situation with France. He concluded that the desires of France could not be reconciled with those of NATO. The issues were consistently the same: French national custody of nuclear weapons; French independent control over those weapons rather than NATO or, for that matter, any collective control; development of France as an independent nuclear military Power. Norstad was convinced that it was contrary to the interests of the US under the Alliance to establish any new system composed of something less than NATO as a whole; e.g. a restricted "Third Force" nuclear bloc. For the US to turn over physical custody of nuclear weapons to other member-states on a bilateral basis or within the framework of a small nuclear bloc, would lessen rather than increase their confidence in the US, thus weakening rather than strengthening the Alliance. Another serious consideration for Norstad was that by permitting detailed multilateral inspection of warheads by such a small bloc, the US would simply be encouraging the growth of additional independent nuclear member-states – especially in those with advanced technology – through this *de facto* sharing of vital information.

For these reasons, Norstad felt that he could not submit counter-proposals to de Gaulle. But he was willing to take steps to improve and broaden the NATO atomic stockpile arrangements. This "Norstad Plan" argued that the US should make even more manifest its commitment to use its nuclear weapons by turning over to the Alliance those US weapons which would normally be deployed in NATO Europe. The criterion for selection of weapons should be what would be required to execute successfully the first intensive and decisive atomic phase of a war – perhaps spelled out in days. The US should undertake not to withdraw these weapons from NATO for the duration of the Treaty, and to deploy them according to agreed NATO plans.[73] The authority for the use of the weapons would derive from NATO, thereby eliminating the unnecessary feature of a double or "two-key" US control. The nuclear weapons transferred to NATO would be immediately available for use by those NATO forces that were actually subjected to direct enemy attack.

This arrangement would place the President of France, for example, on the same footing as the President of the US so far as authorizing the use of the weapons is concerned. Obviously, Norstad was not only trying to appease a disgruntled major NATO member-state – France – that was already reaching for its own independent nuclear weapons capability, but also to appease a suspicious major NATO member-state – the FRG – that might out of frustration and fear embark on acquiring nuclear weapons for itself. This aspect of Norstad's thinking, as he well knew, was bound to get him into trouble with influential politicians and policy-makers in Washington.

Norstad was not adverse to sharing his ideas, including the proposed size and composition of this atomic stockpile, with Spaak, or with a selected committee of Permanent Representatives to the NAC (the three Standing Group members plus appropriate geographic and command representation).[74] In fact, he was even willing to share very high-level NATO nuclear weapons information with de Gaulle, if, for example, this would persuade him of the efficacy of the NATO integrated air defense system. As Norstad reported: "I was particularly pleased to have with me some charts and other information on our NATO weapons resources and a general outline of the NATO Atomic Strike Plan ... I must say that I spoke to him with the utmost frankness and at one time felt required to ask that he restrict the information to himself alone, not even passing it to members of his Cabinet."[75]

Norstad met with Eisenhower on November 4 to discuss the situation with France. He reported that de Gaulle's actions had created some dissension in NATO as a whole, which had come out in the meetings of the NAC. For one thing, the smaller member-states opposed the idea then being bruited about of a Four-Power Western Summit meeting in Paris (US, Britain, France, and the FRG) because they resented what they viewed as the tendency of these larger member-states – and particularly France – to prejudge issues of interest to all of them. They were fearful that de Gaulle was getting his way in wanting a special consultative status in NATO, and thereby denying them a consultative role. Presumably, the Norstad Plan providing for an Executive Committee would have, in part, allayed these resentments.[76] At this meeting, Norstad also brought up his idea of creating an inspection and control regime which would permit reducing forces on both sides of the Iron Curtain. Otherwise, as pointed out earlier, talk of demilitarization in Central Europe was not something Norstad favored. Eisenhower, as usual, expressed concern about the cost of NATO, repeating over and over during this period that "our gold is flowing out and we must not weaken our basic economic strength."

Taking another tack, in the Spring of 1959, de Gaulle escalated his protest another dramatic step by removing abruptly one-third of the French Mediterranean fleet from NATO command.[77] This action caused relations between the US and France to deteriorate badly. Norstad immediately protested this move to de Gaulle; he felt he had a compelling argument because, although the ships flew the French flag, they were in fact legally owned by the US. They had been made available to France for NATO purposes and, under the law that provided this, the SACEUR must certify to the US that equipment of that size and cost was necessary for NATO use. Norstad told de Gaulle that he was prepared to "decertify" – an example of the power of the SACEUR.

Norstad's reasoning had been that: "whosoever has the responsibility for the defense of land areas such as Italy, Greece and Turkey, must also have responsibility for the adjacent sea areas and for the forces necessary for operations in these areas .... Looked at from the political angle, I believe that the withdrawal of the Mediterranean area of the forces committed to that area from Allied Command Europe would be viewed by many of the countries as a mass repudiation of NATO commitments on the part of the parties most directly interested, i.e., the UK and the US."[78] Norstad was advised by his American colleagues, however, that although he could legally do it, decertifying would cause more political trouble than it would be worth, probably even resulting in French withdrawal from NATO, so he did not carry out his threat.[79]

The overall French notion was to "renationalize" the fleets – which de Gaulle had asserted already existed in regard to the position of the US. Sixth Fleet and NATO. Norstad strongly disagreed, pointing out that in fact the first NATO force that was placed under Eisenhower's command when he became SACEUR was the Sixth Fleet.[80]

Publicly, Norstad commented that this withdrawal "does not spell the difference between night and day."[81] Although militarily it was insignificant, Norstad recognized that politically it carried some weight. He told Eisenhower that he felt that de Gaulle was retaliating for Eisenhower's refusal to allow the US to become involved in France's Algerian imbroglio.[82] Norstad added that, in any event, "it would be impossible to satisfy de Gaulle's appetite," so it was no use trying.[83] In other words, de Gaulle's desire for unilateralism, or bilateralism, or trilateralism, could never be reconciled with Norstad's desire for multilateralism.

There was some concern that procedures in the Standing Group might be affected by the French moves. For example, the French member would not refer military questions to SHAPE, and the US member wanted to block anything that was not referable to SHAPE. The underlying issue was command relationships – and equally important politically – the nationality of senior NATO commanders, whether naval commanders in the Mediterranean or army commanders in Central Europe. In the former case, the British were only too willing to step in, and in the latter case the West Germans were already pressing for the post of CINCAFCENT.[84]

Norstad suggested at one point that two commands could be created, one a French national and the other a new NATO command, with a French admiral wearing two 'hats," thus removing French ships from under a British admiral. The Western Mediterranean (MEDOC) could become a separate NATO naval command, under a French admiral reporting directly to Norstad rather than to AFMED at Malta. The idea was not pursued, although at one time Norstad reported to Eisenhower that he was "still tossing this around in my mind."[85] De Gaulle also wanted the US to share its nuclear submarine technology with France. Norstad opposed this, although Dulles had tentatively made an offer concerning an undersea nuclear power plant two years earlier. For Norstad, the change in the French fleet assignment in the Mediterranean ruled out any other forms of naval cooperation between the US and France.[86]

This episode was apparently a sore spot with Norstad, for he also commented to Eisenhower: "I then explained that the French action of not even advising me of a proposal which dealt wholly and solely with an area and function within my cognizance was an unacceptable discourtesy which prejudiced their case in the first instance."[87] It was this imperious side of Norstad that offended the Kennedy Administration – paradoxically reminding them of de Gaulle's own style.

Finally, in December 1959, de Gaulle derailed Norstad's NATO tactical air defense plan that would integrate all tactical fighter forces under his command. De Gaulle insisted that those forces stationed in France could not be armed with nuclear weapons unless the weapons were under French control. Given the fact that Norstad previously had been SACEUR's Air Deputy, he had a special commitment to the notion of strengthening NATO's tactical air defense capability, which included tactical nuclear weapons. He understood very well that de Gaulle's action could cripple NATO's air defenses, so he ordered the withdrawal of some eight squadrons of fighter-bombers from France and repositioned them in the FRG.

Norstad had tried to avoid this confrontation with de Gaulle, even going so far as to say: "I've been around here [NATO] a long time. I know that in NATO, in an international position, one has no authority as a consequence of a body of laws or precedent. You make your own authority and you make it by succeeding not by failing, so I don't force a major confrontation unless I know damn well I can do this."[88] In contrast to his earlier threat concerning the French Mediterranean fleet, Norstad was indeed capable of carrying through on this threat partly, of course, because the US agreed with him that there were no circumstances in which, under US law, France could have control of those nuclear warheads.

There was not much of a prospect that Norstad could arrive at some mutual accommodation with de Gaulle. He was quite aware that it was an uphill road, having noted a speech at this time given by Foreign Minister Couve de Murville in the *Assemblé Nationale*, in which Murville said: "To give, both in peacetime and in war, over the entire French territory, the authority – meaning in particular the right to open fire – to a commander-in-chief [i.e. Norstad] who is not directly under the orders of the French Government, for purposes as vital as Air Defense, that is a matter which poses for our government a problem the seriousness of which I ask the Assembly to understand." Then, in an apparently collateral aside, he noted that "Great Britain faced that question under similar conditions, and a solution was found for her. The solution for France is more difficult, considering her geographical situation. I hope that the discussions which are going to take place will enable a solution to be reached."[89]

Eisenhower, in his meeting in Paris with de Gaulle that December, had made the point about the need for close coordination between the missile and the interceptor, and that the NATO area was none-too-large. If each NATO member-state relied only on itself instead of on a single command, then Eisenhower knew the situation would be hopeless. In fact, he was fearful that de Gaulle "seems to be singularly blind to the fact that if each nation is [g]oing its own way, this automatically destroys NATO." Eisenhower also knew that de Gaulle was objecting to any further integration of French forces into NATO. Nonetheless, he pointed out to de Gaulle that the US forces stationed in Europe, while there, according to a multilateral treaty that provided for the common defense, were also there under an arrangement that kept the various national forces on an equal footing. As he said: "Unless we had a coordinated defense system, it was rather silly for American forces to be in Europe."[90] Unfortunately, Norstad's pessimism was well-founded, for when he met with de Gaulle on January 21, 1960, Norstad could not persuade the President to alter the thrust of his actions.

The fact that Eisenhower appreciated the importance of Norstad's meeting with de Gaulle on January 21 and then with Prime Minister Michel Debré on January 23, was evidenced by the fact that he detailed Lt. Col. Vernon Walters to fly to Paris to be the official interpreter even though Walters was also needed at Eisenhower's side for his forthcoming trip to Latin America.[91]

For one thing, de Gaulle insisted that the French air defense forces had a status analogous to that of the British Fighter Command. De Gaulle spoke of two battles: the overall strategic atomic exchange, and the "battle of Germany." The latter battle would lead to the battle of Britain and the battle of France, and, ultimately, to guerilla warfare, following the pattern of the 1939–1945 war.[92] Although Norstad saw this as an "offense against judgement" he felt that he could rearrange his air defense command relationships so that the French DAT would be directly under SHAPE, which was commanded by a British general who had a French deputy, instead of being under CINCAIRCENT. This arrangement was likely to continue on the unofficial assumption that although no NATO position was earmarked for a particular nationality, the habit was to replace an officer with one of the same nationality.

Norstad reminded Debré in the meeting with him two days later that, under MC/54, national identities were retained, and that aircraft could not be brought in to, or diverted out of, national control, such as Fighter Command or DAT, without prior national consent. Norstad also offered to delegate to CINCENT, who was a French general, his authority as SACEUR for coordination between a new Fifth Region composed of Metropolitan France that would be created for the DAT and Air Defense in the forward areas of the FRG. For Norstad, this arrangement would be more effective from the military point of view than trying to involve SHAPE headquarters in efforts at detailed coordination.[93] This was all to no avail.

By September 1960, the three issues that Norstad had with de Gaulle appeared to be resolving in some way. As to the question of the withdrawal of the Mediterranean French fleet from the NATO command structure, Norstad agreed to accept it as a fact that the French decision was final. Regarding air defense, Norstad had arrived at an agreement concerning the French aircraft stationed in the FRG similar to that with Britain, and he proposed, with Debré's concurrence, that the MC/54/1 amendment be handled in the NAC, with appropriate instructions sent to the French Representative in the Standing Group. Norstad, in his turn, would report the matter to Spaak. Finally, as to atomic stockpiling, since the NATO-assigned USAF strike squadrons were now redeployed outside of France, Norstad did not consider that there was a problem. In sum, it appeared that the military problems between Norstad and de Gaulle – or between NATO and France – were now disposed of. It was not long before Norstad had to regard his own government as his chief adversary in the ongoing NATO dialogue.

Norstad's disappointing attempts to restrain France – and especially de Gaulle – from pursuing a non-integrationist policy toward the creation, location, and intended use of nuclear weapons had a beneficial effect in one sense. These attempts persuaded Norstad that strong Alliance military leadership was needed and had to be provided by the SACEUR. Along with the political leadership that was provided by the Secretary-General, the SACEUR needed to perform the role of a mediator between the reluctance of the Alliance's largest and most powerful member-state to share its control over the use of nuclear weapons with the desire of the Allies to have some influence over their use. Even though de Gaulle's style and methods were deplored, he had struck a chord of nationalist sentiment that lurked not far beneath the surface in many, if not most, of the NATO member-states. Norstad also recognized that in the long term, the US must find a multilateral solution to the problem of providing land-based missiles for Europe.

6
The 1958–59 Crisis Over Berlin: Putting the Consultative Machinery In Place

> ... it is in this area that political and military considerations are so intermingled that neither the statesman nor the soldier is sure that they are his business.[1]

I. Origins of the crisis and the initial response

In December 1958, with tensions on the rise between the US and the USSR over Berlin, Dulles flew to Paris to attend the annual meeting of the NAC. While in Paris, he discussed with Norstad the possibility that Norstad should take certain "tightening up" actions that would not be lost on the Soviets.[2] The source of tension arose from Chairman Khrushchev's pronouncement of November 10, 1958 that he intended to sign a peace treaty "at an early date" with the German Democratic Republic (GDR), thus in his view terminating the Allies' wartime rights in West Berlin. The official Soviet Note said: "the government of the USSR hereby notifies the United States Government that the Soviet Union regards as null and void the 'Protocol of the Agreement between the Governments of the Union of Soviet Socialist Republics, the United States of America, and the United Kingdom on the zones of occupation in Germany and on the administration of Greater Berlin,' of September 12, 1944, and the related supplementary agreements, including the agreements on the control machinery in Germany, concluded between the governments of the USSR, the USA, Great Britain, and France on May 1, 1945, i.e., the agreements that were intended to be in effect during the first years after the capitulation of Germany."[3]

Khrushchev wanted the FRG and GDR to negotiate unification between them. As it was put: "[Khrushchev] wanted to make it clear that the Soviets had not raised the issue of Berlin as such, but rather the question of the conclusion of a peace treaty in order to terminate the state of war with Germany."[4] As a part of this overall settlement he wanted the US, the UK, France and the USSR to withdraw their troops from Berlin. One major objective was to stop the flow of East Germans to the West through Berlin, which was permitted because of the Four-Power agreement after World War II to treat Berlin as a unified city although it had been *de facto* carved up into occupation zones.[5] He had already called upon the Western Powers to begin negotiations with the GDR to achieve the complete withdrawal of all their forces from the city.

Since the West did not recognize the official existence of the GDR, this was obviously not only impossible but also viewed as a provocation. President Eisenhower felt that Khrushchev was bluffing and that he would back down if the West held firm. Perhaps Khrushchev chose this moment to reopen the Berlin situation because he assumed that a condition of nuclear "parity" with the US would mean that the US and NATO would not initiate nuclear war over Berlin.

More specifically, Khrushchev was afraid that the NATO decision of December 1957 to deploy IRMBs in Europe, and in particular in the FRG, could not be forestalled. Possibly Khrushchev was seeking a nuclear-free zone in Europe – a notion that had openly discussed in one form or another for several years, as the so-called Rapacki and Eden Plans demonstrate. Alternatively, Khrushchev's motive may have been simply to force Eisenhower into a summit conference which would "ratify" the Soviet Union's equality as a global Power with the US.[6] But as Eisenhower put it: "In this gamble, we are not going to be betting white chips, building up the pot gradually and fearfully. Khrushchev should know that when we decide to act, our whole stack will be in the pot."[7] This attitude was consistent with his Administration's emphasis on a massive retaliatory nuclear attack in response to any attempt by the Soviet Union to alter the *status quo* in central Europe.[8]

Eisenhower was confident that Norstad could handle the military aspect of this dangerous situation. He was very high on Eisenhower's list, as evidenced by the fact that when, in September 1958, Sherman Adams was forced to resign as the Assistant to the President, Norstad was one of those persons whom Eisenhower considered to replace him. It was Norstad's reputation as being able to handle high-level political-military policy issues effectively that appealed to Eisenhower, but more immediately it was Norstad's value as the most visible and respected American commander in Europe that convinced Eisenhower not to move him back to Washington.[9] As Secretary-General Spaak commented in his *Memoirs*: "Eisenhower said to me one day that he considered Norstad to be the best organizer he had ever met. I know of no reason to question this judgement."[10]

This most serious challenge to the West since the Berlin Airlift of 1948–1949 seemed to be made to order for Norstad, the consumate planner.[11] At the NATO Ministerial Council meeting of December 1958, in response to Khrushchev's "ultimatum," he requested authorization from the Council to accelerate planned increases in Allied divisions, nuclear-armed battalions, and integrated air defense forces.[12]

His goal was to avoid war rather than to fight and win, but in order to accomplish this Norstad had to put in place plans that were both credible to the Soviets and feasible to the US and its nervous NATO Allies. Unfortunately, these plans did not exist, so that in the short run, Khrushchev's "deadline diplomacy" was a major cause of anxiety throughout NATO. Norstad was confronted with the challenge of assisting in putting into place the machinery for Berlin policy-formulation, decision-making and execution, under conditions of political warfare – and perhaps more. He was expected by his NATO "masters" on the Standing Group, the Military Committee and the NAC, and by his "superiors" on the JCS, the NSC, the Department of Defense, and not least of all, the White House, to provide "a rational response to a real threat of a hostile armed attack that might otherwise occur."[13] As it was put: "To deflate [Khrushchev's] expectations, the United States would have had to demonstrate the military capacity to remain in West Berlin without reliance on a starting strategy which simply and horribly called down a nuclear war on Berlin, on all of Europe, and possibly on the United States itself."[14] Through it all Norstad had continually to explore where the inner and outer limits of his authority and responsibility lay both as SACEUR and as USCINCEUR.

In fact, it was to a large extent the NATO Allies' confidence in him to provide such a rational response that at this time maintained Alliance cohesion and protection. The fear was that through intimidation, the Soviets could exploit the obvious geo-military advantage that they enjoyed over Berlin.[15] The dilemma was that, in fact, the Eisenhower Administration did not possess a range of options between negotiating to avoid capitulation, and nuclear war. The search was on for non-nuclear military options; otherwise, what was there to negotiate about? As Eisenhower succinctly put it: "there was little room in the Berlin situation for negotiation or compromise. Militarily, our forces in the city were token garrisons only. Berlin's actual defense lay only in the West's publicly expressed intention that to defend it we would, if necessary, resort to war."[16]

Although Norstad was not a principal party to these negotiations, it was expected that he would, through formulating the various Berlin contingency plans, provide at least a modicum of elbow-room for the negotiators. Every little "salami-slice" move by Khrushchev or by his East German proxies had to be anticipated and responded to without the episode turning into a "tit-for-tat" schoolyard game of "chicken." There was no condition more dangerous than that of Berlin's during the Cold War, and the possibility of Berlin turning into the flashpoint of nuclear Armageddon was on everyone's mind. Small wonder that the means of consultation and decision-making were so cumbersome yet so necessary!

The challenge was taken up on November 14, when the Soviets detained a US military convoy of three trucks for over eight hours at a checkpoint on the autobahn near Berlin. This was the beginning of a series of harassment episodes designed to put pressure on the West both militarily and diplomatically. Their purpose was to exploit differences among the four Western governments – the US, Britain, France and the FRG – both over what to do in specific instances and, on a larger plane, over what provocation should lead the West to contemplate going to war. Norstad, as USCINCEUR, immediately recommended that unless ordered otherwise he would respond by sending a normal convoy from Berlin to Helmstedt, with the US Commander in Berlin (USCOB) being given the authority to "extricate US military personnel and equipment by minimum force necessary if Soviets again detain and prompt protest does not rpt not effect early release."[17] In his request, Norstad defined "early action" to mean four or five days.

He proceeded on the assumption that the incident was a deliberate probe and so if there were a longer response period, the Soviets would assume that the West was recognizing a *de facto* state of blockade. Norstad also felt that by responding promptly, the significance of either the Soviet action or the West's reaction would not be exaggerated; in other words, the entire episode could be viewed as simply a "local incident."[18] Eisenhower apparently saw it that way, although he did not respond publicly until November 21, when he "felt the time had come to make some sort of low-key announcement that the United States would stand on its commitments."[19] He had his press secretary, James Hagerty, address the matter at a regular press conference. Evidently, both Eisenhower and Dulles, along with Norstad, were convinced that, by providing this evidence of Western resolve without appearing hysterical they would help to keep the morale of the Berliners up as well as stiffen the backs of the NATO Allies.

The JCS, although initially agreeing with Norstad's recommendation of an immediate probe, quickly reversed themselves in order to give time for consultation. Eisenhower had ordered that the movement of all convoys to Berlin should be suspended, recognizing that rushing into a confrontation without ensuring the strong support of all the parties concerned could only provide an opportunity for the Allies to show disunity – one of Khrushchev's political goals. Also recognizing this crucial political dimension, both the JCS and Norstad had shortly come to recognize the virtues of caution.[20] Instead, the Allies, through their embassies in Bonn, began composing a Four-Power Note. The USCOB had already sent a letter of protest concerning the incident of November 14 to his Soviet counterpart, General Zakharov. There was brief consideration of the desirability of having Norstad pay a symbolic visit to Berlin, but Dulles thought that this might indicate undue anxiety on the part of the West. Later on, if the tensions persisted, such a visit could be seen as a "concretely reassuring symbol of Western determination to hold Berlin."[21] Very shortly thereafter the ban on Western truck convoys from West Germany to Berlin was lifted.

Regardless of the tactics of the moment, Norstad had already thought through the political steps that he felt needed to be taken. These included providing the public with a clear expression of the West's position and a statement of the rights that the Soviet action had violated. The Soviets should also be warned beforehand what specific steps the US would take to remedy the situation. These steps should be coordinated with the British and French military authorities in Berlin, paralleled by diplomatic consultations with their respective governments. It was vital that the three Allies should be in agreement concerning the level of protest to be made and the time that should be allowed to elapse before a protest would be lodged. For Norstad, this should be no more than two to three hours. Also, the West German authorities, including Adenauer, should be informed beforehand.[22]

The US Ambassador to France, Amory Houghton, after consulting with Norstad recommended that a Four-Power Conference on the German question be arranged, possibly at the foreign minister level. This conference would enable the West to let both the Soviets and the world at large know of the West's determination not to capitulate to Soviet pressures. The dilemma, of course, was how to respond to a series of episodes that might or might not justify the resort to force or other "risky" countermeasures. The Allies' position should be to place the immediate Berlin issue within the context of an overall German settlement, and not to change the *status quo* in Berlin until such a settlement was reached. This position became a consistent objective of Western diplomacy: not allowing the Berlin question as such to become isolated from the overall question of eventual German unity.

Houghton was anxious that such a meeting be arranged soon so that its convening would not appear to be a "last-gasp" measure. The fear was that the Soviets would proceed to turn over the checkpoint responsibility to the GDR and that such an action as this would appear to be forcing the West to negotiate.[23]

Norstad had worked out in his own mind what the general posture of the Western Powers should be and how to go about achieving the *status quo ante* with the Soviets:

> In my view it is essential to inform the Soviets immediately and preferably without public announcement that we do not intend to recognize or deal with GDR; that we will not allow the GDR to impede the exercise of any right we presently hold; that we will not accept any control by the GDR over our movements to and from Berlin; and that we will use force if necessary to enforce our rights.
>
> But at the same time, we should try to seize the initiative while we have the chance and broaden the base of allied support by proposing a four-power conference on Germany (I repeat on Germany not solely on Berlin) ... .
>
> Obviously it is of the highest importance that France and Britain take the same unequivocal line. A major break between allies on this subject could lead to worse disaster than the loss of Berlin itself.
>
> Unless we are willing to begin a humiliating process of yielding step by step to the GDR, we must draw the line now and the Russians must understand we will use force to support this position if necessary. As for the tactics to be employed regarding access to Berlin: first, I suggest that the instructions which Embassy Bonn issued to cover individual travel to Berlin by Autobahn, ... and their instructions covering train travel ... be applied on the broadest basis possible; second, we should continue to operate US military convoys as in the past so long as the checkpoints are under Soviet control, to the extent of even one Soviet representative being present on whom the responsibility can be placed. While we must maintain our rights, we should not now seek to force a test of Soviet control, in light of

1 Dinner honoring General Norstad.

2 A standing ovation for General Norstad.

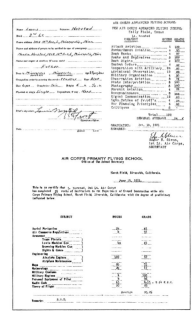

3 Norstad's record at the Air Corps Advanced Flying School.

4 Norstad with General LeMay in the Pacific.

5 Norstad at the Potsdam Conference, 17 July to 2 August 1945, seated between General Eisenhower (*left*) and General Arnold (*right*).

6 Norstad with his mentors – General Arnold (*centre*) and General Marshall (*right*).

7 Norstad at the signing of the proclamation establishing 8 January 1947 as Air Force Day. Doolittle, Vandenberg, President Truman, Norstad, Symington (*left–right*).

8 SHAPE commanders meeting in Paris, 19 June 1952. Admiral Sir Patrick Brind, Lt-General Norstad (US), Lt-General Augustin Guillaume (Fr), Field Marshal Montgomery (UK), General Eisenhower (US), Air-Vice-Marshal Hugh Saunders (UK), Admiral Roal Lemmonier (Fr), Admiral Robert Jaujard (Fr), Admiral Robert B. Carney (US) (*front left–right*): General Wilhelm von Tangen Hansteen (Nor), Lt-General Maurizio de Castiglioni (It), General Alfred Gruenther (US), Major-General Ebbe Gortz (Den), Lt-General Robert K. Taylor (US) (*rear left–right*).

9 Norstad with Isabelle and their cocker-spaniel, Mugsy.

10 Norstad (*left*) with Isabelle and Marshal of the RAF Lord Tedder at the service of commemoration in honor of American World War II dead, 4 July 1952, at St Paul's Cathedral, London.

11 View of the grounds of the villa St. Pierre at Marnes la Coquette, near Paris, 27 September 1951.

12 *Life* cover photograph of Lt-General Norstad, AF Deputy Chief of Staff, Operations, 1 November 1948.

13 *Newsweek* cover photograph of General Norstad, 17 December 1956.

14 Kristin, Isabelle and General Norstad at a garden party, villa St. Pierre, 10 July 1957.

15 General Norstad with Secretary of Defense McNamara (*third from left*), accompanied by Assistant Secretary of Defense for International Security Affairs, Paul H. Nitze (*far right*) and JCS chairman General Lyman L. Lemnitzer (*right*), 23 July 1961.

16 General Norstad with former President Eisenhower.

17 General Norstad being awarded the French Grand Cross of the Legion of Honor by President Charles de Gaulle, 20 December 1962.

18 Invitation issued by the Registrar of Oxford University to award General Norstad a doctorate of civil law, *honoris causa*, 26 June 1963.

19 General Norstad on becoming an executive with Owens-Corning Fiberglas Corporation.

the larger problem which is developing. Third, if the checkpoints have been turned over completely to GDR control, we should choose a time and place to force the issue promptly by dispatching a test convoy supported by appropriate force. It is not a question of the US forces in Berlin being able to defeat any force that could be brought against it, but of forcing into the open the fact that the GDR, backed by the Soviets, is using violence to deprive the US of its established rights.

Ending his remarks to the JCS, Norstad reiterated his previous recommendations:

> The more I study this question the more I become convinced that we must take a very firm position in support of our rights and obligations in Berlin, and that this position be made known to the Russians. We may hope, as we do, that a show of determination may ease the situation, but we cannot expect it to solve the problem. Therefore, we must balance our over-all position, we must make an effort to gain the initiative by more fundamental, longer range action. With all its apparent pitfalls and dangers, the idea of a conference as suggested ... gains weight as we consider the consequences, the strengths and weaknesses of other courses of action. Finally, whatever we decide to do must be done quickly if it is to have any chance of success.[24]

Specifically, Norstad had recommended: "If an attempt is made to replace Soviet personnel with GDR personnel in BASC [the Berlin Air Safety Center], the East Germans will be asked to leave and if need be, escorted out; and flight information on western aircraft continue to be made available ... . The problems which may be anticipated incident to continued air travel between West Berlin and Germany include refusal of civil aircraft to enter into Berlin, with possible manning by US military crews, interference with radar and navigational aid, saturation of corridors by GDR and Soviet aircraft, attempts to force aircraft to land and even interference with aircraft in flights."[25]

To Norstad's undoubted satisfaction the Allies were indeed carrying on discussions dealing with such important considerations as: the degree to which the Western Powers could deal with the East German government without loss of prestige or undue damage to Adenauer; the procedures to be followed (including the degree of force to be used) in the event of serious harassment by East German police; and the timing of Western moves.[26] According to Eisenhower, Adenauer had taken the firmest and most unequivocal position; de Gaulle was uncommitted at this time; and the British, but not necessarily Macmillan, appeared to be the most conciliatory.[27]

There was a sigh of relief in the midst of all of these hasty consultations when on November 27 Khrushchev informed the US that the Soviet Union would not take any action to recognize the GDR for six months, during which time he proposed that negotiations over Berlin should take place. This was, perhaps, an indication of the essentially cautious approach which Khrushchev followed in actuality, his bellicose rhetoric to the contrary notwithstanding.[28] Khrushchev also proposed that West Berlin became a "free city" and placed under the United Nations with all the Occupying Powers' forces being withdrawn from Berlin. It must also not be forgotten that even though Khrushchev's maneuverings seemed threatening to the West, he also had in mind that the existence and integrity as an independent state of the GDR must be protected.

Eisenhower was willing to consider making the United Nations responsible for access to Berlin, but whatever the particular formulations, he insisted that any discussions over Berlin must include the reunification of Germany.[29] This meant that on May 27, 1959, there would be a finale to the crisis that might lead to war. In the meantime Khrushchev would try in every way that he could to divide the West. Fortunately, the deadline was never enforced; instead, on the deadline day the funeral of John Foster Dulles took place, which brought to Washington from Geneva the four foreign ministers who had been attempting unsuccessfully to find a way out of the Berlin impasse. While there they met with Eisenhower, but nothing came of it. Even though Khrushchev wanted a summit regardless of whatever happened in the foreign ministers' Geneva meetings, Eisenhower did not want to meet with Khrushchev unless there had been real progress in ensuring Western rights to West Berlin and guarantees of no further harassment.[30]

As a further show of resolve, the CINCUSAREUR went to Berlin early in December, just four days after the "ultimatum," to conduct a special inspection. The point was to underscore that there were more than 11 000 men in the Berlin garrison, that dependents were not going to be evacuated, and that the US was prepared to defend its position in Berlin.[31]

On December 14 the four foreign ministers, meeting in Paris, found "unacceptable" the Soviet Note of November 27. Then, on December

16, the NAC went on record as considering "that the Berlin question can be settled only in the framework of an agreement with the USSR on Germany as a whole. It recalls that the Western Powers have repeatedly declared themselves ready to examine this problem, as well as those of European security and disarmament. They are still ready to discuss all these problems."[32]

II. Norstad's attempts at coordinated planning

While these diplomatic considerations were going on among the Allies through their embassies in Bonn and in the various capitals, Berlin contingency military planning was also going forward on several fronts. For example, there were tripartite talks among the US, Britain and France to arrive at agreed general principles so that detailed military planning could begin. The principles were in the process of being worked out according to a US *aide-mémoire* of December 11, 1958, which had provided in Paragraph D that the military requirements be laid out along with the possible courses of action designed to respond to the various envisaged contingencies.[33] Norstad, after having met with Dulles in December, asked that the JCS send a team of experts to work in Paris with selected officers of USEUCOM and SHAPE on a US basis. They divided the steps that might be taken into three categories "according to the situation as it may develop."

Category A would include the situation as it existed at the time of what was feared to be a Soviet ultimatum; *Category B* activities that would be taken in response to increased Soviet pressure; and *Category C* would deal with the situation if the Soviets in fact turned over their Berlin responsibilities to the GDR. In the latter eventuality, psychological measures would give way to the actual concentration of NATO forces in the Marienburg area where the autobahn to Berlin crossed the existing boundary between the FRG and the GDR.[34] It was also agreed that the Soviets would be informed in advance of Allied intentions, thus providing a psychological incentive to resolve the matter before the military "scenarios" were actually implemented. These scenarios could include troop redeployments, rescheduling of leave, propaganda and informational campaigns both within NATO and the Warsaw Pact countries, and other forms of psychological warfare.[35]

Most important for Norstad was obtaining complete agreement with the US government that he should be in overall charge of Berlin contingency planning and that this should take place at SHAPE. In this effort he was unsuccessful because essential decisions were made by the governments, and his responsibility was to prepare to carry out these decisions if circumstances justified it, based on the contingency plans that he and his staff were developing. This did not mean, of course, that Norstad did not express his opinion, especially to his own government, as these decisions were being concluded.

Norstad had made it clear that he wanted, first, an American plan in which the US would act unilaterally without any real support from the other NATO Allies, and second, a US–UK–French joint-tripartite plan.[36] He wanted the initial planning done at USEUCOM under his CINCEUR "hat" without the FRG involved, although the West Germans would of course be affected. Adenauer had indeed indicated a desire that NATO should stand firm, but at this point it was not clear whether he would support a Western military response to a closing-off of access to Berlin: would the FRG risk West German troops? Nonetheless, the buildup of the *Bundeswehr* was going forward.

As for France, de Gaulle, since assuming power in 1958, had been highly critical of US policies and actions, and he expressed this when, on September 14, as he put it: "I hoisted my colors."[37] As discussed in the previous chapter, he wanted France to have a role not only in enlarged Alliance deliberations but also in "global" planning through a US–UK–French "Directorate." Eisenhower had responded that "any attempt to organize a coalition of the 'Big Three' NATO nations would be resented by all the others to the point that NATO itself might disintegrate."[38] In discussing de Gaulle with Norstad at the time of Norstad's appointment as SACEUR, Eisenhower had observed: "de Gaulle merely wants to make France the first nation of the world with himself the first Frenchman."[39] But he went on: "In fairness to de Gaulle, on many of these NATO issues, we would react very much as de Gaulle does if the shoe were on the other foot."[40] Norstad commented in response that de Gaulle "is fond of the President personally. This fondness, far from being a comforting matter, can be extremely troublesome," because de Gaulle expected "Eisenhower's reciprocal feeling to help him achieve his goals." But this did not mean that Eisenhower agreed with de Gaulle's aspirations. Nonetheless, de Gaulle was unequivocally supportive of NATO's maintaining a firm stand in regard to Berlin. De Gaulle saw Berlin "as the principal pawn in the rivalry between the two camps."[41]

In contrast, the British were equivocating – they were hinting that a risk of annihilation over the issue of Berlin was not worth it. The British were in favor of "low-level" talks that might lead to the diplomatic recognition of the GDR. The British Foreign Office had even concluded that there need be no necessary connection between recognition of the GDR and the West's expulsion from Berlin.⁴² Fortunately Macmillan repudiated this line of reasoning. He agreed with the US view "that if every test of strength with the Russians is viewed in terms of the risk of total destruction, there can be no agreement on a firm response in any situation."⁴³

As to the legal arguments concerning Western rights of access to Berlin, they had already been put forward. Based on the European Advisory Commission agreements of 1944, and the Paris *Communiqué* of 1949 following the lifting of the Berlin Airlift, the US claimed primary rights based on conquest.⁴⁴ That stemmed as well from the *quid pro quo* established by the US withdrawal from the area which became the Soviet zone in exchange for the agreements over Berlin.⁴⁵

One of the consequences of this crisis atmosphere was the question of the desirability of assigning US forces to Norstad in his SACEUR "hat" in peacetime. It was already established policy that certain forces would automatically pass under Norstad's control with the outbreak of hostilities. The official policy was that US Army major combat units and certain non-organic support and service units located in Allied Command Europe (ACE) were assigned to NATO command, with additional forces stationed in the US also earmarked for assignment to NATO. Furthermore, certain Air Force units were assigned to NATO but no Air Force-level – i.e. USAFE – forces were earmarked for assignment to NATO.⁴⁶ He had: *Assigned Forces, Forces Earmarked for Assignment, Operational Command*, and *Operational Control*. Norstad's role as a "commander" derived from these definitions.⁴⁷

Assigned Forces were those forces-in-being which had been placed under the operational command or operational control of a NATO commander. *Earmarked for Assignment* were those forces which nations had agreed to assign to the operational command or operational control of a NATO commander at some future date in peace or in the event of war; *Operational Command* was the authority granted to a commander to assign missions or tasks to subordinate commanders, to deploy units, to reassign forces and to retain or delegate operational and/or tactical control as was deemed necessary. It did not of itself include administrative command or logistical responsibility. *Operational Control* was the authority granted to a commander to direct forces assigned so that the commander might accomplish specific missions or tasks which were usually limited by function, time, or location; to deploy units concerned, and to retain or assign tactical control of those units. It did not include authority to assign separate employment of components of the units concerned, nor did it, of itself, include administrative or logistic control.[48]

Norstad's broad mandate was:

> All forces of member nations stationed in the area of Allied Command Europe shall be placed under the authority of the Supreme Allied Commander Europe or other appropriate NATO commands and under the direction of the NATO military authorities with the exception of those forces intended for the defense of overseas territory, and other forces which the North Atlantic Treaty Organization has recognized or will recognize as suitable to remain under national command.[49]

As to combat forces – and this is important if Norstad were to decide to force his way to Berlin by ground or air – he was given this mandate:

> In respect of combat forces in the area of Allied Command Europe (ACE), and under the Supreme Allied Commander Europe: (1) all deployments shall be in accordance with NATO strategy; (2) the location of forces in accordance with NATO operational plans shall be determined by the Supreme Allied Commander Europe, after consultation and agreement with the national authorities concerned; (3) forces under the Supreme Allied Commander Europe, and within the area of Allied Command Europe, shall not be redeployed or used operationally within that area without the consent of the Supreme Allied Commander Europe, subject to political guidance furnished by the North Atlantic Council, when appropriate, through normal channels. *Such guidance will not be requested for moves of a routine or administrative nature or in cases of emergency where the degree of urgency precludes following the full procedure.*[50] [Emphasis added]

It should be kept in mind, however, that a decision to use major force to reopen access would require approval of the governments of the three Western Occupying Powers in Berlin, and in 1958 planning was still in a very fluid stage. For example, the US government tended to favor the execution more automatically of certain contingency plans than either the British or French governments were willing to accept. As is true for most commanders, Norstad was very sensitive to any implied challenge to his command authority, and insisted that military directives emanating from Washington should proceed through the military chain of command from the JCS through the unified com-

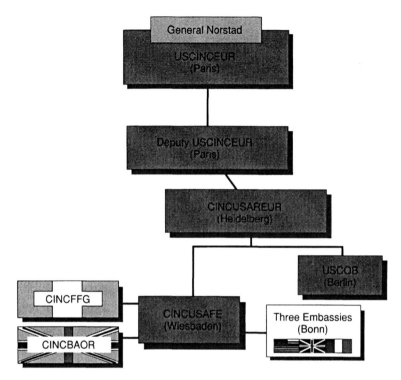

Chart 6.1 USCINCEUR Chain of Command, 1959

mander (USCINCEUR), from whom all subordinate commanders should receive their orders.[51]

Armed with all of this variety of command authority, Norstad believed strongly that NATO had to be "firm but deliberate," so that all possibility of misconception would be avoided. To accomplish this, he felt that the Soviets should know precisely what NATO was planning in order that sufficient negotiating flexibility could be maintained and so taking the "ultimate action" could be delayed as long as feasible.[52] As to exactly what should happen when was of course difficult for the SHAPE planners to anticipate; hence, it was equally difficult for them to know what course of action to recommend to their national authorities if, for example, control of the checkpoints was turned over to the GDR. Nonetheless, in preparing his plans, Norstad pointed out to the national authorities in advance the tasks that he was preparing to perform. He wanted SHAPE to be ready to meet the situation brought about by any of the decisions which the national authorities might take.[53]

It was important that both NATO and the US shared Norstad's attitude when in early February 1959 an American convoy was being held at the Marienborn checkpoint. Norstad had two small US task forces available to counter this apparent effort at intimidation. One was a group of eight light tanks (the A force) located in the FRG which could probably reach the border-crossing point in about twelve hours. The other force (the B force) was a reinforcement battalion of infantry consisting of about 700–800 men. It was assumed that if one convoy was sent through a checkpoint where access was at risk, then more convoys could continue to be sent until some sort of pattern – defined, perhaps, as a period of two weeks or so – was established.[54] Even though there were no substantial Soviet forces in the immediate vicinity of the checkpoint, there were adequate Soviet forces in the general area to create a serious incident.[55] Fortunately, the incident did not blossom into a confrontation thanks to Norstad's calm assumption that the matter probably had involved a local Soviet interpretation of their own inspection procedures. In contrast, Dulles suggested that the purpose of the incident was to provide the Soviets with an excuse to harden their position in anticipation of turning over to the GDR responsibility for the access routes to Berlin. Norstad felt that this possibility would have been more likely if the incident had occurred at the Berlin end of the autobahn.[56]

On February 25, Eisenhower stated at a press conference that "plans" were in place for defending Berlin, thus suggesting that there were alternatives to reacting to provocations with a massive nuclear strike. But Eisenhower went on to say on March 12: "We are certainly not going to fight a ground war in Europe. What good would it do to send a few more thousand or indeed even a few divisions of troops to Europe?" As will be seen, this is exactly what his successor Kennedy decided to do in order to provide an alternative to an "all or nothing" situation. In the March press conference, Eisenhower responded to a question concerning the use of nuclear weapons thus:

> Well, I don't know how you could free anything with nuclear weapons. I can say this: the United States, and its Allies, have announced their firm intention of preserving their rights and responsibilities with respect to Berlin. If any threat, or any push in the direction of real hostilities is going to occur, it's going to occur from the side of the Soviets.
>
> Now if that would become reality, and I don't believe that anyone would be senseless enough to push that to the point of reality, then

there will be the time to decide exactly what the Allies would in turn, expect to do.[57]

Eisenhower's equivocation, although perhaps understandable, nonetheless made it difficult for Norstad to know exactly what the circumstances might be for an all-out military reprisal rather than negotiations.

Prudence was also called for because the JCS held the strong view that an airlift would not settle the Berlin issue and therefore it should be avoided if at all possible in the event that ground or air access routes were severely crippled.[58] One good reason was that Soviet radar installations had been placed around Berlin that could confuse the ground controllers guiding the landings and takeoffs in and out of Berlin.

On March 24, in order to reaffirm the West's intention to stand fast, the US dispatched a high-flying C-130 cargo plane (Lockheed Hercules) along the air corridor into Berlin. The flight plan called for an altitude of 25 000 feet, which immediately resulted in a Soviet protest at the BASC. The maximum altitude permissible according to the Soviets was 10 000 feet, although there was no formal understanding to this effect.[59] The US insisted that flights above 10 000 feet would continue to be made. This was an important point because the higher the flights the more the opportunity to surveil the situation both in the air and on the ground, and this would undoubtedly annoy the Soviets. For Norstad, this test of resolve was not unwelcome, for to a military man intent on his military mission diplomatic negotiations might be fraught with danger. The diplomatic exchanges concerning this matter came just after the West had agreed to convene the conference of the four Foreign Ministers set to begin in Geneva on May 11. Would the West concede important points that might weaken his ability to carry out his responsibilities? Norstad had reason to be uneasy, for one week after Dulles resigned on April 15 due to his cancer, another scheduled C-130 flight was canceled.[60] The new American diplomatic team was apparently less interested in "remaining steadfast" than in "avoiding provocation."

7
The Berlin Crisis Intensifies

The Berlin Crisis was in fact one of the most important episodes in the history of great power politics in the nuclear age.[1]

I. Berlin contingency planning and execution

This crisis over Berlin sparked Norstad to consider how best to coordinate NATO plans and policy in a situation in which the "rights" were non-NATO in origin, even though the "responsibilities" had become SACEUR's. As recalled in the previous chapter, the three "Occupying Powers" – the US, the UK, and France – were still in Berlin by right of conquest. The other member-states of NATO had no direct involvement in the evolution of the status of Berlin stemming from the Yalta Declaration to its *de facto* partitioning.[2] Consequently, in February 1959 Norstad directed the establishment at Headquarters USEUCOM of a "small concealed US only group as nucleus for any tripartite staff he might have to form."[3]

Norstad charged this group to consider any military problems concerned with access to Berlin that might arise. At the same time, he informally let the British know that he would welcome British officers as either members or observers in the USEUCOM group and that he was willing to move forward in this area without formal instructions, provided he was sure that the British, and then the French, governments wished him to do so. This was his cautious way of "sounding out" governments on something that he wanted to do, before "officializing" it. He was, in effect, creating for himself a "third hat" along with those of SACEUR and USCINCEUR.[4] He wanted a tripartite politico-military planning "cell" situated at SHAPE but under his overall direction as USCINCEUR to deal with whatever measures would be taken, working in coordination with the military headquarters of the Tripartite Powers in Berlin under the leadership of USCOB. This was consistent with the creation of what came to be known as "LIVE OAK" because USEUCOM, the joint military headquarters, was located near Paris, as was SHAPE.[5]

Occasionally Norstad jumped ahead of his "political masters" in matters he deemed sufficiently important, and then he would ask for *post facto* authorization.[6] In the present instance, Norstad had approached the British before the French, presumably to stack the cards in favor of French acceptance of his proposal. He did not want to tie this idea to some other French NATO political objective, such as Algeria or de Gaulle's global "Directorate". De Gaulle, as part of his global "vision" had contemplated NATO officially assuming responsibility for dealing with the Algerian insurrection on the ground that Algeria was part of France. This had been rejected by Eisenhower.[7] The State Department, noting that Norstad was not following its policy of dealing with the British and French on an equal footing, requested that the French be approached immediately.

The British responded informally to Norstad's query, stating that they would be happy to participate, and agreeing with Norstad that the LIVE OAK effort should be conducted on a very secret basis. Initially, Norstad used his personal relationship with Sir Frank Roberts, the British Permanent Representative, as his conduit to London, and then he took the matter up with Selwyn Lloyd, the Foreign Secretary, who in turn discussed the LIVE OAK idea with Prime Minister Macmillan. In the case of the French approach, Norstad broached the notion through General Ely, French CINCAFCENT.[8] Shortly thereafter the French also indicated their willingness to participate. As to liaison with the FRG, Ambassador David Bruce was asked to designate a Political Liaison Officer from his staff to participate in the planning discussions along with the British and French Political Liaison Officers designated by their Bonn embassies.[9]

Later, however, Norstad became impatient with the temporizing attitude that the other two Powers took toward creating LIVE OAK. The British Chiefs-of-Staff were concerned about how proper military and political guidance could be given to LIVE OAK. It must be remembered that from the beginning of the Berlin crisis there had been Anglo-American differences over how to handle it. The British had demonstrated more of a willingness to negotiate before introducing force, whereas the Americans were more interested in showing military resolve from the outset.[10]

The French, in contrast and in accordance with de Gaulle's desire to remain aloof, wanted it to be known that their participation was in the form of "coordination" and not "integration". To Norstad, this seemed in practice to be splitting diplomatic hairs. So Norstad prepared a memorandum giving his idea of the terms of reference for LIVE OAK, passed it to the British and French military authorities, neither of whom objected to it. Thereupon, Norstad passed it to the British and French Liaison Officers in LIVE OAK and thereafter considered it as an informally-agreed-upon "charter" for LIVE OAK.[11] He directed that the LIVE OAK Planning Staff would operate under the direct supervision of the Deputy USCINCEUR.[12] It was also agreed that LIVE OAK would utilize NATO communications facilities at SHAPE.[13] Because LIVE OAK was not formally a NATO organization, besides the US, the U.K. and France, no other NATO member-state was involved, although the Canadians received some information.[14] There was also an informal liaison maintained through the FRG National Military Representative at SHAPE.

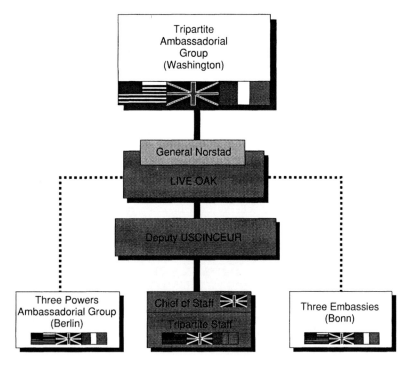

Chart 7.1   LIVE OAK Structure, March 1959

Thus, the structure of developing and executing contingency plans concerning Berlin was in place. Under Norstad's supervision LIVE OAK was responsible for coordinating preparatory military measures and for other measures to restore freedom of access to Berlin, and for assisting the Three Embassies in Bonn to carry out their responsibilities. The Three Embassies unit was responsible for developing recommendations for the identification of Allied movements, instructions for detailed procedures at the two checkpoints, and air access planning.

The Tripartite Ambassadorial Group, the primary decision-making authority, was located in Washington and chaired by the Deputy Under Secretary of State. It was responsible for the overall coordination of Berlin contingency planning.[15] For the British and French, unless action depended on the necessity for coordinating governmental views, their examination of the military and political considerations of an action proposed by Norstad would be sent directly to him.[16] The US procedure for handling Tripartite LIVE OAK staff papers was: upon receipt, the papers were transmitted to the Defense and State Departments for their information; the JCS would also prepare comments and recommendations for the Defense Department; the official US governmental position would then be developed by the appropriate governmental departments; the official US national position would then be presented to the Tripartite Ambassadorial Group.[17]

By this time, contingency planning and procedures had been worked out as follows:

1. Preparatory Military Measures
  a. In view of the possibility that the USSR may withdraw from its function with respect to Berlin and in order to provide evidence of the Three Powers' determination to maintain their free access, the military authorities of the Three Powers will plan quiet preparatory and precautionary military measures of a kind which will not create public alarm but which will be detectable by Soviet intelligence. These measures are to be implemented as soon as they have been agreed.
  b. The military authorities of the Three Powers will also plan more elaborate military measures in Europe, which would be generally observable, including (1) measures to be implemented after the Soviet Government has turned its functions over to the GDR and (2) measures to be implemented after Allied traffic has been forcibly obstructed.

c. The planning of the measures described in paragraphs 1a and 1b above will be carried out on a tripartite basis under the general supervision of General Norstad in his capacity as Commander-in-Chief, United States Forces, Europe. The exact arrangements for the planning will be further concerted between the military authorities of the three countries. These military authorities will also plan measures on a purely national basis in support of the measures referred to above.[18]

To avoid a direct confrontation with the Soviet Union over Berlin, the Three Powers considered adopting what became known as the "Agency Principle." Under this principle, the Soviet Union could expressly authorize GDR personnel to function as Soviet agents in performing Soviet functions concerning access of the Three Powers to Berlin. The Allies would not object to GDR personnel checking vehicles at the checkpoints, even if it meant more vehicle identification would be required. Normal traffic by rail and autobahn would be maintained even if Soviet personnel were withdrawn, except that new procedures would be implemented as necessary for the identification of Allied trains, convoys, or vehicles entitled to unrestricted access so that the flow of traffic would be orderly after the GDR personnel were assigned to man the checkpoints. Furthermore, consideration would be given for the substitution of Allied checkpoint personnel for Soviet personnel.

The Three Embassies at Bonn, in consultation with the appropriate military headquarters, were asked to draft specific instructions to implement these policies, providing both for a situation in which GDR personnel would be designated as Soviet agents with the withdrawal of Soviet checkpoint personnel, and for a situation in which GDR authorities would not be so designated.[19] The US Defense Department was not enthusiastic about making this more-or-less diplomatic distinction.[20] However, if GDR personnel were to operate without a Soviet confirmation that they were acting as Soviet agents, then a crisis would indeed have occurred, and the contingency plans would have been implemented.

Initially, Dulles did not object to the idea, but on second thoughts he retracted his support. Macmillan, on the other hand, seemed amenable to an "Agency" arrangement. De Gaulle was adamantly opposed, as was Adenauer.[21] This is an example of how difficult it was for Norstad to know just which of many proposals floating around among the Allies might be accepted or rejected. In this case, the "Agency" notion died.[22]

Doubtless to Norstad's relief, the Allies came to an agreement on presenting a united front to the Soviet Union, and they instructed their Ambassadors in Moscow to deliver the message:

> The Three Ambassadors ... should inform the Soviet Government at an appropriate time (1) that the Three Powers continue to hold the Union of Soviet Socialist Republics fully-responsible under the quadripartite agreements and arrangements concerning Berlin; (2) that the Three Powers have noted Soviet statements to the effect that the Union of Soviet Socialist Republics will withdraw from its remaining occupation functions with respect to Berlin; they assume this means the Soviets intend to withdraw Soviet personnel from the Interzonal autobahn and railway checkpoints and from the Berlin Air Safety Center; (3) that the right of the Three Powers to unrestricted access to Berlin would remain unaffected by such Soviet withdrawals; (4) that the Three Powers will not tolerate any attempt on the part of the "German Democratic Republic" [sic] to assert any control over or to interfere with their traffic to and from Berlin via quadripartitely established routes, and that they would take all measures necessary to protect their rights in this connection; (5) that, if the Soviets withdraw, the Western Powers will act on the assumption (a) that the Union of Soviet Socialist Republics has decided to abolish unnecessary administrative procedures at interzonal borders, and (b) the Union of Soviet Socialist Republics can and will, without benefit of exchange of flight information in the Berlin Air Safety Center, maintain absolute separation of Soviet aircraft and all other aircraft flying in the Soviet Zone from aircraft of the Three Powers flying in the Berlin corridors and the Berlin control zone; (6) that the Three Powers will expect their traffic to move freely to and from Berlin and will assume the Soviets have given blanket assurance of safety of all Three Power aircraft into the Berlin corridors and the Berlin Control Zone.[23]

With this firm stand now in place, Norstad could proceed with directing the planners at LIVE OAK to get on with their job. Specifically, he charged them with developing the necessary steps that should be taken to accomplish an initial probe effort if Western access were challenged. He wanted the planners to identify the practical difficulties that might be encountered if the Western forces were to disengage once they had encountered substantial opposition. Finally, anticipating the worst, Norstad wanted to know what the military realities would be in order to extricate a force once it had become enmeshed in hostilities with a determined Soviet opposing force. In other words, he wanted LIVE OAK to begin immediately planning what operational steps would be needed to respond to a serious provocation if one were to occur.[24]

One of the possibilities discussed to ease tensions was to negotiate an agreement with the Soviets on quantitative limitations on the Western garrisons in Berlin. The idea was that if the Western military presence were reduced there would be less potential for provocation, and the Soviet forces in turn could be reduced. Not only would this lead to a weakening of the incentive for the Allies to stand firm, however, but it could also play into the hands of those who advocated turning Berlin into an international – or "free" – city under United Nations auspices. To Norstad, these ideas were anathema: he could not see how the West could benefit from starting down the "slippery slope" of partial demilitarization in the isolated context of Berlin without first having achieved an understanding with the Soviet Union over European security as a whole.[25]

Since the three Western Powers regarded their sectors of Berlin as part of "the West," they felt that the overall diplomatic objective should be to ensure that Berlin – and the political-military issues surrounding it – would not be considered as something to be dealt with outside of this larger all-German framework. This did not mean that the FRG should have its legal standing *vis-á-vis* Berlin altered, nor did it mean that NATO as a whole should be formally engaged, but it did mean that the Three Powers were acting not only according to their rights as conquerors and occupiers, but also on behalf of the purposes and goals exemplified by NATO. After all, as Norstad well knew, the overall strategy of NATO and the security of Berlin was deterrence first and foremost: the avoidance of armed conflict. Thus, although he was not acting in his LIVE OAK "hat" as NATO's SACEUR, it was inescapable that Norstad's SACEUR role was inextricably tied up with his other two roles when Berlin issues were involved.

Planning to reinforce the deterrence strategy went forward rapidly once the LIVE OAK machinery had been put in place. For example, Quadripartite Berlin Airlift Plan (QBAL) was being formulated, which included the FRG for ground handling arrangements and construction. LIVE OAK planning dealt with such issues as the dispatch of Tripartite convoys on the autobahn to and from Berlin and of armored personnel carriers (APCs) both alone and in convoy in order to establish precedents and to work out unforeseen procedural matters; the use of NATO staff and communications facilities in connection with Berlin surface access probes; the "serious" use of force to maintain surface access in the event of failure of the probes. Other aspects being dealt with were whether the LIVE OAK planning group and subordinate Air Force Headquarters were being kept fully abreast of Tripartite Berlin air access and airlift planning being conducted at Bonn; what method Norstad should use to announce publicly his intention to give advance notification of Allied corridor flights to the Soviet/GDR air traffic control; which measures should be taken in the event of serious interference with air access to Berlin; and the question of high altitude flights in the Berlin Corridors.[26] It should be remembered that the use of atomic weapons had been ruled out.[27]

II. Issues of command and control

Not long after the creation of LIVE OAK, Norstad had the group prepare a document on Berlin contingency planning entitled, "More Elaborate Military Measures." He wanted to make certain that he could take quick and decisive action when appropriate circumstances arose to justify it.[28] Norstad meant, specifically, when non-military actions had failed after Allied probes had been physically obstructed, he could restore freedom of passage to Berlin through readily observable military measures in such a way that would be restricted to the local areas of rightful passage. In other words, consistent with his general posture of minimizing rather than maximizing the crisis, he wanted the discretion to use minimal force, but to use it promptly – and hopefully – in such a way as to bring about the removal of the physical obstruction. He wanted, at all costs, to be able to demonstrate that the West was determined to maintain its rights to access, and that he could take all measures necessary to protect those rights.

Norstad, as USCINCEUR, informed the Allied Tactical Air Force (ATAF) Commander in the Central European Region that he intended to delegate to him authority to declare a counter-surprise military system state of alert, known as STATE SCARLET, subject to stated conditions. The reason for this delegation was Norstad's assumption that STATE SCARLET would most likely result from radar indications that hostile, or suspected hostile, aircraft were flying over NATO territory. The danger for Norstad's forces was that the time from border crossing to the bomb release would be extremely short, allowing only a few minutes for survival and other emergency actions.[29]

As mentioned earlier, there was always the possibility that the Soviets might withdraw from the BASC. If this were to occur, in Norstad's view, civil air carrier aircraft participation would be doubtful because even with evasive action guidance by the Western Air Traffic Controller, the results could be tragic. Instead, Norstad recommended that "flight plans will be transmitted to the appropriate teletype addressee the Soviets will designate ..." rather than pass the responsibility to the GDR and thus initiate a politically undesirable contact. He wanted to refuse to accept the formal authority of a GDR Controller by notifying the GDR authorities through the Soviets. This would allow the GDR authorities to provide effective flight separation of Western flights without the West appearing to acquiesce in the transfer of the authority to do so from the Soviet Union to the GDR. Norstad also recommended broadcasting flight plans on the open radio repetitiously, on a previously-announced and easily available frequency. Thus not only would flight plans continue to be placed on the Soviet Controller's desk in the BASC, but also a tape recording of the broadcasts could be maintained for record purposes in case it might be necessary to put on the Soviets the onus for any accidents in the Berlin Corridor that might occur.[30]

Norstad wanted, if at all possible, to maintain normal traffic patterns over road access routes to Berlin. He felt that any abnormal traffic on the autobahn, such as APCs, should be avoided, partly because if they moved under their own power their ramps would be up and their doors closed, which would provide for the Soviets an opportunity to raise the closed vehicle issue. They then could insist on looking inside them before granting passage and Norstad would consider this action deliberately provocative, which is why he wanted to avoid the matter altogether.[31] This was in keeping with one of the planned courses of action, which provided that the Western Powers should accept obstructions imposed by the Soviet/GDR forces only after these forces have shown their determination to support their impositions by military means. This might lead to a further course of action, which would include positive Western military action to breach any obstructions without using firepower except in self-defense. In every possible "scenario," Norstad wanted to avoid a shooting incident that could escalate out of control.

With possible courses of action now being formally prepared by LIVE OAK, consideration had to be given to refine further the operational command arrangements. It was proposed to designate Norstad as overall commander for Tripartite operations, with the Commander-in-Chief, British Army of the Rhine (CINCBAOR) as Norstad's direct commander for Tripartite operations. A single commander for the conduct of Tripartite operations in Berlin would be designated, also British, who would report to CINCBAOR, who, in turn, would deal directly with Commander-in-Chief French Forces in Germany (CINCFFG) and CINCUSAREUR for administrative and logistic support of their national forces.[32] The JCS informed Norstad that he would be designated as overall commander for Tripartite operations, with CINCBAOR placed under his direct command for Tripartite operations. Tripartite forces in Berlin would be under the operational control of CINCBAOR for Tripartite operations, providing thus for a single Berlin commander. CINCBAOR would deal directly with CINCFFG and CINCUSAREUR for matters concerning administration and logistic support of national forces.[33]

Information about LIVE OAK was passed to the FRG military through the LIVE OAK Chief-of-Staff to the FRG National Military Representative (NMR) at SHAPE once the planning documents had been approved by Norstad and forwarded to the Tripartite Chiefs-of-Staff.[34] Thus all of the major Western "players" in the struggle over Berlin were effectively integrated into a system of information dissemination that centered on Norstad. Obviously, Norstad wanted to make certain that the lines of authority – both planning and operational – were in his hands. As he put it: "I am in a good position to act as your agent in reviewing and coordinating these [contingency] plans, initiating their implementation when directed by the three governments and maintaining operational control on their execution."[35] Norstad would have authority "to review and control" garrison airlift, civil airlift, QBAL, and TRIPLE PLAY plans, and to coordinate their implementation.[36] This represented a considerable expansion of his responsibilities under his previous two "hats" of SACEUR and CINCEUR. In fact, it made him the most powerful SACEUR in the history of NATO, at least until then.

He felt he needed this authority because he wanted to make clear that the Tripartite Powers were indeed prepared to take military measures to protect and defend their rights of access to Berlin even though the risk of general hostilities might be inherent in these measures in varying degrees.[37] Otherwise, the notion of deterrence would be meaningless, and he would lose his capacity to bring events to a conclusion favorable to the West.[38]

An examination of the relative military strengths of the two sides indicates why Norstad wanted maximum discretion. He was convinced that NATO's forces in Europe were of such strength that the Soviet Union could not win an all-out war on that front. This was because

NATO forces were being equipped with delivery systems that had atomic warheads.[39]

One of the larger issues that Norstad had to put to rest was any notion of East–West disengagement at this time. Obviously, it would be suicidal for Berlin if proposals for disengagement were to gain any diplomatic currency because then the credibility of the West's "resolve" to maintain the status of Berlin would be badly compromised. For this reason, not surprisingly, Adenauer sought to obtain reassurances from Norstad that disengagement was not on the "table." While in London on a formal visit to attend a celebratory service of NATO's Tenth Anniversary in St. Paul's Cathedral, Norstad addressed this issue. In an interview with William Clark of Associated Television Limited (ATL), he was asked this question:

> *Clark*: ... You spoke of the forces, the D-day forces in the central area. That is the area, of course, that is being talked about now in relation to disengagement. Militarily speaking, do you see any safety or merits in disengagement?
> NORSTAD: Disengagement – briefly, no. And categorically, no. But disengagement not only raises great concern, but very properly so from the military standpoint. From the military standpoint it is impossible for me to see any form of military disengagement in the present and existing political context which would not be absolutely disastrous and which would not destroy the really great security that we have developed over the period of the eight to ten years of NATO's existence.
> *Clark*: Could you spell that out a little more? Why would it be so disastrous? Is the forward area particularly important?
> NORSTAD: The forward area – I'm not going into a long discussion of the dangers of a military vacuum, but I think we can agree that most military people, and I think most political observers, would agree that it's a great danger. In addition to that, the forward area from the military standpoint is of the most critical importance, the most critical importance. In the present – again, I'm speaking in the present political context – if there was any disengagement, then there would be the question of removing certain forces. Now some of those forces – notably your British forces, and Canadian forces, which are based in those forward areas – would have to seek some place to go. And some of them almost surely under those circumstances would go home. It would be very hard to resist an argument that they should go home, because their military effectiveness, their

military usefulness would have been decreased to such an extent that it would be very difficult to hold them. If you had this disengagement, the situation would be one where the Russians could correct it from their standpoint. Because they have the initiative. They could bring back the forces, put them in the position where we never could, never – even in the event of a real emergency – never could we get those forces back in time, and in position, and in the numbers that would be necessary to regain the position of security. So there must be some change, and some very important change, in the political context to make even discussion of such a thing anything short of disastrous.[40]

Norstad went on to make the point that the same arguments apply for any "thinning out" of troops on both sides. Any exception would only be feasible if there were control and inspection. As he observed: "Control and inspection itself could be useful: it could eliminate or minimise the dangers, the consequences, of surprise attack; it could relieve us of considerable danger ... . But only on the basis of a guarantee such as is enforceable by us as well as by the other side ... ."[41]

Making these points strong and clear was essential if Adenauer was to be assured that the FRG would not be sacrificed to Soviet military threats. It must be remembered that without the strong West German resolve, any attempt to hold fast in Berlin by the Western Powers would be impossible.[42] This is why, for example, the British Foreign Secretary, Selwyn Lloyd, ignored a query arising from Norstad's radio interview from an opposition member in a House of Commons debate: "Is it not highly deplorable that General Norstad, who should be the servant and not the master of NATO, rejected outright proposals for disengagement and thinning-out the forces in Europe, at a time when the Ministers were actually discussing what proposals they were going to put before the Foreign Ministers' Conference and agree to at the summit conference?"[43] This was in reference to the fact that Macmillan, on a trip to Moscow in February for bilateral talks, had taken up the idea of a partial reduction and limited withdrawal of Soviet and Western forces in a zone incorporating Central Europe – the FRG, GDR, Poland and Czechoslovakia.[44]

Adenauer and de Gaulle had opposed any notion of "decoupling" the FRG from the West because, as has been noted later and as Norstad knew only too well, reinforcing in time from across the Atlantic in the event of an East–West military clash would be impossible given the Soviets' larger conventional forces that would be positioned just over the Polish and

Czechoslovak borders. In this respect, there would have been a natural difference in emphasis on the issue of "thinning out" forces on a volatile front between the military planners, who would want to consider every military-related contingency, and the diplomats, who would want to consider every political option.

At this time, the Norstads' only child, Kristin, was married to Nicholas Craw on July 14 in the American Cathedral in Paris. As is French custom, they were married privately beforehand in a civil ceremony. The bridegroom's father, Col. Demas Craw, had served with Norstad before being killed in action in North Africa. Kristin was known in the French tabloids as "Mlle OTAN." The Norstads were well-known figures in Paris, not only because of the General's position, but also because Isabelle had made her own mark in fashion circles and because of her noteworthy skills in entertaining.[45]

It is quite clear that, aside from dealing with the Soviets along with the change in his family life, Norstad had a formidable problem in planning, coordinating, and executing the various contingency plans. As SACEUR, he reported to the NATO Military Committee, a permanent committee of the North Atlantic Council; as USCINCEUR, he reported to the JCS in Washington; as Commander of LIVE OAK he reported to the Tripartite Ambassadorial Group in Washington.

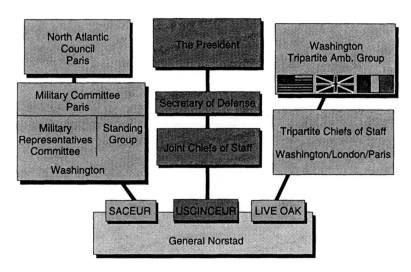

Chart 7.2 Norstad's Three "Hats" as of March 1959 (in August 1961 the FRG joined political discussions and LIVE OAK)

The JCS informed Norstad that a Berlin airlift was to be undertaken only as a last resort and that any impression the US was preparing for an airlift should be avoided. The airlift plan dubbed QBAL had inadvertently become associated with the current Tripartite Berlin contingency planning and in this relationship the QBAL portion had gone beyond the agreement of Tripartite Berlin planning. The US did not want QBAL to infringe on the US policy toward Berlin which stipulated that all references to a Berlin airlift should be avoided in order to preclude giving the Soviets the notion that the US would institute an extensive airlift rather than defend aggressively its legal rights of ground access to Berlin. The result was that planning procedures for QBAL were separated from the planning for other Berlin contingencies.[46]

Planning for the civilian airlift was to be directed toward Tripartite control only to the extent that a central flight operation – or coordinating agency – would be involved; each government would provide substitute flights for the airline associated with that government. Planning for the garrison airlift was to be directed toward the establishment of an operational coordinating agency only, recognizing that the issue of command was a national problem and therefore the needs of each Allied Berlin garrison force would be handled unilaterally. In any event, a policy decision on the advisability of mounting either a civilian or a garrison airlift would be made only in light of the political/military situation at the time. The air evacuation plan for Allied noncombatants and "certain selected aliens" from the Western sectors of Berlin, dubbed TRIPLE PLAY, was not specifically included; nonetheless TRIPLE PLAY could be included in more elaborate military measures.[47]

By late October, after a somewhat shaky start, LIVE OAK's efforts were beginning to bear fruit. The US found Norstad's plan, "Berlin Contingency Planning: More Elaborate Military Measures" to be acceptable. Agreement had been reached, for example, that any countermeasures, to be effective, must be more than punitive and must be conducted in a manner to demonstrate Tripartite unity. Norstad's goal was to demonstrate that the Three Powers could harass the Soviets in return. Having agreed on these general principles, Norstad was now free to prepare military contingency plans for either QBAL or TRIPLE PLAY.[48] Both would include the use of military force to restore access to the autobahn. As to how long Norstad would need to execute an initial probe, he estimated that it would require a seven-day advance warning from the Tripartite Powers for him to assemble and train the probe elements.[49]

The political guidance which the Berlin Ambassadorial Group provided concerning the command structure in the event the QBAL option was chosen, was thus:

> All of these plans (Civil Airlift, Garrison Airlift, Triple Play and QBAL) are designed for use in a situation in which risk of war had been increased and any airlift operation would increase the possibility of having to put into effect more elaborate military measures. A deficiency common to all plans is the lack of a single authority to insure concerted and coordinated control. The possibility is strong that one plan may have to pass into another; it is probable that TRIPLE PLAY will have to be executed concurrently with some other air contingency plan. Although TRIPLE PLAY and QBAL provide authority for appointment of a task force commander, neither plan has the task force commander responsible to one authority. It is therefore essential that a centralised coordinating agency be established from the beginning. The LIVE OAK paper on More Elaborate Military Measures has as one of its conclusions that General Norstad should be placed in command of any tripartite air or ground operations. Therefore, it follows that General Norstad is also in the best position to act for the three governments, as the commander to coordinate planning for these airlift operations and to control their initiation. His designation in this respect would be consistent with his other responsibilities in relation to Berlin contingency planning. The exercise of operational control should be delegated to CINCUSAFE who would be authorized direct communication and coordination with the Allied Ambassadors in Bonn thus enabling them to exercise their special rights and responsibilities in relation to Berlin and Germany as a whole. CINCUSAFE would also be authorized direct communication and coordination with the French and British Commanders in Chief, Germany... .
>
> *The basic difficulty in trying to define a role for General Norstad in connection with air contingency plans, particularly the Civil Airlift and QBAL, lies in the fact that the concept of these contingency plans, the channels for carrying them out, and their purpose are more political and civil than military ... [emphasis added]*
>
> On the other hand, it is fully recognised that since airlift conditions could give rise to overt Soviet/GDR actions interrupting airlift operations, LIVE OAK has a role to play in planning more elaborate military measures to maintain air access to Berlin ... . At that point, combined military action could well call for the single

military commander exercising operational control at the Paris level, particularly if such measures were undertaken in connection with other military measures to reopen ground access to Berlin.[50]

What appeared to be occurring was that as the crisis wore on, a sharper perception was emerging that although Norstad should be kept fully informed about all planning going on at every level and in the several capitals, and that he should have control of steps involving the use of force, the *locus* for operational control should be in Germany rather than in Paris. This would give CINCUSAFE, located in Heidelberg, control of QBAL airlift operations in Germany, working with a coordinating agency, since any decisions concerning airlift plans had to be made at governmental level. This would mean that military decisions would go through national military channels to military commands, and diplomatic/political decisions would go from foreign offices to the embassies in Bonn. FRG concurrence would also, of course, be required.[51]

Norstad, it must be said, did not disagree with this general approach. In fact, what frustrated him was the inability of the Tripartite Powers to come to a final agreement on authority. For example, in a moment of exasperation, he said to Twining: "I feel that the position we take must be a firm one, but, above all else, it must be a united position. Further, it is quite unreasonable to pass to the Military Commandants in Berlin the responsibility for compromising the differences which spring from the varying temperatures of their respective foreign offices. Anything in Berlin can be critical."[52]

As mentioned in the previous chapter, the British had been more hesitant to grant Norstad discretionary operational authority in the event of a "blockage" on the access route. Norstad's B contingency plan, which was to launch a probe if traffic were held up, in their view, should not be executed automatically; instead, the decision to launch a probe should be made by the governments in the light of the situation at the time.[53] At the Foreign Ministers meeting of the three Western Powers and the Soviet Union in Geneva, the British had made the same point. Under Secretary of State Christian Herter, representing an ill Dulles, asked rhetorically whether this unwillingness to reach an advance decision meant that "we [the West] contemplate imposing a blockade on ourselves."[54] Earlier, Norstad had used the same *riposte* to British reservations. Casting every episode in the crisis as presenting an "either/or" – either negotiate a compromise which would mean concessions from the Tripartite Powers, or risk nuclear annihilation – could logically spell capitulation. Neither the French nor the West Germans could agree with this line of thinking and instead argued along with Norstad for a firm posture coupled with careful contingency planning based on giving Norstad flexibility of response.[55]

The Geneva Conference went on intermittently from May to August, 1959. In April Dulles resigned because of colon cancer and Herter was appointed his successor. Douglas Dillon became Under Secretary of State. The elusive goals of these discussions were to provide the basis for a Four-Power summit conference. The notion was that the Four Foreign Ministers were to "narrow the differences ... and prepare constructive proposals for ... a Conference of Heads of Government later in the summer."[56] For example, one of the proposals put forward by Gromyko to his counterparts, Herter, Lloyd, and Couve de Murville, was to set a new deadline – a year (or alternatively two and one-half years) from the date of issuance – at which time all Western rights in Berlin would terminate. Fortunately this proposal was never made public because if it had been, the talks would have completely collapsed.[57] Macmillan, fearing failure after weeks of speechmaking peppered with recesses, had suggested that an "informal" summit be held, an idea Eisenhower firmly rejected as rewarding Khrushchev for his intransigence.

Eisenhower had made it clear to Khrushchev that he was willing to negotiate Berlin's status, and he conceded that his willingness was, in itself, an acknowledgement to Khrushchev's position that the situation in Berlin was "abnormal." Eisenhower wanted nationwide free elections to resolve the situation once and for all, whereas Khrushchev wanted reunification to take place through Four-Power negotiations – in effect, over the heads of the German people.[58] The irony was that, as far as this idea of all-German elections was concerned, Khrushchev could rely on Adenauer to oppose them *de facto* if not publicly. As Eisenhower recounted: "Herter said it was obvious that what Adenauer and the Christian Democrats were scared of was that in a reunified free election the opposition Socialist Party in West Germany would form a coalition with certain East German parties and throw the Christian Democrats out of office."[59]

The issue of the constancy of the British and the Americans to stand fast in Berlin, despite Norstad's efforts to weld together a coalition approach, was still questioned by de Gaulle. In his view, Eisenhower and Macmillan, while believing that Khrushchev was determined to cut Berlin off from the West, were reluctant to define the decisions needed to thwart Khrushchev. De Gaulle especially doubted that Macmillan was willing to have Britain suffer the "appalling destruction" of a war over Berlin. As de Gaulle put it:

> You do not wish to die for Berlin, but you may be sure that the Russians do not wish to either. If they see us determined to maintain the *status quo*, why should they take the initiative in bringing about confrontation and chaos? Moreover, even if any complaisance on our part did not lead immediately to a general aggravation of the crisis, the final consequence might be the defection of Germany, who would go and seek in the East a future which she despaired of being guaranteed in the West.[60]

This dark foreboding proved inaccurate, as Eisenhower remained firm. The problem with the Tripartite Powers was not the overall posture to be struck *vis-á-vis* Berlin, but, as Norstad knew only too well, "the devil was in the details."

After more travelling and communicating among Adenauer, Macmillan, de Gaulle and Eisenhower over Berlin, the impasse, doubtless to Norstad's relief, was finally broken. It occurred during Khrushchev's visit in September to the United States, during which private talks were held at Eisenhower's presidential retreat at Camp David. Time and time again, during the various sessions held between the two men during the course of the visit, Berlin and Khrushchev's ultimatum seemed to come up.[61] Eisenhower insisted that he would not attend any summit conference, which Macmillan along with Khrushchev had wanted – but not de Gaulle – "so long as the Russian ultimatum went unrepudiated."[62] Before leaving the United States, Khrushchev took this important step. As Eisenhower recalled: "the Chairman finally said he recognized my determination in this matter and said he would take steps publicly to remove any suggestion of a time limit within which he would sign a Soviet–East German peace treaty, thus making the future of Berlin a proper subject for negotiation, not one for unilateral action."[63] This concession paved the way for a summit – which turned out to be the abortive Paris Conference of the following May.

From Norstad's perspective, the removal of Berlin from under the threat of East–West confrontation must have come as at least a temporary relief. Perhaps the contingency planning for Berlin, which was vital to demark both the broad outlines of the Allies' political compatibility and the specific military steps that could be taken in response to provocations, also helped to shape Khrushchev's conclusion that whatever it was he had intended to accomplish by making Berlin an East–West flashpoint in the Cold War, must at least be put off until another day.[64]

8
The 1961–62 Berlin Crisis: The Unraveling of a Relationship

> I recognize that you are both an international commander and a United States commander ... . However, as the United States is the leader in the NATO Alliance ... I would not expect the views and attitudes of the United States Government to run contrary to the interests of the Alliance as a whole.[1]

I. A change in presidents and a change in policy and strategy

The negotiations over Berlin continued as the US presidency changed hands. A distinct difference, however, between the Eisenhower approach to European security and the Kennedy approach was the latter's desire to show "strength," and also to provide a "flexible response" concept rather than an – at least articulated – "all-or-nothing" concept to meet a Soviet threat to Berlin.[2] For both reasons, it was obvious to the Kennedy Administration that more planning, effort and resources should be given to a conventional military buildup in Europe, even while not neglecting the nuclear dimension.

One major nuclear policy issue was whether to retain IRBMs in Europe in light of the fact that ICBMs were now coming "on line." As it was put: "If the Communists blocked access [to] or drew a noose around the city, the only thing to do, it seemed, would be to defend with the crude tactical nuclear weapons along the border, which the United States had been installing since Eisenhower's day."[3] This new approach was not necessarily incompatible with what Norstad had been advocating for years. In fact, he had continually wanted a stronger conventional military alternative to a Soviet threat, whether in Central Europe or over Berlin access, so that the

West's response could be at a minimal rather than a maximum effective level of force.

It should also be pointed out that the Bay of Pigs fiasco had sorely embarrassed the new Administration (for which Kennedy had blamed both Eisenhower and his own military and intelligence people). For Kennedy to give the appearance of weakness in Europe where the vital interests of the US clearly lay would not only encourage Soviet "adventurism" elsewhere, but also demoralize the Berliners, the West Germans, and the NATO Allies generally. In this respect, strong encouragement was given for a more rapid West German military buildup.[4] Norstad favored this approach since he had consistently encouraged Adenauer and especially Adenauer's politically powerful Minister of Defense, Franz-Joseph Strauss, to meet the FRG's conventional force goals as soon as possible.

The difference between the Kennedy and Norstad approaches to such a buildup was a matter of scale. Norstad continued to believe in a restrained, gradual military strengthening in the face of continued Soviet threats, whereas Kennedy believed that more forceful steps were needed immediately, both at home and abroad, to convey to Khrushchev that he was "serious." The infamous meeting in Vienna in June 1961 between Khrushchev and Kennedy had only served to reinforce Kennedy's conviction that strong steps were needed to allay any Soviet misunderstanding or miscalculation concerning a "weak" Kennedy.[5] Khrushchev, before meeting Kennedy on June 3, had already warned him that he intended to sign a separate peace treaty with the GDR by the end of the year. As the US Ambassador to Moscow Llewellyn Thompson reported: "[Khrushchev] realized this would bring [a] period of great tension but he was convinced would not lead to war. I told him ... it was my duty as ambassador to see that he was under no misunderstanding of our position and that if he signed [a] separate treaty and force was used to interfere with our communications it would be met with force. He replied if we wanted war we would get it but he was convinced only madmen would want war and western leaders [were] not mad ... ."[6]

To help Kennedy reformulate his policies after the Vienna meeting, Secretary of State Dean Rusk formed a Berlin Task Force led by the Assistant Secretary of State for European Regional Affairs Foy Kohler and his deputy Martin Hillenbrand. They prepared a draft reply for Kennedy to Khrushchev's Vienna *aide-mémoire*, emphasizing negotiations rather than confrontation. Dean Acheson, from whom Kennedy sought advice at this time, advocated a rapid buildup of both conventional and nuclear forces.[7] Tensions were rising, however, as Soviet harassing activities concerning Berlin accelerated to such an extent that Norstad concluded they were amounting to an infringement of Allied rights and vital interests. Then, on August 23 Khrushchev sent a Note to the Tripartite Powers threatening the restriction of air access to Berlin for all but military personnel.[8] The contrasting approaches that confronted Kennedy at this juncture were concisely put to him: "The US [Eisenhower] chose to build strength at a moderate pace, to avoid provoking the Soviets and alarming Allied populations. The Soviets have quickened the pace and accused us of war-mongering nevertheless. It is unlikely that changes in the pace of our build-up would bring any worse Soviet reaction. As to Allied alarm, the most likely source now is the success of Soviet belligerence to date. More rapid build-up seems now more apt to reassure than disturb Allied publics."[9]

Back in July, the JCS had reluctantly agreed to Norstad's contingency plans FREE STYLE and TRADE WIND, which posited a ground response of first an Army company and then a battalion to a clear Soviet provocation.[10] The JCS felt that if no land action were to be taken in the event of a ground access obstruction, and that instead if Norstad were to proceed straight to an airlift, the West would be in danger of surrendering its land access rights.[11] They felt that the West's right of access to Berlin both by land and by air had to be maintained. Although ground operations at the battalion and smaller level might be unsound militarily, they could provide an alternative from jumping straight from a Soviet probe to nuclear war. Norstad had consistently wanted to provide for a "pause" or a "trip-wire" in order that there be time to weigh the consequences more carefully if a Soviet thrust was a prelude to full-scale war or merely a feint. What the JCS wanted was to plan for a *succession* of operations on an increasing scale of force to serve as a method of proving Allied determination. They were skeptical that a manifestly weak ground military response would be effective.

The Kennedy Administration viewed the issue of land access to Berlin and the impact of an airlift in response to a challenge as a matter of political rather than military policy. For example, Kennedy disagreed with the British position that the sole aim of land operations was to compel the Soviets to be the first to resort to military force. Kennedy wanted to build up the range of ground alternatives so that he could have more options – or rungs on the escalatory ladder. Consequently, Kennedy did not agree with either Norstad or the British that the size of the ground force used against the Soviets was irrelevant – that the West's aim could be achieved as well by an Army company as by a division or even larger force.¹²

Norstad's LIVE OAK planners had, of course, assumed that it would be wrong to proceed directly to all-out war in response to a ground provocation without suitable graduated escalation, even though militarily the escalation would probably result in the loss of up to a division if the Berlin garrison were reinforced significantly as Kennedy desired, or if this size force were used to compel the restoration of Western ground access to Berlin. Whether Kennedy would have sacrificed a division to gauge Soviet intentions lay, of course, with his and Norstad's estimation of the degree of the Soviet's determination to deny access.¹³

Kennedy's predilection for turning to his civilian colleagues for military advice, which was a sharp contrast to Eisenhower's system, was probably more important to Norstad's relationship with the new Administration than any differences over tactical military considerations considering Berlin. Since the Bay of Pigs, Kennedy had decided not to trust the advice of the JCS, whose Chairman was General Lyman Lemnitzer, an old friend of Norstad's and soon to be his successor.¹⁴

Consequently, in July 1961 Kennedy had asked McNamara rather than the JCS to revise the Berlin contingency plans. He wanted "a plan which would permit non-nuclear resistance on a scale sufficient both to indicate our determination and to provide the communists time for second thoughts and negotiation ..." so that Kennedy could avoid the early resort to nuclear weapons.¹⁵

Furthermore, Kennedy brought Army General Maxwell Taylor out of retirement to occupy a new position as "Military Advisor to the President" and charged him with dealing with the JCS. Taylor had resigned as Eisenhower's Army Chief-of-Staff over the issue as to what military posture the US should take *vis-à-vis* the Soviet Union. In his book, *The Uncertain Trumpet*, written after he had retired, Taylor rejected the Eisenhower – Dulles doctrine of massive retaliation. He disagreed with Eisenhower's preoccupation with maintaining a strong economy as a mainstay of national security, which meant tight military budgets. Taylor felt that budgetary constraints should not be at the expense of the buildup and modernization of conventional forces.¹⁶ Clearly, bringing Taylor in did not bode well for Norstad, who did not have the same cachet with the Democratic President as he had enjoyed with his Republican mentor, Eisenhower.¹⁷

One thing was clear: the Kennedy Administration was more interested in keeping to the fulfillment of NATO's previously agreed-upon conventional force goals as contained in MC/70 of May 1958 than being diverted either by planning for the Berlin crises or by negotiating the MRBM program. As discussed in earlier chapters both of these activities had been major preoccupations for Norstad. In fact, Norstad believed that undertaking steps such as a speed-up of the overall NATO military buildup at the expense of giving priority to steps relating directly to the GDR's actions concerning Berlin would be a mistake.[18] Kennedy disagreed; he wanted a "controlled partial mobilization," which included calling to active duty 250 000 Reservists and National Guardsmen and increasing the US troop level in Europe from 230 000 to 270 000.[19] McNamara met with Norstad at SHAPE on July 22 and 23 to hear Norstad's responses to the following two questions: 1) To what extent should US and/or Allied forces be expanded in connection with the Berlin crisis?; 2) What military action should the Allies take if the Soviet Union and/or the GDR were to deny the West access to Berlin?[20]

McNamara's meeting with Norstad had been preceded by a visit on July 18 to Norstad of the West German Ambassador to France, Herbert Blankenhorn. Norstad suspected Adenauer was conducting a "fishing expedition" to obtain a sense of Kennedy's intentions and priorities. Blankenhorn pointed out to Norstad that the West German people still had clear memories of the devastation of World War II and that they were inclined to hesitate before the prospect of war over Berlin. Adenauer believed that it was virtually inevitable that the Soviets would sign a peace treaty with the GDR. In his opinion, this event would immediately be followed by the transfer of rights over access to Berlin to the GDR, which would continue to follow the Soviet policy of "push, squeeze and play by ear" – as Norstad put it. This episode underscores how Norstad was gradually being caught between the Kennedy Administration's harder-line attitude toward overall European security through a more aggressive conventional military force buildup and the concerns of some of the major NATO Allies that this change could lead to all-out war rather than to a negotiated settlement over Berlin.

Like the British, Adenauer believed that negotiations must take place with the Soviets concerning Berlin, and that these negotiations should continue in the framework of the all-German problem – i.e. eventual German unification. But Adenauer was willing to accept some concessions, such as a de-emphasis on propaganda and intelligence activities and claims that Berlin was the "capital" of the FRG. It was even possible that the Oder-Niesse line could be accepted as the border between the FRG and the GDR if this concession could be worked into a package of mutual concessions that would over time make clear without formal acknowledgment that there existed *de facto* recognition of the GDR by the FRG.[21]

II. The erection of the wall provides new "opportunities"

Much diplomatic activity took place at this time to develop a common Western position on how to handle Berlin provocations after the GDR constructed a barrier on the night of August 13 that cut off the Western zones from the Soviet zone of Berlin. As it was reported: "East German regime took extensive security precautions morning August 13 when implementing decision prevent travel East Germany West Berlin. Between 4:00 and 5:00 a.m., VOPOs [East German *Volkspolizei*, paramilitary state police] at sector crossing points were heavily reinforced. Barbed wire and other barriers were laid ... *Kampfgruppen* units entered almost all buildings on streets adjacent to East/West sector lines ... . Many Soviet-licensed cars making observation tours."[22]

This bold and desperate action was largely in response to the increasing flow of East German refugees through East Berlin into the FRG and a life in the West. In the weeks between the Kennedy–Khrushchev Vienna meeting and the construction of the Wall, more than 20 000 of the best-educated and most youthful East Germans passed through the twenty-eight border points between Soviet-occupied East Berlin and West Berlin.[23] Although for several years there had been such an exodus, the numbers fleeing grew as rumors spread that this gap in the GDR's ring of barriers to the West might be closed.[24] Kennedy had himself observed earlier in the month: "Khrushchev is losing East Germany. He cannot let that happen. If East Germany goes, so will Poland and all of eastern Europe. He will have to do something to stop the flow of refugees – perhaps a wall. And we won't be able to prevent it."[25] In fact, Kennedy was more interested in preserving the Allies' rights of access to West Berlin than he was in preserving the right of free movement between the two Berlins, and Khrushchev was careful to draw that distinction. As one observer put it: "Finally, diplomacy caught up with the facts and, only then, settled in to await the creation of new ones."[26]

To probe Soviet intentions and as a symbolic move to raise Allied and especially the West Berliners' morale, on August 18, Norstad (as USCINCEUR) was directed by Lemnitzer on behalf of the JCS to

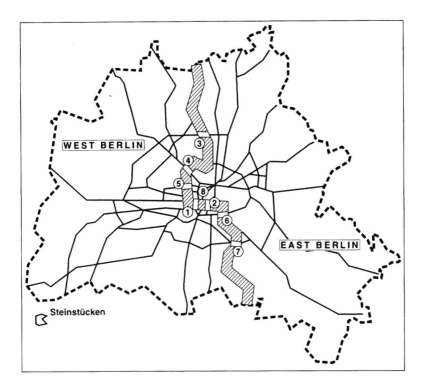

Chart 8.1   The Berlin Wall and Crossing Points, August 1961

augment the Berlin garrison by sending in one US battle group, reinforced to include appropriate artillery and engineer contingents. The duration of the deployment of the battle group in Berlin was not determined.[27] It was to pass the Helmstedt crossing-point shortly after daylight on Sunday, August 20, with no publicity pending an announcement in Washington. In addition, on August 19 Lemnitzer informed Norstad and the CINCUSAREUR, Lt. General Bruce C. Clarke, that they could expect to encounter four types of resistance: administrative, undefended or passive obstacles, lightly defended obstacles or harassing fire, or superior military forces. Norstad was instructed that in the event undefended or passive obstacles were placed in the way of the battle group, the obstacles should be removed and the column should continue. If lightly defended obstacles or harassing fire were encountered, the column should take appropriate defensive action and

European newspaper cartoons: reflections of public attitudes (courtesy of the Norstad family)

attempt to proceed. Otherwise, the column commander should halt, report and request further instructions.[28]

A taste of how Norstad handled the situation with his commanders is reflected in the following telephone conversation he had with Maj. General Albert T. Watson 2nd, US Commander in Berlin (USCOB), on August 24:

GEN NORSTAD: Any change since I talked to you last?
GEN WATSON: Not a bit.
GEN NORSTAD: If you will go along on that basis – where you are held up where an individual or a vehicle can ease through by using some easy force, if I can put it that way, that should be done; but where it means running over people, stop at that point for the time being, and demand to see the Soviets; and then let me know just as fast as you can because, as you know, the atmosphere on the other side of here is changing by the minute. If you will do that so that if any individual can shrug this off, or ease somebody off a fender, go ahead, but don't use a military force, as such, for this purpose and don't run over people for the time being, but demand in the strongest terms to see the Soviets. Coming back, if these people are blocked, just tell them to slowly ease their way and shove these guys off and come through. If there is great opposition, then again I think you will have to call the Soviets; but if it is a matter of just pushing people and running over their toes, run over their toes.
GEN WATSON: We don't want to knock them down.
GEN NORSTAD: I don't think it is a question of whether you want to at this particular point, but it is not desired on the other side that this should be done. Don't overdo the gentleness.
GEN WATSON: I understand.
GEN NORSTAD: I think you understand better than I.
GEN WATSON: I certainly do.
GEN NORSTAD: If there is anything I can do, call at any time.
GEN WATSON: Don't have any worry about this.
GEN NORSTAD: I don't have any. I couldn't be more pleased having you up there, my friend, and for your assurance. I have just talked to Lem [General Lemnitzer] and told him the instructions I gave you and he had nothing to add, so everything is okay on that.
GEN WATSON: May I review my instructions now? The first step when held up, the individual will ease around and if he can go ahead, go ahead, avoid knocking anybody down, don't use military force or actually run over people until I check with you. If that takes

place – being held up – I personally demand strongly that I be given a Soviet contact and demand the right to exercise my rights here in the city.

GEN NORSTAD: That's right.[29]

The operation passed without incident, to the relief and satisfaction of everyone who was involved.

On his part, Norstad planned to go ahead with the NATO exercises CHECKMATE and CHECKMATE II that had been scheduled for September. The purpose of CHECKMATE was to test the utility of the newly-created ACE Mobile Force, comprised of units from six NATO member-states. By not being restricted to NATO's regional command formations the force could be immediately available to deal with any flashpoint within the NATO area in Europe. Operation CHECKMATE II, to be held in the southern region by CINCSOUTH would employ AFSOUTH Army and Air Force units augmented by AFMED, British and American units. The American contribution would include an airborne battle group deployed from the US for the exercise. In his view, not to go ahead with these exercises would, under the crisis atmosphere over Berlin, be seen by the Soviets as a sign of weakness.[30]

The flurry of Western diplomatic activity concerning the Wall continued, with messages being exchanged between Kennedy, Macmillan and de Gaulle. Kennedy, after some hesitation which angered Adenauer and perplexed de Gaulle, decided as a first step to send Vice President Lyndon Johnson to Berlin via Paris. General Lucius Clay, the hero of the first Berlin crisis of 1948–1949 accompanied Johnson.[31] They would act as the personal representatives of the President. At the same time Norstad was told that he should not place any aircraft on alert status or order the movement of troops until he had received instructions from Kennedy as transmitted to him through the JCS. Kennedy was keeping a tight hand over this crisis, presaging how he would handle the Cuban missile crisis a year later.[32]

Johnson was asked to cover the following subjects in his discussions with Ambassadors James Gavin (France) and Thomas Finletter (NATO), and with Norstad or his deputy: the effect of the Berlin crisis on NATO cohesion; the facilities for the buildup of US forces in Europe; the NATO country buildup to meet the Berlin crisis; emergency authority to stockpile atomic weapons in France.[33] Kennedy was concerned that, in contrast to other crises in NATO that had always before tended to unify the Alliance, the Berlin garrison buildup was testing NATO cohesion, doubtless much to Khrushchev's satisfaction.

At his meeting with Johnson, Norstad was quite blunt in saying that he had been opposed to the sending of Johnson to Berlin along with a battle group because he thought such steps should have been saved for a later date as part of a calculated "build-up" program in the "war of nerves." He commented that: "we have committed our reserves and I believe committed them too early." Speaking in unusually colorful terms, Norstad said that if he had been the military commander on the scene in Berlin when the Wall went up, he: "would have slung a hook across the barbed wire when it was erected, attached the hook by a rope to a jeep and torn down the wire." By the same token: "he would have felt justified under the same circumstances in battering down the Berlin wall with a tank."[34] Norstad felt that Clay should have been sent first to Berlin, reserving a Vice Presidential visit at the next occurrence of a slump in the morale of the West Berliners.

Somewhat to Norstad's discomfiture, shortly thereafter Kennedy appointed Clay to be his "Personal Representative" on the scene, which was one more piece of evidence that the command and communications structure built up by Norstad during the earlier phase of the Berlin crisis was being either ignored or bypassed by Kennedy and his associates.[35] Kennedy, on his part, was impatient with what he viewed as the rigidity of the military to respond with alacrity in a fast-moving crisis situation.

Contrasting this crisis with the 1948 Berlin crisis, Clay saw the problem as:

> Another increase in the chain of command came with the establishment of NATO. This moved the [US] Army commander down a step. When I was the Army commander, I also commanded all American forces in Europe: Air Force, Navy, anything that was in Europe. But with NATO, that became the NATO commander's job. And in 1961, it was Norstad. And that was a problem, because Norstad couldn't make a decision as the US commander without making it as the NATO commander, and none of the European nations wanted [to take] any action in Berlin. So he was being pulled back all of the time by the fact that he was wearing a NATO hat.[36]

Tensions inevitably began to rise between Kennedy and Adenauer.[37] This situation doubtless made Norstad's job harder, for he knew only too well that strong and trusting relations with the FRG were essential

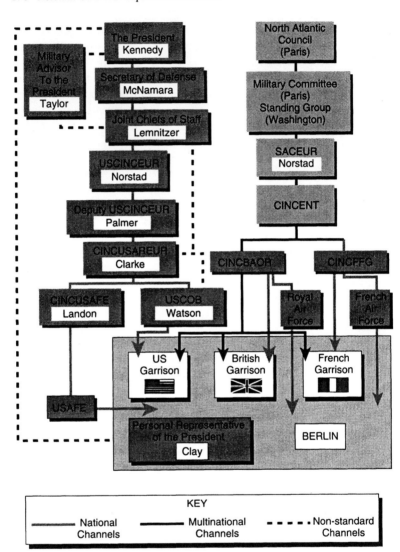

Chart 8.2 Operational Command Channels for Berlin, 1961–62 (in August 1961, the FRG joins political discussions and LIVE OAK)

for him to carry out his responsibilities effectively. For example, there was some anxiety in the FRG about what new instructions were to be given to Norstad under these dramatic circumstances. In Washington on August 17 the Quadripartite Powers – the FRG having joined the Tripartite Ambassadorial Group – addressed three priority tasks:

revision and agreement on contingency planning; clarification of the relationship between LIVE OAK operations and NATO, with suitable agreed instructions to Norstad; and the reply to the Soviet Notes of August 3 concerning access to Berlin. At the same time, NATO representatives in Paris were working on two additional subjects: the NATO military buildup; and possible economic countermeasures by NATO members.[38]

Basic planning was required after the construction of the Wall because a vastly new political-military situation now existed. On August 26 Rusk and McNamara attended a meeting in Bonn of the Ambassadorial Group where they pushed for a revision of Norstad's terms of reference. Consequently, the Group's military representatives sent two directives to Norstad. One directive amplified and modified the terms of reference for the Tripartite Berlin contingency planning that had been adopted in April 1959, and the second directive in effect called for an extension of JACK PINE plans. The Rules of Engagement (ROE) agreed to under the JACK PINE Tripartite plan had sought to force the other side to fire the first shot; the US adapted this to permit a USAF pilot to fire first. Norstad wanted further revisions to the JACK PINE counter-action plans to include authorizing him to decide when to initiate counter-action against enemy airfields, anti-aircraft, surface-to-air missile sites and ground installations in or near the corridor.[39] This discretion was considered by Norstad to be necessary because it was unlikely that the particular gun position or missile site could be identified which would have engaged Western aircraft. Norstad was given the responsibility for expanded non-nuclear air and ground operations, and the selective use of nuclear weapons.[40]

Norstad was continually faced with this difference in approach among the Quadripartite Powers – the British and West Germans (but not the West Berliners) more inclined to seek a basis for compromise, and the Americans and French more inclined to show military strength with its implied threat of conflict breaking out and escalating to general (i.e. nuclear) war. For the British, these changes were annoying because: "this decision perpetuated the unsatisfactory basis for planning which had always characterized LIVE OAK and, in particular, that once again a British Commander-in-Chief would be required to prepare plans which did not enjoy the support of HM Government."[41]

It was put thus:

> [Norstad] was also still caught between his NATO "hat" and his US "hat." Clay attributed this to the difficulties that he felt that he encountered while he was in Berlin: "In point of fact, the NATO com-

mander had never even visited Berlin [immediately after the Wall]. I think that was for political reasons ... because all of NATO wasn't involved in Berlin. But on the other hand, when he was wearing his American hat, he was the commander of US forces in Berlin. He did visit it after I had rather pointedly called his attention to this omission. And I'm not being critical. Because this is where these two hats that the NATO commander wears sometimes conflict.[42]

The general principle was that the new directives to Norstad concerning his Berlin responsibilities would be issued to him by the Ambassadorial Group in his capacity as USCINCEUR. Also, since many of the plans required by these directives were beyond the scope of the LIVE OAK staff to prepare, it was left to Norstad to allocate responsibilities and to work as he chose between his LIVE OAK and NATO staffs.

He included the following provisos regarding attacking ground sites: the sites must be clearly identifiable; the sites must be located within the corridors; and the sites must not be located in populated areas.[43] If these conditions were met, Norstad wanted to counter-attack immediately following a provocation. Failing such conditions, counter-attacks could be regarded only as political gestures of Western determination because attacks on selected sites would not maintain Western freedom of passage through their air corridors since the Soviets had such a large number of airfields. These airfields were located at distances up to 200 miles from the air corridors from which their fighter attacks could be mounted.[44]

These circumstances, made it unlikely that the West could maintain regular air service to West Berlin in the face of air and ground opposition, but Norstad thought that it might be possible to push through individual escorted convoys.[45] In any event, the JCS instructed Norstad that without permission from Washington he should not retaliate against Soviet anti-aircraft fire or against surface-to-air missiles launched against Western planes nor should he attack the sites.[46] An idea that Norstad opposed was the French position that military air transports without escorts should be substituted if civil air traffic were stopped by military action. He preferred the JCS instructions giving him discretion in the use of escorts. While the decision could only be made in the light of circumstances at the time, Norstad believed that if civilian airplanes were stopped by military action, it would not be reasonable to send in any kind of transport plane immediately thereafter without escort.[47]

But he objected to JCS instructions proposed to him that, in the event that civilian aircraft were blocked, he should immediately substitute military aircraft for civilian aircraft. Norstad believed that such action might result in the automatic degradation of the West's flights. Instead, he recommended that in the event civilian air traffic were stopped consideration should be given to continuing the operation of some civilian aircraft with, if necessary, the substitution of military for civilian crews. In Norstad's view, this action would be sufficient to show the West's determination to continue civil air service in the face of threats or harassment.[48]

What all this amounted to was that the Western Allies had acquiesced in the final stage of creating an independent German state in the East, paralleling the FRG. Although formal diplomatic recognition of this fact by the FRG was to await the Brandt initiatives in his "Ostpolitik" foreign policy, as long as the Soviet Union did not tamper with the West's rights of access to West Berlin, the situation was considered stabilized.

III. Organizational and policy responses to the wall

As the Berlin situation appeared to take on more of a diplomatic than a military cast, questions continued to arise about the relevance and efficacy of the planning machinery Norstad had put in place since 1958. The Tripartite governments were very sensitive to any suggestion that their prerogative to decide political questions – and Berlin was viewed as a political question – would be surrendered to Norstad.[49] There was also the recurring question as to whether the Berlin contingency plans should be implemented by Norstad through his LIVE OAK "hat" or through his SACEUR "hat." If the former, then the LIVE OAK staff would take on operational as well as planning responsibilities. If the latter, then Norstad would use regular NATO operational command channels. He continually had difficulty making clear to the Tripartite governments that LIVE OAK was essentially a planning body because questions of implementation continually would arise as one crisis episode would follow another.

On his part, Norstad saw no major problem concerning the mechanics of transferring military control between LIVE OAK and NATO. He intended to maintain LIVE OAK as a separate entity from

SHAPE with independent national representatives who would not be integrated into the SHAPE staff. As he said:

> The transfer of political control from tripartite to NATO authority should if possible occur "before the first probe is launched." If it is not possible at this time to obtain agreement that NATO will, in an emergency, assume responsibility for controlling the implementation of tripartite contingency plans, the very limited operational capability I plan to develop in LIVE OAK could be used to assist me in directing minor operations ... . In addition, the planned LIVE OAK operational capability will provide a reservoir of qualified personnel that can be absorbed into the NATO control structure on short notice. This will facilitate effective NATO assumption of control without necessitating prior detailed NATO staff participation in all levels of LIVE OAK planning.[50]

The purpose was not to absorb LIVE OAK into NATO but to facilitate Norstad's control over LIVE OAK planning in order to achieve better coordination of NATO and LIVE OAK activities. The move would also facilitate the transition of Norstad's operational control of NATO on short notice. In fact, the assumption was that if operations should occur on any significant scale they would require the resources of NATO and should therefore become Norstad's responsibility in his SACEUR "hat."

Norstad did request that the Ambassadorial Group in Bonn advise him, prior to the initiation of any probe or military action, whether he could plan on NATO's assuming control over the implementation of Tripartite plans in an emergency – a solution which he found preferable – or whether this question should be left undecided until the emergency occurs, thus requiring that Norstad should be prepared to conduct minimum initial operations.[51]

As suggested earlier, another point of tension was that those NATO member-states that did not have direct responsibility in Berlin were insisting on fuller participation in the planning that could well determine how and when they went to war, partly because they had been engaging in their own buildup. The existing 211–12 divisions in the Central Region was to be increased to 241–43 by January 1, 1962, with most of these divisions having high combat potential. A strategic reserve of 123–5 divisions was to be available outside of continental Europe depending upon improved transportation and logistic support, which the US was working on. The air strength was to be augmented by the addition of 225 aircraft by January 1, and of at least 177 more during 1962.[52] Yet the Tripartite Powers could not afford to consult because to do so would invite a small-Power veto in the early stages of a crisis. How to bridge this situation was one of Norstad's biggest challenges – working, of course, with Secretary-General Stikker.[53]

For these reasons, Kennedy's efforts to bring the Alliance as a whole much more fully into Berlin contingency-planning made Norstad nervous. This was especially true over the role of nuclear weapons in a conflict over Berlin.[54] Indeed, it was especially difficult for Norstad to find himself negotiating and disagreeing with his own government on so many issues concerning Berlin, NATO and European security.

To the dismay of Adenauer and the uneasiness of the European Allies, Kennedy's overall response to the Berlin situation was to minimize the crisis so that it would not become a full-scale East–West military confrontation. As mentioned, the concern of the Tripartite Powers was not to retaliate for the building of the Wall, but to continue to insure their rights of access to West Berlin. This put Norstad in the uncomfortable position of carrying out a policy which was, of course, viewed by Adenauer as a retreat.

For example, in order to bring FRG divisions up to 90 percent effectiveness, he was urging Adenauer to extend for three months those West German conscripts whose twelve-month service obligation ended on September 1. One of Norstad's arguments was that he could not persuade the other NATO member-states to meet their requirements if the FRG did not meet its requirements. After some hesitation, Adenauer agreed.[55] In fact, after having opposed the extension twice in his Cabinet meetings, Adenauer proposed to reverse himself if Norstad would state that the measure was necessary, which, of course, Norstad did. Adenauer also agreed that other contingents scheduled for release would also be held for an additional three-month period if this appeared necessary. This is an example of how Norstad let himself be used by the governments of the member-states to enable them to accomplish something Norstad wanted but which was unpopular at home.[56]

Norstad met with Adenauer in Bonn in early September at which time Adenauer remarked that "sometimes he is worried about Washington." Adenauer's worry was that on some aspects of the Berlin problem Kennedy might be insufficiently firm. He was referring to Kennedy's emphasis on conventional forces which Adenauer suspected implied a reluctance to use nuclear weapons to defend the FRG. Norstad reassured him that the US would indeed use atomic weapons if necessary, and mentioned the four F-100 squadrons and the additional B-47s that Kennedy was sending to Europe. This appeared to appease Adenauer, who also wanted to draw a distinction between stabilizing the situation in Berlin and deterring any Soviet territorial designs on the FRG. He was worried, for example, that there might be an uprising in the GDR in which Adenauer did not want to become involved precisely to avoid any possibility that such an intervention could lead to all-out war.[57] Although Adenauer was reluctant to force a showdown with Khrushchev over access rights to Berlin that might escalate into general war, he remained adamant against any formal recognition of the GDR, even though there had evolved over time considerable interzonal trade.

Adenauer was not aware of the fact that on August 23 Kennedy had approved National Security Action Memorandum (NSAM) 109, which established as formal policy that the Kennedy Administration would use nuclear weapons to hold Berlin if diplomatic and economic pressures were to fail, and after full mobilization.

> If despite Allied use of substantial non-nuclear forces, the Soviets continue to encroach upon our vital interests, then the allies should use nuclear weapons, starting with one of the following courses of action but continuing through C below if necessary:
> A. Selective nuclear attacks for the primary purpose of demonstrating the will to use nuclear weapons.
> B. Limited tactical employment of nuclear weapons to achieve in addition significant tactical advantage such as preservation of the integrity of Allied forces committed, or to extend pressure toward the objective.
> C. General Nuclear War.[58]

Whether the reality of the actual situation would lead to this, no one will ever know, but doubtless this formal commitment helped Kennedy to stand fast with Khrushchev in the nuclear standoff over Cuba. Norstad, in his turn, probably had misgivings, although such resolve in his own government could have led him either to search more earnestly for "measures short of general war," or to feel confident that in all three of his "hats" he had done everything he possibly could to prepare NATO and his own country to fight and prevail. Whatever his feelings, he had to live every day with this awesome responsibility.

On September 8 Kennedy had posed ten questions to his military and intelligence communities, and to Norstad as USCINCEUR. On September 13 McNamara instructed Norstad to ignore those aspects of Lemnitzer's replies concerning the buildup and deployment of non-nuclear forces that were at variance with McNamara's. It was clear that McNamara was putting his own imprint on the evolving policy debate. He made the point to Norstad that "in particular the General should note differences of interpretation, shifts of emphasis, nuances, which the General would see and which are very important." Ominously, McNamara stated: 'If you do not agree with me, and you may not, I am anxious to know that." McNamara also suggested that "it might be wise" for Norstad to come to Washington to discuss things with Kennedy, the JCS and with him.[59] The ten questions were:

1. What will the presence in Europe of 6 additional US divisions accomplish: a. In meeting the Berlin situation? b. In vitalizing NATO and strengthening the long-term defense of Western Europe?
2. Will an increase in our conventional forces in Europe convince Khrushchev of our readiness to fight to a finish for West Berlin, or will it have the opposite effect? What other steps of all kinds may help to carry conviction on this point?
3. [Not declassified]
4. It has been my understanding that we would need to call additional divisions only as we actually decided to send existing divisions to Europe. Since our current plan is to send only one such division, why is it necessary now to call 4 divisions from the Reserve?
5. If we call up four additional National Guard divisions now and do not send them to Europe, how can they be usefully employed? How long would it take to convert them to Army of the US divisions? How long would it take to create effective AUS divisions by other means?
6. How much of the 4 division build-up would be justified in view of the over-all world situation if Berlin were not an immediate issue?
7. What tactical air support is needed for the planned forces in Europe and what is the plan for providing such support?
8. The reduction in terms of days of combat of the supply backup of US forces in Europe which will result from increasing our forces and from supplying the West Germans has been noted. Would this result in putting US troops in a possible combat situation without adequate supplies?

9. If we add six divisions to NATO, may not Khrushchev add six or more divisions to the conventional forces facing NATO? Or will logistical problems, fear of attack by atomic weapons and preoccupations in the Satellites set a limit on the Soviet conventional forces available for immediate use against NATO?
10. What is the estimated net gold cost per year of the movement of six divisions to Europe and what can be done to reduce it?[60]

On September 16 Lemnitzer sent Norstad his reactions to Norstad's proposed answers, and they were not far from Norstad's views. In fact, Lemnitzer's and Norstad's responses in many cases used almost identical language. Because this exchange between McNamara and these two principal military commanders marked another milestone in the somewhat tense relationship between Norstad and the Kennedy Administration, it is desirable to have Norstad's complete answers:

1. I have studied your proposed answers to the ten questions which will be considered in connection with your recommendations to call to active duty four national guard divs. Our respective reactions to the principal questions posed are conditioned by the basic views we hold, both with respect to future NATO strategy, and to the measures required to meet the current threat to Berlin and elsewhere. I believe that your paper reflects to a large degree my thoughts on these broader questions. It is in degree rather than in principle that our views may vary. I hope that the answers eventually submitted will contribute to a better understanding of both principle and detail. To this end, I will first outline my views on what I consider to be the basic issues, since these are largely the source of the related specific comments.
2. I fully appreciate and support the need to create a position from which we would be able to respond, within reasonable limits, to any form of Soviet aggression in the NATO area, forcefully, but in such a way as to minimize the risk of general war. I believe, however, that realistic planning must seek to exploit our strengths without overlooking our weaknesses; above all, it must weigh immediate needs against interests of the long-term defense posture of the West. While preparing to exploit any favorable developments, we must not confuse the wish with the fact. We should therefore consider, very carefully, our ability to enforce a graduated, controlled development of the battle, and not overestimate the extent to which we can dictate the Soviet response,

particularly in a situation where it is unlikely that we would have the initiative. To assume that we could exercise independent, unilateral control over the battle would be as wrong in 1961 as it was wrong in 1953 to speak of "a time and place of our own choosing."

3. Based upon the principle that it is sound practice to be confident in execution but questioning and concerned in planning, I am disturbed by what may be over-optimism with respect to: A. The alternatives that will, in fact, become available to use by measures that essentially meet force goals previously established by NATO as the minimum required for an effective defense of Europe, with nuclear support when necessary. B. What more we can achieve, because of the conventional force build-up envisioned, in terms of either deterring Soviet action against our access routes to Berlin, inducing them to reopen access if it is denied, or actually forcing a reopening of access against determined opposition. C. Our ability to defend Western Europe against a massive conventional attack by the Soviet Bloc for as much as a month or more, without having to resort to the use of nuclear weapons. D. The impact of the measures which we propose to take on both the short-term and long-term efforts of our Allies.

4. Our force posture should be such as to permit us to respond to the whole range of the Soviet threat. In this connection, the credibility of the deterrent can be destroyed by emphasizing a policy that could be construed by the Soviets as permitting them to become involved, and then, if they decide the risks are too great, to disengage. That there is a real possibility of such a misconception is evidenced by the questions in the minds of some of our Allies as to our concepts and our policy. It is absolutely essential that the Soviets be forced to act and move at all times in full awareness that if they use force they risk general war with nuclear weapons.

5. The Soviet capability to augment forces in Europe is clearly greater than ours. Our build-up to the 30-division level will greatly increase our flexibility, extend the period over which we could defend successfully and raise the threshold at which nuclear weapons would have to be introduced into the battle. It will not, however, provide a real basis for assurance that we could successfully sustain a defense against massive conventional attack for an extended period of time. It certainly will not permit

us to consider conducting any major conventional offensive operations against determined Soviet resistance.
6. While not wishing to overestimate Soviet capabilities or to underestimate our own, we must recognize that the Soviets may well start with superior forces, will almost certainly have the initiative and would enjoy superiority in conventional air operations from the outset. Assuming a normal Allied combat loss rate, to gain and maintain air superiority over Western Europe presents a serious problem for the Alliance. Under this condition, our conventional defenses and our ability to carry out atomic defense plans would deteriorate quickly.
7. Lastly, we must keep in mind the fact that our NATO strategy must be generally acceptable to our Allies if they are to have either the will to face up to possible military operations or the inclination to build up their forces. Unreasonable as such an interpretation would be, any policy which might appear to suggest trading large areas of Europe for time in which to seek to avoid the spread of war to the US or which appears to deny the use of capabilities and weapons which might divert or destroy the Soviet threat to European lives and territory, will have hard going. I am sure you agree that nothing we do should suggest that our goal is to confine the fight for Allied rights in Europe to Europe.
8. I fully endorse the strengthening of our capabilities and our efforts to get our Allies to do likewise. I have always advocated a posture here in Europe which would provide an appropriate response across the full range of threats, and thus one which must be based upon a balance of conventional and nuclear forces.[61]

Having laid down his general comments, which, especially in regard to point 2, unwittingly were a harbinger of the US failure in Vietnam that was to come, Norstad then went on to demark how his views differed from McNamara's. By doing so Norstad probably sensed that his days as SACEUR would be numbered. As Norstad put it:

Where divergence of views appears to exist, in most cases it springs from differing estimates as to the extent of the benefits to be derived from the planned increases in military strength, national and NATO, and of the degree of dependence we are warranted in placing on these benefits. The strengthening of NATO forces to deal in a flexible manner with lesser acts of aggression as well as meet major threats to Allied Command Europe is badly needed, and is long over-due. I have advocated such strengthening of our capability for at least five years. I specifically endorse the early deployment of the planned 40,000 US troop augmentation in Europe, the proposed increase in US strategic reserve capabilities and the development of suitable means to deploy rapidly these reserve forces.

In the light of the situation existing today, I would suggest no further deployment to Europe until we have been able to absorb effectively the 40,000 augmentation now planned. Should the political or military situation change, as it might well do over any 24-hour period, the initial overseas deployments should be made on an exercise basis, several of which have been planned. In this way, a substantial build-up could be achieved without freezing us in a "for the duration" position so destructive of military and political flexibility. In case of very serious deterioration, these forces should be moved as rapidly as possible.[62]

On September 18 Kennedy received the State–Defense–Treasury replies to the ten questions, which recommended that the President to call up four National Guard divisions immediately and deploy to Europe one division of the present Strategic Reserve Army Corps (STRAC).[63] The point was to convey to the Soviets and to NATO the US's determination to defend its interest in Berlin, with the ultimate objective of increasing NATO defensive capability. To accomplish the latter, the US pressed NATO to achieve the thirty division goal of MC/70 by the end of 1961. From the US global point of view, if it turned out that this increase was not needed in Europe, then this increase in overall readiness could be applied to other trouble spots, such as Iran and Southeast Asia.[64]

The memorandum made the observation that the Soviets – regardless whether the US buildup would occur – might engage in a similar or larger reinforcement in the GDR. Significantly, it also pointed out that: "[Norstad] is against deployments at this time, but endorses the planned troop augmentation in Europe and the four division call up."[65] Essentially, Norstad was arguing that the West could not multilaterally control any conflict with the Soviet Union, and thus may not be able to enforce a gradual, controlled development of the battle. He felt that the US must be prepared for "explosive escalation" to general war. Following from this, Norstad was skeptical about how the buildup to the MC/70 force goals could provide additional alternatives for the use of force. These goals were the *minimum* required, with nuclear support when necessary, and therefore they should not be overestimated. Norstad was concerned about these points because they bore on his ability to implement a "controlled escalation" strategy, and on the degradation of his own forces in combat. What Norstad consistently did – and which Kennedy did not want him to do – was to resist separating into different entities any Berlin probes he might make from his general war capabilities. He was always looking at the Soviet *capability* to escalate from a Berlin probe to general war, rather than any calculations of Soviet *intentions*. Norstad's thinking ran counter to Kennedy's desire to impose a "controlled development of any conflict." The Administration embraced the concept that a limited ground conventional effort was possible to achieve the limited objective of inducing the Soviets to re-open access to Berlin, without necessarily contemplating ending up in a general war situation.[66]

Norstad felt strongly that "we are in a position from which we can move forward, backward, perhaps sideways, but we cannot sit still."[67] He was genuinely alarmed that a Berlin incident could lead to "an inevitable clash of arms." To avoid this, he recommended:

a. That we exploit to the maximum by every possible propaganda means, and get our Allies to do the same, the note struck yesterday afternoon to the effect that the responsibility of the Russians in East Germany and East Berlin, and their sovereignty in fact in that area, have now been clearly established by the presence of Soviet tanks and troops near the Friedrichstrasse check point.
b. That we restrict Russian entrance and exit to and from West Berlin to one gate, preferably other than Friedrichstrasse. Since the Soviets have done this to us, they must put up with a little pushing around on this point from us.
c. That the rules governing Soviet entrance into the Western sectors and the entrance of Tripartite personnel into the Soviet sector be placed on a completely reciprocal basis, emphasizing the fact that the Soviet personnel will show identification to West Berlin police where identification is required under the reciprocal arrangements. This is substantially the proposal made by [US Ambassador Llewellyn] Thompson ... . In this connection, we should emphasize the fact that we will show identification to the police at the check point, since the presence of Russian forces has established the fact that whether the police are German or Russian, they are still symbols of Russian authority.[68]

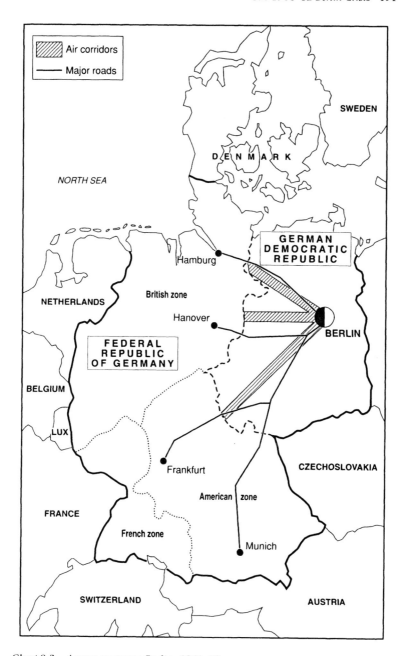

Chart 8.3 Access routes to Berlin, 1961–62

Norstad wanted this policy implemented within twenty-four hours so that it would not be seen as a "step backward" rather than, as he put it, a "step sideways."[69] Dealing directly with Berlin, Norstad had suggested changing the location of the West's entry point into East Berlin, along with making the policy of showing passes consistent for both the roads (where they were not required) and the subways (where they were) in order to reduce tensions as well as display some initiative.[70]

This internal US policy debate notwithstanding, it had already been agreed in Paris, at French insistence, that negotiations by Rusk or anyone else with the Soviet Union should only be of a preliminary nature to determine whether any basis for negotiations existed.[71] In any event, the signing of a peace treaty between the Soviet Union and the GDR would not be considered a *casus belli*, whereas the stoppage of interzonal trade would unavoidably lead to actions affecting access to Berlin, which would be regarded as *casus belli*.[72]

There had been a provocation concerning passes on August 24, when the senior American diplomat in Berlin, Allan Lightner, although he was in civilian clothes, had been detained at the Friedrichstrasse Gate checkpoint between the Western and Eastern zones of Berlin because he had refused to show his identification. Norstad at this time placed a temporary ban on the movement of officially-connected civilians to East Berlin pending talks in Moscow through Ambassador Thompson.[73] The dilemma was, as Norstad put it: "While it is absolutely clear that we cannot under any circumstances change the present procedure under direct pressure or the appearance of direct pressure, there appears to be general agreement that we are willing to show identification under the conditions and circumstances indicated ... . Since this is the case, should we not seek the first opportunity to accomplish this rather than *find ourselves involved in shooting over a point in which even we ourselves do not believe?*"[74] This question would be asked time and time again as the crisis dragged on from year to year. Always, for Norstad, it was a major preoccupation. The overall cause of this particular crisis was maneuvering on the part of the Soviets concerning East–West Berlin access rather than West German–West Berlin access. As it turned out, these maneuvers were a harbinger of something more drastic to come.

The US military authorities in Berlin did not agree with Norstad's recommendations. In their opinion, the US would be in a stronger position if the Soviets were still forced to stop US civilians to demand seeing their identification cards, rather than offering to show them to VOPOS. Instead they felt that bringing in West German police to supplant West Berlin police to do the checking on the Western side of the checkpoint was what Norstad intended. There had recently been a Tripartite agreement to demand identification from Soviet civilians entering West Berlin and restricting them to one crossing. Since, as a result of this episode, US civilian travel was now stopped by Soviet forces rather than by VOPOS, and was now accompanied by an armed escort, it appeared that the West was in an improved posture.[75] This exchange illustrates how difficult it had become for Norstad to obtain rapid agreement among all the various US diplomatic and military parties involved. To a lesser extent the same was true for the French and the British.

9
The End Nears

> Since you are the senior American commander and symbolize the role of the United States in NATO, you have an unusual responsibility in expounding the United States position and convincing our Allies of its soundness.[1]

I. The strains persist and intensify

In order to facilitate rapid communications, Norstad reluctantly departed from his insistence that normal military command channels be followed in dealing with episodes over Berlin. He authorized the CINCUSAREUR, Lt. General Clarke, to communicate directly with the USCOB, Maj. General Watson. Norstad also insisted, of course, that he and his Deputy USCINCEUR, Lt. General Willis W. Palmer, be kept fully-informed about developments in Berlin.[2] Norstad's reasoning was that prompt decisions in the face of a Soviet–East German provocation were essential to stave off any sign of weakness or hesitation on the part of the Tripartite Powers. This deviation from normal communications procedure was to apply only to episodes in Berlin itself, and not to any activities on the autobahn. By giving operational control to CINCUSAREUR, located in Heidelberg, Norstad as USCINCEUR had removed himself from being directly involved in such decisions, unless there was a sharp change in the Berlin situation that might result in more extensive or unique responses than had already been authorized or contemplated.[3]

Norstad went even further by proposing that if circumstances so warranted, he be authorized to designate, without prior consultation if necessary, USCOB as the single commander for the three Allied Berlin garrisons. The British, aware of the political implications involved, wanted national approval before Norstad could make this designation. The French, in their turn, wondered what circumstances could justify such a designation. Norstad envisioned two cases where the designation might be justified. One would be an overt armed attack on any scale whatsoever against West Berlin, and the other would be a grave civil disturbance suddenly fomented in West Berlin.[4] This explanation seemed to mollify the two Allies.

Not much later, however, Norstad became very irritated that the JCS or "higher authority" were communicating directly with Clarke and Watson. He complained to Lemnitzer: "I question seriously the wisdom of resorting to such an improper procedure ... such a practice tends to erode command integrity at a time when the slightest shift in the wind could create a crisis in which success could depend to a very large extent on the respect, confidence and strength which characterize good command relationships."[5] Lemnitzer replied that: "For many weeks I have been resisting strongly the constant hounding and harassment to take these and other actions which I regard as serious violations of the US traditional and tested system of military command relationships ... . In some cases I succeeded in resisting but in these two cases [about which Norstad was complaining] the point was reached where further resistance was impossible without being in direct violation of the specific instructions of the Commander-in-Chief."[6]

Lemnitzer had tried to explain to the White House, to no avail, that it takes longer to draft a carefully-worded operational message to implement a decision, than merely to give general information on the gist of a decision. Lemnitzer finally had to agree that all action messages having to do with Berlin which he dispatched to Norstad would be repeated for information directly to both Clarke and Watson.[7] This procedure related to subjects on which the State Department or the White House might be sending messages to their own representatives in Berlin. The arrangement had the practical effect of foreclosing an opportunity for Norstad to assess such directives before the operational commanders would initiate actions to implement them. In other words, Kennedy and McNamara were taking Norstad "out of the loop."

Norstad's grievance rested on the obvious fact that the responsibility for action should continue to rest with him, and so it was essential that his command status not be eroded.[8] As Norstad put it, doubtless with clenched teeth: "since a decision appears to have been taken, no further comment is offered at this time. I assume that the responsibility for action is still vested in this command." But it was also true that at the Pentagon McNamara was riding roughshod over the military community in general, and that Norstad was not an exception although he felt as an international commander he probably should have been.[9]

Added to this, however, was the fact that the broad political configurations against which specific military decisions could be made were not yet in place. There was, for example, tension between Norstad at SHAPE/Fontainebleau and Ambassador Thomas Finletter, the US Permanent Representative who was located at NATO Headquarters in Paris. This situation became increasingly apparent, even though Norstad still carried more prestige in NATO circles than any other American. In one episode, Finletter took a position in the deliberations in the Military Committee before Norstad had had a chance to comment on it. When he read about it, Norstad expressed the view that Finletter's statement went so far that it might prove embarrassing to US military authorities. His observation was ignored, which could not have pleased him. He was told that "the statement had been properly cleared and was therefore visible evidence of progress."[10]

This was but one of the many ways by which the Administration was clipping Norstad's wings. Kennedy wanted him to stick more closely to military affairs – and these as a US commander – rather than "meddling" in political–diplomatic affairs, and therefore acting more as NATO's SACEUR.[11]

As early as January 1961 – before the Wall had gone up – Norstad's former Air Force colleague General Nathan "Nate" Twining, who was Chairman of the JCS in the second Eisenhower Administration, perceived what was happening:

> You have done a tremendous job as the Supreme Allied Commander, and everyone knows it and, of course, would like to have you stay there forever. My worry is, Laurie, that the politicos – and this is with all due respect – sometimes get a little irked with us military folks, because they feel that maybe we are getting too strong a position as military people, which many of them resent. I know you appreciate that and fully understand why I have had some worries about your case because you have been very strong on numerous occasions.[12]

Aside from personalities, the heart of the matter was the Administration's desire to create in NATO an ability to respond to "less-than-total" aggression with "less-than-total" force. The idea was to raise the threshold that would lead to general nuclear war. Understandably, the US's NATO Allies suspected that an emphasis on a buildup of conventional forces might suggest that the US was moving toward the abandonment rather than reinforcement of Western Europe. This is why they were not convinced that an MRBM buildup was necessarily desirable. So it became one of Norstad's major preoccupations to bridge a sense of mutual suspicion concerning the general strategy that the Kennedy Administration considered was the most appropriate for NATO.[13]

On another sensitive command and communications matter, Norstad met with Kennedy, McNamara and General Maxwell Taylor on November 7 to discuss, among other matters, Norstad's relations with General Clay, who was still in Berlin as the President's Personal Representative. The problem was that there was no official document that specifically outlined Clay's mission and authority. There were only the statements in the Kennedy news conference of August 30:

> I am appointing General Lucius Clay to be my personal representative in Berlin with the rank of Ambassador. The situation in Berlin is a serious one, and I wish to have the advantage of having on the scene a person of General Clay's outstanding capacity and experience.
>
> While this appointment will not change the existing responsibilities of our military and diplomatic officers in Germany and Berlin, General Clay will be in close touch with such men as Ambassador (Walter C.) Dowling in Bonn and General Watson (Albert Watson, 2nd), our Berlin Commandant, and the appointment adds to our resources of judgment and action by placing in a most important city an American in whom the Secretary of State and I have unusual confidence.
>
> We are most grateful to General Clay for once again resuming his long career of public service. General Clay will take up his duties on Sept. 15, will proceed to Berlin, and will serve as long as this special arrangement seems desirable.[14]

Norstad had earlier remarked that "as he understood the matter, Clay had no authority and his presence in Berlin complicated an already complicated administrative problem." Adding to the confusion Norstad had rejected a request in late September by Clay that a motor convoy be sent from West Berlin to Steinstuecken – a small section in East Berlin under Allied control that acted as a magnet for refugees from East Berlin. This situation had not only been long-standing but had arisen during the first Berlin crisis. Norstad had already authorized helicopter flights of groups of refugees from Steinstuecken to West Berlin. Clay wanted the convoy to serve as a means of asserting Allied ground access rights, but Norstad felt that probing Soviet intentions in this way in regard to very vulnerable territory presented a high risk of launching a war.[15] Under other circumstances, such differences might have seemed minor and tolerable, but with tensions so high and the consequences of miscalculation so great, Norstad had to monitor constantly every significant or insignificant event that took place concerning Berlin.

The confusion between Norstad and Clay was such that it had been necessary for the CINCUSAREUR, who had been given the operational responsibility over Berlin access, to reaffirm his authority over the command, control, and procedures in place to handle military probes and other such activities along the borders and outside of West Berlin proper. For Berlin, Clarke had proposed that either Norstad as USCINCEUR or Palmer as Deputy USCINCEUR should take operational control of the US Army in Berlin and that the headquarters of USCOB and USBER be combined.[16] One possible reason for this was that Clay had been ordered to stop the autobahn patrols, and this angered him. As he said later: "Norstad ordered Clarke to stop the autobahn patrols. He sent Clarke up to break it to me gently that he'd been ordered to stop the patrols. Silliest damn order I'd ever heard."[17] Clay went on to comment harshly: "So far as Norstad is concerned, I don't think he was capable of handling anything. But that is just a personal opinion."[18]

The conversation at the November 7 meeting then turned to NSAM 109 concerning Berlin. Norstad felt that further mobilization was not needed at this time. In fact, earlier he had written Kennedy: "You will recall that in the conference over which you presided on the 3rd of October, I did not request that additional divisions be deployed to Europe to augment my ground forces." It is this stated reluctance to support enthusiastically a decision already made – although at the same time he stressed that taking some dramatic political action was desirable – that gave the impression to the Kennedy Administration that Norstad was not a "player." Norstad did go on to say, however: "After studying the inclosure to your letter, I sense a suggestion that the United States may desire to send additional forces to Europe, perhaps two or more divisions. If this impression is correct and if, after this further consideration, the United States wishes to strengthen our forces in this manner, we are prepared to receive such an augmentation and will support it as a sound military step."[20]

In this instance Norstad was addressing Kennedy as an international commander – in his SACEUR "hat" – rather than as a US commander. Intentionally or not, the tone of the letter probably conveyed the impression that in some ways as a NATO commander he would have preferred not to have gone along with the President's decision. This tone would not have gone down well with either Kennedy or with McNamara. It reinforced their perception that the NATO Europe members trust Norstad because he is one of them, and not merely an advocate of American policy. As for Norstad, he regarded himself as a NATO commander first, and an American commander second; for Kennedy, he regarded Norstad as an American commander first, and a NATO commander second. This would become even more clear as tensions between the NATO commander and the leader of the Alliance's most powerful member-state persisted.

For example, Norstad suggested to Kennedy that Kennedy might "summon" Khrushchev to an emergency meeting in Berlin to discuss the crisis on a bilateral rather than on a multilateral basis.[21] When Norstad was asked how he expected to persuade the NATO Allies to accept this notion, he "expressed confidence" that he could do this. But he felt that the draft memorandum prepared by the State Department to inform the Allies of this initiative would need some revising, especially to account for West German concerns.[22] In any event, nothing came of the notion.

Shortly thereafter, Norstad reminded Kennedy that about four years previously he had formulated a system of control and inspection to facilitate de-escalating the military confrontation between the two Germanies and the two alliance systems, and that the NAC was taking an active interest again in this plan. Norstad felt that with some changes to bring the plan up to date, the papers prepared earlier could be used again. The geographic area in which the respective forces could be "thinned out," for example, in Norstad's later view, could be extended to include some part of the US (such as Alaska) in exchange for an equivalent area of the Soviet Union. Unfortunately however, as discussed in the previous chapters, Adenauer had not agreed with this idea when he had been briefed by Norstad in May 1960, and he continued to disapprove of it.[23] Adenauer had consistently insisted that the front line of NATO should be the Elbe.

Another tense episode between Kennedy and Norstad occurred during Adenauer's visit to Kennedy on November 22, when Adenauer was given a very detailed briefing of US military strength together with a discussion of that strength *vis-à-vis* the capability of the Soviet Union. The purpose of this briefing was to help resolve some of the differences between the FRG and the US concerning relative strengths and commitments. Norstad was very upset when he found out about the briefing, that Adenauer had received some very highly classified information that went far beyond anything that he had been given up to that time.[24] Kennedy's policy of sharing more nuclear-related information, including targeting, both with Allies and with the Soviet Union, in order to reassure the Allies and to deter the Soviet Union, was one of the many items that caused discomfort between Norstad and the Administration.

On November 16, Norstad had transmitted to Kennedy, "SACEUR's Instructions to SHAPE Planners." It reached the White House over the weekend of November 18–20. When, on December 1, Rusk and McNamara sent their comments to Kennedy on Norstad's November 16 letter, they included this remark: "The General may continue to have reservations on US policy. However, the proposed reply would nevertheless require him in any event to take the minimum necessary planning steps to make the US preferred course of military action feasible from a military point of view, Soviet reactions permitting."[25] Taylor, who reviewed all the papers, had this to say: "The Secretaries of State and Defense find General Norstad's proposed instructions to NATO planners, ... only in part consistent with US policy on military actions in a Berlin conflict. I agree ... ."[26] Taylor then listed the areas of concern or perhaps he was offering several possible explanations.[27] Because this probably is the point at which the Administration concluded that Norstad was more of an impediment than an asset, Taylor's remarks to Kennedy are worth quoting:

Reason General Norstad does not yet completely understand the full thrust of agreed US policy; if he did, he would modify the draft instructions and conduct himself differently in the future.

Action Send General Norstad a rather detailed letter of follow-up to your October 20 letter and its enclosure, to be signed either by you or by the Secretary of Defense (the Secretaries of State and Defense have prepared such a letter; it is available, along with a few changes which I would propose).

Reason General Norstad holds strong views which have caused him consciously or unconsciously to resist accepting US policy, and probably will continue to do so unless rather drastic action is undertaken.

Action Send a personal emissary to General Norstad to talk through in detail the full range of US policy in a Berlin conflict, using as a primary vehicle the joint draft letter prepared by the Secretaries.[28]

Obviously the Administration was becoming testy with Norstad. So Kennedy wrote him that he was sending Rusk and McNamara to see him the following week to discuss the Administration's position paper, "US Policy on Military Actions in a Berlin Conflict."[29]

Norstad told Rusk and McNamara that he would inform Kennedy that he would not issue formal instructions to the SHAPE planners based on Kennedy's letter and the position paper, but instead he would use it as general background and guidance rather than as specific directions to the LIVE OAK staff. Norstad then went on to observe that, when the paper is used to support the US position in the NAC, "great skill and delicacy" will be needed to overcome the opposition to the limited actions that the Administration proposed. After making this not-too-subtle comment, adding that the opposition in NATO is "certainly not diminishing" despite the Administration's recent efforts, he felt sure that a generally acceptable solution could be achieved.[30] This attitude could not but add to the Administration's awareness that the US's chief military leader in Europe was not overly enthusiastic about the new approach.

While in Paris, McNamara urged the NATO Allies to "make a major effort to build conventional forces for checking Soviet pressure in Europe."[31] The foreign, defense and finance ministers were McNamara's audience, and he forthrightly put forward the Kennedy Administration's view that "it was essential for the alliance to close the great gap between its formidable total nuclear power and its growing but still inadequate conventional forces." He then went on to recapitulate what the Deputy Secretary of Defense, Roswell L. Gilpatric, had said a short time earlier, that the US was so heavily armed with nuclear weapons that no conceivable first strike could cripple the US's retaliatory capacity.[32]

Later, Kennedy's Special Assistant for National Security Affairs, McGeorge Bundy, while circulating Norstad's letter to Kennedy to Rusk and McNamara for further comment, observed: "If you feel that this most recent letter is inadequate in major respects, would you also jointly recommend to the President an appropriate further action? In this latter connection I am under the impression that there was fairly general agreement within the government to avoid, if possible, any further proliferation of correspondence between the President and General Norstad on this subject."[33]

In fairness to Norstad, the emphasis on a conventional buildup had been evolving for several years, and both the US and NATO had been searching for a way to avoid nuclear war by miscalculation. As Norstad put it: "We must have a conventional force adequately manned and equipped with modern weapons. However, it is also agreed that we must have, associated with these formations, a nuclear capability which could, if the situation demands, be joined promptly and effectively with the conventional effort to force a pause and to halt aggression – to halt and defend."[34] The gap between inadequate conventional forces in Europe and the resort to strategic nuclear forces would be filled by the MRBMs that were being employed in some of the NATO countries.

Because Norstad in his LIVE OAK "hat" was formulating the contingency plans for Berlin, it was of great interest to the NAC what his views were concerning the prospect of either NATO's conventional ground forces suffering defeat or the superpowers engaging in a mutually-destructive nuclear exchange. Norstad's solution had been to plan to use nuclear weapons placed in Europe in small numbers to strengthen the "pause" that would bring about a break in which hostilities could be stopped. As he put it: "By the presence of effective strength, we must be in a position to prevent, if possible, an act of aggression, large or small, intentional or unintentional. If such an act were to take place, however, we must, in a minimum, be able to force a pause in which to identify the action as aggression in fact or intention, a pause to emphasize the cost and significance of such an aggression. The aggressor must be required to make a conscious decision as to whether or not he will expand the incident so that it would constitute an act of war."[35]

What all this meant was that the US was significantly strengthening its conventional forces, but the NATO Allies were still unpersuaded that it was in their best interest to significantly match the American effort. There was a suspicion that the Kennedy Administration was building up conventional forces and ancillary European-based nuclear weapons precisely in order to avoid the need to make good on the threat of going from a possibly ambiguous thrust and counter-thrust to all-out nuclear war. Adenauer, in particular, was convinced that in this event the FRG would become the battlefield. This view persisted even though Norstad insisted that the buildup only meant that NATO was reaching closer to the force goal of 30 divisions agreed upon in 1958 in MC/70.[36]

II. Relationships improve in spite of provocation

By February 1962 the LIVE OAK staff had completed their plans on what to do in the event that the air corridors to West Berlin were harassed. This was none too soon because on February 8 and 9, the Soviets had indicated an intention to constrict Allied air travel in the corridors to 10 000 feet. This was a familiar problem, having first arisen during the Eisenhower period. Not surprisingly, Norstad had anticipated that the corridors would be interfered with again in order to disrupt normal Allied civil air schedules. Norstad believed that if the Soviets were to declare their intention to ban travel in air corridors up to 10 000 feet, this would represent an intention on their part to push the West hard, and that the West's response should not be limited to simple probes below 10 000 feet. What Norstad wanted was that the Tripartite Powers should "push hard" in return, and that flights should immediately fly above 10 000 feet as well as below. Because the civil airlines probably could not be persuaded to fly civilian crews above 10 000 feet, Norstad planned to use military crews on empty civilian planes.

What Norstad was proposing to do was to raise the stakes at the outset to show that NATO's reaction would be prompt and positive. Specifically, he proposed:

(a) In case of more declaration by Soviets, bring all pressure to bear on civil airlines to continue to fly in accordance with normal schedules and at normal altitudes. (This would represent clear-cut political victory if they met with no interference.) Military air transports would also fly in corridors at critical altitudes.
(b) If civil airlines refuse to do this, then have civil planes with military crews fly at critical altitudes; also encourage civil airlines to fly above 10,000 feet, if necessary with military crews and without passengers. Military transports would not RPT not fly above 10,000 feet.
(c) However, if civil airlines agree to fly normal schedules, then no RPT no civil air transports, with or without military crews, would fly above 10,000 feet.[37]

Although the British and French agreed "in principle" with his plans, the British specified that the actions proposed by Norstad regarding flights above 10 000 feet must be considered in Washington by the Ambassadorial Group.[38]

On February 14, three US military transports flew the northern corridor to Berlin in and out at the altitudes that deviated from 10 000 feet, and two RAF transports along with one French transport flew the central corridor. This prompted the Soviet Controller in the BASC to tell the British Controller that if "your aircraft" continued to fly at these altitudes, they would be considered "trespassers," with resulting consequences. Norstad immediately apprised the Tripartite governments through LIVE OAK channels of the situation, and directed CINCUSAFE to bring up to twelve the number of F-104s on alert.[39] However, he did not have US unilateral or Tripartite delegated authority to direct fighter protection of the transports flying in the critical air corridors unless Soviet/GDR fighters actually physically harassed them. If such harassment were to occur, however, then at his discretion Norstad could use fighter protection in line with basic JCS instructions.[40]

Even though the notion of fighters orbiting at the entrances to the air corridor was considered, Norstad decided not to do this unless it became more clearly necessary. He also would not at this time order fighters to escort civil aircraft in the event of hostile buzzing. If buzzing were to occur as a warning, Norstad would have ordered a limited number of fighters to orbit at the corridor entrances. Of course, if an Allied transport were shot at and hit or were physically rammed, then he would have ordered subsequent flights to be escorted.[41]

It was, of course, very important that Kennedy authorize whatever plans Norstad proposed to implement as USCINCEUR. This authorization was given on February 14 in NSAM 128. Kennedy stated:

1. That the State Department is authorized to seek Ambassadorial Group agreement to delegate to General Norstad authority (a) to urge the civil airlines to fly over 10,000 feet if the Soviets seek by declaration to prevent all flights below 10,000 feet, and if, as a result, the civil airlines are unwilling to fly below that limit; and (b) to fly civil aircraft (initially without passengers) with military pilots over 10,000 feet, if the civil airlines decline to fly either above or below 10,000 feet. (General Norstad already has authority also to fly civil aircraft with military crews below 10,000 feet, if the civil airlines decline to do so.)[42]

On February 15 the Allies continued to fly at the critical altitudes in the southern corridor despite the Soviet position that such flights should not be made, and despite buzzing by Soviet fighters. Norstad considered these operations as successful, and therefore the West was in a good tactical position because if the Soviets were to deny further flights, they must take decisions to interfere with them by force. The Soviets would bear the clear onus for using force if they were to press their claims to a showdown in the face of the West's having refrained from provocative or aggressive actions.[43]

On February 16 operations in the northern corridor went as planned, with the participation of Tripartite military aircraft and with US and British commercial aircraft flying at the critical altitudes. Because of adverse weather conditions, there was no hostile Soviet activity.

So as not to surrender the initiative, Norstad considered the desirability for the West to begin low-key harassments of the Soviets in other areas not directly connected with Berlin. For example, he contemplated subjecting Soviet cargo ships and fishing fleets to certain controls or harassments on the assumption that, while they would not be major incidents, their import to the Soviets about the West's resolve would be clear.[44] Norstad was also anxious that the Ambassadorial Group resolve the issue of border-crossing times, although he was not strongly convinced that this was an issue on which the West should be prepared to stand firm.

The way that Norstad handled the Berlin situation at that time helped to repair his relations with Kennedy. Doubtless he was very pleased to receive the follow personal letter: "Now that there is, at least for the moment, a lull in Soviet activity in the air corridors, I want to write to tell you personally that, in my judgment, your handling of this affair in the last two weeks has been outstanding. Your alert and skillfully measured response, and your combination of coolness with determination, seem to have communicated themselves to all concerned, and I want you to know that those of us who have been watching in Washington are full of admiration."[45]

Norstad responded gracefully: "On behalf of all those who have worked directly on the Berlin air traffic problem since February, as well as myself, I thank you for the very generous comments in your letter of 26 February. We are all pleased that you feel the action we have taken has been in compliance with your thoughts and has furthered your objectives." Then Norstad went on to pay himself a compliment: "As you probably know, the Governments of the United Kingdom and France have also been quite satisfied with the manner in which these operations have been conducted. As a matter of fact, we believe that there has been greater harmony and a clearer sense of common purpose in this particular exercise than in almost any other field in which the three countries have worked together over a period of at least several months."[46]

Norstad went on to offer Kennedy his thoughts regarding the Soviet motives for having provoked the crisis: "My own thought is that this started out as a reminder that Berlin is a problem and as an attempt to undermine the confidence, particularly of the West Berliners, in the one secure means of transportation. Perhaps it continues for one or both of these reasons, although a new factor may have been added: that is, the difficulty of discontinuing something that has not proved to be a success."[47] This is, of course, what Khrushchev's threats came down to in 1958–1959, and it was to be replicated again later in 1962, although under vastly different circumstances. But for the moment the pause in provocations was short-lived.

On March 9, and repeated on March 13 and 14, a Soviet high-flying aircraft was observed by electronic means making a run from north to south across the three Berlin air corridors. During the day a total of three Soviet aircraft made this run, some forty miles west of Berlin both north to south and south to north. Extensive Soviet chaff drops east of Berlin were observed as well, the purpose of which was to interfere with Allied Berlin radar control. The chaff drops, in Norstad's opinion, were a direct and deliberate offensive threat to the safety of flight. He saw no justification for dropping chaff in or near the corridors, and especially in the let-down area of the Berlin air control zone. Therefore Norstad urged that the Tripartite Powers should protest in the strongest terms either in Geneva or in Moscow against this attempt at interference with the air corridors, and should demand that it not be repeated.[48]

Norstad felt that because of timing, nature and especially the altitude of the drops, together with the status of the Soviet actions in the corridors at that time, strong protests were merited. He also saw them as good propaganda underscoring the West's resolve, since the chaff drops occurred during the Geneva Disarmament Conference of Foreign Ministers.[49] Nonetheless, the Tripartite Powers chose not to protest because chaff drops were not considered that unusual.

At the same time, Norstad received authority from the British and French to schedule flights above 10 000 feet, but only if absolutely necessary because, as Foreign Secretary Lord Home put it, this would inform the Soviets that they would have forced the Tripartite Powers to depart from their normal procedures. At his request, Norstad briefed the NAC on these developments. He said that if necessary, flights would be sent under 10 000 feet and if forced, consideration would be given to flights above 10 000. The important point was that the Tripartite Powers show their determination to do whatever was necessary to maintain flight access to Berlin. Although he was not under a formal obligation to consult with the NAC prior to instituting flights above 10 000 feet, Norstad felt that he was under a personal obligation to do so.[50]

An illustration of Norstad's sensitivity at this time on this question of flight altitudes was his instruction to the US Controller at the BASC to deny Clay's request to fly above 10 000 feet on a return flight from Berlin to Bonn. Clay did not like this at all, and complained about it. The matter went all the way to Kennedy, who felt constrained to write Clay a soothing letter supporting Norstad's decision – but it was also an indication that Clay's usefulness to Kennedy was drawing to a close, doubtless much to the relief of the various commanders involved in the Berlin situation. Kennedy put it firmly: "We are of course following the situation in the corridors on an hourly basis here, and I am aware of your differences with General Norstad. On balance, in the situation as it stands so far, I have found myself in agreement with General Norstad and I have accordingly approved his recommendations. I believe we have sustained our essential positions coolly and effectively, but each day may bring new tests and new decisions, and if stronger measures appear to me to be necessary, I shall not hesitate to order them."[51]

The depth of the tension between Clay and Norstad can be inferred from Kennedy's forthright addressing of the situation to Clay, as he continued:

> Meanwhile, I want to say three things to you. One is that when your opinion is not shared and your advice not taken, your candid and determined comments are of great value. We need to know what alternative courses are available, and what the contending arguments are, in this kind of situation, and it is a matter of great importance to me that your voice, which must always be heard, is on the line from Berlin. This importance may not be easy for you to understand, in situations in which you might well feel that mistakes are being made and your own convictions lightly overridden – but I assure you that it is so.[52]

Kennedy then went on to praise him for supporting the whole course of action "even when parts of it do not command your personal approval."⁵³ Nonetheless, Clay was convinced that both Norstad and Clarke had resented his coming. Kennedy ended by informing Clay that he was sending General Maxwell Taylor to meet with Clay and to discuss with him: "all matters of importance relating to Berlin and to your own position." Clay departed from Berlin on May 2, 1962, after a huge rally was staged in his honor on the Platz der Republik.⁵⁴

III. A new doctrine for NATO

In Europe, by the late 1950s, the role of the NATO forces was changing; it was conceived more and more in terms of limited military operations and no longer, as earlier, as defense against a massive, calculated invasion. General war seemed unthinkable and totally self-defeating. Instead of being perceived as conducting a holding operation while the sword of the US Strategic Air Command was wielded in massive retaliation, the NATO ground force shield was now thought to have the more modest task of preventing limited aggression by ruling out the possibility of early gains. As mentioned earlier, Norstad, to support this thesis, had advanced the concept of the "pause." In the event of large-scale fighting in Central Europe, which he envisaged would come about as the product of miscalculation or "momentary rashness," the NATO ground forces, both nuclear and non-nuclear, would "enforce a pause" in the hope that diplomacy could avert the recourse to strategic air attack.⁵⁵

The Kennedy Administration, however, believed that if the role of the NATO ground forces was conceived in these terms, the policy of immediate tactical nuclear response was inappropriate because it would tend to expand or escalate the conflict, which was the opposite of the outcome being sought.⁵⁶ Taylor, who replaced (some might say displaced) Lemnitzer as Chairman of the JCS, took the position that a doctrine of flexible response was required to forestall, by the use of conventional forces for as long as possible, the recourse to nuclear weapons.

Earlier, the Eisenhower Administration, under Secretary of State Christian Herter, had recommended a two-part program whereby POLARIS missile submarines would be assigned to Norstad, to be manned by a multinational crew from at least three NATO memberstates.⁵⁷ The purpose was to create a multilateral strategic force (MLF) that would enable the European Allies – and especially the FRG – to have a share in nuclear command and control. This became known as the Herter Plan. Norstad publicly opposed the MLF proposal (and also the companion British ANF proposal) because, as he said: "We should not for almost a thousand reasons think of creating a new strategic force, because you just cause more trouble than it is worth."[58]

In both plans – the Norstad Plan for the control of MRBMs and the Herter Plan – the underlying issue was how to involve the West Germans without putting their "finger on the trigger." By 1961 the FRG was the only NATO European member-state that had increased substantially its conventional forces. The Kennedy Administration's desire to move toward making flexible response more plausible gave the FRG more leverage in support of their desire to be more involved in the formulation of overall NATO military doctrine. For the FRG this meant more, rather than less, integration. The MLF, incidentally, was also bitterly opposed by the Soviet Union on the grounds that it would in effect make the FRG a nuclear Power, which would violate international agreements.[59]

Nonetheless, Norstad told the British Minister of Defence, Harold Watkinson, that he hoped that "the new Administration ... would back the general principles enunciated by Mr. Herter."[60] The Macmillan government had not been very enthusiastic about an MRBM force or the thought of other NATO member-states sharing in the control of nuclear weapons. After initial meetings in March 1961 with McNamara and his two key associates, Paul Nitze and Roswell Gilpatric, Watkinson was happy to report that they "did not really like the Herter offer at all, nor do they seem very enthusiastic about a large MRBM force ... . They do not like the idea of creating any kind of NATO nuclear force, tactical or strategic."[61] The Administration was thinking in terms of tighter, more centralized controls upon nuclear weapons, and the Herter Plan as well as Norstad's calls for NATO to be the fourth nuclear power did not fit into the new strategy then evolving in Washington.

The clash between Norstad and his own government was thus over profoundly important issues of NATO policy. But on another level, it also became a clash of personalities and of styles. As has been seen, Norstad did not like to be upstaged by, what seemed to the Europeans, the brash and inexperienced McNamara and his "whiz kids."[62] What NATO called long-term planning, the Pentagon now called strategy. Norstad had played a key role in the debate over long-term planning, and therefore felt that he had been shut out of the Administration's declarations on a changed "strategic concept" for NATO. As Stikker said: "It was clear that the new President wanted to change current NATO strategy. This, of course, the American government had every right to propose and to discuss. Unfortunately, however, the new ideas reached the Council more in the form of *faits accomplis* than of proposals for collective consideration."[63] The Administration felt that its policy of nonproliferation and centralized control ruled out a NATO nuclear force that was not ultimately subject to US veto.[64] To Norstad this was almost a vote of nonconfidence in the SACEUR.

The issue centered around viewing the MRBM as a complement to a larger conventional buildup. One of the grievances which the NATO Allies had was that under the "sword" and "shield" concept, the "sword" was primarily the US-controlled nuclear deterrent, whereas the "shield" was the European-provided conventional "trip-wire." And the heart of this shield was, from the Kennedy Administration's perspective, the *Bundeswehr*. Kennedy had made no secret that he regarded a Washington–Bonn axis as more important than a Washington–London axis, and this shift away from an "Anglo-Saxon"/Atlantic focus was causing some disquiet within the Alliance. But Adenauer did not agree with this shift because its purpose was to build up the FRG's conventional forces and to minimize FRG participation in nuclear affairs.

Adenauer also suspected – as did the other NATO Allies – that the two nuclear superpowers would negotiate over their heads to avoid the possibility of catastrophic war on their respective homelands, while being willing to sacrifice the territories of their European Allies. He was alarmed that his small yet strategically-placed country would inevitably become the exclusive battleground. An indication of the delicate position this put Norstad in was the fact that Rusk felt it necessary to request that Kennedy designate a personal emissary to try to persuade Norstad that the interests of NATO as well as those of the US would be better served if he would "exercise his great influence" to secure NATO's agreement on the Administration's new policy of flexible response.[65] The recommendation underscored the gap between Norstad and Kennedy: "The man selected should (ideally): (1) Enjoy the full confidence of the President. (2) Enjoy the full confidence of Norstad, as nearly as can be determined. (3) Believe fully in the NATO military policy of this Government, as nearly as can be determined."[66]

McNamara had said he "would not favor" Norstad's plan. "I think it would be unwise," he said, "to divide the nuclear force of NATO into two categories without a proper linkage between them, granting to one group of nations authority to use one category and ... another group of nations or a single nation authority to use the other category. Nuclear war is indivisible." He continued: "I know of no single member of

NATO who would recommend that the authority to utilize nuclear weapons be granted to three to five other nations of NATO ... . Nor do I know of any member of NATO that would wish to see the US delegate its veto power to any other member of NATO or to any grouping of NATO nations."[67]

The diversity of viewpoints concerning how and when to use nuclear weapons was crystallized over Berlin. Norstad rejected the notion that NATO could engage in armed conflict for an extended period of time without using nuclear weapons. As he put it: "The use of armed force, even in limited quantity, risks the danger of explosive expansion to higher levels of conflict, including the highest level. This risk is accepted, and therefore we stand ready to use all forces and weapons available, including nuclear weapons, if necessary, to protect the territory and people of the NATO nations and to defend our other vital interests."[68] The reaction in Washington was summed up by Lawrence Leger in his somewhat cynical observation:

> Had lunch today with Cy [sic] Weiss of State and Dee Armstrong of Defense, both active and influential working-level officers in the NATO business. They feel that General Norstad remains basically opposed to the "graduated-response" defense concept which this Administration has adopted for the NATO area, especially in a context of increasing crisis over Berlin. They may be right, but they will have a hell of a hard time, in my opinion, proving it to their more detached bosses; Norstad's latest paper is almost foolproof in covering all bets, or "all things to all men."[69]

Norstad's SHAPE study contained an implied criticism of the decision in August, which Norstad had opposed, to send a battle group to Berlin that month. In his opinion, this weakened the front-line forces in the FRG. He stated: "Whatever action is taken, political or military, should if possible improve our over-all military position, but under no circumstances can it be permitted to detract therefrom." Kennedy signed a brief covering letter to Norstad with Rusk's and McNamara's evaluation of the SHAPE study as an enclosure. His note merely stated that Norstad's study "has resulted in comments which I have approved and now enclose for your guidance in planning and in future relations with your NATO colleagues."[70]

Norstad refused to adopt Kennedy's new policy, embodied in NSAM 109, as official policy to guide the work of the SHAPE planners. As a NATO commander, Norstad was under no obligation to accept

guidelines from the US government for use by his Allied staff; his policy directives came from the NAC in which the US was only one of the fourteen members. But in his USCINCEUR "hat" he served at the pleasure of the President, so his rejection of NSAM 109 placed him on a collision course with his Commander-in-Chief.

Unfortunately for him, as far as the US was concerned, Norstad continued to ignore the new strategic thinking coming out of Washington. Instead, in the Autumn of 1961, he and his staff developed a new NATO Emergency Defense Plan (EDP) that continued to assume that nuclear weapons would be used, if necessary, after a brief pause. He did note that "there was also a place for conventional forces." It is no wonder that Norstad remained popular with NATO's European Allies even as he was increasingly unpopular at home. As Watkinson put it: "the concept expressed in SACEUR's new Emergency Defense Plan was very closely linked to British thought, whatever its relation to US thinking might be."[71]

By then, Norstad's days were numbered, but he had amassed a legacy which would be unmatched by any of his successors, as worthy as they might be. Former NATO Ambassador Robert Hunter summed it up:

> The most extraordinary SACEUR of all was one of America's most extraordinary officers, General Lauris Norstad. It was clear which hat he preferred to wear: that of the naturalized European presiding over a coalition of states in a tradition more appropriate, it might seem, to the 18th century. Indeed, he came so well to reflect the needs and demands of the NATO organization itself – the "compleat" organization man and a superb politician – that during his tenure the grip of the United States on the Alliance was weakened, and NATO enjoyed its finest hours as a coalition where political problems could also be tentatively advanced, instead of being confined to external bilateral forums.[72]

Conclusions

> God knows, I have been accused of everything ... I figured I was doing the most I could do... by being a good and effective officer. I have been very pleased, the way that has worked out, to be in a key spot at a *very* difficult, sensitive time and to be involved in so damned many controversies ... .[1]

I. Norstad as a man of his generation

Lauris Norstad's career spanned some of the most tumultuous years of the twentieth century. With the development and use of the atomic bomb followed by the creation of an ever-larger and diversified arsenal of nuclear weapons, these years were witness to the achievement of the pinnacle of industrial warfare – the possibility of the ultimate destruction of human civilization. If ever-more complex nuclear-armed manned and unmanned "delivery systems" proved not to be the panacea for peace, then long-suffering mankind seemed ripe for yet more suffering on a scale heretofore unimagined. The dilemma that confronted Norstad and his generation of Cold War military leaders was that, if nuclear weapons failed to deter the Soviet Union, the world might have to endure incredibly brutal national and personal immolation.

These years were also further witness to the rise of ideological warfare, which threatened to eclipse the liberal and humane achievements of Western civilization. The West needed NATO to forestall yet another ideological catastrophe after Fascism and National Socialism. Small wonder, then, that for Norstad the imperatives of first, achieving military and ideological victory over Fascism and then, of waging the Cold War against global Communism, provided the moral basis for his career.

Fortunately for him, his personal religious instincts were not incompatible with this moral basis. It is doubtful that Norstad, as he grew up in small upper mid-Western communities, the son of a Lutheran minister and the descendant of devout Scandinavian immigrants, ever contemplated the conundrum of reconciling the New Testament values of compassion and forbearance with the "darker," more destructive, warlike human imperatives.[2]

In these respects he was not different from his Air Force contemporaries. If they had any ideological predilections other than a generalized belief in liberal democracy, and in preserving the American "way of life," it was probably their common belief that the massive use of air power, which they considered to be the backbone of modern warfare, could destroy the enemy "root and branch." Norstad undoubtedly agreed with "Jimmy" Doolittle's observation that: "the main thrust [of AWPD-1] was to blueprint the way for air power to undermine the capacity and the will of our enemies to wage war."[3] But instead of lowering the enemy's morale and the will of both combatants and noncombatants to resist, as Norstad and his colleagues had assumed, strategic aerial bombardment of this sort in World War II resulted in a more resolute attitude of resistance on the part of the victims.[4] Nonetheless, as Michael Sherry put it: "rational calculations about damaging the enemy were never the sole motivation for the strategic bombing ... ."[5]

These gifted airmen – among them Cabell, Kuter, LeMay and Vandenberg – were, in their own way, whether they realized it or not, reflecting in their attitudes and actions the prevailing American social concept of what came to be known as pragmatism. Stripped to its bare essentials, these pragmatists were believers in the notion that "if it works, it must be right." It also must be utilized – they were all in this sense utilitarians. How to "solve a problem," or how to "get things done," was what motivated them. The earliest days of military aviation "... was a time when flying was learned by doing. ["Hap"] Arnold initiated the use of goggles after being hit in the eye by a bug; a colleague devised the seat belt after almost being thrown from the airplane."[6] Risking – and overcoming – the dangers of flight had left an indelible imprint in their psyches that mankind could continue to prevail over machines, even as they encouraged the development of ever-more-lethal war-making machines that threatened at least to destroy mankind's quality of life (whatever that may mean) if not mankind itself. The simple answer, for them, must have been that enlightened mankind could only be saved from its mean-spirited, militaristic, tyrannical "other" through overwhelming countervailing technological means. This meant that nuclear weapons were viewed as necessary instruments of defense against a totalitarian threat that would make life as known in the West not worth living.

For Norstad, however, it was policy pragmatism rather than technological pragmatism that appealed to him. He was a good flyer, as they all had to be to advance during the somnolent days of the interwar period. But Norstad also possessed a capacity – probably inherited from his forebears – to reach out and to influence others through analytical persuasion. He was not a power-hungry bureaucrat by any means, but he also was not satisfied with being just a good "operator" in the military sense of "planning" and "operations." It did not matter that Norstad had an outstanding, if limited, combat record. Then as now the true *kudos* of the professional military were more likely to go to those general officers whose success come from operations.[7] Solving the technological, bureaucratic, and warfighting problems of military aviation became neither his primary intellectual interest nor his professional forté, which is perhaps why in retrospect he has not been remembered by the Air Force as one of its "warriors."[8] He gravitated relatively early in his career to the larger platform of the politics of command.

Furthermore, Norstad's personality was distinctive. For example, picking up on his father's example of preparing and delivering weekly sermons, Norstad realized early on the power of language. Identifying the "heart of the matter" in any given policy issue and then articulating it persuasively to others – as in a sermon – became his hallmark. He excelled at analyzing complex policy issues, which is why he was known as a "thinker" more than as a "doer," although he thought of himself as both. As he remarked: "I wanted to get things done. I didn't want to just go through the exercise of working things out, thinking about ideas. I wanted to carry them into effect."[9] This quality also enabled him to be an effective negotiator and in a multinational environment, an effective commander.

From the time when "Hap" Arnold selected him as a young officer to be one of his "boys" on his Advisory Council, Norstad had been a "marked man." In that assignment, he performed a trouble-shooting and problem-solving role that could have been seen as threatening to those other officers who worked within the bureaucratic establishment. This, in itself, made him "different." Then Arnold recalled him from operational duties in the Mediterranean Theater to help him run the Twentieth Air Force, which purposely had been created outside the normal command channels. Norstad, on behalf of Arnold, was charged with ensuring that the B-29 Superfortress would be the instrument to win the war against Japan. If this meant cashiering on behalf of Arnold some of his closest colleagues, so be it.

Norstad excelled in the sometimes bitter internecine budgetary and roles and missions struggles that characterized postwar Washington military politics. He knew how to cultivate the "movers and shakers" of the city's political elite and this brought to him the kind of public attention not usually accorded a very young general officer – especially one who had not won his reputation by being in harm's way on the battlefield or in the air as World War II drew to a triumphant conclusion.

It certainly did not hurt his career when he won the gratitude of President Truman after he, along with Vice Admiral Forrest Sherman, concluded the difficult negotiations that led to the passage of the National Security Act of 1947. His role in the pivotal negotiations for the War Department in the struggle for Armed Forces unification and the creation of an independent Air Force, accorded him a reputation as a tough and effective diplomat on top of a well-established reputation as a brilliant planner. Norstad's ability to reach out beyond his own Service's interests to articulate the interests of the competing Services undoubtedly brought for him both career benefits and liabilities. As he recounted: "I was enough of a political animal to sense that, having been around Washington, you could get anything done if you were reasonably intelligent and you knew your subject and had the votes. You could get anything done."[10]

One important benefit was having established a close working relationship with Eisenhower.[11] Being in the right place at the right time had indeed brought him early promotion and subsequent recognition, but by now Norstad had shown that he was worthy of the trust vested in him first by Arnold and then by Eisenhower.

II. Norstad's leadership

It was therefore almost a natural evolution in Norstad's career that he would be involved in creating a four-star Air Force position in Europe and would then find himself occupying it. In this new command he become two-hatted – both a national commander as CINCUSAFE and an international commander as CINCAAFCE. Then, as Air Deputy to SACEUR, he had become a major "player" in nuclear affairs, which was the centerpiece of the politics of the Cold War and by extension of

NATO. Although Norstad was as much a "nuclear general" as was his famed contemporary LeMay, he also was, for better or worse, an "international general." He tried to be at the international level what LeMay had become at the national level. He was convinced as both a "nuclear" and an "international" general that the command and control of tactical nuclear weapons in NATO had to be multinational in character in order to preclude their further proliferation.

Owing to their World War II experience, both Eisenhower and Norstad believed firmly not only in the principle of unity of command, but also that effective multinational military cooperation required a truly integrated international headquarters and command structure. Modern coalition warfare demanded it. This belief set Norstad apart from many of his Air Force contemporaries, some of whom would have resented this departure from the parochialism of a young Service with weak traditions and a debatable doctrine. The instinctive Service parochialism and almost jingoistic nationalism that accompanied the victory of World War II, and which was being played out in Washington during the late 1940s in the competition for roles and missions, was gradually – being challenged by an ideal of international military cooperation that would not, and for that matter could not, ever be fully realized.

The command and control of nuclear weapons was too great an issue to be resolved within the framework of the still-evolving postwar international system, especially under Cold War conditions. It was for this reason that during Norstad's tenure as SACEUR, after *Sputnik*, US political-military thinking swung back toward more exclusively national control of the nuclear strike mission. Moreover, as Andreas Wenger concludes: "[t]he development of the [Berlin] crisis during the summer of 1961 confirmed to the Kennedy administration the lesson (which Eisenhower too had learned) that nuclear superiority had only limited psycho-political meaning. The nuclear balance counted for very little with respect to military planning."[12] Without a doubt, the protracted and recurring crises over Berlin were the high-point of Norstad's influence as a military diplomat and Cold War general. But the Kennedy Administration, especially after the Cuban missile crisis, could not accept the rationality of the assumptions concerning waging nuclear war on which Norstad had relied as a basis for his multinational leadership.

The fundamental reality for Norstad was that it was their *uncontrollable* nature that made nuclear weapons so decisive in the East–West struggle. Escalation was the true deterrent. If nuclear weapons could be controlled in war, then their value as the absolute deterrent as well as the absolute weapon was compromised. In response to a question as to whether he would have automatically gone to nuclear war, he replied: "Not automatically. No, it was never automatic, but it was almost inevitable because it was unlikely that the Soviets, if they had launched a clear attack, would accept failure. It was unlikely that we would accept destruction without doing what we could do to avoid it."[13] Sir Solly (later Lord) Zuckerman put it in a nutshell: "If the NATO high command were to consider that MRBMs [equipped with nuclear warheads] with a range of some 1000 miles were part of its effective armory, the planning of land battles would become totally befuddled by the Douhet-Trenchard doctrine of strategic air power."[14]

War for Norstad had to be a function of diplomacy – but it was more the diplomacy of absolute deterrence rather than of graduated deterrence, or flexible response. Controllable escalation would, in the final analysis, be self-defeating. This is why the clash between the Allied Supreme Commander and the Kennedy Administration encompassed contrasting rationalities.

Whether or not he succeeded in his various diplomatic endeavors should not diminish the fact that Norstad was, during his tenure as SACEUR, the pre-eminent spokesman for the Alliance. After Paul-Henri Spaak's departure as NATO Secretary-General, Norstad shared the diplomatic spotlight with only the irascible and enigmatic de Gaulle after he returned to power in 1958 because they both raised difficult questions concerning East–West and trans-Atlantic political-military relationships. Probably more irritating to the US was that they were also offering, each in his own way and from differing perspectives, often unsolicited solutions. Norstad's so-called "Norstad Plans" were not intended as final solutions to the intensely political problem of the command and control of nuclear weapons stationed in Europe; instead the plans were attempts to influence a necessary, if at times disconcerting, intra-Allied dialogue over by whom – and how – the decision to use NATO's nuclear weapons would be made.

For this reason Norstad was not reluctant to engage in a diplomatic *démarche* if to do so would advance his conception that NATO as a collective body should play a role not unlike that of a Great Power. In other words, NATO's political-military institutions should acquire more discretionary authority to engage in war/peace *decision-making* – as distinct from the *war-planning* functions already allocated to SHAPE and later LIVE OAK.

Norstad also had clear views on the art of negotiation. For reasons of both substance and tactics Norstad would, in the first instance, put forward proposals that fell within the framework of existing positions. He was leery of staging dramatic diplomatic "breakthroughs" that might raise unrealistic expectations. Norstad preferred that a foundation be laid that would provide for him maximum negotiating leverage in the early stages of the negotiations and from which incremental, implementable results could be achieved. But he was also willing to improve or refine his proposals in the cause of simplicity and of clarity in order to enhance their public impact. He was keenly aware that East– West negotiations were as much a function of propaganda as they were of threat-reduction and risk-avoidance.

Consequently, his diplomacy combined elements of the appearance of power with the substance of power. Put another way, as SACEUR he maximized to the greatest extent that he could a fundamentally weak power base, dependent as he was on the support of the North Atlantic Council and in particular, of the US government. In the end he overreached his actual power. In this respect, the attractively persuasive and public relations conscious SACEUR and the grandiose President of the Third Republic utilized similar diplomatic strategies but de Gaulle was a Head of State, which made a vast difference. Secretary-General Dirk Stikker provided a good illustration of this:

> There are, first of all, what are now called the Norstad proposals. These proposals were for the first time discussed at my house in Menaggio between Adenauer, Norstad, Spaak and myself. The main reason for these proposals was of a political nature. De Gaulle had just made his speech in Grenoble, where he stated that those countries which had no atomic weapons could only be considered as satellites. This statement had angered Adenauer in the extreme. But he was not only angry; he feared even more that the growing nationalism in France would have similar repercussions in Germany, and he could not believe that after his death there would be a successor strong enough to oppose the creation in Germany of a national atomic force. According to Adenauer, the chance to prevent the resurrection of a national German army was once missed when France turned down the European Defence Community, and if now the possibility of creating a multilateral European nuclear weapons system were not accepted, nobody would be able to prevent Germany in the future from creating such a system for itself. And Germany could do that better and sooner than France![15]

Norstad forgot that he was, in the final analysis, only an agent of the governments – and especially of his own. When his sponsor Eisenhower left office, Norstad's independent access to the White House was gone. Literally for the first time in his career he was bereft of powerful political-military patronage. Not only was McNamara determined to bring the Pentagon's military bureaucracy to heel, he was also determined to have an American general officer in NATO who would not forget that the ultimate basis of his power, and also perhaps of his authority, was his appointment as USCINCEUR as well as SACEUR. Without that national political underpinning SACEUR's role in NATO would lose its *raison d'être*, which is why any suggestion that a non-American should be SACEUR has fallen flat – neither the US nor the European Allies, including France, have truly wanted the US to disengage militarily from Europe. The best insurance against this is retaining an American as SACEUR who also is USCINCEUR.[16]

First and foremost, SACEUR is a military commander, the head of an international military bureaucracy whose purpose during the Cold War was to plan for contingencies in the hope that the plans would never be executed. Norstad was a planner *par excellence*. He had made his mark as a planner before coming to NATO; that track of his career had provided the substance which enabled him to attempt, through his various "Plans" and his LIVE OAK perambulations during his Berlin crisis years, to transcend personally the very planning system that he had helped construct in NATO. Along with this function, and deriving from it, was SACEUR's diplomatic role and responsibility to keep the Allies militarily united against a common enemy rather than divided among themselves.

As a study group once observed, in elaborating on the point that personalities make an important difference:

> how individuals viewed nuclear weapons and what their specific responsibilities were had an impact on the policies they espoused. Eisenhower, as a military man, had major reservations about the role of nuclear weapons as a military instrument. Even so, he was clearly determined to use them if the USSR forced a major war in Europe. Further, he preferred to very strongly capitalize on their deterrent effects, and as a former SACEUR he could see their importance as a means of assuring the NATO allies that their security was being protected by the United States. Kennedy's views were less clear ... .[17]

Norstad carried Eisenhower's conception as far as it was possible when he was SACEUR. His effort contributed to what for him was an unsatisfactory end to his military career. Every SACEUR has the dilemma of being both an "American" commander and a "European" leader. According to the outlook of the respective American Chief Executive of the time, the SACEUR has to achieve a proper balancing of these two roles that enables him to be an effective voice in Washington for NATO as a whole, while at the same time to be an effective voice in NATO for Washington. The transition of Chief Executives from Eisenhower to Kennedy altered this balance from a more European-orientation to a more nationalistic American-orientation. Norstad either could not, or would not, adjust his role accordingly. Perhaps this dilemma is inherent in the position of SACEUR which even the most politically-sensitive incumbent cannot avoid.

Nonetheless, there was no other military leader of his generation who had more success in transcending, in the general public's perception as well as in the perceptions of the various governments engaged in the East–West struggle, both his own Service and his national command responsibility. One would have to look back to General MacArthur to find a parallel.[18] In both cases, their downfalls had as much to do with their inclination to argue with their own government – often in public – rather than to display a more solicitous attitude toward their "political masters." It was therefore not too surprising, as a reaction, that Norstad was succeeded by Lemnitzer, whom Kennedy considered the prototypical military bureaucrat (in the best sense of the term) as well as being reliably "American" rather than "European." To put it bluntly, "Lem" could be relied upon to "know his place" in the national scheme of things. Also, his personal loyalty to the Kennedy Administration was not in question.

In Army circles, the only general officer who came close to Norstad in both career profile and in personal charisma was Maxwell Taylor, who also was comfortable as an "outsider". Although having been a hero in World War II, he was also known as a man of personal appeal who was almost too handsome for the battlefield. Taylor could write and articulate policy, and did so fearlessly, to the annoyance of the Eisenhower Administration. It is worth recalling that in July 1962 Kennedy sounded out Taylor as to whether he would be interested in succeeding Norstad as SACEUR. As it was put: "The president thought it was the perfect assignment and hoped that Taylor's experience as a commander on the Continent and his recommendations on NATO would dampen the growing divisions among America's European allies."[19] Although he had grown frustrated serving as the President's Military Advisor, Taylor demurred; nonetheless, shortly thereafter

Kennedy named him Chairman of the JCS and later as Ambassador to South Vietnam.

Another famous general who was sometimes compared to Norstad was James Gavin, who was at the time of Norstad's retirement the American Ambassador to France and considered pro-de Gaulle. Like Taylor, Gavin had made his reputation in World War II as an airborne unit commander, and also could express himself well in writing as well as in speech. He had that same "glamour" appeal that Norstad and Taylor possessed. Seeing them possibly as rivals, Norstad observed: "Gavin was an appointee of Kennedy's and was pretty much a fair-haired boy ... Kennedy was enamored of two officers – Max Taylor and Jimmy Gavin – because during his [electoral] campaign, it was useful from his standpoint to criticize Eisenhower."[20] It is not unlikely that if a Republican had been in the White House at the time of Norstad's retirement, he might also have received an ambassadorship.

In sum, Lauris Norstad was indeed a special man for his times. He never forgot the adage about allies (or colleagues) that hanging together against a common enemy was preferable to hanging separately. He should be ranked as one of the great commanders produced by the United States Air Force during one of the most – if not *the* most – potentially self-destructive period in twentieth century history. During this period, to him must go the credit that "it is an extraordinary fact that the politics of the alliance never really became a politics of mutual resentment."[21]

Appendix: A New Career as Corporate Executive

As Norstad approached the end of his military career, he was still a young man. He had made many important contacts both at home and abroad, and was therefore in a strong position to embark on a promising second career. But, as he said: "I ruled out exploiting my military connections, and I am going completely away from the armaments business."[1] In fact, he was attracted, but not seriously, toward a university appointment, which is why Professor Norman Gibbs, the Chichele Professor of the History of War at All Souls College, Oxford, offered to arrange for him a visiting appointment at All Souls.[2] He found himself more attracted to a career as a corporate executive. His criteria were: "I wanted to work with some company that had no significant business with the Government. I wanted to work with a big company because I had always worked with big organizations. I wanted to work with a company where I could feel that I could learn enough about it to be a factor in it, to be an influence."[3]

The former US Ambassador to France, Amory Houghton, head of the Corning Glass Works, wrote to him in August 1962: "Your resignation saddens me as I realize so clearly what a gap in the NATO picture your departure will mean ... . I cannot let this moment go by without telling you how greatly I admire the job you have done. Perhaps having seen you at work first hand I can to an unusual degree appreciate the intelligence, vigor, skill and patience that were a part of your leadership as Supreme Commander. You should get great satisfaction out of your performance."[4] Norstad replied that he did not "at the moment" have any firms plans for the future, which might have sent a signal to Houghton to so inform Harold Boeschenstein, the head of the Owens-Corning Fiberglas Corporation (OCF). Boeschenstein recounted how Norstad was recruited: "Everybody was bidding for Norstad before he retired. But I flew over to Europe for a weekend and he agreed to come even though we never even talked salary until later."[5]

Norstad joined OCF on January 17, 1963 when he was named President of OCF International and at the same time was elected to the Board of Directors of the parent company. *Time Magazine* reported on January 25: "Nattily turned out in a grey civilian suit complete with vest, former NATO Supreme Commander Lauris Norstad, 55, showed up in Manhattan to take on a new post: president of the international division of Owens-Corning Fiberglas Corp."[6] An interesting aspect of the new post was that OCF International was planning at that time to open a branch office and distribution operation in Belgium as a forerunner to establishing a wholly-owned subsidiary with manufacturing facilities in Western Europe.[7] Probably not coincidentally, one of Norstad's first appointments was to name Roger van den Perre as his Vice President. Van den Perre, a French citizen, had been with the French Petroleum Company as its US representative since 1945. He undoubtedly would be effective in the Western European activities of the company.[8]

On December 19, 1963, only eleven months later, Norstad was elected President of the parent company, succeeding Harold Boeschenstein who had been President since OCF was organized.[9] The Norstads then moved to a large apartment in Toledo, where they participated in the civic life of the community and continued, of course, to play golf regularly. Boeschenstein was elected Chairman of the Board, and continued as Chief Executive Officer, with Norstad as Chief Operating Officer.[10]

Norstad was to perform a very important role in transitioning the company from the corporate culture of the 1930s and 1940s to a culture that was more attuned to the rapidly-changing manufacturing and marketing conditions of the 1960s. He had to do it under some delicate "executive suite" circumstances. As it was put: "Harold Boeschenstein has not so much stepped aside as he has *moved over* to make room for Norstad; for though he is 67, Boeschenstein shows no sign of retiring to the golf course."[11]

Norstad not only established cordial relations with the father but also with Boeschenstein's son, William, who was at that time Vice President-Marketing. As a military man accustomed to undergoing frequent changes of command, he understood that here was a situation over which he had little control. In the event, Norstad and William became allies. With Norstad's support, William changed OCF's marketing focus from one oriented to product lines, to an orientation along marketing lines. This was accomplished by concentrating on particular markets and specializing in their needs and characteristics. For example, to meet the needs of the automotive market, William recruited sales people with an automobile background so that they could approach people in the automobile industry with the facts, figures, and experiences that would be of particular meaning to that industry. He noted that this marketing strategy was particularly important to a company that had a broad product line in which it must pioneer to have its products accepted.[12]

One way that Norstad contributed to management improvement was to change the system under which the divisions made their sales and cost projections. "In the army," Norstad observed, "a general maintains control or leverage by the way he uses his reserves. This new projection system allows us to hold more of the available dollars in reserves to exploit opportunities or to shore up danger spots." The system forced the division managers to make two sets of projections, one based on what they were sure that they were going to do in the way of business and the other reflecting what they hoped to get. "You'd be amazed how a relatively crude system like this disciplines our men to weed out the sheer guesses."[13] Norstad also worked to improve both the quantity and quality of the information upon which the top management based their decisions. In February 1966, for example, he established the position of operations analysis manager, who was responsible for the development and the administration of corporate operating plans for major profit improvement programs.[14]

On October 19, 1967 OCF experienced a major transitional shift as Harold Boeschenstein retired as Chairman and Chief Executive Officer, although he continued as Chairman of the Board's Executive Committee. Norstad moved up to Chairman of the Board and Chief Executive Officer. These two experienced executives – although a generation apart not only in age but also in professional managerial outlook – continued to work together effectively even if at times uneasily. When the new 28 story Fiberglas Tower, built on the river front in downtown Toledo, was completed in 1968, they both signed their names on the gold-painted top-of-the-tower steel beam in the ceremony that marked its completion.[15]

Norstad organized three groups, each with vice presidents. There was the Textile and Industrial Group, headed by Fowler Blauvelt, with responsibility for the production and marketing of fiber glass materials for industrial markets; the Construction Group, headed by Charles E. Peck; and the International Group, headed by Richard Muzzy.[16] In moves toward further consolidation, Norstad created two new positions, those of Corporate Economist and Corporate Security Director. The Corporate Economist would analyze business conditions and economic factors influencing the company's organization, operations, and development. Undoubtedly, this position had a direct relationship to the increasing emphasis on corporate planning – planning being, of course, Norstad's forte.[17]

Norstad also took a strong personal interest in the Owens-Corning Technical Center, located in Granville, Ohio. He frequently visited the Granville operation and established ties with the local college, Dennison University. Norstad inaugurated the first of several public lectures at Dennison under the sponsorship of OCF, which brought distinguished friends of Norstad to the mid-west campus.[18] In 1968–69, the Owens-Corning Lecturers were former Secretary of State Dean Rusk, and Senator J. William Fulbright who at the time was Chairman of the Senate Foreign Relations Committee. Other lecturers that Norstad obtained were Helmut Schmidt, George Kennan, and Dean Acheson.[19]

Everything was not positive during Norstad's time as CEO. For example, in the fall of 1970, he had to report a drop in sales and net earnings. He explained: "Our sales have been adversely affected by the general softness that has characterized the national economy this year. Sales weakness, spread across many areas of consumer interest, has limited our growth in 1970, while the costs of essential goods and services have materially increased."[20] Strikes in the automobile industry were an important contributing factor, because this resulted in reduced sales in textiles.

In August 1971 Harold Boeschenstein retired from the board and his son William was elevated from Executive Vice President to President and Chief Operating Officer of OCF.[21] It was said at the time: "Few corporate executives in [Harold Boeschenstein's] time plunged more deeply or with more energy and dynamism into doing their job well – spectacularly well in his case – than did Mr. Boeschenstein .... As Mr. Boeschenstein ends a 50-year career in the glass industry, the presidency – and the challenge of leading this corporation in the years ahead – falls to his son, William, of whom he once said that he had demanded more in the way of performance than of anyone else in the company."[22]

Only a year later, in August 1972, Norstad announced that he would retire on January 1, 1973. He remained a member of the Board of Directors, with William Boeschenstein becoming Chief Executive Officer while the Chairmanship of the Board, held by Norstad, was left unfilled.[23] His contribution to OCF was aptly put:

> At Owens-Corning, he has headed a company that was "making a transition from being a small large company to a large company. " ... He says he wasn't hired to be a governmental diplomat for Owens-Corning. "And I haven't

been," he commented. "It was very clear from the beginning that I was not going to be a representative to the United States Government ... . We do very little business for the government. I'm terribly sensitive about taking advantage of my government associations."

Part of his philosophy of business is that "you have to be very intolerant of low standards." "I hope I've influenced these young people to live up to their own highest standards," he added. "All my life I've been afraid of what mediocrity can do to a good organization. Somebody caught me young and taught me never to be satisfied."[24]

Norstad's contribution to OCF quite clearly derived from his military career. He felt that both business and military organizations should practice delegation, pushing authority and responsibility to the lowest practicable level. To do this, Norstad realigned OCF's management, making the corporate Groups that he created virtually autonomous.[25] He told this story on himself: "Another somewhat militaristic feature was added [during Norstad's tenure] – a formal planning system. Shortly after the initiating of the planning procedure, the general recalls, 'three young men appeared in my office and wanted to know what I did. I thought this was damned impertinent at the outset.' However, the planning system grew out of his directive. Rules were rules. So he went along."[26] Norstad's final observation was: "We're getting confident in our predictions," he said. "We know where we're going."[27]

When asked what he considered to be his most important personal contribution to the direction of OCF, Norstad replied: "I would like to think my most important contribution has been to create a context where more of our people could really operate up to their full capacity. Generally, that was done by establishing a new direction; by organizing to accomplish objectives. We established a planning system which gave us direction, and then we used it to monitor our progress. We altered the organization to delegate authority down and then helped lower levels of management to do their job."[28]

Afterword: Some Thoughts on NATO's Future Leadership Challenges

Beyond the cold war

The Cold War is now long since over and, with it, the nuclear doctrines and most of the deployments that were central to its conduct. Even though deterrence as a concept persists and could still be implemented – deterrence remains "existential" so long as the weapons exist – the nuclear issue has long since faded, both in US policy and in that of the Alliance. Yet even with the passing of the Cold War and the threats that produced nuclear doctrines and deployments, NATO has endured. To be sure, it is a very different NATO in many respects; indeed, during the past several years, the Alliance has gone through a fundamental adaptation and transformation almost equal in scope and extent to the work at the time of its creation. But in other ways, the Alliance has remained the same. And it is in both these differences and similarities that can be seen the primary characteristics of the role of SACEUR as it has evolved well into the post-Cold War period.

What is the same

First, the similarities. Security in Europe during the Cold War period was not just about deterring Soviet and Warsaw Pact aggression and preparing to implement a strategy to counter that aggression, should it occur (primarily through so-called "intra-conflict deterrence," the continuing threat that a conventional attack from the East would be met, at some point, by initiation of the use of nuclear weapons). It was also about the pursuit of humane values that were peculiar to the West indeed, it can be argued that, without the value-base to the realpolitik of the NATO Alliance, it could never have been sustained through the lulls as well as the crises that recurred at intervals for about four decades. Of course, pursuit of these humane values continues today, and is one reason that NATO is embarked on policies that have taken it beyond the old geographic limits imposed by the Iron Curtain and into Central Europe, where it seeks to help give the peoples of that region the chance to take part in Western society. It might even be argued that the final proof of the validity of the West's goals in the Cold War – and hence the *raison d'être* of NATO through all those years – is to be found in continued efforts to complete the work of integrating societies that were cut off for so long. In brief, the task today is to carry the principles of the Marshall Plan past the limits imposed by Joseph Stalin in 1947–48.

At one level, therefore, NATO's continued existence is about the pursuit of values and the construction of a security system critically informed by those values; but it is also about the effort to create stability, confidence, and predictability in the center of Europe – Mackinder's European Heartland; in effect, to take these countries, newly reborn to history, out of the history of contest for dominance or spheres of influence. Thus the Alliance launched both Partnership for Peace and the process of taking in new members (enlargement); and both help to provide the Alliance with a compelling rationale for the future. For the same underlying reasons, NATO has also taken responsibility for preserving the peace in Bosnia, site of the one great conflict in Europe since 1945.

The inertia of institutions

At the same time, NATO has continued to exist – indeed, to thrive – into the post-Cold War period precisely because of the strength of its institutional development. At the most simple, economic level, decades of military cooperation have so intertwined the forces, planning, practices, and operations of Western establishments in Europe that the "entry price" of going it alone has become, in practice, prohibitive. An ally would need to have a most compelling political reason to detach itself from the bureaucratic structures at Brussels and in the various military commands, and it would pay a substantial price in the process. Indeed, both Spain and France, allies outside the integrated structure, have been moving toward it since the end of the Cold War, with Spain fully joining Allied Command Europe.

The role of the military commands is part of the institutional inertia that continues to bind the allies together. Among the commands, Allied Command Atlantic (ACLANT) in Norfolk, Virginia, and the Supreme Allied Commander, Atlantic (SACLANT) – like SACEUR, always an American four-star officer – have long played an essential part. But this is a lesser part than is true of SHAPE and SACEUR, since ACLANT is located an ocean away from Europe; it engages only a few of the allies, it is overwhelmingly dominated in all aspects by the United States, and it is primarily engaged at sea – with the essence of navies being that they can sail in and then sail out again: not the stuff to demonstrate commitment. By contrast, SHAPE and SACEUR are very much part of the European military and political scene situated on the Continent, with visible subordinate commands, and the Supreme Commander's regular, almost daily presence at NATO headquarters or in allied capitals that his counterpart in Norfolk could not hope to rival.

American commitment and leadership

Another key factor is also very much the same in the post-Cold War NATO and impacts on the role and importance of SACEUR: the continued, critical importance to the Alliance of the US military presence in Europe and American leadership of NATO. Neither was foreordained. Indeed, after 1989, there were efforts on both sides of the Atlantic to reduce the role played by the United

States in European security. This included some arguments in America that NATO could even be dissolved and that institutions like the Conference on Security and Cooperation in Europe (CSCE; now the OSCE) would be sufficient to meet residual security tasks in Europe. And this included efforts in Europe, especially led by France, to reduce the American military, strategic – and hence political – role on the Continent through the enhancement of European institutions, especially the European Union's Common Foreign and Security Policy (CFSP), the development of a European Security and Defence Identity (ESDI), and the lodging of this ESDI primarily in the Western European Union (WEU).

But US role in European security – and hence in NATO, America's chosen instrument for projecting military power and influence to the Continent – has remained central. Of course, US interests in a free, stable, and prosperous Europe remain; but at least for the moment, challenges to that order are few and far between. Even more important, it became apparent in the early years of the 1990's that the European Allies were still not ready to undertake major security efforts on their own. What happened in Bosnia was a dramatic illustration of this point. It is not necessary to review all the details – including the fact that 9 NATO Allies were involved in UNPROFOR (United Nations Protection Force) while the United States stood aloof from engagement on the ground – to recognize that the Bosnia war only came to an end when the US view of NATO strategy there prevailed and when the United States took effective control of the diplomacy. Similarly, virtually all the ideas and leadership of NATO's transformation in the 1990s have been "Made in America". Nor is this out of place; after all, the enlargement of NATO is first and foremost about the security guarantees that the United States is prepared to make to new members; and, in strictly geo-political terms, it is widely recognized that the nurturing of Russia's future cannot be safely achieved without a central role for the United States.

Thus there is again a need to demonstrate the staying power of the US commitment to European security. It is less in degree, of course, than in the days when US strategic engagement was seen to be so vital to preserving the independence of Western Europe from the Soviet and Warsaw Pact threaten "crisis" looms in which US security could be seen to be "decoupled" from that of its allies. But patterns of expectations about the demonstration of American commitment are nonetheless real and compelling, however attenuated in terms of the immediacy of risk. These expectations take many forms, including the continuation of a substantial US force presence on the Continent – now in the vicinity of 100 000, a far cry from the 326 000 American troops that garrisoned Europe during the last several years of the Cold War. The US president is still expected by the European allies to pay frequent visits, and while on the Continent to stress the enduring nature of transatlantic ties. And the United States is still expected to provide the Supreme Allied Commander, Europe.

SACEUR as American

On this last point, there continues to be a clear Allied consensus, even though, in 1996, France did consider for a time the proposition that there should be a supreme-supreme commander – a US officer on top of all NATO commanders, with SACLANT and SACEUR as subordinates and both Europeans. This proposition gained no support within the Alliance, however. Indeed, France has joined all the other Allies in underscoring the importance that an American commander be a visible demonstration of US commitment to the Alliance, even while Paris has sought to reduce the relative predominance of the United States in the overall NATO command structure and, in fact, the weight of US political influence in Western security strategy. Thus in his December 1995 decision to move France toward reintegration in NATO's military structure, President Jacques Chirac accepted a continued role for SACEUR and, in pursuing the European Security and Defense Identity within NATO as opposed to outside the Alliance, the French have accepted SACEUR's role in all Allied military operations.

By the same token, there is no opposition to the concept that SACLANT should remain an American; indeed, on reflection, continuing this tradition should be virtually as important as retaining an American SACEUR, since the Alliance's Atlantic Command is integrated with the US Atlantic Command – the "force provider" for Europe and the most extensive military command in the West, at well over a million men and women. In a world no longer dominated by nuclear weapons, the capacity to "provide" such conventional forces to the European theater has an important political as well as strategic quality.

Differences in the post-Cold War era

With all of these similarities in the qualities of NATO and the critical role of SACEUR as a significant emblem of the US military commitment to European security, the end of the Cold War has brought with it a number of critical differences. Most obviously, US forces – and SACEUR – no longer connect the fate of Europe to the fate of the United States in any immediate sense. For its part, for the first time since before Pearl Harbor, the United States has no natural enemies, potentially posing a lethal threat to the American homeland. To be sure, the weapons of utter devastation still exist (Russian, Chinese), but there is no encompassing political and strategic conflict within which these weapons have significance as palpable threats. Meanwhile, for their part, the European allies no longer fear an attack westward from the Soviet Union that could bring into play the US nuclear commitment, as the culmination of a series of escalatory steps that would perforce center on conventional forces under SACEUR's command – to say nothing of the instrumental role that he would play in the transition to the use of nuclear weapons in the European theater. Thus SACEUR's role as strategic connector to the United States has been radically diminished, even if a significant measure of his politically symbolic role continues to be important.

The impact of Bosnia

With NATO-led operations in Bosnia, however – first the Implementation Force (IFOR) and then the Stabilization Force (SFOR) – SACEUR has taken on a wide range of tasks that were never contemplated during the Cold War, dominated as it was by concern about so-called Article V responsibilities. In Bosnia and Kosovo by contrast, the Alliance has been acting "out of area" – beyond the territory defined by Article VI of the Treaty of Washington as subject to the common defense. SACEUR's role is thus not to focus on a single threat (however many branches it might have had) – namely, to deter (or defeat) aggression from the Soviet Union and Warsaw Pact – but rather to lead a coalition force in day-to-day operations of great complexity and without even a hint that there might have to be a recourse to nuclear weapons. The "C" in SACEUR, in effect has finally come into its own.

This role was not foreordained, however. During the debates on NATO's role in Bosnia, it was not clear that a "non-Article V" operation would require the full panoply of NATO's military structure; nor was there immediate consensus that SACEUR should be included in a command chain for military actions that were not specifically envisioned in the Treaty or in Cold War practice. The latter point was more about politics than performance, however – including the (then) concerns of France about the role of the integrated structure in NATO military actions that did not impact on Article V. Good sense prevailed, however, and the command chain for SFOR passed from the North Atlantic Council to the military Committee to SACEUR, and thence to the theater commander, COMSFOR – as it happens, also an American four-star officer. With preparations for NATO operations in Kosovo in 1999, the issue of SACEUR's critical role in the command chain was not even raised.

SACEUR as operational commander

This arrangement produced at least four major differences from those regarding SACEUR's role during the Cold War. In the first place, with the deployment of IFOR he had to assume the functions of an operational commander, not just on paper – for NATO did not fire a shot in anger during the preceding 46 years – but on a day-to-day basis. This was not an abstraction, but reality, subject to trial and error, experiment and correction. As it happened, the NATO-led military operation in Bosnia was able to be effective in part precisely because there had been more than four decades of preparation for a war that never came; but the application of the lessons learned from the Cold War, and also from the Persian Gulf War of 1990–91 that was "non-NATO" but vitally supported by the Alliance, substantially informed what NATO was able to do in the radically different circumstances of the Balkans. So, too, SACEUR adapted to the new circumstances as an operational commander, as he also had to do for Kosovo operations.

Diminished specialness of US power

By the same token, the absence of either an Article V or a nuclear component to Bosnia operations – except in the remotest contingency – meant that SACEUR performed no special role in connecting US power and commitment to NATO's engagement. To be sure, there was a substantial American force presence on the ground, as part of an Allied-wide requirement that the risks of potential combat be fairly shared by Allies on both sides of the Atlantic, but the demonstration of US fealty was made by the troops themselves, or, in the Kosovo air campaign, by the preponderance of US aircraft, not by their commander.

Reassurance for all the allies

At the same time, the role played by SACEUR in commanding IFOR/SFOR has been important to reassure Allied leaders across the board – both Europeans and Americans – that the rules of engagement were adequate to provide the forces with the maximum degree of protection, and that the forces were being employed in ways that would expose them to minimal risk in a mission that was about peacekeeping, not active combat. Likewise, in Kosovo air operations, a similar rule applies. Thus,unlike the Cold War period, SACEUR's reassurance function was directed equally to all the Allies – indeed, perhaps more to the United States than to the Europeans, because in Bosnia the US was most reluctant to become engaged on the ground in the first place or, in Kosovo, to take casualties.

SACEUR and civilian leadership

Finally and perhaps most significantly, NATO's Bosnia and Kosovo operations have betokened a dramatically revised relationship between SACEUR and his political masters at NATO headquarters. During the Cold War, he nominally took his instructions from the North Atlantic Council, passed through the Military Committee. But there was little doubt that, in the terms that would matter most, the potential use of nuclear weapons, SACEUR functioned as an arm of American strategic power and authority. Despite the polite fiction that some nuclear weapons belonging to the United States and the United Kingdom were at NATO's disposal, release authority for these weapons was always jealously guarded by the national capitals. So, too, during the Cold War the Alliance's formal political leadership, embodied in the North Atlantic Council, set the outlines of the employment of force if the Alliance were attacked. There were many plans to cover many contingencies. But even though not all contingencies could possibly be covered, and even though political decisions to use force remained in civilian hands, it was generally assumed that, in practice, once a major conflict in Europe began, the focus of decision would pass effectively from the North Atlantic Council to the military commanders – in the European theater, primarily SACEUR. Radical steps up the so-called escalation ladder would call for further civilian intervention and decision, but as likely as not, these would be focused in Washington and in conversations between capitals rather than in Brussels, at least regarding the use of nuclear weapons.

There was good reason for assuming that, once hostilities began in earnest, SACEUR would play the predominant role in what would than transpire. The pace of combat would most likely be so intense that there could be little practical opportunity for the North Atlantic Council to exercise effective control over military operations. Indeed, an element of deterrence during the Cold War was the demonstration that authority to act rapidly had been delegated, so that a potential aggressor could not count on his victim's delay in responding as an incentive to initiate hostilities. Obviously, this need no longer obtains, and the strings by which civilian authorities control the military are again held tightly, in the classic manner.

The examples of Bosnia and Kosovo

All the practices of the Cold War changed when that era passed, certainly regarding circumstances such as those in Bosnia and, later, in Kosovo. Political guidance for military commanders is not just something to be determined in advance, written down and ratified, and then essentially dispensed with as allied forces, under SACEUR's command, went about the business of prospecting high-intensity combat. Quite the contrary, from the outset, the NATO allies approached their engagement both in the Bosnia crisis and then in the Kosovo war air operations, with the most cautious concern to retain political control over all allied military activities. In the early days in Bosnia, when NATO was only providing sea and air support for UNPROFOR, the North Atlantic Council went to great lengths to inhibit independent action by NATO commanders.

This led not just to fine-tuning of rules of engagement and targeting, but also to the requirement that the commanders – SACEUR – return to the Council for further guidance and authority to act past certain well-defined points. These limitations, coupled with those imposed by the United Nations for those operations that were jointly controlled ("dual key") at times produced the absurd spectacle that NATO forces were ineffectual in meeting any challenge.

This experience helped shape the terms in which the mandates for IFOR and then SFOR were crafted. The "dual key" was dispensed with and robust rules of engagement were adopted that would enable the NATO-led force to protect itself, without the need for SACEUR to return to the North Atlantic Council for further authority. But the range of IFOR/SFOR actions was well circumscribed, essentially to the military aspects of implementing the Dayton Peace Accords (Annex 1-A). And there was constant concern to avoid so-called mission creep, the assumption by IFOR/SFOR of additional duties that could create increased risk to the force. Nor was this just a requirement imposed by civilian authority, given that the objective was peacekeeping and not securing of objectives held vital by allies, NATO's military leadership was at least as concerned as the civilians to avoid taking responsibilities that could lead to increased risks to the forces on the ground. SACEUR could not, in fact, be just a strategic commander, but had also to relate to the forces in the field to an extent hardly contemplated in the Cold War – to be a "soldier's soldier." Thus the North Atlantic Council was clearly in charge, but it was imposing its discipline on a SACEUR and subordinate commanders who were of a like mind in terms of caution.

Looking for reassurance

At the same time, during the Bosnia operations, SACEUR went even further to ensure that he was not proceeding beyond the limits desired by NATO's political authorities. During the UNPROFOR period, the 16 allies regularly took decisions regarding air strikes in support of UN Safe Areas, but with major doubts in some allied capitals about whether these operations should actually be conducted. These doubts were often reflected in orders given to U.N. commanders, at variance with decisions taken in the North Atlantic Council. Against this background of ambiguity and ambivalence, SACEUR regularly sought reassurance that the orders he was given actually reflected the will of the Council; at times, he discovered that it did not, and he responded accordingly. Similarly, in Kosovo, the allies were concerned to have this regular relationship with SACEUR, even though there was no problem such as had been posed with the UN command in Bosnia.

The North Atlantic Council ascendant

As a general proposition, the Bosnia and Kosovo experiences indicate that, in the absence of Article V threats to members of the Alliance, the new relationship between SACEUR and NATO's civilian leadership is likely to be the standard. He is an American general, carefully selected to be responsive to US views of the future of the Atlantic Alliance; but he is also very much a creature of the North Atlantic Council – of all the allies – with some need to take his distance from the United States in fulfilling his mandate.

SACEUR will also need to be responsive, on a regular and continuing basis, to the guidance of the Council and of individual allied capitals. Regarding the latter, however, post-Cold War SACEURs have not had the same effect in pursuing policies directly with allied capitals that was true in Norstad's day. In major part, this reflects the fact that the Council has become a functioning, deliberative institution to a degree never seen in the Cold War, and for the same reasons that SACEUR's relationship to civilian authority has changed, many of the contemporary issues do require give-and-take, consensus-building and creative outcomes, to an extent rarely seen during the Cold War, save at moments when great issues were at stake, such as the decision to deploy medium-range nuclear missiles in Europe (and diplomacy on this issue had a heavy component of US bilateral contacts with allied capitals). In a word, the North Atlantic Council has come into its own, and this has affected – in effect, diminished – the role of SACEUR as a soldier-diplomat to individual capitals.

US leadership from military to civilian channels

By the same token, in the early 1990s the role of representing the United States at NATO – both substantively and symbolically – largely passed from SACEUR to the US representative on the Council, whether at the ambassadorial,

236 Afterword

ministerial or head of state level. Indeed, all the initiatives and debates on NATO's transformation during the 1990s have centered on the US Mission to NATO in Brussels; there has been nothing comparable to the role General Norstad played regarding nuclear policy. Nor, given the greater "allied" as opposed to "American" role played by SACEUR in the post-Cold War, post-nuclear era, would this have been appropriate, in terms of the advancing of American policy within the Alliance. Only with Kosovo, with its rapidly-changing military situation, has SACEUR again come to play the leading US role at NATO in Brussels.

Symbolizing American power to the partners

Even with this shift in SACEUR's special role in dealing with allied capitals, such contacts have assumed great importance in the capitals of the Partners for Peace, where the weight of the American strategic commitment to European security is still very much in play and very much desired for classic reasons of national independence, integrity, and engagement in the West. This is a logical extension of the major training responsibilities that SACEUR – and SHAPE – have assumed in regard to the Partnership for Peace. While technically, the Partnership Coordination Cell (PCC) that is the locus of this relationship was, from the outset, "outside the (SHAPE) fence" and is just "at Mons", in reality it has always been very much connected to SHAPE and has relied upon the Allied headquarters for most of its resources. Also, the PCC has a director who is subordinate to the North Atlantic Council. But in debate about the PCC's creation, a role was reserved for SACEUR, and his proximity and command of resources has ensured him a major place in determining the direction and course of the PCC's work.

SACEUR and the Secretary-General

Some of SACEUR'S new, day-to-day relationship with civilian authorities in Brussels is directly with the Secretary-General, however, as opposed to the Council. This has been a practical requirement imposed by NATO's operations in Bosnia and Kosovo. The Council provides the guidance and refines it as need be – relying heavily on the Military Committee, which also has come into its own in the post-nuclear era and provides the Council with an extra source of military advice and commentary on commanders' views. But SACEUR often finds it prudent to gain a second opinion regarding the application of the Council's guidance, or to seek counsel about the limits of his mandate or the wisdom of a particular course of action in any situation because of the complexity of IFOR/SFOR or Kosovo operations as no set of principles or rules of engagement can cover all situations. Whether the Secretary-General chooses simply to act as a conduit for SACEUR, in his turn seeking the advice and consent of the full Council, or to provide interpretations of existing guidance, is a matter of judgement, both about the substance and about the relationship which the Secretary-General develops with the members of the Council, whom he serves.

Hands-on political skills

In one further area, the post-Cold War SACEUR needs special political skills in the conduct of operations. Bosnia – and Kosovo also – may prove to be an exception but so far it has been instructive. The Dayton Accords defined the mandate for the NATO-led IFOR/SFOR, and the North Atlantic Council has provided the guidance and the rules of engagement. But the peacemaking effort in Bosnia is only partly about military matters, and COMSFOR is only one authority in the country. The High Representative of the Peace Implementation Conference (PIC) – Carl Bildt and then Carlos Westendorp – has widespread authority for implementing other aspects of Dayton; the local parties have major responsibilities; and perhaps more non-governmental organizations (NGOs) have been involved there than in any other international crisis. NATO's local commanders must deal with all of these entities on a regular, daily basis; and, from time-to-time, the same is true of SACEUR. Within his NATO mandate, therefore, he has a diplomat's role in the implementation of provisions of the Dayton Accords, in relating IFOR/ SFOR to other institutions, and in dealing with political leadership of Bosnia and the neighboring countries.

ESDI and SHAPE

In a final area, the role of SACEUR – or at least of SHAPE – in the post-Cold War era has changed. The United States and France each took decisions in the mid-1990s that have led to a new relationship between NATO and the Western European Union, enabling the latter, for the first time, to have a true capacity to take military action, by drawing upon NATO manpower and other assets, according to a principle of "separable but not separate" from the NATO command structure. Thus elements of the NATO command – double-hatted officers, Deputy SACEUR, and various categories of NATO capabilities such as communications, transport, and intelligence – can, under certain circumstances, be made available to the WEU. But these arrangements have been crafted so that they do not diminish SACEUR's authority or the ability of the NATO military structure to function. Key to the relationship with WEU is adherence to the principle of unity of command and a continuing role for SACEUR, so that nothing that is done will interfere with the ability of the NATO military commands and commanders to fulfill their allied responsibilities.

The new NATO

This New NATO within which today's Supreme Allied Commander, Europe operates thus reflects some continuing themes from the past; but these are overlaid with some radically different practices and procedures, relationship and responsibilities, as befits the renewal of an Alliance to meet fundamentally changed circumstances. This could be seen as an environment alien to the likes of, for example, the pre-eminent Cold War-era SACEUR (other than Eisenhower)/

General Lauris Norstad. Yet it is very likely that Norstad would be able to operate effectively in today's times as he did in times past.

Norstad was, at heart, a soldier-statesman who understood the uses of power, was comfortable in his dealing with political leaders, applied himself to contemporary political and strategic problems, and saw that coalition diplomacy meant exactly that NATO could only function if all the Allies, not just the one providing the essential political glue of the Alliance, were prepared to act as one. In these senses, Norstad's qualities are also those that guide today's SACEUR to success in fulfilling his NATO mission.

ROBERT E. HUNTER
US Permanent Representative on the North Atlantic Council,
1993–98; Senior Advisor, RAND Corporation

Notes

Chapter 1

1. Robert L. O'Connell, *Of Arms and Men: A History of War, Weapons, and Aggression* (New York: Oxford University Press, 1989), p. 7.
2. J. Bryan III, "SHAPE and its Shapers," *National Review*, dtd 6/28/58, p. 36.
3. Ltr Norstad–Eisenhower, dtd 1/16/61 (EL, NP).
4. The "handing over" from Eisenhower to Kennedy was notably cool, as illustrated by this remark from Ann C. Whitman, Eisenhower's Personal Secretary to Norstad: "Although your telegram to the President arrived before we were rudely evacuated from the White House, ..." (Ltr, Whitman–Norstad, dtd 1/27/61 [EL, NP]).
5. For a summation of the impact of McNamara on the Pentagon, see Douglas Kinnard, *The Secretary of Defense* (Lexington, KY: The University Press of Kentucky, 1980), ch. 3.
6. Norstad had first met McNamara when McNamara was a Lieut. Colonel in charge of a statistical section for XX Bomber Command when its planes were flying the China "Hump." (See Wesley Frank Craven and James Lea Cate, *The Army Air Forces in World War II: Men and Planes*, Vol. VI [Washington, D.C.: Office of Air Force History, New Imprint, 1983], Vol. V, p. 90.)
7. Lawrence S. Kaplan, "The Berlin Crisis, 1958–1962: Views from the Pentagon," in William W. Epley, ed., *International Cold War Military Records and History* (Washington, D.C.: Office of the Secretary of Defense, 1996), p. 67.
8. Frank Costigliola, "Kennedy, the European Allies, and the Failure to Consult," *Political Science Quarterly*, Spring 1995, p. 108.
9. DDEL, NP, Box 73, McNamara, Robert (1) (GP). Portions of the following pages are drawn with permission from Gregory W. Pedlow, "General Lauris Norstad and the Second Berlin Crisis," paper presented to the Nuclear History Program Author's Conference on the Second Berlin Crisis, Washington, D.C., May 20–21, 1993. The relevant citations are indicated by the initials "GP." Dr. Pedlow is Chief, Historical Office, SHAPE.
10. Ltr Schuckburgh–Macmillan, dtd 4/27/62.
11. DDEL, NP, Box 73, McNamara, Robert (1) (GP).
12. He had his first, and "substantial," heart attack in 1955, which was concealed from public notice. Norstad's appointment as SACEUR had been announced but he had not yet taken command. In spite of Air Force regulations, he remained on active duty. His second heart attack occurred in May, 1960 which kept him from attending the ill-fated and aborted Paris Summit between Eisenhower and Khrushchev. (Norstad, Lauris, *Oral History Interview*, February 13–16 and October 22–25, 1979, USAF Historical Research Center, Maxwell AFB, AL, pp. 347–352.)

240 *Notes*

13. Oral interview of Axel Holm with Mrs. Norstad, dtd 10/16/95. (Holm is compiling an oral history of Mrs. Norstad's life, drafts of which he has shared with the author.) There was a lot of entertaining, both for neighbors and for visitors to the islands. From these early years surrounded by the hospitable, easy-going environment of the islands in the 1920s and 1930s, Isabelle came to enjoy going to, and giving, parties. These were also the days of the afternoon tea dances, and the high school "proms." By the time she came to Paris, she had become a noted hostess who planned and supervised her dinner parties herself.
14. PRO, PREM dtd 11/3695, Extract from Record of a Conversation in the British Embassy, Washington, dtd 4/29/62, at 11:30 a.m. Minute 4 (GP).
15. Quoted in Deborah Shapley, *Promise and Power: The Life and Times of Robert McNamara* (Boston: Little, Brown and Co., 1993), p. 143.
16. Shapley, *Promise*, pp. 143–144.
17. Shapley, *Promise*, p. 145.
18. Norstad, *Oral History*, p. 305.
19. Norstad, *Oral History*, p. 308 [his emphasis].
20. The meeting probably occurred at the time of the NATO ministerial meetings at NATO headquarters in June 19–21, 1962. Norstad had refused to attend the Spring ministerial meeting of the NAC held in Athens in May. For Norstad's version of how matters came to a head, see Norstad, *Oral History*, pp. 306–310.
21. Norstad, *Oral History*, see pp. 309ff.
22. DDEL, NP, Interview with General Lauris Norstad by Dr. Thomas Soapes dtd 11/11/76 for DDEL Library, pp. 50–52 (GP). See also Norstad, *Oral History*, pp. 309–310.
23. This was recounted to Dr. Pedlow (see note 9 above).
24. See Mark Perry, *Four Stars* (Boston: Houghton Mifflin Co., 1989), p. 120.
25. See, for example, *Le Monde*, dtd 7/20/62.
26. Norstad, *Oral History*, pp. 312–313.
27. Shapley, *Promise*, p. 145.
28. Norstad, *Oral History*, p. 310.
29. Norstad wrote his letter dtd 7/18/62, to which Kennedy replied on 7/19/62. See *Congressional Record*, Vol. 108, No. 183, dtd 10/6/62, p. A7367 for reprints of the letters. Obviously, neither party had wasted any time in concluding the formalities, which is one reason that the European press characterized Norstad's resignation as "unexpected."
30. Ltr Kennedy–Norstad, dtd 7/19/62, ibid. Because of the exigencies of the Cuban missile crisis of October 1962, he lingered on until the end of 1962, but his impact on the ongoing crisis over the Western allies' rights of access to Berlin was henceforth quite low. In fact, the crisis itself moved to the political-military "back burner" during the second half of 1962. On October 26, with the Cuban missile crisis still underway, Kennedy decided to extend Norstad as SACEUR until the end of the year. Lemnitzer, who had been named his successor with Taylor succeeding him as chairman of the JCS, started work as USCINCEUR on November 1, as scheduled. So for two months the positions of SACEUR and USCINCEUR were separated, as they had been in Eisenhower's day.
31. *Le Monde* broke the story of Norstad's resignation before Kennedy's regular Monday morning press conference. Kennedy had planned to have the

announcement telecast live to Europe via the Telstar communications satellite. (Warren Rogers, Jr., "Norstad Quits as NATO Chief: Lemnitzer will Succeed Him," *New York Herald-Tribune*, dtd 7/20/62.)
32. In fact, after his retirement, there was some public speculation about a possible candidacy for the Republican nomination in 1964, but nothing came of it. See, for example, Victor Lasky, "A Dark Horse for the GOP?" *Jacksonville, Fla. Journal*, dtd 5/25/63; Victor Lasky, "Norstad's Talk to GOP Group Expected to Stir Speculation," *Fort Worth Star-Telegram*, dtd 5/25/63. Lasky was a syndicated columnist based in New York.
33. For a discussion of the dilemmas of being SACEUR/USCINCEUR, see Robert S. Jordan, ed., *Generals in International Politics: NATO's Supreme Allied Commander, Europe* (Lexington, KY: The University Press of Kentucky, 1987), esp. the Conclusions.
34. For more on this point, see Robert S. Jordan, *Political Leadership in NATO: A Study in Multinational Diplomacy* (Boulder, CO: Westview Press, 1979), Ch. 3.
35. Quoted in Robert S. Jordan, *Generals*, p. 92. The original source is Franz A.M. Alting von Geusau, *Allies in a Turbulent World: Challenges to U.S. and Western European Cooperation* (Lexington, MA: Lexington Books, 1982), p. 163.
36. Ltr Norstad–Isabelle, dtd 10/21/42 (EL, NP).
37. Philip Ziegler, *Mountbatten* (New York: Alfred A. Knopf, 1985), pp. 599–600. Ziegler went on to report that Norstad reciprocated the admiration, and at one stage maintained that Mountbatten ought to succeed him as SACEUR (p. 600).
38. *Newsweek*, dtd 7/62.
39. Charles de Gaulle, transcript of luncheon address, dtd 12/20/62, NATO Public Information Division.
40. The formal letter, dtd 10/25/62, was signed by Maj. Gen. C.I.H. Dunbar (U.K.), Maj. Gen. Albert Watson II (U.S.), and General de Division E. Toulouse (Fr.).
41. Reported in *The New York Times*, dtd 8/17/62.
42. *The New York Times*, dtd 7/17/62. At a luncheon in Norstad's honor, Adenauer called him a "guardian of the temple of peace."
43. J. Res. 902, 87th Congress, 2d Session, dtd 10/4/62.
44. Quoted in Jane E. Stromseth, *The Origins of Flexible Response: NATO's Debate over Strategy in the 1960s* (London: The Macmillan Press, 1988), p. 26.
45. Stromseth, *Origins*, p. 27.
46. To put it into perspective, it should be noted that similar debates were taking place over whether the aircraft carrier had supplanted the battleship as the capital ship, and over whether tank warfare – or the attack – was superior to trench warfare – or the defense.
47. Phillip S. Meilinger, *Hoyt S. Vandenberg: The Life of a General* (Bloomington, IN: Indiana University Press, 1989), p. 202.
48. See Alfred F. Hurley, *Billy Mitchell: Crusader for Air Power*, 2nd edn. (Bloomington, IN: Indiana University Press, 1975).
49. Norstad, *Oral History*, p. 52.
50. Norstad, *Oral History*, p. 29.
51. Ltr Norstad–Johnson, dtd 10/13/27 (EL, NP).

52. Norstad, *Oral History*, p. 4.
53. Norstad, *Oral History*, pp. 15–16. For life at West Point, see Dale O. Smith, *Cradle of Valor: The Intimate Letters of a Plebe at West Point* (Chapel Hill, NC: Algonquin Books, 1988). Air Force Major General Smith entered West Point in 1930, just after Norstad had graduated.
54. Norstad, *Oral History*, p. 52.
55. Ltr Norstad–Johnson, dtd 2/23/28 (EL, NP).
56. Oral interview of Axel Holm with Mrs. Norstad, dtd 10/16/95. The ceremony took place in the Jenkins's home.
57. This boat trip, on an Army transport, was characterized by Isabelle as "doomed", because strange things happened, such as the captain throwing himself overboard upon arrival in San Francisco, a Catholic priest dying of leprosy, and herself coming down with the chicken pox and being confined to her cabin for most of the trip. (See Oral interview of Axel Holm with Mrs. Norstad, dtd 10/10/95.)
58. The officers are Frederick L. Anderson, Henry H. Arnold, Lewis H. Brereton, Charles P. Cabell, James H. Doolittle, Ira C. Eaker, Muir S. Fairchild, Harold L. George, Barney McK. Giles, Haywood S. Hansell, Jr., George C. Kenney, Laurence S. Kuter, Curtis E. LeMay, Lauris Norstad, Thomas S. Power, Elwood R. Quesada, Carl A. Spaatz, Nathan F. Twining, Hoyt S. Vandenberg, Kenneth N. Walter, Thomas D. White, and Donald Wilson. (Since these men went through various promotions during the period treated in this chapter, their ranks are omitted here).
59. Further background on many of these officers can be found in John L. Frisbee, *Makers of the United States Air Force* (Washington, D.C.: Office of Air Force History, 1987). It is noteworthy that in an official Air Force history publication, Norstad was not included in the group of "makers."
60. Frisbee, *Makers, passim.*
61. For a useful summary of the leadership of the "air power" school of thought, see Frisbee, "Introduction: Men with a Mission", *Makers*, pp. 1–9.
62. Haywood S. Hansell, Jr., *Air Plan That Defeated Hitler* (New York: Arno Press, 1980), p. 3.
63. David R. Mets, *Master of Airpower: General Carl A. Spaatz* (Novato, CA: Presidio Press, 1988), p. 116.
64. DeWitt S. Copp, *Forged in Fire: Strategy and Decisions in the Air War over Europe, 1940–1945* (Garden City, NY: Doubleday and Company, 1982 [for The Air Force Historical Foundation]), p. 201.
65. Norstad, *Oral History*, pp. 109–110.
66. Craven and Cate, *Army*, vol. VI, p. 40.
67. Craven and Cate, *Army*, Vol. VI, pp. 32, 38–39.
68. Craven and Cate, *Army*, Vol. VI, p. 39.
69. See, for example, I.B. Holley, Jr., *Ideas and Weapons* (Washington D.C.: Office of Air Force History, 1983).
70. Craven and Cate, *Army*, Vol. VI, p. 41.
71. Craven and Cate, *Army*, Vol. VI, pp. 36–38.
72. See, for example, Michael H. Gorn, *Harnessing the Genie: Science and Technology Forecasting for the Air Force 1944–1946* (Washington D.C.: Office of Air Force History, Air Staff Historical Study, 1988). See also G. Pascal Zachary, *Endless Frontier: Vannevar Bush, Engineer of the American Century*

(New York: The Free Press, 1997). Bush was instrumental in the creation of the Office of Scientific Research and Development during World War II. He was also the designer of electromechanical analog computers and was an early exponent of the notion of a military–university–industrial complex.

Chapter 2

1. Perry M. Smith, *Taking Charge: A Practical Guide for Leaders* (Washington, D.C.: National Defense University Press, 1986), p. 123.
2. H.H. Arnold, *Global Mission* (New York: Harper and Brothers, Publishers, 1949), pp. 356–357.
3. Recounted in Thomas M. Coffey, *Hap: The Story of the U.S. Air Force and the Man Who Built It, General Henry H. "Hap" Arnold* (New York: Viking Press, 1982), pp. 254–255. Cabell, one of Norstad's closest friends, was a B-17 command pilot in World War II and became director of plans for the U.S. Strategic Air Forces in Europe, planning the air support for the invasion of Normandy. After the war, he was appointed Director of Intelligence, Headquarters USAF, and later, Director of the Joint Staff, OJCS. He was selected in 1953 as Deputy Director of the CIA. General Cabell retired in 1962.
4. Norstad, *Oral History Interview*, February 13–16 and October 22–25, 1979, USAF Historical Research Center, Maxwell AFB, AL., pp. 483, 487.
5. Jacob E. Smart, *Oral History Interview*, November 27–30, 1978, USAF Historical Research Center, p. 45. Smart concluded: "... the role of the Advisory Council was that of adding a new dimension to the consideration of problems that confronted the Army Air Corps and its Chief in particular. We were not expected to second guess the Air Staff or the major commands, but instead to review and assess their proposals to General Arnold in light of those four considerations ..." (p. 46). Smart made special missions for Arnold to the China–Burma–India and Middle East theaters. He also attended the Casablanca and Quebec Conferences. In early 1944 he went to Italy, commanding the 97th Bomb Group. In May, he was shot down, captured, and remained a POW until late 1945. After the war, Smart was Assistant Vice Chief of Staff, Headquarters USAF; Vice Commander, Tactical Air Command; Commander of the U.S. Forces in Japan; CINCPAC, and Deputy CINCEUCOM.
6. Richard G. Davis, *HAP: Henry H. Arnold, Military Aviator* (Washington, D.C.: Air Force History and Museums Program, 1997), p. 1.
7. Memo Lt. Cols. Cabell and Norstad–Arnold, "Status of Flying School Graduates," dtd 3/13/42. The memo passed through Brig. Gen. Kuter, who was Deputy Chief of Air Staff. Taking another tack, General Kuter would ask Cabell and Norstad to comment informally on various problems. One such problem was how to handle officers returning from combat theatres. (See exchange dtd 3/31/42, "Handling of Officers Returning from Combat Areas." [EL, NP]
8. Memo Cabell and Norstad–Arnold, "Plane-borne Rockets," dtd 6/29/42 (EL, NP).

9. On the Combined Chiefs of Staff Committee, see Hastings Ismay, *The Memoirs of General Lord Ismay* (New York: The Viking Press, 1960).
10. For more on Ismay, see Robert S. Jordan, *The NATO International Staff/Secretariat, 1952–1957: A Study in International Administration* (London: Oxford University Press, 1967).
11. A glance at the list of the first five NATO SACEURS – other than Eisenhower – stretching from 1950 to 1968, makes this point. They all had served together with distinction during the war. See Robert S. Jordan, ed., *Generals in International Politics: NATO's Supreme Allied Commander, Europe* (Lexington, KY: The University Press of Kentucky, 1987).
12. Norstad, *Oral History*, p. 95.
13. Ibid., p. 88
14. Quoted in Ronald Schaffer, *Wings of Judgment: American Bombing in World War II* (New York: Oxford University Press, 1985), p. 17. Schaffer cites several examples of how constant exposure to death "hardens" flyers.
15. Phillip S. Meilinger, *Hoyt S. Vandenberg: The Life of a General* (Bloomington, IN: Indiana University Press, 1989), p. 86.
16. Schaffer, *Wings*, pp. 18–19.
17. See Robert Frank Futrell, *Ideas, Concepts, Doctrine: Basic thinking in the United States Air Force, 1907–1960* (Maxwell Air Force Base, AL: Air University Press, 1989).
18. Haywood S. Hansell, Jr., *The Strategic Air War against Germany and Japan: A Memoir* (Washington, D.C.: Office of Air Force History, USAF Warrior Studies, 1986), p. 10.
19. John Newhouse, *War and Peace in the Nuclear Age* (New York: Alfred A. Knopf, 1989), p. 42. See also Schaffer, *Wings*.
20. Michael S. Sherry, *The Rise of American Air Power: The Creation of Armageddon* (New Haven and London: Yale University Press, 1987), p. 208. Sherry quotes several sources, from public information officers to social psychologists, affirming how the airmen's preoccupation with the intricacies of modern technological air warfare – and its attendant detached destruction – helped to remove much concern about the feelings of the enemy, whether civilian or military.
21. Quoted in Christopher Harvie, "Technological Change and Military Power in Historical Perspective," George Edward Thibault, ed., *The Art and Practice of Military Strategy* (Washington, D.C.: National Defense University, 1984), p. 510.
22. Curtis LeMay, *Mission with LeMay: My Story* (Garden City, NY: Doubleday and Co., Inc., 1965), p. 347.
23. LeMay, *Mission*, pp. 347–348.
24. For more on this point, see Richard Rhodes, *Dark Sun: The Making of the Hydrogen Bomb* (New York: Simon and Schuster, 1995; also Richard Rhodes, *The Making of the Atomic Bomb* (New York: Simon and Schuster, 1986).
25. For more on this point, see Sherry, *Rise*, ch. 7.
26. Arnold firmly believed that, with the heavily-armed B-17 and the new Norden bombsight, it was possible to engage in precision daylight bombardment, rather than, as the British believed, that heavy bombers could only do night indiscriminate bombardment in order to avoid heavy losses.
27. Coffey, *Hap*, p. 252.

28. See Daniel R. Mortensen, *A Pattern for Joint Operations: World War II Close Air Support North Africa*, Historical Analysis Series (Washington, D.C.: Office of Air Force History and U.S. Army Center of Military History, 1987), Ch. 2. I am grateful for the support of Dr. Mortensen in the early stages of preparing this manuscript.
29. Norstad, *Oral History*, p. 486. A few weeks earlier, Arnold had promoted him to full colonel.
30. Norstad, *Oral History*, p. 499. While in London, Doolittle, Vandenberg, Norstad, and several other officers lived together.
31. Ltr Norstad–Isabelle, dtd 9/28/42 (EL, NP). He also wrote a separate letter to Kristin, and appeared to take an active interest in Kristin's development over the years.
32. Ltr Norstad–Isabelle, dtd 9/28/42 (EL, NP).
33. Wesley Frank Craven and James Lea Cate, *The Army Air Forces in World War II: Europe: Torch to Pointblank August 1942 to December 1943*, Vol. II (Washington, D.C.: Office of Air Force History, New Imprint, 1983), pp. 52–53.
34. Eisenhower had requested either Spaatz or Eaker. When Eisenhower reluctantly acquiesced, Arnold personally chose Doolittle's staff, an unusual act since commanders usually pick their own staffs. (See Meilinger, *Vandenberg*, pp. 29–30.)
35. James H. Doolittle, *I Could Never Be So Lucky Again: An Autobiography* (New York: Bantam Books, 1991), p. 304.
36. Norstad, *Oral History* p. 500. He was still in London at that time.
37. Meilinger, *Vandenberg*, p. 30.
38. Ltr Norstad–Isabelle, dtd 1/42 (EL, NP).
39. Ltr H. Vandenberg, Jr.–Isabelle, dtd 8/13/88 (EL, NP).
40. Mortensen, *Pattern*, pp. 51–52.
41. Mortensen, *Pattern*, p. 52. Norstad, shortly after the war, when chief of plans for the AAF, observed that "... the conception of the tactical air force was 'one of the greatest developments' of World War II." (Quoted in Futrell, *Ideas*, Vol. 1, p. 173.)
42. Mortensen, *Pattern*, pp. 53–55. Norstad did not have an Air Support Command, which probably indicated that conclusions had not been made about the kind of aircraft to be used for close air support in North Africa.
43. Norstad, *Oral History*, p. 503.
44. Norstad, *Oral History*, p. 509. See also Lowell Thomas and Edward Jablonski, *Doolittle: A Biography* (Garden City, NY: Doubleday and Co., Inc., 1976), pp. 209–210.
45. Norstad, *Oral History*, p. 516. It was also shaky because before the French surrendered to Norstad at Tafaraoui they had destroyed the sewer system. This had turned the airfield into a muddy patch that could not support the heavy medium bombers, which were soon relocated in the drier interior. In fact, when Doolittle landed at Tafaraoui in his B-17, it sank into the mud when it left the runway, and had to be pulled out by four tanks. (Recounted in Meilinger, *Vandenberg*, p. 31.)
46. Meilinger, *Vandenberg*, p. 31. The 31st Fighter Group is also mentioned.
47. For a full account of the political-military circumstances of North Africa at this time, see Robert Murphy, *Diplomat Among Warriors* (Garden City, NY: Doubleday and Co., Inc., 1964).

48. Norstad, *Oral History*, p. 515.
49. Ltr Doolittle–Arnold, dtd 11/19/42. In this letter, Doolittle describes the magnitude of the situation confronting Norstad: "Yesterday at Oran we had fourteen thousand men and about one thousand officers. These are all stationed at Tafaraoui and La Senia at the moment ..."
50. Ltr Arnold–Doolittle, dtd 12/21/42, (EL, NP).
51. Ltr Norstad–Isabelle, dtd 3/15/43 (EL, NP).
52. Mortensen, *Pattern*, p. 55. The bomber and fighter commands were on call for close air support and other ground tasks, but when not on alert, they would engage in planned interdiction to fulfill Air Force objectives.
53. Norstad, *Oral Histoy*, p. 517.
54. Quoted in Mets, *Master*, pp. 151–152.
55. Statement by Major General Lauris Norstad, "Air Power in the Mediterranean, 1942–1945," Air Force Historical Center, Maxwell, Air Force Base, Alabama, undtd, pp. 2–3.
56. David Syrett, "The Tunisian Campaign, 1942–1943," in Benjamin Franklin Cooling, ed., *Case Studies in the Development of Close Air Support* (Washington, D.C.: Office of Air Force History, 1990), pp. 184–185. Arnold had copies sent to every Air Force officer.
57. Walter J. Boyne, *Beyond the Wild Blue: A History of the U.S. Air Force, 1947–1997* (New York: St. Martin's Press, 1997), p. 23.
58. On February 4, "Headquarters, North African Theater of Operations, U.S. Army," was created under Eisenhower.
59. Alan F. Wilt, "Allied Cooperation in Sicily and Italy, 1943–1945," in Cooling, *Case Studies*, p. 195.
60. Meilinger, *Vandenberg*, p. 32. He cites G.O. No. 1, Hq Mediterranean Air Command, February 18, 1943; Craven and Cate, *Army*, Vol. II, pp. 115–116. In December 1943, Tedder's command was redesignated "Mediterranean Allied Air Forces (MAAF)." When Tedder became Eisenhower's deputy for OVERLORD he was succeeded by Lt. Gen. Eaker.
61. Statement, *Air Power*, p. 8. [Norstad's emphasis] Norstad did not attend the Casablanca Conference, although he gave some preparatory briefings to Eisenhower. (See also Mets, *Master*, p. 152.)
62. Quoted E.K.G. Sixsmith, *Eisenhower as Military Commander* (New York: Stein and Day, Publishers, 1983), p. 65.
63. There were also P-38s and P-40s for escort, and four wings of British Wellingtons. (Meilinger, *Vandenberg*, p. 32.)
64. Meilinger, *Vandenberg*, p. 33.
65. Norstad, *Oral History*, p. 519.
66. Norstad, *Oral History*, p. 519. See also Diane T. Putney, ed., *ULTRA and the Army Air Forces in World War II: An Interview with Associate Justice of the U.S. Supreme Court Lewis F. Powell, Jr.* (Washington, D.C.: Office of Air Force History, 1987), pp. 12–13.
67. Ltr Norstad–Isabelle, dtd 8/3/43 (EL, NP).
68. See Mets, *Master*, pp. 152–157.
69. Listed in Meilinger, *Vandenberg*, pp. 32–33. Ploesti was on the list because of the efforts of Col. (later General) Jacob E. Smart. (Smart, *Oral History*, pp. 70–84.)
70. For more on the Ploesti raids, see Smart, *Oral History*, pp. 70–84.
71. Ltr "Commendation", Spaatz–Norstad, dtd 6/13/43 (EL, NP)

72. Ltr Norstad–Isabelle, dtd 3/27/43 (EL, NP).
73. See Craven and Cate, *Army*, Vol. II, p. 114. The other commander placed under Tedder was Air Chief Marshal Sir Sholto Douglas as air commander for the Middle East. The NAAF was organized along functional lines, manned by both British and U.S. officers.
74. He participated in several major operations including ANVIL, DIADEM, SHINGLE, and FRANTIC, which was an attempt to obtain the Soviet Union's cooperation in shuttle bombing operations.
75. Norstad, *Oral History*, p. 498.
76. Statement, *Air Power*, p. 9.
77. R.J. Overy, *The Air War, 1939–1945* (New York: Stein and Day, 1981), p. 17. Overy goes on to discuss the influence of air power doctrine on grand strategy. (See pp. 18–25.)
78. Norstad's tenure was from 7/20/44 to 5/8/45. Both he and Hansell occupied dual positions as Deputy Chief of Staff, AAF and Chief of Staff, Twentieth Air Force. As will be seen in the following chapter, Norstad was drawn into planning for the postwar Air Force in his former role.
79. Ltr Norstad–Isabelle, dtd 7/44 (EL, NP).
80. Norstad, *Oral History*, p. 95. Kuter, also a gifted planner although not so much an operational commander, returned to Washington "too soon" and so also did not emerge as one of the "heroes" of World War II. In mid-May 1943, after commanding the Allied Air Support Command and then Deputy Commander of the Northwest African Tactical Air Force (NATAF), Kuter was reassigned by Arnold to be his Assistant Chief of Staff for Plans. Kuter was an advocate of tactical air support. (See Mortensen, *Planning*, pp. 67 and 78.)
81. Ltr Norstad–Isabelle, dtd 3/16/44 (EL, NP). Later that year, he raised with Isabelle the possibility of trying for a "son and heir." His view was to wait until they could talk it over so that they would be in harmony, but he did comment: "I must admit that the very thought of this subject gives me great pleasure." (Ltr, Norstad–Isabelle, dtd 7/26/44.) Tragically, Isabelle had one more child, a son, who did not live.
82. George C. Kenney, *General Kenney Reports: A Personal History of the Pacific War* (Washington, D.C.: Office of Air Force History, USAF Warrior Studies, 1987), p. 526. (The book was originally published by Duell, Sloan, and Pearce of New York in 1949.)
83. Quoted in Ronald H. Spector, *Eagle Against the Sun: The American War with Japan* (New York: Vintage Books, 1985), pp. 489–490. For Hansell's version of events, see Hansell, *Strategic Air War Against Germany and Japan*, *supra*.
84. Craven and Cate, *Army*, Vol. V, pp. 566–567.
85. Craven and Cate, *Army*, p. 567. Hansell had been: "Arnold's top planner for awhile, and something of a protégé, and Arnold was not without a streak of sentiment for his 'boys.'" (p. 566.) For a good short summary of the role of the Twentieth Air Force in the surrender of Japan, see Herman S. Wolk, "General Arnold, the Atomic Bomb, and the Surrender of Japan," in Gunter Bischof and Robert L. Dupont, eds., *The Pacific War Revisited* (Baton Rouge: Louisiana State University Press, 1997), pp. 163–178.
86. Spector, *Eagle*, p. 491. The description first appeared in St. Clair McKelway, "A Reporter with the B-29s," *New Yorker*, dtd 6/16/45, p. 32. See Sherry,

Rise, pp. 408–409, notes 113–130 for further sources concerning Norstad's and McKelway's roles and the various published reactions to the change in bombing tactics of senior American officials. See also Thomas M. Coffey, *Iron Eagle: The Turbulent Life of General Curtis LeMay* (New York: Crown Publishers, Inc., 1986), p. 163.
87. He retired in 1953. Quoted in Meilinger, *Vandenberg*, p. 87. For a summary of Vandenberg's accomplishments, see Meilinger, *Vandenberg*, Ch. VIII.
88. Norstad, *Oral History*, pp. 203 and 194. Partly because of temperament – Norstad was articulate although not ebullient, and LeMay was taciturn – they were not particularly close.
89. Schaffer, *Wings*, pp. 130ff. Schaffer cites extractions from McKelway, "Reporter," pp. 36–37, 39; Bruce Rae, "300 B-29's Fire 15 Square Miles of Tokyo," *The New York Times*, dtd 3/10/45, pp. 1, 6; LeMay, *Mission*, p. 348 (PM).
90. McKelway, "Reporter," pp. 30–31. LeMay discussed the raid after the bombers had departed.
91. Thomas S. Power, *Design for Survival* (New York: Coward–McCann, 1964), p. 28 (quoted in Schaffer, *Wings*, p. 132).
92. Quoted in Schaffer, *Wings*, p. 132. For more on Norstad's role in justifying to the American public the "cost-benefits" of mass firebombing, see Sherry, *Rise*, pp. 288ff.
93. See Major James F. Sunderman, USAF, ed., *World War II in the Air: The Pacific* (New York: Franklin Watts, Inc., 1962), p. 261.
94. Quoted in Schaffer, *Wings*, p. 37; Moscow, "Center of Tokyo," p. 1; LeMay, Report of Operations, dtd 3/10/45; ARP Tokyo, p. 3 (RS).
95. Spector, *Eagle*, p. 505.
96. Schaffer, *Wings*, p. 123.
97. Quoted in Schaffer, *Wings*, p. 123.
98. In meetings that Norstad chaired of the Joint Target Group (JTG) and the SBS staff, he wanted to know especially the impact of refugees from bombings on transportation, food, medical attention, and morale. (Conrad C. Crane, *Bombs, Cities, and Civilians: American Airpower Strategy in World War II* (Lawrence, KS: University Press of Kansas, 1993), p. 138.
99. Franklin D'Olier, et al., *The United States Strategic Bombing Surveys*, September 30, 1945 (Maxwell AFB, AL: Air University Press, October 1987), pp. 82ff.
100. Schaffer, *Wings*, p. 138.
101. For a discussion of Churchill's rationale for area bombing, see Christopher C. Harmon, *"Are We Beasts?": Churchill and the Moral Question of World War II "Area Bombing"* (Newport, RI: Naval War College, The Newport Papers, #1, December 1991).
102. Quoted in Gar Alperovitz, *The Decision to Use the Atomic Bomb* (New York: Vintage Books Edition, 1996), pp. 322–323, Alperovitz's bracketed comments. The debate over whether the bomb was needed to end the war is still going on. See, for example, *Newsletter* of The Society for Historians of American Foreign Relations, Vol. 29, No. 3 (September 1998).
103. Quoted in Jeffrey Barlow, *Revolt of the Admirals: The Fight for Naval Aviation, 1945–1950* (Washington D.C.: Naval Historical Center, 1994), p. 19.
104. Quoted in Schaffer, *Wings*, p. 138.
105. See Davis, *HAP*, p. 32.

106. For more on this point, see Sherry, *Rise*, pp. 173ff.
107. Norstad, *Oral History*, p. 101.
108. Norstad, *Oral History*, p. 106. See also Dean Acheson, *Present at the Creation: My Years in the State Department* (New York: W.W. Norton and Co., 1969), p. 218.
109. Solly Zuckerman, *Monkeys, Men, and Missiles: An Autobiography 1946–1988* (New York: W.W. Norton and Co., 1988), p. 283.
110. Quoted in Schaffer, *Wings*, p. 40.
111. Quoted in Alice Kimball Smith, *A Peril and A Hope: The Scientists' Movement in America: 1945–47* (Chicago: University of Chicago Press, 1965), p. 53.
112. Zuckerman, *Monkeys*, p. 186. Zuckerman also criticizes the USSBS in his review, "The Silver Fox," in *The New York Review of Books*, dtd 1/19/89. He reviewed Strobe Talbot, *The Master of the Game: Paul Nitze and the Nuclear Peace* (New York: A.A. Knopf, 1988).
113. See Rhodes, *Dark*, p. 224; also Marc Trachtenberg, *History and Strategy* (Princeton: Princeton University Press, 1991).
114. Mets, *Master*, pp. 314–315.
115. Mets, *Master*, p. 315. See also Rhodes, *Dark*, p. 226.
116. Rhodes, *Dark*, p. 228.

Chapter 3

1. H.H. Arnold, *Global Mission* (New York: Harper and Brothers, Publishers, 1949), p. 615.This chapter is written with the collaboration of Herman S. Wolk, Senior Historian, Air Force History Support Office, whose invaluable assistance to me while I had cardiac health problems, I wish to acknowledge. His notes are designated (HW). For more on this subject, see Herman S. Wolk, *Planning and Organizing the Postwar Air Force,1943–1947* (Washington D.C.: Office of Air Force History, 1984). Also useful was Wolk's article, "The Defense Unification Battle, 1947–1950: The Air Force,"*Prologue: The Journal of the National Archives*, Spring 1975 (Vol. 7, No.1). Other articles in this issue by Philip A. Crowl ("What Price Unity: the Defense Unification Battle, 1947–50), Paolo E. Coletta ("The Defense Unification Battle, 1947–1950: the Navy"), and Richard F. Haynes ("The Defense Unification Battle, 1947–1950: The Army") were also consulted.
2. Ltr Arnold–Eaker, dtd 6/29/43 [Arnold's emphasis].
3. Ltr Giles–B/G Howard C. Davidson, dtd 12/3/43. He went on to comment: "Along that general line a study concerning the best type of permanent service journal for the AAF is in process of preparation."
4. Walter J. Boyne, *Beyond the Wild Blue: A History of the U.S. Air Force, 1947–1997* (New York: St. Martin's Press, 1997).
5. Memo Gen. Arnold–Maj. Gen. Norstad (AC/AS, Plans, Subj: Daily Activity Rpt, Dec 11, 1945, in RG 18, AAG 3191, Plans Daily Activity Rpts, 1945, 370, Modern Military Br, NA.)
6. Norstad, *Oral History*, p. 97.
7. Ibid., p. 96.
8. Memo Arnold–Air Staff, "Organization for Unification," dtd 11/13/45 (HW).

9. This was in keeping with Arnold's determination to maintain top priority for postwar organizational planning for an independent Air Force. As early as 1943, he formed groups within AAF Headquarters to accomplish postwar planning.
10. Norstad, *Oral History*, p. 98.
11. Ibid., pp. 94–95.
12. Memo Norstad–Spaatz, "Comments on AAF VJ Plan as of 7/15/45," dtd 7/11/47 (HW).
13. Arnold, *Mission*, p. 348.
14. Memo Norstad–Chief of Air Staff, dtd 9/15/45 (HW). There also had been studies underway during this time by the Patch Board and the Simpson Board.
15. Memo Norstad–Spaatz, dtd 8/11/45 (HW). Interim Air Force planning should include provision for an Air Academy; an Air Intelligence Service; and a Flying Safety Service. Also, it was probable that a substantial increase would be required in the ratio of civilians to military personnel.
16. See also Boyne, *Beyond the Wild Blue*, pp. 24ff.
17. Memo Norstad–Eaker, "Committee on Reorganization of the AAF," dtd 12/14/45 (HW).
18. Memo Norstad–Spaatz, "Comments on AAF VJ Plan as of 7/15/45," dtd 7/1/47 (HW).
19. Arnold, *Mission*, p. 541.
20. War Department Ltr AG 322, "Establishment of Air Defense, Strategic Air and Tactical Commands," dtd 3/21/46 (HW). Spaatz and Norstad referred to this reorganization as "functional," meaning that they had created a major command to conduct each of the air roles described in Field Service Regulation 100–20.
21. Norstad, *Oral History*, p. 122–123.
22. For a brief analysis of Eisenhower's strategic thinking, see Steven Metz, *Eisenhower as Strategist: The Coherent Use of Military Power in War and Peace* (Carlisle Barracks, PA: Strategic Studies Institute, U.S. Army War College, February 1993). As will be seen in the chapters which follow, Norstad's thinking was derived from Eisenhower's.
23. For an excellent summary of the convolutions of committee reports and the Services's responses thereto, see Wolk, *Planning*, pp. 58–61.
24. Ltr Forrestal–Harold D. Smith, Director, Bureau of the Budget, dtd 3/12/45 (HW).
25. Memo R.S. Edwards–King, "Comment on Rpt of JCS Special Committee for Reorganization of National Defense," dtd 4/14/45 (HW).
26. Memo CSA–CINC Army and Navy, "Reorganization of National Defense", Encl B to memo Pres fr. Adm. William D. Leahy, C/S to CINC of Army and Navy, dtd 10/16/45 (HW).
27. Statement by Forrestal, Hearings on S.84 and S.1482, p. 97, dtd 10/22/45 (HW). The Report recommended that the Navy retain its aviation. Ferdinand Eberstadt had been an investment banker friend of Forrestal's.
28. Testimony of Eisenhower, Senate Military Affairs Committee, dtd 11/16/45 (HW).
29. Testimony of Eisenhower, the Senate Military Affairs Committee, dtd 11/16/45 (HW).

30. Ibid.
31. Harry S. Truman, *Memoirs: Years of Trial and Hope*, Vol II (Garden City, NY: Doubleday and Co., Inc. 1956), p. 46 (HW).
32. *The New York Times*, dtd 8/31/45, p. 16 (HW).
33. "Special Message to the Congress Recommending the Establishment of a Department of National Defense," in *Public Papers of the President of the United States: Harry S. Truman, 1945* (Washington, D.C.: U.S. Government Printing Office, 1961), p. 547, dtd 12/19/45 (HW).
34. *Public Papers*, p. 555 (HW).
35. *Public Papers*, p. 559 (HW).
36. General Lauris Norstad, "The National Security Act of 1947: Implications and Interpretations," in Paul Schratz, ed., *Evolution of the American Military Establishment Since World War II* (Lexington, VA: The George C. Marshall Research Foundation, 1978), p. 24 (HW).
37. Norstad, *Oral History*, p. 159 (HW).
38. Ltr Norstad–Arnold, dtd 3/20/46 (HW).
39. Memorandum for Record, "Conferences re Military Representation in the Office of the Secretary of Defense," dtd 5/11/48 (EL, NP, Box 21, Memo for Record). Norstad mentioned that General Omar Bradley was, in his opinion, best suited for the position, and that Secretary Forrestal was considering appointing him. When sounded out, however, Bradley declined, and the entire matter was dropped. (See Omar N. Bradley and Clay Blair, *A General's Life* [New York: Simon and Schuster, 1983], pp. 494–495.)
40. Memo Norstad–Div. Chiefs, "Unification," dtd 5/15/46 (HW).
41. Norstad, *Oral History*, p. 231 (HW).
42. Townsend Hoopes and Douglas Brinkley, *Driven Patriot: The Life and Times of James Forrestal* (New York: Alfred A. Knopf, 1992), p. 369. They recounted that at one point, Symington gave this advice to an Air Force staff officer about Pentagon politics: "Don't ever let your honesty interfere with your judgment." (p. 369.)
43. See episodes recounted in Hoopes and Brinkley, *Driven*, pp. 367–370. The authors claim that Symington's harassment of Forrestal contributed to Forrestal's mental breakdown and suicide.
44. Ltr Norstad–Arnold, dtd 3/20/46 (HW). The correspondence files for Norstad at this time are replete with assertions from naval sources and denials of senior Air Force officers concerning reported episodes where Air Force officers allegedly spoke in offensive terms about the Navy.
45. Ltr Truman–Patterson and Forrestal, dtd 6/15/46 (HW).
46. Quoted in Michael A. Palmer, *Origins of the Maritime Strategy: American Naval Strategy in the First Postwar Decade* (Washington, D.C., Naval Historical Center, 1988), p. 34 (HW).
47. Norstad's appointment was symbolic as well. Over a decade earlier, General Marshall had appointed Brigadier General Frank M. Andrews – the only other airman – to the same post. (See DeWitt S. Copp, *A Few Great Captains: The Men and Events That Shaped the Development of U.S. Air Power* [Garden City, NY: Doubleday and Co., Inc., 1980], p. 483.)
48. Ltr Robert Proctor–Norstad, dtd 6/21/46 (EL, NP, Box 23, Personal 1946 [4]).

252 *Notes*

49. See Ralph B. Jordan, *Born to Fight: The Life of Admiral Halsey* (Philadelphia: David McKay Co., 1946) for a lively account of the exploits of another major naval hero of the Pacific war.
50. Testimony of Eisenhower, Senate Military Affairs Committee, dtd 11/16/45.
51. Ltr Norstad–Brig. Gen. J.D. McIntyre, dtd 7/6/46 (EL, NP, Box 23, Personal 1946 [4]). Norstad went on to observe: "My view, for what it is worth, is that unification in substantially the form indicated by the President is right and sound and therefore inevitable."
52. Ltr Norstad–Arnold, dtd 4/18/46 (EL, NP, Box 23, Personal 1946 [5]).
53. Ltr Norstad–Robert Proctor, dtd 6/25/46 (EL, NP, Box 23, Personal 1946 [4]).
54. Ltr Norstad–Baldwin, dtd 1/28/47 (EL, NP, Box 23, Personal 1947 [5]). Baldwin was suspect in Army and AAF circles partly because he was an Annapolis graduate and former naval officer.
55. Hoopes and Brinkley, *Driven*, p. 369.
56. Norstad, *Oral History*, p. 129.
57. Ltr Norstad–Isabelle, dtd 7/24/48 (EL, NP)
58. Norstad, *Oral History*, p. 130
59. Ltr Norstad–Eleanor Whitney, dtd 1/31/47 (EL, NP)
60. Ltr Norstad–Reid, dtd 5/9/46 (EL, NP, Box 23, Personal 1946 [5]).
61. David Lawrence, "Air Force vs Navy Enmity Seen Rising," *Washington Star*, dtd 3/22/46. This particular article was prompted by a purported anti-Navy remark made by Spaatz at a private dinner of the Aviation Writers Association.
62. Gen. Lauris Norstad, "The National Security Act of 1947: Implications and Interpretations," in Schratz, *Evolution*, p. 25. Norstad provided important Congressional testimony in support of the Act. (See: "Statement of Major General Lauris Norstad, Director of Plans and Operations Division, War Department General Staff," before the Committee on Expenditures in the Executive Departments, House of Representatives re H.R. 2319, National Security Act of 1947; "Statement of Major General Lauris Norstad, Director of Plans & Operations Division, War Department General Staff," before Armed Services Committee of U.S. Senate, re S. 758, creating National Defense Establishment.) (HW)
63. Ltr Norstad–Proctor, dtd 6/25/46 (EL, NP, Box 23, Personal 1946 [4]). These delicate matters were hammered out at inter-Service conferences held from March 11–14, 1948 at Key West, Florida and from August 20–22, 1948 at the Naval War College in Newport, Rhode Island.
64. Ltr Norstad–Arnold, dtd 4/18/46 (EL, NP, Box 23, Personal 1946 [5]).
65. Norstad, *Oral History*, p. 167 (HW).
66. Norstad, "The National Security Act of 1947: Implications and Interpretations," in Schratz, *Evolution*, p. 25 (HW).
67. Ltr Patterson and Forrestal–Truman, dtd 1/16/47; Ltr, Truman–Patterson and Forrestal, dtd 1/16/47 (HW).
68. The first independent Chairman was General Omar Bradley. The Chairman need not necessarily be named from one of the three incumbent Chiefs of Staff/Chief of Naval Operations.
69. Statement of Eisenhower, Senate Committee on Armed Services, "Hearings on S.758," dtd 3/25/47 (HW).

70. Executive Order 9877, "Functions of the Armed Forces," Sec IV, par 4, dtd 7/16/47 (HW).
71. Quoted from Alfred Goldberg, ed., *A History of the United States Air Force, 1907–1957* (Princeton, NJ: D. Van Nostrand Co., Inc., 1957), p. 103.
72. Norstad, *Oral History*, p. 176 (HW).
73. Ibid., pp. 175–176 (HW).
74. Norstad, *Oral History*, p. 183 (HW).
75. Ibid., p. 184 (HW).
76. Ibid., p. 181 (HW).
77. Memorandum for the Record, "Conference with General Eisenhower," dtd 5/1/48 (HW).
78. See Chapter 4 for more about Norstad on this subject. He also worked closely with General Gruenther, who represented the Army in these negotiations, and with whom Norstad would work in setting up SHAPE.
79. Ltr Lilienthal–Norstad, dtd 8/4/47 (EL, NP, Box 23, Personal 1947 [2]).
80. Ltr Representative James W. Wadsworth–Norstad, dtd 7/24/47 (EL, NP, Box 23, Personal 1947 [3]).
81. Ltr Norstad–Sherman, dtd 11/2/48 (EL, NP, Box 22, Official-Classified 1948).
82. Ltr Sherman–Norstad, dtd 11/18/48 (EL, NP, Box 22, Official-Classified 1948). Sherman had been promoted by then to Vice Admiral, and sent to sea as Commander of the Sixth Task Fleet in the Mediterranean.
83. For a summary of the Soviet motives for initiating this crisis, see Vojtech Mastny, "Stalin and the Militarization of the Cold War," *International Security*, Winter, 1984–85 (Vol. 9, No. 3), pp. 109–129.
84. For a readable short history of the occupation of Germany and of Berlin in particular, see Philip Windsor, *City on Leave: A History of Berlin, 1945–1962* (New York: Frederick A. Praeger, 1963).
85. For the diplomatic aspects of the crisis, see Charles E. Bohlen, *Witness to History, 1929–1969* (New York: W.W. Norton and Co., Inc., 1973), Chapter Sixteen.
86. Lucius D. Clay, *Decision in Germany* (New York: Garden City, NY: Doubleday and Co., Inc., 1950).
87. Harry S. Truman, *Years*, Vol. Two, p. 123.
88. Bradley and Blair, *Life*, p. 477. Although the National Security Act of 1947 established a National Security Council to coordinate crisis policy, it was not convened at this early stage. Instead, the crisis was handled through informal meetings between Secretary of Defense Forrestal, Undersecretary of State Lovett, Secretary of the Army Kenneth Royall, Eisenhower, and the JCS (Bradley and Blair, *Life*, p. 478).
89. Quoted in Bradley and Blair *Life*, p. 477.
90. See Steven L. Rearden, *History of the Office of the Secretary of Defense*, Vol. 1: The Formative Years, 1947–1950 (Washington, D.C.: Historical Office, Office of the Secretary of Defense, 1984), pp. 292–295.
91. Norstad, *Oral History*, p. 198.
92. Dean Acheson, *The Struggle for a Free Europe* (New York: W.W. Norton and Co., 1969), pp. 36–37.
93. For a brief discussion of U.S. diplomacy *vis-à-vis* the UN at this time, see Bohlen, *Witness*, pp. 281–287.

254 Notes

94. John H. Backer, *Winds of History: the German Years of Lucius DuBignon Clay* (New York: Van Nostrand Reinhold Company, 1983), pp. 239-240.
95. Quoted in Phillip S. Meilinger, *Hoyt S. Vandenberg: The Life of a General* (Bloomington, IN: Indiana University Press, 1989), pp. 96-97. Meilinger describes the limited capacity of the Air Force to carry out any engagement using atomic weapons. The Berlin crisis was a catalyst to revitalize the Strategic Air Command (SAC). (See pp. 102-107.)
96. Quoted in Backer, *Winds*, p. 240.
97. There were two Groups, each composed of three Squadrons.
98. See ltr, Norstad – Vandenberg, "Trip to U.K.," dtd 2/16/49 (EL, NP, Box 22, Official File 1949-50[4]). Vandenberg was to make the trip on behalf of the JCS in March.
99. See Jean Edward Smith, *Lucius D. Clay: An American Life* (New York: Henry Holt and Co., 1990), for Clay's career.
100. Meilinger, *Vandenberg*, p. 98.
101. Msg USAFE, 12148, dtd 6/48. (AFHO) This Operation followed the plan of the initial Task Force Berlin operations of 4/4/48.
102. Msg Vandenberg–LeMay, 12936, dtd 6/28/48. This was in response to LeMay's msg to Norstad UAX 8552, dtd 6/26/48 (AFHO).
103. Msg LeMay–Norstad, UAX 8714, dtd 7/9/48 (AFHO).
104. See Truman, *Years*, Vol. Two, pp. 125-126; also Meilinger, *Vandenberg*, p. 98.
105. There already were facilities at Tempelhof and Gatow, whose runways had been improved; Tegel, in the French sector, was to be built. (See Backer, *Winds*, p. 246.)
106. Truman, *Years*, Vol. Two, p. 126.
107. G.O. Number 1, Hq. Air Task Force (Provisional), dtd 7/31/48 (AFHO).
108. For a description of how and why Vandenberg picked Tunner, see Meilinger, *Vandenberg*, p. 99. The CATF replaced the Berlin Airlift Task Force, which was under the command of Brigadier General Joseph Smith, who had been designated on 6/29/48. He served for only four weeks. Both units were located at Headquarters USAFE in Wiesbaden. (Msg Kissner–Smith, "Designation of Project Commander," dtd 6/29/48; also msg Kissner–Tunner, "Instructions to Commander, Airlift Task Force (Provisional)," dtd 7/30/48 [AFHO]).
109. Meilinger, *Vandenberg*, p. 101.
110. Bohlen, *Witness*, p. 279.
111. See Windsor, *City*, pp. 99-114.
112. Windsor, *City*, p. 126.
113. See Bohlen, *Witness*, pp. 283-287.
114. Bradley and Blair, *Life*, p. 481.
115. See Hoopes and Brinkley, *Driven*, pp. 372-374. Forrestal was irritated also that Truman would vacillate over what to do next concerning Berlin, and he was still unwilling to approve sharp increases in the military budget. This had to wait for a supplementary appropriation.
116. For a detailed discussion of these negotiations, conducted by a Seven-Power Working Party, see Sir Nicholas Henderson, *The Birth of NATO* (Boulder, CO: Westview Press, 1983). Robert A. Lovett, the Undersecretary of State, represented the U.S. From the State Department came Charles A. "Chip" Bohlen, Counselor of the Department; George Kennan, Chief of the Policy Planning Staff; George Butler representing Kennan; John A.

"Jack" Hickerson, Chief of the Division of European Affairs; and Theodore "Ted" Achilles, Hickerson's Deputy. Lt. Gen. Alfred Gruenther represented Secretary of Defense Forrestal. (See also Theodore C. Achilles, "The Omaha Milkman: The Role of the United States in the Negotiations," in Andre de Staercke, *et al.*, Nicholas Sherwen, ed., *NATO's Anxious Birth: The Prophetic Vision of the 1940s* [London: C. Hurst and Co., 1985]).

Chapter 4

1. Douglas L. Bland, *The Military Committee of the North Atlantic Alliance: A Study of Structure and Strategy* (Westport, CT: Praeger, 1991), p. 186.
2. See ltr Twining–Norstad dtd 1/19/50 (EL, NP, Box 22, Official File 1949–50 [4]). One responsibility for the Alaska Commander was to look after the fishing camps that senior government officials would come to for their recreation. Norstad, like the other senior officers of his generation, loved to go up to Alaska for fishing. Fly-fishing was his first love. In the correspondence among them, there were frequent references such as: "I trust that your recent trip to Alaska was enjoyable and that you caught a lot of big ones." Ltr Brig. Gen. W.R. Wolfinbarge–Norstad, dtd 6/23/50 (EL, NP, Box 22, Official File 1949–50 [4]).
3. Ltr Norstad– Barton Leach, dtd 1/30/50 (EL, NP, Box 21, Leach File [1]). W. Barton Leach, of the Harvard Law School, had been a consultant to the Secretary of the Air Force for several years, playing, for example, a leading role in the Air Force's political maneuvering over the unification issue. He was also a reserve Air Force Brigadier General. Later Leach directed the Defense Studies Center at Harvard, which was subsequently led by Henry Kissinger. It was one of the earlier university-based "think tanks" concerned with what came to be known as "Security Studies."
4. Three informative unpublished papers by Dr. Michael O. Wheeler should be noted here: "The Evolution of Harry Truman's and Dwight D. Eisenhower's Views on Nuclear Weapons as an Instrument of National Security Policy, 1945–1955," dtd June 1997; "Nuclear Weapons and European Security: The Evolution of American Politico-Military Views, 1945–1954," dtd July 1997; "Early U.S. Nuclear Doctrine and Command and Control," dtd 8/97.
5. For a succinct description of the various efforts at pre-NATO and early NATO war planning, especially as concerns Germany, see Christian Greiner, "Strategic Concepts for the Defence of Western Europe, 1948–1950,"in Norbert Wiggershaus and Roland G. Foerster, eds., *The Western Security Community, 1948–1950: Common Problems and Conflicting National Interests during the Foundation Phase of the North Atlantic Alliance* (Oxford: Berg Publishers, 1993), pp. 313–341.
6. To assist him in his advocacy role, Norstad considered setting up a special, permanent policy presentation group. In some ways his action is reminiscent of Arnold's Advisory Council, membership on which had given Norstad his real start.
7. This is paraphrased from Jeffrey G. Barlow, *Revolt of the Admirals: The Fight for Naval Aviation, 1945–1950* (Washington, D.C.: Naval Historical Center, Department of the Navy, 1994), pp. 86ff.

8. For more about PINCHER and subsequent plans, see Steven T. Ross, *American War Plans, 1945–1950* (New York: Garland Publishing Inc., 1988). There was a subsequent edition printed in London by Frank Cass in 1996. See also Michael Sherry, *Preparing for the Next War: American Plans for Postwar Defense, 1941–1945* (New Haven: Yale University Press, 1977).
9. Barlow, *Revolt*, p. 84.
10. Barlow, *Revolt* p. 84. In note 83, Barlow cites: "Presentation Given to President by Major General Lauris Norstad on 29 October 1946. 'Postwar Military Establishment'," 30 Oct. 1946, 3–4, File No. 28, box 9, TS AAG Files, DCS/O General File 1944–53, RG 341, NA.
11. Quoted in Barlow, *Revolt*, p. 88. The document became JCS 1725/1.
12. Ltr Norstad–Mr. Thomas M. Johnson, dtd 5/22/46 (EL, NP).
13. For a detailed *exposé* of LeMay's efforts to protect the autonomy of SAC in relation to the defense of Europe in the early days of SHAPE, see Peter J. Roman, "Curtis LeMay and the Origins of NATO Atomic Targeting," *Journal of Strategic Studies*, March, 1993, pp. 46–74.
14. Quoted by Barlow, *Revolt*, p. 91. For a readable account of American and British war planning during this period, see Sean M. Maloney, *Securing Command of the Sea: NATO Naval Planning, 1948–1954* (Annapolis, MD: Naval Institute Press, 1995), Chs. 2 and 3.
15. HALFMOON itself became in various versions FLEETWOOD.
16. For more on this, see Robert S. Jordan, *Alliance Strategy and Navies: The Evolution and Scope of NATO's Maritime Dimension* (New York: St. Martin's Press, 1990).
17. Jordan, *Alliance*, p. 120.
18. Lawrence S. Kaplan, in Wiggershaus and Foerster, *Security*, p. 53. See also Greiner, in Wiggershaus and Foerster, *Security*. He discusses the French-inspired concept of the "Rhine Zone Defence," or the "Elbe Defence," favored by the Germans.
19. The text can be found in Thomas H. Etzold and John Lewis Gaddis, eds., *Containment: Documents on American Policy and Strategy, 1945–1950* (New York: Columbia University Press, 1978).
20. Omar N. Bradley and Clay Blair, *A General's Life: An Autobiography* (New York: Simon and Schuster, 1983), pp. 488–489. Later versions were called FLEETWOOD and DOUBLESTAR.
21. See Barlow, *Revolt*, p. 320 for full citation.
22. Maloney, *Securing*, pp. 83–84. See also Kaplan, "Western Union and European Military Integration 1948–1950 – An American Perspective," in Wiggershaus and Foerster, *Security*, pp. 45–67.
23. Barlow, *Revolt*, p. 95. See his page 321, note 151 for citations. A good source for this section is Walter S. Poole, *The History of the Joint Chiefs of Staff, The Joint Chiefs of Staff and National Policy, vol. 4, 1950–1952* (Washington, D.C.: Historical Division, Joint Secretariat, Joint Chiefs of Staff, 1979).
24. George Baer, *One Hundred Years of Sea Power: The U.S. Navy, 1890–1990* (Stanford, CA: Stanford University Press, 1994), p. 303). For a closer examination of U.S. planning as the Cold War got underway, see Ernest R. May, ed., *American Cold War Strategy: Interpreting NSC-68* (New York: Bedford Books of St. Martin's Press, 1993).

25. Greiner in Wiggershaus and Foerster, *Security*, pp. 326ff.
26. Maloney, *Securing*, p. 89. CROSSPIECE was the American designation, and GALLOPER was the British designation for this EWP. Core planning for the West was focused around Anglo-American war plans. (See Jordan, *Alliance* pp. 6ff.)
27. John Newhouse, *War and Peace in the Nuclear Age* (New York: Alfred A. Knopf, 1989), pp. 108–109.
28. Barlow, *Revolt*, p. 152.
29. Quoted in Bradley, *General*, p. 491.
30. *Life Magazine*, dtd 11/1/48, pp. 87, 90.
31. *Life Magazine*, dtd 11/1/48, p. 90.
32. Ltr Norstad–Air Chief Marshal Sir John C. Slessor, dtd 3/21/50 (EL, NP, Box 22, Official File 1949–50 [4]).
33. Jordan *Alliance*, pp. 8–9. This post should not be confused with the joint-service position of USCINCEUR heading the new Headquarters, U.S. European Command (USEUCOM), created in 1952; at that time the Army's command in Europe was renamed U.S. Army Europe (USAREUR) and its commander's title was changed to CINCUSAREUR. On NATO's naval command, see Maloney, *Securing*.
34. CINCEUR was in Heidelberg, and CINCNELM was in London.
35. Ltr Norstad–Cannon, dtd 9/27/50 (EL, NP, Box Official File 1949–50 [1]). The Air Force at this time consolidated the Air Defense Command and the Tactical Air Command into the Continental Air Command (CONAC). Each of these posts would be given four-star status, along with SAC, and USAFE.
36. For the U.S. Air Forces in Europe–U.K.–North Africa, it was planned to allocate nineteen general officers. The Deputy Commander would be three-star; the three numbered Air Forces commanders respectively for Europe, Britain, and the Mediterranean, would be two-star. In the headquarters, there would be a Chief of Staff and a Deputy for Operations, each two-star; the Director for Operations, the Deputy for Plans and the Deputy for Material would be two-star. See ltr, Maj. Gen. Nugent, A.F. Deputy Chief of Staff, Personnel–Norstad, dtd 12/4/50 (EL, NP, Box 21, Miscellaneous 1950 [1]).
37. Alfred Goldberg, ed., *A History of the United States Air Force, 1907–1957* (Princeton, NJ: D. Van Nostrand Co., Inc., 1957), pp. 111–112.
38. Douglas Kinnard, *President Eisenhower and Strategy Management: A Study in Defense Politics* (Washington: Pergamon–Brasseys, 1989), pp. 12–13; also Robert R. Bowie and Richard H. Immerman, *Waging Peace: How Eisenhower Shaped an Enduring War Strategy* (New York and Oxford: Oxford University Press, 1998).
39. Quoted in Timothy P. Ireland, *Creating the Entangling Alliance: The Origins of the North Atlantic Treaty Organization* (Westport, CT: Greenwood Press, 1981), p. 194. For an overview of the evolving SHAPE command structure, see Gregory W. Pedlow, "The Politics of NATO Command, 1950–1962," in Simon W. Duke and Wolfgang Krieger, eds., *U.S. Military Forces in Europe: The Early Years, 1945–1970* (Boulder, CO: Westview Press, 1993), pp. 15–42.
40. For a brief but authoritative summary of the creation of Eisenhower's new command, see the Introduction, "The Development of SHAPE: 1950–1953,"

by Andrew J. Goodpaster, in Robert S. Jordan, ed. *Generals in International Politics: NATO's Supreme Allied Commander, Europe* (Lexington, KY: The University Press of Kentucky, 1987), pp. 1–7. Norstad thought very highly of Goodpaster, having brought him to Eisenhower's attention when Eisenhower was Army Chief of Staff, and Norstad had recommended Goodpaster to join a special unit for long-range plans. Goodpaster, like Norstad, made his reputation as a planner, albeit with a good World War II combat record. (See John Prados, *Keepers of The Keys: A History of the National Security Council from Truman to Bush* [New York: William Morrow and Co., Inc., 1991], pp. 66–67).

41. Goldberg, *History*, p. 112. The Seventeenth was created in April 1953. By 1957, these three air forces had control of all USAFE combat units – fighter, fighter-bomber, light bomber, and reconnaissance. The combat units of the tactical air forces were allocated to one or another of the major international air commands established under SHAPE. The Third Air Force, in the U.K., also supported SAC's 7th Air Division; the Twelfth Air Force directed the operations of all USAFE tactical air units in Europe; the Seventeenth AF's area of responsibility was the Mediterranean and North Africa, including the SAC 5th Air Division in Morocco. (Goldberg, *History*, p. 112.)

42. Paralleling SACEUR's policy of delegating his day-to-day USCINCEUR responsibilities to the Deputy USCINCEUR, Norstad delegated his CINCUSAFE responsibilities to his deputy, Major General Truman H. Landon. Barney Oldfield, who was a public affairs/information officer/international affairs consultant both in the Air Force and in corporate life, recalls that he arranged to have Norstad activate his AAFCE command on April 2 rather than April 1,1951 to avoid ridicule from the European Communist press. (Ltr, Oldfield–Jordan, dtd 6/26/89) Oldfield also established the "General Lauris Norstad Political and Military Science Scholarship" at the University of Nebraska. The Iron Gate Chapter of the Air Force Association endowed a General Lauris Norstad Falcon Foundation scholarship to give prep school assistance to aspirants for appointment to the Air Force Academy. (See Barney Oldfield, *Never a Shot in Anger* [Santa Barbara, CA: Capra Press, Inc., Battle of Normandy Museum Edition, 1989], note 19, p. xxxvii.)

43. See Lord Ismay, *NATO The First Five Years 1949–1954* (Paris: NATO Information Services, 1954). Norstad had advocated planning for the use in Europe of tactical atomic weapons as early as August 1951 (See also Robert A. Wampler, *NATO Strategic Planning and Nuclear Weapons, 1950–1957*, Occasional Paper 6, Nuclear History Program, Center for International Security Studies, School of Public Affairs, University of Maryland, 1990, p. 53. Wampler cites a series of "red line" messages between Norstad and Vandenberg.)

44. Quoted in Wampler, *Planning*, p. 7. Dr. Wampler was very helpful in sharing some of his writings with the author during the early stages of this project.

45. Wampler, *Planning*, p. 6. See also Timothy Stanley, *NATO in Transition: The Future of the Atlantic Alliance* (New York: Frederick A. Praeger, 1965). Stanley mentions that there were at times proposals for a "Supreme Commander, Nuclear Weapons (SACNUC)", or "Supreme Commander Deterrent (SACDET)" (p. 232.)

46. Ltr Norstad–LeMay, dtd 9/25/50 (EL, NP, Box 22, Official File 1949–50 [1]); ltr Norstad–LeMay, dtd 9/28/50 (WL, NP, Box 22, Official File 1949–50 [4]). This letter went through several revisions by Norstad, obviously reflecting its importance in demarking relationships and command authority that involved two major Air Force components. The Third Air Division would be assigned to CINCUSAFE.
47. Quoted by Bland, *Military*, p. 190. As Bland pointed out: "In these circumstances the Military Committee and the Standing Group, isolated in Washington, could not play any significant role." See also Sir Peter Hill-Norton, *No Soft Options: The Politico-Military Realities of NATO* (Montreal: McGill-Queen's University Press, 1978), pp. 88–89.
48. *New York Herald-Tribune*, dtd 10/31/56, as quoted in Robert S. Jordan, *Political Leadership in NATO: A Study in Multinational Diplomacy* (Boulder, CO: Westview Press, 1979), p. 46.
49. Jordan, *Generals*, pp. 50–51.
50. See Jordan, *Generals*, pp. 28.
51. For a description of the so-called Annual Review process by which the military requirements were reconciled with the economic capacities of the member-states, see Robert S. Jordan, *The NATO International Staff/Secretariat, 1952–1957: A Study in International Administration* (London: Oxford University Press, 1967).
52. Quoted in Jordan, *Generals*, pp. 43.
53. For an excellent discussion of the evolution of nuclear policy *vis-á-vis* NATO, see Marc Trachtenberg, *History and Strategy* (Princeton: Princeton University Press, 1991), pp. 107ff.
54. See Wampler, *Planning*, p. 11. This was called Project Solarium. See Kinnard, *Strategy*, for a discussion of the Eisenhower Administration's "New Look" – or attempt to get "more bang for the buck." Also Bowie and Immerman, *Waging Peace*.
55. Kinnard, *Strategy*, p. 14.
56. Robert S. Allen, "Bob Allen Reports," *New York Post*, dtd 7/18/52. Allen's column was nationally syndicated, so it appeared all over the country. In some newspapers, it was noted as a factor in Norstad's favor: "When Norstad graduated from West Point in 1930, he was first commissioned as a 2nd lieutenant of Cavalry and didn't get his wings until the following year. LeMay is not a West Pointer. He was graduated as an engineer from Ohio State University and entered the regular Army as a pilot in 1928."
57. *Washington Post*, dtd 8/2/52. Winchell put it under the heading, "The Washington Ticker." The rumors persisted in the gossip columns for several months. (See, for example, Danton Walker, "Broadway," *Boston Traveller*, dated 11/52.)
58. Some of this access came when he was working closely with James Forrestal, the first Secretary of Defense. Forrestal had excellent Washington connections. (See Townsend Hoopes and Douglas Brinkley, *Driven Patriot: The Life and Times of James Forrestal* (New York: Alfred A. Knopf, 1992); also C.L. Sulzberger's memoirs, *A Long Row of Candles*, and *An Age of Mediocrity* (New York: Macmillan Publishing Company, 1969 and 1973, respectively).

59. *Air Force Times*, dtd 7/15/52. Norstad's close friend, Charles Cabell, received his third star at this time.
60. *Courrier de L'Ouest Angers*, dtd 7/9/52.
61. *Chicago Tribune*, dtd 7/20/52.
62. Because of his assignment as Vice Chief of Staff of the Air Force, Norstad had played an important role in the creation of a CINC instead of a Commanding General (CG) position which insured the Air Force's independence from the Army. For more on Vandenberg's desire to maintain a strong independent Air Force role in SHAPE, see Roman, *LeMay*, pp. 58–59.
63. For more detailed information on the many changes in NATO's command system during this period, see Pedlow, "The Politics of NATO Command, 1950–1962," in Duke and Krieger, *Forces*.
64. For more on NATO's regional military structure, see Jordan, *NATO*, and Bland, *Military*. For more on the formation of the NATO naval commands, see Jordan, *Alliance*; Maloney, *Securing*; and Robert S. Jordan, "U.S. Naval Forces in Europe and NATO," in Duke and Krieger, *Forces*, pp. 66–82.
65. See Chapter 2, and also Daniel R. Mortensen, *A Pattern for Joint Operations: World War II Close Air Support North Africa* (Washington, D.C.: Office of Air Force History and U.S. Army Center of Military History, Historical Analysis Series, 1987).
66. Benjamin Welles, "Norstad Discussed as NATO Air Chief," *The New York Times*, dtd 8/17/52.
67. See Bradley and Blair, *General*, pp. 655 and 659–660. Admiral Arthur Radford's name was also prominently mentioned for CNO.
68. *Daily Telegraph* (London), "Next Chief," dtd 12/11/52.
69. Bob Considine, "Loss by Early Retirement Snarls Choice of Air Force Chief," *Omaha World Herald*, dtd 3/31/53.
70. Ibid.
71. Harvey Hudson, "'Boy Wonder' General Fast Building European Air Defenses," *Port Arthur (Tex) News*, dtd 11/16/52. This was filed through the Associated Press.
72. Trachtenberg, *Strategy*, pp. 162–165.
73. Quoted in David N. Schwartz, *NATO's Nuclear Dilemmas* (Washington, D.C.: Brookings Institution, 1983), p. 24. Norstad's career, starting with his service with the Twentieth Air Force in World War II was, of course, virtually built around the development and use of atomic and nuclear weapons.
74. Quoted in *Flight*, "NATO Air Power Lacking," dtd 1/16/53.
75. See Maxwell D. Taylor, *The Uncertain Trumpet* (New York: Harper and Brothers, 1960).
76. *Daily Mail*, dtd 3/6/53.
77. Ltr Gruenther–Eisenhower, dtd 2/14/53. Major General William H. Tunner, of Berlin Air Lift fame, succeed Norstad as CINCUSAFE. He had replaced Major General Landon as Deputy CINCUSAFE the previous May. When Norstad became SACEUR, he had a Belgian general officer as his Air Deputy, but this person was advisory only.
78. Don Cook, "Norstad, Juin Given Broader Commands," *New York Herald-Tribune*, dtd 7/4/53.

79. Ibid. The long delay in bringing the changes about was caused partly by the cumbersome decision-making structure in NATO. The reorganization plan had to go to the Standing Group and then to the NAC, which could only act after the governments had provided the Permanent Representatives with their instructions.
80. *Continental Daily Mail*, "Big SHAPE ReShuffle," dtd 2/28/53.
81. Don Cook, "1953 is Pay-Off Year for NATO Air Planners," *New York Herald-Tribune*, dtd 3/15/53.
82. Taken from NSC 162/2, in *Foreign Relations of the United States* (FRUS), 1952–1954, II. 577–597. See Wampler, *Planning*, pp. 13–14. In NSC/68, the Truman Administration's policy rationale for the buildup, the expectation was that a rapid military buildup was needed to meet a period of "maximum danger" which was posited as being 1952–54. See Ernest R. May, ed., *American Cold War Strategy* (New York: Bedford Books, St Martin's Press, 1993), p. 14; also Paul H. Nitze, *From Hiroshima to Glasnost: At the Center of Decision, A Memoir* (New York: Grove Weidenfeld, 1989), pp. 93–100; Richard H. Immerman, ed. *John Foster Dulles and the Diplomacy of the Cold War* (Princeton: Princeton U.P., 1990), p. 32.
83. Harry S. Truman, *Memoirs: Years of Trial and Hope*, Vol. Two (Garden City, N.Y.: Doubleday and Co., Inc., 1956), p. 304.
84. Ltr Eisenhower–Gruenther, dtd 10/27/53. Eisenhower used the term "Roman wall" frequently in protesting that the commitment militarily of the U.S. to Europe could be permanent in the sense of being a garrison. (See also Stephen E. Ambrose, *Eisenhower the President*, Vol. Two [New York: Simon and Schuster, 1984], p. 143.) For more on the Ridgway–Gruenther–Eisenhower relationship in NATO, see Jordan, *Generals*, Chs. 2, 3.
85. Quoted in Jordan, *Generals*, pp. 58–59. Testimony to U.S. Senate, Committee on Foreign Relations on 3/26/55.
86. "Gen'l Gruenther's Support for Atomic Weapons," *The Times* (London), dtd 6/9/54, p. 6. (Quoted in Jordan, *Generals*, p. 59.)
87. Ibid. For a general discussion of the place of atomic weapons in the Alliance, see Francis A. Beer, *Integration and Disintegration in NATO* (Columbus, OH: Ohio State University Press, 1969), Ch. 2.
88. *NATO Final Communiques, 1949–1974* (Brussels: NATO Information Service, 1974), p. 16. The language was: "The Council expressed the firm determination of all member governments to see the Atlantic forces equipped with the most modern weapons" (p. 96).
89. Memo Gruenther–Radford, "USEUCOM Joint Capabilities Plans, 1-55," dtd 11/12/55 (NA, JCS, CDF, 1954–56, Box 113). The plans were prepared in accordance with JCS guidance for the 1995 planning cycle and the JCS's comments on the USEUCOM Joint Capabilities Plan for 1954. Ridgway's "SACEUR's Estimate on the Situation and Force Requirements for 1956" had put the main weight of NATO's atomic counter-offensive on non-NATO territory, in accord with the desire of the FRG that it not be the atomic battlefield. (See Wampler, *Planning*, p. 9.)
90. Memo JCS–Norstad, "USEUCOM Joint Capabilities Plan 1-55," dtd 1/17/56 (NA, JCS, CDF, 1954–56, Box 113).

91. Alfred Gruenther, "The Defense of Europe," address at the Alfred E. Smith Memorial Foundation Dinner, New York City, 10/8/53, reprinted in the *Department of State Bulletin*, dtd 11/9/53.
92. Ltr Gruenther–Eisenhower, dtd 4/3/54.
93. *NATO Final Communiques*, p. 102.
94. Eisenhower had obtained from his National Security Council a new statement of policy that broadened the extent of the U.S.'s sharing with its Allies information concerning nuclear weapons. This was NSC/151/1. (See Ambrose, *Eisenhower the President*, pp. 145–146.)
95. Marc Trachtenberg, *A Constructed Peace: The Making of the European Settlement 1945–1963* (Princeton: Princeton University Press, 1999), p. 177.
96. Ltr Eisenhower–Gruenther, dtd 10/27/54, in Gruenther Papers, Eisenhower Library. For the motives for the "New Look." see Kinnard, *Strategy*, ch. 1. The reference to Dulles is on pp. 35–36. Also see Bowie and Immerman, *Waging Peace*.
97. *NATO Final Communiques*, p. 113–114. This is also cited in Lawrence S. Kaplan, *NATO and the United States: The Enduring Alliance* (Boston: Twayne Publishers, 1988), p. 62. At the December 1956 NAC Ministerial Meeting, the Defense Ministers of Britain, France, the Netherlands, and Turkey, had requested that tactical nuclear warheads under the control of the U.S. be made available to NATO Europe – other than the FRG. (See also Kinnard, *Strategy*, p. 40.)
98. Statement of General Norstad before the Senate Foreign Relations Committee, dtd 3/26/58.
99. This was one important reason for NSC 151/1. Quoted in Ambrose, *Eisenhower the President*, pp. 146.
100. *Illustré*, dtd 6/28/56. This article is a good summary of the lifestyle of the Norstad family during their time in Europe (EL, NP).
101. "NATO Commander Norstad: Thinning Line Against Russia," *Newsweek*, dtd 12/17/56, p. 15.
102. Margaret Biddle, "General Norstad: A Portrait of the Supreme Commander, Allied Powers in Europe," *Realities*, dtd 9/56, p. 12. Her husband, Brig. Gen. Anthony Biddle, was on the staff at SHAPE. He had been appointed by Eisenhower to be his staff liaison with the National Military Representatives (NMRs). The NMRs represented national points of view to Eisenhower and his successors. (See Jordan, *Generals*, p. 3.)
103. See ltr dtd 4/3/56 from President Eisenhower to Lord Ismay, Vice Chairman, NAC. (EL, EP, Box 3, WH, NATO File No. 1.[1])
104. White House Press Release, dtd 4/12/56 (EL, Papers of D.D.E. [EP], Box 3, White House Office, NATO File No. 1 [1]).
105. Ltr. Norstad – Eisenhower, dtd 4/17/56.
106. *New York World – Telegram and Sun*, dtd 4/21/56.
107. Ltr Baruch–Norstad, dtd 5/16/56 (Norstad's personal letters [NPL] concerning his appointment as SACEUR are deposited with the Papers of Lauris Norstad at the Eisenhower Library).
108. Ltr Cabell–Norstad, dtd 4/16/56 (NPL). Cabell at that time was Deputy Director of the CIA.
109. Ltr Quarles–Norstad, dtd 4/15/56 (NPL).

110. Ltr Hamilton–Norstad, dtd 4/16/56 (NPL).
111. Ltr Ganey–Norstad, dtd 4/19/56 (NPL).
112. Ltr Hutchinson–Norstad, dtd 4/17/56 (NPL).
113. Ltr van Vredenburch–Norstad, dtd 4/20/56 (NPL). Van Vredenburch had been Deputy Secretary-General of NATO under Lord Ismay.
114. Quoted from a reply to a letter of congratulations from The Rt. Hon. The Viscount Swinton, dtd 4/17/56 (NPL). Swinton had played a very important role in British defense policy over much of Norstad's career.
115. To get an idea of just how turbulent it was, see Dean Acheson, *Present at the Creation: My Years in the State Department* (New York: W.W. Norton and Co., 1969), and Hoopes and Brinkley, *Driven*.
116. Ltr w/encl., Wilkinson–Jordan, dtd 11/23/88. See Burke Wilkinson, *Night of the Short Knives* (New York: Charles Scribner's Sons, 1964). Wilkinson was Public Affairs Adviser to Norstad from 1958 to 1962.

Chapter 5

1. Text of interview with Norstad by Robert Kleiman, Western European Editor, *U.S. News and World Report*, undtd.
2. Marc Trachtenberg, *History and Strategy* (Princeton: Princeton University Press, 1991), p. 163.
3. Eisenhower to Sen. Henry M. Jackson, dtd 5/17/66, Senate Committee on Government Operations, Hearings, *The Atlantic Alliance*, pp. 224–225.
4. Norstad's testimony, U.S. Congress, Joint Committee on Atomic Energy, Subcommittee on Agreements for Cooperation, Amending the Atomic Energy Act of 1954, Hearings, 85th Congress, 2nd Session, 1958, p. 519. But, when President Kennedy and Secretary of Defense McNamara *de facto* declassified such sensitive information as numbers of warheads, their locations, and their targets to Chancellor Konrad Adenauer and others – friend and foe alike – Norstad felt that matters had gone too far.
5. Elizabeth Stabler, "The MLF: Background and Analysis of Pros and Cons," *Congressional Record*, U.S. House of Representatives, dtd 1/5/65, p. 81.
6. Memo Elbrick–Dulles, "NATO Atomic Stockpile," dtd 10/23/57 National Archives (NA), Records of the Department of State (State Dept.), Office of European Regional Affairs (Eur. Reg. Aff.), Office of Atlantic Political and Military Affairs, Records Relating to NATO, 1957–64, Box 1.
7. Ltr Dulles–Wilson, dtd 7/2/57 National Archives (NA), Records of the Department of State (State Dept.), Bureau of European Affairs (Eur. Aff.), Office of European Regional Affairs Eur. (Reg. Aff.), Political-Military Numerical Files (Pol-Mil) NF, Box 6.
8. *NATO Final Communiques, 1949–1974* (Brussels: NATO Information Service, 1974), p. 113. See also MC/14/2, dtd 12/57.
9. The true name for this concept of stockpiling was the NATO Special Ammunition Storage Program. The purpose of the Program was for the U.S. to provide nuclear weapons support to several delivery systems assigned, or to be assigned, to national forces made available to NATO.
10. Memo Elbrick and Smith–Dulles, dtd 7/1/57 (NA, State Dept., Eur. Aff., Eur. Reg. Aff., Pol-Mil. NF, Box 6). See also, in connection with the "New

Look," NSC 162/2 (October 1953) and NSC 5501 (January 1955); the two policy statements and a subsequent "interpretation" of March 1955 specified that whereas planning should go forward on the assumption that nuclear weapons would be used, alternatives should also be considered, and furthermore there would be no decision in advance that nuclear weapons would be used (For a further discussion, see Leon Sloss and Kemper Vest, *Nuclear Weapons and the Berlin Crisis*, Lessons from Nuclear History Project, Center for National Security Negotiations Occasional Paper, Monograph #2, April 1995.)

11. See memo Elbrick–Dulles, "NATO Atomic Stockpile," dtd. 10/23/57 (NA, State Dept., Eur. Aff., Office of Atlantic Political and Military Affairs [Atl. Pol-Mil. Aff.], Records Relating to NATO [NATO], 1957–64, Box 1).
12. Memo to Chairman, JCS, "Brief of Comparison of Views on 'NATO Atomic Stockpile Concept'", dtd 10/28/57 (NA, Records of the Joint Chiefs of Staff [JCS], Chairman File/General Twining [CF/GT], 1957–60, Box 10). The initial planning called for a buildup to a total of 240 missiles, or 16 squadrons by the end of fiscal Year 1962. Included would be the 60 missiles (four squadrons) for the U.K. Norstad would not be given any control over atomic warheads stored in the U.K. for strategic purposes. See ltr Sec. Defense Wilson–Sec. State Dulles, dtd 11/14/57 (NA, JCS, CF/GT, 1957–60, Box 10).
13. See Chapter 6 for the Berlin crisis and Norstad.
14. This entire question is discussed fully in James L. Richardson, *Germany and the Atlantic Alliance* (Cambridge, MA: Harvard University Press, 1966), esp. Ch 1 and 3. As early as Autumn 1949, the U.S. Army General Staff had drafted a plan for the creation of German divisions that was endorsed by the JCS in April 1950. The plan was not adopted as official policy because the State Department claimed that European objections would be too strong. (Richardson, *Germany*, pp. 18.)
15. "Text of Norstad's TV Interview," dtd 2/25/58 (NA, Stste Dept., Eur. Aff., Eur. Reg. Aff., Pol-Mil. NF, Box 7).
16. However, if further NATO requirements demand, it was understood that two additional squadrons of JUPITERs could be introduced, providing that Mutual Security Program (MSP) funds were made available. The introduction of IRBMs into the NATO armory under Norstad as SACEUR initially was limited to five squadrons of THOR and three squadrons of JUPITER missiles. Norstad's overall plan called for a total of ten IRBM squadrons, with four provided to Britain and two for Italy. This left two additional squadrons, and possibly four, that might be deployed either in Europe or in the U.S. or U.S.-controlled territory. Norstad wanted one squadron each in Greece and Turkey, presaging a *de facto* escalation of NATO's deterrent threat to the Soviet heartland from NATO's southern flank. A not-unimportant political consideration for Norstad was that by sending this latest weaponry to Greece and Turkey these member-states would know that they were being treated as "first-class" partners in NATO.
17. Quoted in Richardson, *Germany*, pp. 50–51.
18. "Text of Norstad's TV Interview," dtd 2/25/58 (NA, State Dept., Eur. Aff., Eur. Reg. Aff., Pol-Mil. NF, Box 7).
19. Memo Yingling–Raymond, "Circular 175: Authority to Conclude Agreement with the United Kingdom re Atomic Stockpile in Germany,"

dtd 5/8/59. This agreement was concluded as an Executive Agreement according to the President's inherent constitutional authority as Chief Executive and Commander-in-Chief of the Armed Forces, which meant that it did not need ratification by Congress.
20. "Defending Europe without France," interview with General Lauris Norstad, *Der Spiegel*, dtd 4/18/66, reprinted in *The Atlantic Community Quaterly* 4, no. 2 (Summer 1966), p. 183. After his retirement, however, in a pamphlet published by the Critical Issues Council of the Republican Citizens Committee of the U.S., and prepared by a task force under the chairmanship of Norstad, he appeared to back away from his earlier position. The pamphlet stated: "It can no longer be taken for granted that what is good for the narrow circle of countries seeking a powerful political merger will necessarily serve the purposes of those other allies with whom they are aligned in the crucial task of collective Atlantic defense ... . We must now reappraise our view of European unity ... in terms of America's own interest."
21. Memo of Meeting, Norstad–Quarles, dtd 1/18/58 (NA, State Dept., Eur. Aff., Atl. Pol-Mil. Aff., NATO, 1957–64, Box 1). But Norstad was very sensitive to his own command prerogatives, and this meant that he did not want to have to obtain the express approval of the NAC for every step that he took to implement NATO policy concerning nuclear weapons. By reporting his progress to the Standing Group, he obtained, in effect, the implicit approval of the NAC, thus avoiding to some extent having to contend with the endless political wrangling that went on in the NAC. (See Memo, Norstad–OSD ALO 260, dtd 2/20/58 [NA, State Dept., Eur. Aff., Atl. Pol-Mil. Aff., NATO, 1957–64, Box 1]). Spaak was kept in the picture through the State Department when NAC business on these matters from the U.S. national angle was involved.
22. An agreement had been negotiated between Eisenhower and Macmillan in Bermuda, dtd 2/22/58, which committed the U.S. to provide IRBMs to the U.K. on a grant basis under the Mutual Weapons Development Program (MWDP). In accordance with the agreement, the U.S. undertook to provide the weapons systems for four squadrons of THOR IRBMs, to be equipped with atomic warheads.
23. Memo of Meeting, Norstad–Quarles, dtd 1/18/58 (NA, State Dept., Eur. Aff., Atl. Pol-Mil. Aff., NATO 1957–64, Box 1).
24. Memo, "U.S. Policy on IRBMs for NATO," dtd 11/24/58 (NA, State Dept., Eur. Aff., Eur. Reg. Aff., Records of NATO advisor [NATO ad.], Box 1). Also, in fairness to the French, it took time for Norstad to work out what would appear to be very simplified arrangements.
25. Ltr Dulles–McElroy, dtd 3/3/59. The original target number was for twelve squadrons for NATO Europe, and this was maintained.
26. Memo Timmons–Murphy, "Second Generation IRBMs for Europe," dtd 2/5/59 (NA, State Dept., Eur. Aff., Eur. Reg. Aff., NATO ad, Box 1).
27. Ibid.
28. The funding was terminated in March 1959 because the U.S. did not consider BLUE STREAK an operationally effective weapon.
29. Memo for the Files, "Second Generation IRBM's for Europe, dtd 2/12/59 (NA, State Dept., Eur. Aff., Eur. Reg. Aff., NATO ad., Box 1).

30. For a survey of Britain's attempts to stay in the ballistic missile field, see William P. Snyder, *The Politics of British Defense Policy, 1945–1962* (Columbus, OH: Ohio State University Press, 1964), pp. 24ff.
31. Memo for the Files, "Second Generation IRBMs for Europe."
32. Memo Timmons–Murphy, "Second Generation IRBMs for Europe," dtd 2/5/59 (NA, State Dept., Eur. Aff., Eur. Reg. Aff., NATO ad., Box 1). The other options were: U.S. technical assistance and limited financial support, but no insistence on NATO control; U.S. technical assistance and limited financial support conditioned upon NATO control; U.S. provision of POLARIS missiles without insistence on NATO control.
33. Memo of Norstad–Quarles Meeting, "Second Generation IRBMs for Europe," dtd 2/6/59 (NA, State Dept., Eur. Aff., Eur. Reg. Aff., NATO ad., Box 1). When Greece declined to accept MRBMs on its territory, there occurred a discussion as to where the eighth IRBM squadron should go. For budgetary reasons, Norstad decided not to press for moving the squadron elsewhere.
34. Memo Timmons–Murphy, "Attached Telegram re NATO Atomic Stockpile," dtd 2/21/59 (NA, State Dept., Eur. Aff., Eur. Reg. Aff., Pol-Mil. NF, Box 6).
35. Memo for the Chairman, JCS, "Comments on General Norstad's Message Re Soviet Note on Development of an Atomic Capability in Germany and Other NATO Countries," dtd 4/24/59 (NA, JCS, Central Decimal File [CDF], 1959, Box 107).
36. "Soviet Note dtd 4/21/59 to the US Government on Modernization of Armaments of US Allies," Soviet Note Number 28/OSA (NA, State Dept., Eur. Aff., Eur. Reg. Aff., Pol-Mil. NF, Box 6).
37. Associated Press, dtd 12/18/59. Norstad, address to the NATO Parliamentarians' Conference, *Addresses by Speakers*, 1960, p. 36 (NATO Information Service).
38. U.S. Senate. Hearings, pp. 82–84. Norstad also commented emphatically: "The critical and immediate problem was not with some new longer-range strategic force of yet undetermined purpose and pattern, not with the deployment of weapons which do not bear directly on the NATO task, not with an MLF, for instance ... . Rather the problem was 'how do we answer the European questions as to the availability and the control of weapons already deployed and, in a way, engaged.'" (Hearings, pp. 70, 86.)
39. U.S. Senate. Committee on Government Operations. Hearings, *The Atlantic Alliance*, pp. 82–84.
40. Hearings, pp. 82, 84. There were variations on the notion, as Norstad maneuvered among various national sensitivities to find a broadly acceptable formula.
41. See the following section of this chapter for more on de Gaulle's proposal. In a speech at the University of Southern California in Los Angeles on 12/6/59, Norstad continued his attempt to influence American opinion in favor of making NATO the "fourth nuclear power" through the creation of a multinational atomic authority.
42. A complete discussion of types of alliances can be found in Julian Freedman *et al.*, *Alliance in International Politics* (Boston: Allyn and Bacon, 1970). See esp., K.J. Holsti, "Diplomatic Coalitions and Military Alliances," pp. 93–103.

43. Norstad, comment at Eisenhower Library conference. For a good discussion of the French view, see General Pierre Gallois, *The Balance of Terror: Strategy for the Missile Age* (Boston: Houghton-Mifflin, 1961).
44. Holsti, "Diplomatic" p. 103. [Holsti's emphasis]
45. Paul–Henri Spaak, address to the Imperial Defense College, dtd 10/21/60 (mimeographed) (NATO Information Service).
46. As far back as the previous November, Norstad had proposed it to Adenauer's Minister of Defense, Franz–Josef Strauss, who had indicated his support. The military staff in Bonn under general Adolf Heusinger also favored it.
47. Ltr Eisenhower–Norstad, dtd 4/29/60 (EL, NP, Box 28, Norstad–Gen. Lauris [1]).
48. This summary is extracted from a Memo of Conference with the President, recording Norstad's conversation with Eisenhower, dtd 3/15/60 (EL, NP, Box 28, Norstad–Gen. Lauris).
49. Paul–Henri Spaak, *The Continuing Battle: Memoirs of a European 1936–1966* (Boston: Little, Brown and Co., 1971), pp. 341–342.
50. Msg Norstad–Quarles SH 21218, dtd 2/2/58 (NA, State Dept., Eur. Aff., Atl. Pol-Mil. Aff., NATO, 1957–64, Box 1). Donald Quarles was Deputy Secretary of Defense.
51. Ibid.
52. Msg Norstad–Quarles ALO 230, dtd 2/12/58 (NA, State Dept., Eur. Aff., Atl. Pol-Mil. Aff., NATO, 1957–64, Box 1).
53. Memo for the Record, Attachments, dtd 3/25/58 (NA, State Dept., Eur. Aff., Eur. Reg. Aff., Pol-Mil. Aff., Box 7). This document references the following: (1) S/AE-2771/5-Paris 4376 3/22, (2) S/AE-2189/5-Paris 4016 2/27, (3) S/AE-2186/5-Paris 3999 2/26.
54. Edgar S. Furniss, Jr., "The French Military Position," unpub. paper presented to a Study Group of the Council on Foreign Relations, dtd 3/11/58. It was contained as an enclosure to a letter introducing Furniss to SHAPE. Ltr, Col. Richard A. Yudkin–Gen. C.V.R. Schuyler, SHAPE Chief of Staff, dtd 4/11/58 (EL, NP, Box 9, Freeman thru Furniss).
55. This draft went from Norstad to Ely on 3/21/58 (NA, State Dept., Eur. Aff., Atl. Pol-Mil. Aff., NATO, 1957–64, Box 1). This was drawn from DOD Draft No. 3 "Agreement." Since France wanted all of the three IRBM squadrons to be assigned to France to be French manned, at least a calendar year would have been required to make the IRBM capability operational.
56. Under the arrangement, the technical teams would have been under Norstad as USCINCEUR, but the French noted that the first Thor squadron in Britain was operated and controlled by the RAF.
57. Memo Jandrey–Dulles, "Developments Since Your Talks with General de Gaulle on the French IRBM and Nuclear Storage Questions," dtd 7/24/58 (NA, State Dept., Eur. Aff., Atl. Pol-Mil. Aff., NATO, 1957–4, Box 2).
58. Quoted in McGeorge Bundy, *Danger and Survival: Choices About the Bomb in the First Fifty Years* (New York: Vintage Books, 1988), p. 473. Bundy felt that if Norstad had requested permission from Eisenhower to provide the information de Gaulle wanted, he would have received it.
59. Charles De Gaulle, *Memoirs of Hope: Renewal and Endeavor*, trans. Terence Kilmartin (New York: Simon and Schuster, 1971), pp. 257–258.

60. Secretary-General Spaak in his memoirs also claims to have had in his possession a copy, passed to him in his capacity as Secretary-General, but that this copy subsequently disappeared mysteriously from his files (Spaak, *Continuing Battle*, p. 312).
61. Dwight D. Eisenhower, *The White House Years: Waging Peace, 1956–1961* (Garden City: Doubleday and Co., Inc., 1965) p. 427.
62. Department of State, Memo of Conversation, "Tripartism," dtd 2/4/59 (NSA, Berlin, Norstad). It should be pointed out, however, that at this time other voices were suggesting thoughts similar to de Gaulle's "globalist" conception for NATO. One, in fact, was Spaak's, who advocated that NATO should be geared to meet the Soviet Union's economic challenge in the underdeveloped countries. In fact, Spaak soon resigned as Secretary-General to resume the Premiership of Belgium precisely over his concern about the effects of decolonization on global politics. (See Robert S. Jordan, *Political Leadership in NATO: A Study in Multinational Diplomacy* (Boulder, CO: Westview Press, 1979) pp. 91ff.).
63. Spaak, *Continuing Battle*, pp. 339.
64. Memo Lyon–Dulles 1652, dtd 11/4/58 (NSA, Berlin, Norstad).
65. Associated Television Limited, March 31, 1959, "General Norstad: Supreme Allied Commander, Europe, interviewed by William Clark in ATV's 'Right to Reply' series on the Independent Television Network."
66. For more on the Anglo-American relationship and NATO, see Robert S. Jordan, *The NATO International Staff/Secretariat 1952—1957: A Study in International Administration* (London and New York: Oxford University Press, 1967); Don Cook, *Forging the Alliance: The Birth of the NATO Treaty and the Dramatic Transformation of U.S. Foreign Policy Between 1945 and 1950* (New York: Arbor House/William Morrow, 1989). NATO's "doyen" during this period, compiled a useful book – André de Staercke, *NATO's Anxious Birth: the Prophetic Vision of the 1940s*, ed. Nicholas Sherwen (London: C. Hurst and Co., 1985).
67. The expectation was to complete the deployment to Turkey of a JUPITER squadron which originally had been slated for Italy, but for training and logistics reasons could be better utilized by the end of 1959 in Turkey. During 1960 the DOD planned to deploy either a JUPITER or THOR squadron in Greece, with a second squadron, either JUPITER or THOR, then going to Turkey.
68. See Internal State Department memo, "Problems to be Discussed at Meeting on IRBMs," dtd 1/8/59 (NA, State Dept., Eur. Aff., Atl. Pol-Mil. Aff., NATO, 1957—64, Box 1). The State Department wanted to await the completion of this study before going beyond the commitment for the four squadrons planned for the U.K. and the one squadron for Italy already committed.
69. For more discussion on this matter, see ltr Dulles–Secretary of Defense Neil H. McElroy, dtd 2/3/59 (NA, State Dept., Eur. Aff., Atl. Pol-Mil Aff., NATO, 1957–64, Box 1).
70. For a complete discussion, see Robert S. Jordan, *Political Leadership in NATO: A Study in Multinational Diplomacy* (Boulder, CO: Westview Press, 1979), pp. 86–94.
71. See SHAPE Memo for General Norstad, dtd 6/15/59 (EL, NP, Box 96, Atomic Nuclear Policy [3]). For a cogent analysis, see Thomas Cadett, "General de Gaulle and Nato," *The Listener*, dtd 6/18/59.

72. In order to facilitate NATO's adoption of the strategy of tactical nuclear response, the U.S. had, by then, revised the restrictive Atomic Energy Act of 1946 (the McMahon Act), enabling atomic weapons to be supplied to NATO Allies provided the warheads remained under American control.
73. To maintain physical custody of the weapons, the U.S. would make available to NATO appropriately trained military personnel who would be reponsive to NATO authority–meaning Norstad's.
74. Memo Nolting–Dulles, dtd 8/21/59 (NA, JCS, CDF, 1959, Box 107).
75. Ltr Norstad–Eisenhower, dtd 1/27/60 (EL, EP, Box 28, NATO–Norstad–De Gaulle).
76. Memo of Conference with the President, dtd 11/6/59 (NSA, Berlin, Norstad).
77. It had been established in 1958 that SACLANT's requirements in the European theater were to be closely coordinated with those of SACEUR and covered by whatever arrangements were worked out between the United States and the host countries concerned with respect to European elements of the NATO atomic stockpile. In other words, there were to be no separately arrived at arrangements for the SACLANT atomic stockpile, or separate negotiations between SACLANT and the European countries involved. Ltr, Timmons–Wolf, dtd 9/23/58 (NA, State Dept., Eur. Aff., Atl. Pol-Mil. Aff., NATO, 1957–64, Box 1). See also Robert S. Jordan, *Alliance Strategy and Navies: The Evolution and Scope of NATO's Maritime Dimension* (London: Pinter Publishers; New York: St. Martin's Press, 1990), for a more detailed discussion of these events.
78. Ltr Norstad–Twining, dtd 1/7/60 (EL, EP, Box 28, Norstad–Gen. Lauris [1]). Norstad hinted that this action by de Gaulle presaged further steps that had not yet been completely thought through – meaning further withdrawal of French military forces from the NATO command structure, possibly in connection with the formation of some kind of African security organization.
79. Norstad, remarks at conference on "Leadership in NATO: Past and Present," Dwight D. Eisenhower Presidential Library, unpub., dtd 12/15/82.
80. For more on these points, see Jordan, *Alliance*.
81. He went on to observe that the naval forces involved are relatively small, comprising only about one-third of the French Mediterranean fleet.
82. Memo of Conference with the President, dtd 6/9/59 (NSA, Berlin, Norstad).
83. Memo of Conference with the President, dtd 6/9/59 (NSA, Berlin, Norstad).
84. See msgs Twining–Norstad ALO 1173 and ALO 1258, dtd 11/27/59 and 12/28/59 (NA, JCS, CDF, 1959, Box 108).
85. Ltr Norstad–Eisenhower, dtd 1/19/60 (EL, EP, Box 28, Norstad–Gen Lauris [1]). Norstad went on to comment: "I must say that it might be workable. My main criticism would be that making a greater monstrosity out of an already monstrous organization is something of an offense against common sense." See also Simon Duke and Wolfgang Krieger, eds., *U.S. Military Forces in Europe, the Early Years* (Boulder, CO: Westview Press, 1993), p. 35.
86. See Memo of Conversation, "Nuclear Submarine for France," dtd 9/13/60 (NA, State Dept., Eur. Aff., Euro, Reg. Aff., Pol-Mil., Box 7).

87. Ltr Norstad–Eisenhower, dtd 1/19/60 (EL, EP, Box 28, Norstad–Gen Lauris).
88. Quoted in Norstad, Eisenhower Library conference.
89. Quoted in ltr Norstad–Eisenhower, dtd 1/7/60 (EL, EP, Box 28, Norstad–Gen Lauris [1]).
90. Ltr Eisenhower–Norstad, dtd 1/11/60 (EL, EP, Box 28, Norstad–Gen Lauris [1]).
91. See Memo Goodpaster–Norstad CAP 5013, dtd 1/11/60 (EL, NP, Box 99, De Gaulle [1]).
92. Ltr Norstad–Eisenhower, dtd 1/26/60.
93. Memo of Conversation, "Meeting Norstad–Debre," dtd 1/23/60 (EL, EP, Box 28, NATO–Norstad–De Gaulle). See also msg, Houghton–Dulles 3395, dtd 1/28/60 (EL, EP, Box 28, NATO–Norstad–De Gaulle).

Chapter 6

1. Memo Legere–Bundy, "Differences among NATO Allies on Broad Strategy," dtd 10/24/61 (National Security Archive [NSA], The Berlin Crisis 1958–1962 [Berlin], Name Index: Norstad, Lauris [Norstad]).
2. Ltr, B.E. Lane Timmons, Director, Office of European Regional Affairs, Department of State–Ray L. Thurston, Counselor of Embassy, American Embassy, Paris, France, dtd 1/6/59 (NSA, Berlin, Norstad). The Dulles–Norstad conversation is recorded in Memo of Conversation, USDEL/MC/8 dtd 12/15/58 (NSA, Berlin, Norstad).
3. "Note by the Government of the Union of Soviet Socialist Republics to the Government of the United States of America on the Situation in Berlin, November 27, 1958," as contained in Wolfgang Heidelmeyer and Guenter Hindrichs, *Documents on Berlin, 1943–1963* (Munich: R. Oldlenbourg Verlag, 1963), pp. 190–191.
4. Quoted in Marc Trachtenberg, *Strategy and Policy* (Princeton: Princeton University Press, 1991), pp. 171. Discussed later will be the problem of refugee flows through West Berlin as a motivation for Krushchev's action (See also Trachtenberg, *A Constructed Peace: The Making of the European Settlement 1945–1963* [Princeton, NJ: Princeton University Press, 1999]).
5. For documentary background, see Heidelmeyer and Hindrichs, *Documents*.
6. See previous chapter for a discussion of this deployment.
7. Quoted in Stephen E. Ambrose, *Eisenhower the President*, Vol Two (New York: Simon and Schuster, 1984), p. 503. Although the JCS initially had recommended to Eisenhower that they were planning to force their way into Berlin with a division if the autobahn were closed, Eisenhower categorically disagreed; he wanted a force large enough for a probing operation, not a force "... far too weak to fight its way through to Berlin against serious opposition, yet far too strong for a mere show of force" (ibid.)
8. See for example, Jack M. Schick, *The Berlin Crisis, 1958–1962* (Philadelphia: University of Pennsylvania Press, 1971), pp. 47–48. As will be seen later, the Berlin crisis also rekindled a debate over whether the Eisenhower–Dulles doctrine of "massive retaliation" was still appropriate to the circumstances. This debate was led by former Secretary of State Dean Acheson

and later by Gen. Maxwell Taylor (see his *The Uncertain Trumpet* (New York: Harper and Row, 1960); also Douglas Brinkley, *Dean Acheson: The Cold War Years, 1953–1971* (New Haven: Yale University Press, 1992); Robert A. Divine, *The Sputnik Challenge* (New York: Oxford University Press, 1993.)

9. Dwight D. Eisenhower, *The White House Years: Waging Peace, 1956–1961* (Garden City: Doubleday and Co., Inc., 1965), p. 318.
10. Paul–Henri Spaak, *The Continuing Battle: Memoirs of a European, 1936–1966*, transl. Henry Fox (Boston: Little, Brown and Co., 1971), p. 263. Spaak went on to say: "I was determined to follow Norstad's advice in all defence matters. I could not but bow to his technical expertise and very soon became convinced of his utter loyalty to the Atlantic Alliance." For a discussion of the relationship between the Secretaries-General of NATO and the SACEURs, during this period, see Robert S. Jordan, *Political Leadership in NATO: A Study in Multinational Diplomacy* (Boulder, CO: Westview Press, 1979), esp. Chs 2 and 3.
11. The Airlift probably provided the final incentive to the U.S. and its newfound allies to create NATO in April 1949. See Chapter 2 *supra* for background.
12. *The New York Times*, dtd 12/18/58, p. 16 (cited in Schick, *Berlin*, p. 47.)
13. For an excellent discussion of the evolution and the efficacy of NATO's machinery for political-military consultation, see Douglas L. Bland, *The Military Committee of the North Atlantic Alliance: A Study of Structure and Strategy* (New York: Praeger, 1991). See also Robert S. Jordan, *The NATO International Staff/Secretariat, 1952–1957: A Study in International Administration* (London and New York: Oxford University Press, 1967), for a discussion of the political-military consultative machinery that NATO had put in place.
14. Schick, *Berlin*, p. 49.
15. Barry Buzan, ed., *The International Politics of Deterrence* (London: Frances Pinter, 1987), p. 176. This book provides a clear exposé of the perceptions of deterrence held by the West and by the Warsaw Pact.
16. Buzan, *International*, p. 330.
17. Msg Norstad–Dulles, 1799, dtd 11/17/58 (NSA, Berlin, Norstad). In fact, the JCS had already made the issue moot on November 18 by suspending all convoys.
18. Msg Norstad–Dulles, 1799, dtd 11/17/58 (NSA, Berlin, Norstad).
19. Eisenhower, *Waging Peace*, pp. 331–332.
20. Eisenhower, *Waging Peace*, p. 331.
21. Msg, Dulles–Thurston 1647, dtd 11/14/58 (NSA, Berlin, Norstad).
22. Msg Norstad–Dulles, 1799, dtd 11/17/58 (NSA, Berlin, Norstad).
23. Msg, Houghton–Dulles, 1911, dtd 11/21/58 (NSA, Berlin, Norstad).
24. Msg, USCINCEUR–JCS EC9-6265, dtd 11/23/58 (NSA, Berlin, Norstad).
25. Ibid.
26. Eisenhower, *Waging Peace*, p. 333.
27. Eisenhower, *Waging Peace*, pp. 332–333.
28. For more on Krushchev's motives, see Vladislav Zubok and Constantine Pleshakov, *Inside the Kremlin's Cold War: From Stalin to Krushchev* (Cambridge, MA: Harvard University Press, 1996).

29. Ambrose, *Eisenhower the President*, p. 521. The UN Secretary-General, Dag Hammarskjold, did not agree with these ideas concerning the UN and Berlin. He could not, for example, envision how the UN could provide political guidance to such a UN presence, whether in the form of a garrison force or even of administering the city, which had been suggested at one time. Joseph P. Lash, *Dag Hammarskjold: Custodian of the Brushfire Peace* (Garden City, NY: Doubleday and Co., Inc., 1961), p. 183.
30. Ambrose, *Eisenhower the President*, pp. 525–526.
31. Jean Edward Smith, *The Defense of Berlin* (Baltimore: The Johns Hopkins Press, 1963) pp. 185–186.
32. See Heidelmeyer and Hindrichs, *Documents*, pp. 210–211; also Smith, *Defense*, pp. 188–189.
33. See "Substance of Discussions," of State–JCS Meeting, dtd 1/14/59 (NSA, Berlin, Norstad). Careful coordination within the U.S. government was, of course, necessary, in order that a common position be put forward both to the British and the French, and to Norstad. In the respect, Robert Knight, Assistant Secretary of Defense for International Security Affairs (ISA), was present at most of these coordinating meetings. He retained his interest in Norstad after Knight had left government service to become a partner in the New York law firm of Shearman and Sterling, serving for many years as Norstad's personal attorney. He also was a member of the Board of Directors of Owens–Corning Fiberglas Corporation during the time when Norstad was serving as Chairman and Chief Executive Officer. See also Sean M. Maloney, "Notfallplanung für Berlin: Vorlaufer der Flexible Response, 1958–1963," in *Militar Geschichte*, First Quarter 1997, pp. 3–15.
34. See Ltr Thurston–Timmons, dtd 1/9/58.
35. These steps would, of course, be coordinated with the FRG, probably using the American Ambassador in Bonn, David Bruce as the channel, as well as through formal Alliance channels. See, for example, JCS 1735/363, dtd 1/7/59, Memo for USCINCEUR, "Psychological Warfare Liaison with the French." (National Archives [NA], Records of the Joint Chiefs of Staff [JCS], Central Decimal File [CDF], 1959, Box 104).
36. See Memo for the Record, dtd 1/21/59, signed by Lt. Gen. Glenn O. Barcus, USAF, JCS Chief of Staff (Eisenhower Library [EL], The Papers of Lauris Norstad [NP], Box 1, Baker thru Beckwith [1]). In this memorandum, General Barcus confesses that the U.S. is "starting for scratch ," and that the JCS are "just bringing out [contingency plans], dusting them off and bringing them up to date."
37. Charles De Gaulle, *Memoirs of Hope: Renewal and Endeavour*, transl. Terence Kilmartin (New York: Simon and Schuster, 1971), p. 202.
38. Eisenhower, *Waging Peace*, p. 427.
39. Ambrose, *Eisenhower*, p. 539.
40. Quoted in Ibid.
41. De Gaulle, *Memoirs*, p. 166. (See also Simon Serfaty, *France, De Gaulle and Europe: The Policy of the Fourth and Fifth Republic Toward the Continent* (Baltimore: The Johns Hopkins Press, 1968).) In March 1959, de Gaulle withdrew the French Mediterranean fleet from NATO. Norstad merely shrugged this off, viewing the act as not significant militarily because of

the small number of ships, although having some symbolic significance. De Gaulle did agree to cooperate fully with SACEUR in time of war. (Eisenhower, *Waging Peace*, p. 428; Robert S. Jordan, *Alliance Strategy and Navies: The Evolution and Scope of NATO's Maritime Dimension* [London: Pinter; New York: St. Martin's Press, 1990, pp. 109–110].)
42. Ambrose, *Eisenhower the President*, p. 502; Eisenhower, *Waging Peace*, p. 333. British Foreign Secretary Selwyn Lloyd reported to Ambassador John Hay Whitney that the French Foreign Minister, Maurice Couve de Murville, also favored such a course (Ibid). This was not shared by de Gaulle.
43. "Substance of Discussions," of State–JCS Meeting, dtd 1/14/59 (NSA, Berlin, Norstad).
44. See Heidelmeyer and Hindrichs, *Documents*. In December 1958, the State Department issued a press release on the legal aspects of the Berlin situation, in which it was stated that the Allied rights "do not depend in any respect upon the sufferance or acquiescence of the Soviet Union. Those rights derive from the total defeat of the Third Reich and the subsequent assumption of supreme authority." (Quoted in Smith, *Defense*, p. 190.)
45. See Heidelmeyer and Hindrichs, *Documents*.
46. See JCS Briefing Sheet, 2073/1709 dtd 2/3/59 (NA, JCS, CDF, 1959, Box 104). For SACLANT, U.S. naval forces were earmarked for NATO command in three categories: Category A were those forces available between D-Day and D + 2; Category B were those available between D + 2 and D + 30. Category C were those available after D + 30. Practically all of CINCLANT's and CINCEUR's ready forces were made available under Categories A and B.
47. NATO MC 57/1, quoted in JCS 2073/1709, 1958, "Assignment of U.S. Forces to NATO Supreme Allied Commanders in Peacetime," Encl. "A." (NA, JCS, CDF, 1959, Box 104).
48. Ibid.
49. Ibid.
50. NATO MC/53, quoted in JCS 2073/1709, 1958, "Assignment of U.S. Forces to NATO Supreme Allied Commanders in Peacetime," App. "A." (NA, JCS, CDF, 1959, Box 104.) The emphasis is to underline Norstad's discretionary scope. As USCINCEUR, Norstad was the U.S. military commander having area responsibility in Germany in accordance with Executive Order 10608 dtd 5/5/1955. In a way, this is simply a reiteration of the emergency decision-making authority that existed from when atomic and then nuclear weapons were included in NATO planning. This is discussed further in the previous chapter.
51. See, for example, msg from USCINCEUR–CJCS, EC 9–1082, dtd 2/20/59 (NSA, Berlin, Norstad).
52. See Memo of Conversation, "Memorandum of Conclusions to White House Conference re Berlin," a meeting held in the American Embassy Residence, London, with the Secretary of State, dtd 2/4/59 (EL, NP, Box 86, Berlin–Live Oak 1958–60 [4]).
53. See ltr Thurston–Timmons, dtd 2/1/59 (NSA, Berlin, Norstad).
54. See Memo of Conversation, "Berlin," a meeting held in the American Embassy Residence, London, with the Secretary of State, dtd 2/4/59 (EL, NP, Box 86, Berlin–Live Oak 1958–60 [4]).

55. Department of State Memo of Conversation of a meeting held in the Embassy Residence in London, with the Secretary of State, dtd 2/4/59 (EL, NP, Box 86, Berlin–Live Oak 1958–60 [4]). There had been a flurry of messages around this time. See Note JCS 1907/162, dtd 1/13/59, with amendments of 1/22 and 1/27, which took account of Norstad's preliminary views and was passed to the Secretary of State; EC 9–10120 to the JCS from Norstad, dtd 1/31/59, giving Norstad's detailed comments on JCS 1907/162; JCS 954356, dtd 2/2/59, from Chairman JCS to USCINCEUR (Exclusive for Norstad), which in Part III includes a memorandum of 2/2/59 prepared for the Secretary of Defense on Berlin. This was also sent to Dulles, so both Norstad and Dulles had copies when they met in London. See Thurston–Timmons, dtd 2/4/59 (EL, NP, Box 86, Berlin–Live Oak 1958–60 [4]).
56. Ltr Thurston–Timmons, dtd 2/11/59 (NSA, Berlin, Norstad).
57. Quoted in Schick, *Berlin*, p. 52. See also Eisenhower, *Waging Peace*, pp. 348–349.
58. See, for example, "Substance of Discussions," State–JCS, meeting. dtd 1/14/59 (NSA, Berlin, Norstad).
59. See Smith, *Defense*, pp. 201–202. This issue of restricting flights to 10 000 feet came up again in the 1961–1962 crisis.
60. Smith, *Defense*, pp. 201–202.

Chapter 7

1. Marc Trachtenberg, *History and Strategy* (Princeton: Princeton University Press, 1991), p. 169.
2. For a summary of the developments that led to the partitioning of Berlin between the Soviet Union and the three Western Powers, see Daniel Yergin, *Shattered Peace: The Origins of the Cold War and the National Security State* (Boston: Houghton Mifflin Co., 1977), Ch. XIV; also Wolfgang Heidelmeyer and Guenter Hindrichs, *Documents on Berlin, 1943–1963* (Munich: R. Oldlenbourg Verlag, 1963).
3. Msg Thurston–Secretary of State, 3075, dtd 2/29/59.
4. Norstad had already sounded out the JCS, whose backing, of course, was essential. See msg from Thurston–Secretary of State, 3076, dtd 2/25/59 (NSA, Berlin, Norstad). See also Sean M. Maloney, "Notfallplanung fur Berlin, Vorlaufer der Flexible Response, 1958–1963," *Militar Geschichte*, First Quarter, 1997, p. 4.
5. The Headquarters, USAREUR, was located at Heidelberg. Regarding LIVE OAK, see Gregory Pedlow, "Allied Crisis Management for Berlin: The LIVE OAK Organization, 1959–1963," in William W. Epley, ed., *International Cold War Military Records and History: Proceedings of the International Conference on Cold War Military Records and History Held in Washington, D.C. 21–26 March 1994* (Washington, D.C.: Office of the Secretary of Defense, 1996), pp. 87–116. Also see note 12 below.
6. In the preceding chapter was described how he opened discussions with the Greek government about locating IRBMs in Greece before obtaining American approval, which he knew might not be as forthcoming as he desired because of budgetary uncertainties, especially the availability of Mutual Security Program (MSP) funding.

7. In fact, de Gaulle's memo to Eisenhower concerning a global "Directorate" had its origins in the debates in the French National Assembly concerning the ratification of the North Atlantic Treaty in 1949.
8. See USRO–Secretary of State, Msg 3200, dtd 3/4/59 (NSA, Berlin, Norstad); Ambassador Amory Houghton–Secretary of State, msg 3295, dtd 3/11/59 (NSA, Berlin, Norstad).
9. See Simon Serfaty, *De Gaulle and Europe: The Policy of the Fourth and Fifth Republic Towards the Continent* (Baltimore: The Johns Hopkins Press, 1968), pp. 33–39; Frank Costigliola, *France and the United States: The Cold Alliance Since World War II* (Boston; Twayne Publishers, 1992).
10. See ltr Thurston–Kohler, dtd 4/20/59 (NSA, Berlin, Norstad). The British Chiefs-of Staff Committee (COS) is not to be confused with the American Joint Chiefs-of-Staff (JCS).
11. See ltr Thurston–Kohler, dtd 4/20/59 (NSA, Berlin, Norstad).
12. Norstad's Memorandum, "LIVE OAK Planning Staff," was dated 4/14/59 and was attached to the letter cited above (NSA, Berlin, Norstad). LIVE OAK was set up as military staff, with liaison for the FRG and with representatives of the appropriate Army and Air Force commanders in Germany. A British Major General and a French Brigadier General were to be assigned as immediate directors of staff activity.
13. This had to be cleared with the North Atlantic Council. For U.S. approval, see Note by the Secretaries to the JCS, "Meeting of U.S. Coordinating Group, Berlin Contingency Planning," dtd 7/13/59 (NSA, Berlin, Norstad); also JCS 1907/222, dtd 7/15/59 (NSA, Berlin, Norstad).
14. Maloney, "Notfallplanung," p. 5.
15. The Assistant Secretary of State for European Regional Affairs looked after the day-to-day affairs. It was commonly agreed that the Standing Group, also located in Washington, would not be involved in Berlin contingency-related affairs.
16. Msg, Dillon–U.S. Embassy Paris, dtd 5/20/59 (NSA, Berlin, Norstad).
17. Msg JCS–USCINCEUR, JCS 959771, dtd 5/18/59 (EL, NP, Box 86, Berlin-Live Oak 1958–60 [3]).
18. State Department Instruction, "Berlin Contingency Planning," CA-8581, dtd 4/6/59 (EL, NP, Box 86, Berlin-Live Oak 1958–60 [3]). Earlier papers on contingency planning were the U.S. *aide-mémoire* of 12/11/58, U.S. memorandum of 12/11/59, which were intended for basic guidance for detailed planning by the three embassies in Bonn. See State Department Instruction, "Berlin Contingency Planning," CA-8581, dtd 4/6/59 (EL, NP, Box 86, Berlin-Live Oak 1958–60 [3]).
19. State Department Instruction, "Berlin Contingency Planning," CA-8581, dtd 4/6/59 (EL, NP, Box 86, Berlin-Live Oak 1958–60 [3]).
20. See Memo of Meeting with the President, prepared by the Special Assistant to the President, Gordon Gray, dtd 4/18/59 (NSA, Berlin, Norstad).
21. Schick, *Berlin*, p. 55.
22. Schick, *Berlin*, p. 54.
23. State Department Instruction, "Berlin Contingency Planning," CA-8581, dtd 4/6/59 (EL, NP, Box 86, Berlin-Live Oak 1958–60 [3]).
24. Msg Norstad–Twining, ALO408, dtd 4/15/59 (NSA, Berlin, Norstad).
25. See msg, Houghton–Dulles, 4469, dtd 6/4/59 (NSA, Berlin, Norstad).

276 Notes

26. Memo Kohler–Murphy, "Discussions with General Norstad: (A) Berlin Contingency Planning ...", dtd 6/6/59 (NSA, Berlin, Norstad); for more details, see Maloney, "Notfallplannung," p. 5.
27. Maloney, "Notfallplannung," p. 5.
28. See Note by the Secretaries to the JCS, "Meeting of U.S. Coordinating Group, Berlin Contingency Planning," 5034, dtd 7/13/59 (NSA, Berlin, Norstad). Also see JCS 1907/222, dtd 7/15/59 (NSA, Berlin, Norstad).
29. Msg Norstad (USCINCEUR)–OSD/ISA EC 9-4064, dtd 10/3/59. (NSA, Berlin, Norstad)
30. Msg USCINCEUR–CJCS, EC 9-3715, dtd 7/12/59 (NSA, Berlin, Norstad).
31. See msg, USCINCEUR–CJCS, EC 9-10807, dtd 6/9/59 (NSA, Berlin, Norstad).
32. See msg, Dillon–Thurston, 4778, dtd 6/8/59 (EL, NP, Box 86, Berlin-Live Oak 1958–60 [3]).
33. Msg Dillon–Live Oak 4778, 6/8/59.
34. Msg USCINCEUR–JCS EC9-10915, dtd 7/13/59 (NA, State Dept., Eur. Aff., Atl. Pol-Mil. Aff., NATO], 1957–64, Box 1).
35. Msg Norstad–CJCS EC 0-5302, dtd 10/6/59 (NSA, Berlin, Norstad). Norstad went on to say: "If you agree with my being given this responsibility, I intend delegating to the Commander in Chief, United States Air Forces in Europe, the authority to coordinate planning for these military airlift operations and to exercise operational control over the airlifts if they are executed."
36. See msg, Herter–Bonn Embassy, dtd 10/14/59 (NSA, Berlin, Norstad).
37. Ltr Thurston–Kohler, dtd 6/23/59 (NSA, Berlin, Norstad).
38. One example of how Norstad's "hats" both complemented and supplemented one another was the concept of the SACEUR's Alert System. Reference SHAPE 60/58, quoted in Memo for the CJCS from Robert H. Knight, Acting Assistant Secretary of Defense, "SACEUR Alert System," 1-14497/9, dtd 7/1/59 (NA, JCS, CDF, 1959, Box 113). As USCINCEUR, Norstad was authorized as the representative of the U.S. Defense Department to work out detailed procedures of the Military Vigilance and Counter Surprise Military Systems of SACEUR's Alert System. Reference Memo for the CJCS from Robert H. Knight, Acting Assistant Secretary of Defense, "SACEUR Alert System," 1-14497/9, dtd 7/1/59 (NA, JCS, CDF, 1959, Box 113).
39. A summary of Western strength is as follows: 21.5 combat divisions, including 5 U.S., 4 British, 2 French, 3 Belgian and Dutch, 0.5 Canadian, 7 West German; 6 000 military aircraft, located on 175 air bases in Western Europe; several types of atomic weapons, including missiles – 1800-mile THORS, 600-mile Matadors, 200-mile Redstones, 90-mile Corporals, plus battlefield missiles of many kinds. These forces were intended to slow any invasion attempt, with the conventional forces providing the "shield" and the nuclear forces the "sword." See "East VS. West: The Force Behind All The Talk," *U.S. News & World Report*, 4/13/59, pp. 37–39. The article summarized: "Communist strength in ground forces is great, could be overwhelming in a surprise attack, utilizing the Soviet edge in armor, airborne units and manpower. But satellite forces are unreliable, so Russian forces would have to be used in large numbers to win on the ground. This, in turn, would bring on, in

retaliation, quick H-bomb attacks, able to 'break the back' of the Soviet Union in an all-out nuclear war ... . Allied strength is composed of more than token forces, can slow any Communist attack by use of tactical nuclear weapons and a few well-equipped divisions – but cannot expect to hold an all-out Russian attack on the ground, would have to use all-out nuclear war."

40. Transcript, "General Norstad, Supreme Allied Commander, Europe, interviewed by William Clark in ATV's 'Right to reply' series on the Independent Television Network," dtd 3/30/59.
41. Ibid.
42. See Chapter 5 for a discussion concerning Allied and Soviet anxiety over the FRG acquiring from the U.S. weapons with atomic capabilities.
43. *Hansard*, House of Commons, 4/8/59. In fact, Norstad had proposed a "thinning out" approach in March 1958.
44. See Jack M. Schick, *The Berlin Crisis, 1958–1962* (Philadelphia: University of Pennsylvania Press, 1970), p. 54; also Nigel Fisher, *Macmillan: a Biography* (New York: St. Martin's Press, 1982), pp. 212–214; for more on Macmillan, see Alistair Horne, *Macmillan 1894–1950: Volume One of the Official Biography* (London: Pan Books Ltd., 1988). Macmillan characterized the visit as a "reconnaissance" rather than a negotiation.
45. See "Mademoiselle OTAN signe la grande alliance," *Jours de France*, dtd 9/26/59; "Monsieur Shape joue le pére de la marié," *Paris Match*, dtd 9/26/59; "General's Pride in the Bride," *Life Magazine*, dtd 10/5/59. They were divorced within a year; Kristin later married Andrew Jaffe, by whom she had a son, Christopher, who was a great favorite of the Norstads. The Jaffes also divorced.
46. Msg JCS–USCINCEUR JCS 967551, dtd 10/28/59 (EL, NP, Box 86, Berlin–Live Oak 1958–60 [2]).
47. Msg JCS–USCINCEUR JCS 967551, dtd 10/28/59. (EL, NP, Box 86, Berlin–Live Oak 1958–60 [2]).
48. Msg, JCS–USCINCEUR 967199, dtd 10/21/59 (EL, NP, Box 86, Berlin–Live Oak 1958–60 [2]). These plans would, of course, be reviewed by the national military authorities of all three Powers.
49. Msg Norstad–Lemnitzer EC 9–11280, dtd 1/20/59.
50. Msg Radius–State, G-181, dtd 10/22/59 (NSA, Berlin, Norstad).
51. Ibid.
52. Msg Norstad–Twining ALO 1098, dtd 10/27/59 (NSA, Berlin, Norstad). He seemed to be lecturing to Twining: "This subject should be considered on a high enough political level to insure a common Tripartite solution and this solution should be passed in clear and simple language to the Military Authorities involved."
53. State Department, Memo of Conversation, "Contingency Planning," EO 11652, 8/4/59. The meeting was between Robert Murphy, Deputy Under Secretary of State and Sir Harold Caccia, British Ambassador to the U.S. and their aides. While in London for the Tenth Anniversary celebrations, Norstad met privately with Macmillan, who said that he had been thinking of a possible "summit meeting" on the German problem. Norstad took the position that the foreign minister level would be more appropriate. Msg Houghton–Dulles 1983, dtd 11/27/58 (NSA, Berlin, Norstad).

54. Msg Herter–State, SECTO 324, dtd 7/15/59.
55. See "Substance of Discussions," of State–JCS Meeting, dtd 1/14/59 (NSA, Berlin, Norstad).
56. Fisher, *Macmillan*, p. 215.
57. Eisenhower, *Waging Peace*, pp. 402–403.
58. Ambrose, *Eisenhower*, Vol. Two, p. 521.
59. Ibid.
60. De Gaulle, *Memoirs*, p. 223.
61. See Eisenhower, *Waging Peace*, p. 444.
62. Eisenhower, *Waging Peace*, p. 446.
63. Ibid., p. 447.
64. For a fresh examination of Khrushchev's motives, see Vladislav Zubok and Constantine Pleshakov, *Inside the Kremlin's Cold War: From Stalin to Krushchev* (Cambridge, MA: Harvard University Press, 1996).

Chapter 8

1. Draft Memo Kennedy–Norstad, dtd 10/10/61.
2. For background, see Jane E. Stromseth, *The Origins of Flexible Response: NATO's Debate over Strategy in the 1960s* (London: The Macmillan Press, 1988.) McNamara publicly articulated the flexible response doctrine at the Athens Ministerial Meeting of the NAC in May 1962.
3. Deborah Shapley, *Promise and Power: the Life and Times of Robert McNamara* (Boston: Little, Brown and Co., 1993), p. 117. McNamara had prepared a memo for Kennedy, "Military Planning for a possible Berlin Crisis," that affirmed in Kennedy's mind that the real plan of the U.S. and its Allies was to counter almost any Soviet military action concerning Berlin by using nuclear weapons. See Richard Reeves, *President Kennedy: Profile of Power* (New York: Simon and Schuster, 1993), p. 125.
4. See, for example, msg Rusk–Stoessell 2298, dtd 10/21/61 (NSA, The Berlin Crisis 1958–1962 [Berlin], Norstad, Lauris [Norstad].
5. For background on the change of approaches to foreign and national security policy between the two Administrations, see Thomas J. Schoenbaum, *Waging Peace and War: Dean Rusk in the Truman, Kennedy, and Johnson Years* (New York: Simon and Schuster, 1988), esp. Ch. 11.
6. Quoted in Reeves, *President*, p. 136.
7. Schoenbaum, *Waging Peace and War*, pp. 337.
8. Msg Lemnitzer–Norstad JCS 1235-61, dtd 8/26/61, reprint of Memo Nitze–McNamara, "Subject: Berlin Build-up," dtd 8/24/61 (NSA, Berlin, Norstad).
9. Msg Lemnitzer–Norstad JCS 1235-61, dtd 8/26/61 (NSA, Berlin, Norstad).
10. Useful information concerning these operations can be found in Gregory Pedlow, "Allied Crisis Management for Berlin: The LIVE OAK Organization, 1959–1963," in William W. Epley, ed., *International Cold War Military Records and History: Proceedings of the International Conference on Cold War Military Records and History Held in Washington, D.C. 21–26 March 1994* (Washington, D.C.: Office of the Secretary of Defense, 1996), pp. 87–116.

11. JCS views summarized in British Chiefs of Staff Committee Annex, COS (61) 45th Meeting, dtd 7/18/61 (NSA, Berlin, Norstad).
12. I am grateful to Dr. Gregory Pedlow for pointing out to me this contrast in views in his FAX message of 9/25/97.
13. The British wanted the West's response to be through negotiations, believing "it would gravely interfere with the later implementation of NATO war plans, should the crisis escalate to war, if we had first to commit our forces tripartitely in the ways suggested by Live Oak." See BCOS Committee Annex, COS (61) 45th Meeting, dtd 7/18/61 (NSA, Berlin–Norstad).
14. Shapely, *Promise*, p. 116.
15. Quoted in Stromseth, *Response*, p. 36.
16. Maxwell D. Taylor, *The Uncertain Trumpet* (New York: Harper and Row, 1960). Dean Acheson also brought new ideas to Kennedy, after having been openly critical of the Eisenhower Administration's policies. See Douglas Brinkley, *Dean Acheson: The Cold War Years, 1953–1971* (New Haven: Yale University Press, 1992).
17. Norstad undoubtedly had mixed feelings when, with some reluctance, Kennedy appointed General Curtis LeMay to be Chief of Staff of the Air Force in June 1961. See Reeves, *President*, p. 183.
18. Msg Lyon–Rusk 832, dtd 8/16/61 (NSA, Berlin, Norstad).
19. Stromseth, *Response*, p. 36. On July 25 Kennedy requested a $3 billion increase in the defense budget to expand the Army. Kennedy also hoped, perhaps, that the threat of an arms race with the U.S. might serve as a deterrent to continuing Soviet pressure in Berlin.
20. Memo McNamara–Norstad DEF 999160, dtd 7/18/61 (NSA, Berlin, Norstad).
21. For example, this could follow from various FRG–GDR contacts, such as technical cooperation. See msg Gavin–Rusk, dtd 7/29/61 (EL, NP, Box 86, Berlin–Live Oak 1961–30 Aug. [30]).
22. Quoted in Reeves, *President*, pp. 209–210.
23. Reeves, *President*, p. 185.
24. Since 1945, for example, the entire population of the Soviet zone had suffered a net loss of over two million. A fear of war, shortages of food staples, and anxiety that free movement in Berlin would be permanently curtailed, had led by June and July 1961 to a massive flow of people from East to West. The Ulbricht regime was desperate. In July the total of refugees fleeing was 30 444. For more background, see Jean Edward Smith, *The Defense of Berlin* (Baltimore: The Johns Hopkins University Press, 1963), pp. 256–266.
25. Quoted in Frank A. Ninkovich, *Germany and the United States: The Transformation of the German Question Since 1945* (Boston: Twayne Publishers, 1988), p. 129. See also Walt W. Rostow, *The Diffusion of Power 1957–1972* (New York: Macmillan, 1972), p. 231.
26. Ninkovich, *Germany*, p. 141.
27. Msg Lemnitzer–Norstad (as USCINCEUR) JCS 1168, dtd 8/18/61 (EL, NP, Box 86, Berlin-Live Oak 1961–30 Aug. [2]). The movement was to be regarded as classified until the public announcement was made.
28. Msg Lemnitzer–Norstad and Clarke–JCS 1185, dtd 8/19/61 (EL, NP, Box 86, Berlin-Live Oak 1961–30 Aug. [2]).

29. Memo for Record, "Telephone Conversation between General Norstad, SHAPE, and General Watson, Berlin," dtd 8/24/61 (NSA, Berlin, Norstad).
30. Msg Gavin–Dulles 693, dtd 8/761 (NSA, Berlin, Norstad). CHECKMATE II, although bearing a similar name, was not directly connected with CHECKMATE, which was only concerned with the central front and the testing of the ACE Mobile Force.
31. See Lucius D. Clay, *Decision in Germany* (New York: Doubleday and Co., Inc., 1950); also Thomas A. Schwartz, *America's Germany: John J. McCloy and the Federal Republic of Germany* (Cambridge, MA: Harvard University Press, 1991).
32. Msg Lemnitzer–Norstad [number deleted], dtd 8/18/61 (EL, NP, Box 86, Berlin-Live Oak 1961–30 Aug. [2]).
33. Memo for the Vice President from Paul H. Nitze, dtd 9/27/61 (NSA, Berlin, Norstad).
34. Memo "Memorandum of Conversation between Vice President Lyndon B. Johnson, Ambassador Gavin, Ambassador Finletter and General Norstad at the United States Embassy, Paris, France, dtd 9/30/61" (NSA, Berlin, Norstad).
35. Lawrence W. Kaplan, "The Berlin Crisis, 1958–1962: Views from the Pentagon," in Epley, *International*, p. 67. As Kaplan observed: "The administration's reservations about Norstad and the JCS extended to all aspects of the machinery which the Eisenhower administration had assembled ... it simply by-passed them. Ad hoc policy studies and special investigations under new advisers took their place ... ."
36. Quoted by Jean Edward Smith, *Lucius D. Clay: An American Life* (New York: Henry Holt and Co., 1990), p. 647.
37. It was reported, for example, that Adenauer once described Kennedy as a "cross between a junior naval person and a Roman Catholic boy scout." (Memo of Conversation dtd 9/30/61, *Supra*).
38. See msg Rusk–Embassies in Moscow, Paris, London, Bonn and Berlin 911, dtd 8/16/61 (EL, NP, Box 86, Berlin-Live Oak 1961–30 Aug. [2]).
39. Norstad went about obtaining this authorization by asking the British to favor it because he did not want to risk having his hands tied by his own government. See letters Norstad sent to Lord Mountbatten and to General Ely. Also see U.K. COS (61) 299 quoted from "Chiefs of Staff Committee – Confidential Annex to C.O.S. (61) 56th Meeting Held on Monday, 28th August, 1961," dtd. 8/28/61 (NSA, Berlin, Norstad). The Soviet Note August 23 over air access of required that Norstad give priority for aircraft planning.
40. Kaplan, "The Berlin Crisis, 1958–1962: Views from the Pentagon," in Epley, *International*, pp. 76ff. Kaplan mentions "horse blanket" – meaning the list of scenarios to respond to Soviet provocations.
41. Memo U.K. COSC, "Annex to C.O.S. (61) 56th Meeting held on Monday, 28th August, 1961," dtd 8/28/61 (NSA, Berlin, Norstad).
42. Smith, *Lucius*, p. 652. Clay had much broader powers in the earliest Berlin crisis, and he regretted not having them during this period.
43. Msg Lyon–Rusk 1342, dtd 9/8/61 (EL, NP, Box 86, Berlin-Live Oak 1961 [1]).
44. Memo U.K. COS (61) 299 quoted from "Chiefs of Staff Committee – Confidential Annex to COS (61) 56th Meeting Held on Monday, 28th August, 1961," dtd. 8/28/61 (NSA, Berlin, Norstad).

45. Ibid.
46. Msg Lyon–Rusk 1342, dtd 9/8/61 (EL, NP, Box 86, Berlin-Live Oak 1961 [1]).
47. Ibid.
48. Msg Lyon–Rusk 1342, dtd 9/8/61 (EL, NP, Box 86, Berlin–Live Oak 1961 [1]). By September 19, the British Air Ministry had completed arrangements with BEA for the training of five air crews on Viscounts. These crews would be kept available to take over Viscount service at short notice, with two of the crews flying supernumerary with BEA air crews. See memo U.K. COS (61) 299 quoted from "Chiefs of Staff Committee – Confidential Annex to C.O.S. (61) 56th Meeting Held on Monday, 28th August, 1961," dtd. 8/28/61 (NSA, Berlin, Norstad).
49. A West German liaison officer was included in the LIVE OAK staff in 1961. West German forces would not participate in Berlin contingency response forces; consequently, the FRG would be given sets of plans but not access to the LIVE OAK files. Prior to 1961, Norstad passed some information on LIVE OAK to the West Germans through the FRG's National Military Representative at SHAPE, Brigadier General Peter Butler (FAX, Pedlow-Jordan, dtd 9/25/97.)
50. Msg Norstad–Nitze and Lemnitzer ALO 707, dtd 8/19/61 (NSA, Berlin, Norstad). Nonetheless, the British were concerned that the procedure for military crews to take over civil aircraft should be incorporated into JACK PINE in order to avoid any possibility of unilateral implementation. They also wanted the Ambassadorial Group and LIVE OAK informed accordingly. See memorandum U.K. COS (61)299 quoted from "Chiefs of Staff Committee – Confidential Annex to C.O.S. (61) 56th Meeting Held on Monday, 28th August, 1961," dtd. 8/28/61 (NSA, Berlin, Norstad).
51. Msg Norstad–Nitze and Lemnitzer, dtd 8/19/61 (NSA, Berlin, Norstad).
52. See memo for the Vice President from Paul H. Nitze, dtd 9/27/61 (NSA, Berlin, Norstad).
53. The concerns of the Europeans were reflected in the NAC, which is the political forum for NATO policy-making, and were considered in the Standing Group, which was composed of the representatives of the U.S. British and French Chiefs-of-Staff.
54. Msg Norstad–Nitze and Lemnitzer, dtd 8/19/61 (NSA, Berlin, Norstad).
55. Msg Gavin–Rusk 1194, dtd 9/1/61 (NSA, Berlin, Norstad).
56. See Msg Lyon–Rusk 1313, dtd 9/7/61 (NSA, Berlin, Norstad).
57. Ibid.
58. Quoted in Shapley, *Promise*, p. 122. See also Paul Nitze, *From Hiroshima to Glasnost: At the Center of Decision: A Memoir* (New York: Grove Weidenfeld, 1989), pp. 202, 203; Richard J. Barnet, *The Alliance–America, Europe, Japan: Makers of the Postwar World* (New York: Simon and Schuster, 1983), p. 231.
59. Memo for Record, "Telephone Conversation – Secretary of Defense McNamara calling General Norstad from Washington," 9/13/61 (NSA, Berlin, Norstad).
60. Memo for the President from the Secretary of Defense, "Military Build-up and Possible Action in Europe," dtd 9/18/61 (NSA, Berlin, Norstad). This was in response to Kennedy's memo of 9/8/61.

61. Memo "Military Build-up ...", dtd 9/18/61 (NSA, Berlin, Norstad). Norstad's commentary is attached as Appendix A to this referenced document. In hindsight, it is regrettable that McNamara and his colleagues did not take more seriously Norstad's strictures in point 2 above when plunging the U.S. military deeper into Vietnam a few years later.
62. Memo "Military Build-up ...," dtd 9/18/61 (NSA, Berlin, Norstad).
63. McNamara estimated that the four National Guard divisions could be completely converted to Active Army divisions within six to twelve months.
64. Memo for the President from Maxwell D. Taylor, 9/18/61 (NSA, Berlin, Norstad). As an illustration of the direct connection between the Kennedy Administration's response to Berlin and to its subsequent activities in the early stages of the war in Vietnam, it was the availability of this general military buildup that gave the Administration the means to escalate the war in Vietnam without provoking an atmosphere of crisis in the U.S.
65. Memo from Taylor, dtd 9/18/61 (NSA, Berlin, Norstad).
66. See Memo for General Taylor, "General Norstad's Views." dtd 9/28/61 (NSA, Berlin, Norstad).
67. Msg Norstad–McNamara PRS2741, dtd 10/28/61 (NSA, Berlin, Norstad).
68. Ibid.
69. See Msg Gavin–U.S. Mission Berlin, 1750, dtd 10/31/61 (EL, NP, Box 86, Berlin-Live Oak 1961 Sept–31 Dec [2]).
70. Memo for the Record, "Meeting with General Norstad," dtd 11/7/61 (NSA, Berlin, Norstad). There was also a suspicion that the Soviets and the GDR were considering changing the cross points from East to West Berlin from Friedrichstrasse to Mauer or Charlottenstrasse.
71. The West's negotiating position could not vary much from that agreed to in 1959, as discussed in the previous chapter. These talks, in any event, reached a dead end as the Cuban Missile Crisis took center stage.
72. Memo for General Taylor, "General Norstad's Views," dtd 9/28/61 (NSA, Berlin, Norstad).
73. Msg Norstad–Clarke (CINCUSAREUR) 2589, dtd 10/26/61 (NSA, Berlin, Norstad).
74. Msg Norstad–Lemnitzer PRS2691, dtd 10/24/61 (NSA, Berlin, Norstad). Clay felt that moving tanks up, after Lightner had been extricated by a U.S. military patrol, was a good move. The episode brought the Soviets into confrontation with the U.S., thus dispelling the myth that these actions in Berlin were only GDR-inspired. (See Smith, *Lucius*, p. 660.)
75. Msg Watson–Norstad NIACT 637, dtd 10/31/61 (NSA, Berlin, Norstad).

Chapter 9

1. Draft ltr Kennedy–Norstad, dtd 10/10/61 (NSA, The Berlin Crisis 1958–1962 [Berlin], Norstad, Lauris [Norstad]).
2. Msg Norstad–Clarke (CINCUSAREUR), dtd 10/30/61 (EL, NP, Box 86, Berlin-Live Oak 1961 15 Sept–31 Dec. [2]).
3. Msg Clarke–Watson HBG 3333, dtd 10/31/61 (EL, NP, Box 86, Berlin-Live Oak 1961 15 Sept–31 Dec [2]).

4. See Ltrs Norstad–Mountbatten ECLO 600/76, undtd. (EL, NP, Box 86, Berlin-Live Oak 1958–60 [1]), and Norstad–Ely ECLO600/73, undtd (EL, NP, Box 86, Berlin-Live Oak 1958–60 [1]).
5. Memo Legere–Bundy, "Differences among NATO Allies on Broad Strategy," dtd 10/14/61.
6. Msg Lemnitzer–Norstad JCS 0116-62, dtd 1/18/62 (NSA, Berlin, Norstad).
7. Msg Lemnitzer–Norstad 115049, dtd 12/30/61 (EL, NP, Box 86, Berlin-Live Oak 1961 1 Sept–31 Dec [1]).
8. Msg Norstad–Lemnitzer dtd 1/3/62 (EL, NP, Box 86, Berlin-Live Oak 1962 [3]).
9. For a summation of the changes in decision-making and execution under McNamara, see Douglas Kinnard, *The Secretary of Defense* (Lexington, KY: The University Press of Kentucky, 1980), pp. 85ff.
10. Ltr Hamilton–James dtd 11/7/61 (NA, SD, Eur. Aff., Eur. Reg. Aff., Pol-Mil. NF, Box 21).
11. See Memo Legere–Bundy 2582, dtd 10/14/61. Kennedy and McNamara would not have been comfortable with this flattering description of Norstad made during the Eisenhower period: "Like the American president, Norstad has to be many men: an expert soldier, a diplomat, a backstage politician, a perfect host, a considerate guest, a tireless traveler, a careful reader, a budget student and a complete chamber of commerce in at least half a dozen languages." Doris Fleeson, "Norstad, Man of Many Talents," *Washington Evening Star*, dtd 3/25/59.
12. Ltr Twining–Norstad, dtd 1/9/61 (EL, NP).
13. Eisenhower understood clearly his dilemma: that the more the U.S. committed itself to Europe, the less motived the Allies would be to sacrifice for their own defense. Understandably, given this situation, the Kennedy Administration policy would create some anxiety with the Allies. See, for example, Marc Trachtenberg, *History and Strategy* (Princeton: Princeton University Press, 1991), pp. 166–167.
14. "Partial Transcription of the Prepared Statement by the President Appointing General Clay as Personal Representative in Berlin." Clay said that there was another paragraph in the letter that gave him full authority in Berlin, but that the State Department had it excised. (See Jean Edward Smith, *Lucius* ..., [New York: Henry Holt and Co., 1990] p. 651.)
15. Memo "Memorandum of Conversation between Vice President Lyndon B. Johnson, Ambassador Gavin, Ambassador Finletter and General Norstad at the United States Embassy, Paris, France, Sept. 30, 1961," dtd 9/30/61 (NSA, Berlin, Norstad). Clay had flown into and out of the enclave by helicopter to symbolize the West's resolve, without having gained prior authority. (See Smith, *Lucius*, pp. 658–659. He spelled it "Steinstucken").
16. Ltr Decker–Clarke, dtd 11/13/61 (NSA, Berlin, Norstad); msg Clarke–Norstad 3297, dtd 11/13/61).
17. Smith, *Lucius*, p. 657.
18. Ibid.
20. Memo Kennedy–Rusk, dtd 11/8/61 (NSA, Berlin, Norstad). In fact, taking up the idea of dramatic political action, Kennedy had directed Rusk to look into this idea, asking: "Would such a direct meeting between the Chairman and myself be a good idea at this or at some other stage of the

crisis? Would Berlin be a good place? Should other Western statesmen be included? Should we privately prepare a contingency plan?"
21. Memo Kennedy–Rusk, dtd 11/8/61 (NSA, Berlin, Norstad).
22. Norstad sent his proposed revisions to Kennedy on 11/16/61 (NSA, Berlin, Norstad).
23. See msg to the Standing Group from Norstad for the NAC, Nr. SH 40405, and SHAPTO 1492, both dtd 6/20/57, quoted in ltr Norstad–Kennedy, dtd 11/17/61 (NSA, Berlin,Norstad).
24. See ltr Lemnitzer–Norstad, dtd 11/25/61 (EL, NP, Box 103, JCS Nov 1961–Dec 1962 [5]).
25. Memo for the President, "General Norstad's Letter of November 16," dtd 12/1/61 (NSA, Berlin, Norstad).
26. Memo for the President, "Response to November 16 Letter from General Norstad," dtd 12/4/61 (NSA, Berlin, Norstad).
27. See FAX Pedlow–Jordan, dtd 9/25/97.
28. Memo "Response to November 16 Letter from General Norstad,"dtd 12/4/61 (NSA, Berlin, Norstad).
29. Ltr Kennedy–Norstad, dtd 12/5/61 (EL, NP, Box 86, Berlin-Live Oak 1961 1 Sept–31 Dec [1]). Because of the importance of this exchange, a "Memorandum for the Record" dtd 12/6/61 was prepared by Bundy's assistant, Lawrence Legere, detailing the various meetings that took place (NSA, Berlin, Norstad).
30. Ltr Norstad–Kennedy, dtd 1/10/62 (NSA, Berlin, Norstad). On January 10, 1962 he informed the Administration of his decision: "I have decided not to issue formal instructions to the SHAPE Planners. Thus the position paper 'U.S. Policy on Military Actions in a Berlin conflict' will serve as general background and guidelines but will not be translated into specific directions to my Allied staff."
31. Robert C. Doty, "M'Namara Spurs NATO's Build-Up of Ground Units," *The New York Times*, dtd 12/15/61.
32. Ibid.
33. Msg Bundy–Rusk, National Security Action Memorandum No. 112, dtd 1/15/62 (NSA, Berlin, Norstad).
34. Quoted in Leonard Beaton, "NATO Strength Up by a Quarter," *The Guardian*, dtd 11/14/61.
35. Beaton, "NATO." As mentioned earlier, the Kennedy Administration had already called up reserves, with 200 000 men being added to the armed forces, with over 40 000 being sent to Europe to reinforce the Seventh Army and its supporting forces. Six regular Army divisions were made available in the U.S. to move to Europe if needed, and the Marine Corps and Navy air power and anti-submarine capacity were being strengthened.
36. Earlier, in a speech to the NATO Parliamentarians in Paris, Norstad had reported that NATO would soon have about twenty-five divisions on the Central Front, but that there would still be deficiencies in training and equipment.
37. Msg Gavin–Rusk 3835, dtd 2/12/62 (EL, NP, Box 86, Berlin-Live Oak 1962 [3]).
38. Msg Gavin–Rusk 3825, dtd 2/10/62 (EL, NP, Box 86, Berlin-Live Oak 1962 [3]). The British wanted to know more precisely what Norstad had in mind;

further, their view was that in response to a Soviet declaration regarding reservation of air space, Norstad should first send in probes at altitudes below 10 000 feet to ascertain if the Soviets really intended to cause interference.
39. Msg Gavin–Rusk NIACT 3866, dtd 2/14/62 (EL, NP, Box 86, Berlin-Live Oak 1962 [3]).
40. Msg Gavin–Rusk NIACT 3881, dtd 2/14/62 (EL, NP, Box 86, Berlin-Live Oak 1962 [3]). He had been given JCS instructions on 8/31/61 and had also JACK PINE II rules of engagement.
41. Msg Gavin–Rusk NIACT 3881, dtd 2/14/61 (EL, NP, Box 86, Berlin-Live Oak 1962 [3]). Norstad would order escort operations by RAF and USAF fighters in accordance with his delegated powers, and also request the French government to authorize French fighters to participate.
42. Bundy–Rusk, National Security Action Memorandum No. 128, "Response to Soviet Action Regarding Air Corridors," dtd 2/14/62 (NSA, Berlin, Norstad). There was an introductory comment in the memorandum: "Since there has been a little confusion in the White House with respect to the precise meaning of your recommendations, I wish to restate what the President understands that he has approved ..." Throughout this period, as is already clear, the lines of communication and authority were constantly getting tangled up. This was also true for Allied coordination. For example, the British were anxious that the Ambassadorial Group and LIVE OAK should be informed that the procedures for military crews to take over civil aircraft should be incorporated in JACK PINE so as to avoid any possibility of unilateral implementation.
43. Msg Gavin–Rusk NIACT 3894, dtd 2/15/62 (EL, NP, Box 86, Berlin-Live Oak 1962 [3]). By this time Norstad had a better conception of the available resources to him. For example, the French told him that for the present they would be unable to place military crews on French civilian aircraft because there were no French military crews checked out to fly the types of plane used by the Air Force. Although regular Air France crews could be converted to military duty, this process would take time and presented some complications. Avoiding this, Norstad did not request the French authorities to fly commercial transport with military crews, although he might want this in the future. As for the British, they could provide a military crew for a BEA aircraft, although the aircraft would have to be brought to West Germany from Britain.
44. Msg Gavin–Rusk, American Embassy Bonn 3901, dtd 2/16/62 (EL, NP, Box 86, Berlin-Live Oak 1962 [3]).
45. Ltr Kennedy–Norstad, dtd 2/26/62 (NSA, Berlin, Norstad). Kennedy also wanted to honor some of the individual pilots who did their jobs "with such unflinching courage in the face of harrassment."
46. Ltr Norstad–Kennedy, dtd 3/9/62 (NSA, Berlin, Norstad). Norstad went on to recommend that a personal congratulatory letter should be sent to General Truman H. Landon, CINCUSAFE. He also recommended that a brief note or telephone call be made to Juan Trippe of Pan American Airways thanking through him the Pan Am crews who were willing to fly aircraft "even in the danger areas at the critical times ..." (ibid).
47. Ltr Norstad–Kennedy, dtd 3/9/62 (NSA, Berlin, Norstad).

48. Norstad's message went through the LIVE OAK channel, to the U.S. Embassy in Moscow with the request that the message be shared there with the British and French, and to Geneva for the attention of Rusk and Lord Home. They were in Geneva at the Disarmament Conference. Msg Gavin–American Embassy Moscow 222, dtd 3/10/62 (EL, NP, Box 86, Berlin-Live Oak 1962 [3]). The authority to Norstad was under the provisions of par. 4 SHLO-5-00199.
49. Msg Gavin–Rusk 4352, dtd 3/17/62 (EL, NP, Box 86, Berlin-Live Oak 1962 [2]).
50. Msg Gavin–Rusk 4270, dtd 3/13/62 (EL, NP, Box 86, Berlin-Live Oak 1962 [3]).
51. Ltr Kennedy–Clay, dtd 3/15/62 (NSA, Berlin, Norstad).
52. Ltr Kennedy–Clay, dtd 3/15/62 (NSA, Berlin, Norstad).
53. See Smith, *Lucius*, p. 654.
54. For the circumstances surrounding his departure, see Smith, *Lucius*, pp. 662–665.
55. Lauris Norstad, "NATO Strength and Spirit," *NATO Letter*, dtd 1/60, pp. 7–11.
56. Norstad felt compelled to pursue a policy of forward strategy because *not* to do so would have sacrificed the FRG almost in advance of hostilities. Some of his policies that hinted at forms of disengagement understandably met strong West German opposition.
57. See David N. Schwartz, *NATO's Nuclear Dilemmas*, (Washington, D.C.: Brookings Institution, 1983), pp. 82–85; Robert E. Osgood, *The Case for the MLF: A Criticial Evaluation* (Washington, D.C.: Washington Center for Foreign Policy Research, 1964). Lemnitzer was particularly scornful of plans of mixed-manned crews for the *POLARIS* submarines. He claimed "he could not see it for dust," primarily because the close quarters of a submarine required a closely-knit, integrated crew. (See interview of LTC Bickston with Lemnitzer at the Pentagon, 5/4/72, Oral History Collection, Army War College, Carlisle Barracks, p. 38.)
58. Quoted in Francis A. Beer, *Integration and Disintegration in NATO* (Columbus: Ohio State University Press, 1969), p. 111. Specifically, the non-proliferation agreement, and the requirement that to join NATO the FRG would not acquire nuclear arms.
59. Portions of the following pages are drawn with permission from Gregory W. Pedlow, "General Lauris Norstad and the Second Berlin Crisis," paper presented to the Nuclear History Program Author's Conference on the Second Berlin Crisis, Washington, D.C., May 20–21, 1993. The relevant citations are indicated by the initials "GP."
60. PRO, DEFE 13/211, dtd 12/16/60 (GP).
61. PRO, DEFE 13/211, MM 20/61, dtd 3/21/61 (GP).
62. For an examination of Robert McNamara's managerial style as Secretary of Defense, see Kinnard, *Secretary*, pp. 85ff.
63. Dirk U. Stikker, *Men of Responsibility: A Memoir* (New York: Harper and Row, Publishers, 1965), p. 330.
64. See Hanson Baldwin, *The New York Times*, dtd 7/25/62.
65. Ibid.
66. Memo Legere–Taylor, "The Middle of 1961," dtd 6/30/62 (GP)

67. U.S. Senate. Committee on Government Operations. Hearings, *The Atlantic Alliance*, p. 206. The smaller member-states were not anxious to see the U.S. share its veto, either.
68. DDEL, NP, Box 104, Kennedey, John F. (4), "SAUCEUR's Instructions to SHAPE Planners," dtd 11/15/61 (GP).
69. Memo Legere–Taylor, "The Middle of 1961," dtd 6/30/62 (GP). The reference is to Seymour Weiss.
70. Memo Bundy–Norstad, dtd 12/5/61 (enclosing text of Kennedy's letter), NSA (GP).
71. PRO, DEFE 13/211, MM: 59/61, dtd 11/1/61 (GP). Not long after, the British had a taste of the disinclination of the Kennedy Administration to consult with Allies in advance of decisions in the famous Skybolt affair. For a brief summary of this episode, see Frank Costigliola, "Kennedy, the European Allies, and the Failure to Consult," *Political Science Quarterly*, Spring 1995, pp. 118–123. Out of this came the British sharing the U.S.'s *POLARIS* submarines, which tied the British nuclear force more tightly with the American, which was consistent with the Administration's desire to control nuclear management.
72. Robert Hunter, *Security in Europe* (Bloomington, IN: Indiana University Press, 1969), p. 62.

Conclusions

1. Norstad, *Oral History*, p. 338.
2. He was not himself intensely devout; theological abstractions were not of much concern to him.
3. General James H. "Jimmy" Doolittle with Carroll V. Glines, *I Could Never Be So Lucky Again: An Autobiography* (New York: Bantam Books, 1991), p. 272.
4. Franklin D'Olier et al., *The United States Strategic Bombing Surveys*, September 30, 1945 (Maxwell AFB, AL: Air University Press, October 1987), pp. 82ff.
5. Michael Sherry, *The Rise of American Air Power: The Creation of Armageddon* (New Haven: Yale University Press, 1987), p. 15.
6. Walter J. Boyne, *Beyond the Wild Blue: A History of the U.S. Air Force, 1947–1997* (New York: St. Martin's Press, 1997), p. 11.
7. In this respect, Norstad and General Alexander Haig had something in common. It was a well-known secret that the Army hierarchy was dead set against Haig becoming Army Chief of Staff, and to avoid this happening, lobbied hard for his appointment as SACEUR after the Watergate debacle.
8. See, for example, John L. Frisbee, *Makers of the United States Air Force* (Washington, D.C.: Office of Air Force History, 1987). Norstad did not affect a "hail fellow well met" *persona* nor did he cultivate an image of being a "high flyer," or "throttle jockey." He did not drink to excess, was never known as a "lady's man," was fastidious almost to a fault, and generally exuded an aura of extreme self-discipline. He was reserved by nature,

and curiously, in a professional environment populated by exuberant extroverts, this trait proved, on balance, to be more of an asset than a liability.
9. Norstad, *Oral History*, p. 306.
10. Ibid., pp. 305–306. This was the period when the Norstads became experienced in the art of official entertaining, which was (and still is) a necessary component of political and military advancement, and which served them well when they went on to Europe to engage in the practice of coalition diplomacy.
11. In fact, Norstad helped persuade Eisenhower to leave the presidency of Columbia University to return to Europe as NATO's Supreme Allied Commander Europe (SACEUR) and to create the Supreme Headquarters Allied Powers Europe (SHAPE). (Norstad, *Oral History*, pp. 277–278.)
12. Andreas Wenger, *Living with Peril: Eisenhower, Kennedy, and Nuclear Weapons* (New York and Oxford: Rowman and Littlefield, 1997), p. 318. In fact, Norstad had a select group of the SHAPE Staff engaged in an analysis of the situation that might exist at the completion of an initial atomic exchange. He saw this as an important factor in the consideration of the strategy for continued operations in the event of a general war. Eventually he gave up on the effort because of the dearth of classified information which could be shared multinationally from U.S. sources. There might also have been undesirable morale and political repercussions if it were known to the Allies that the U.S. was indeed contemplating – and even planning – what life would be like if Europe were laid waste, and presumably the U.S. were not.
13. Norstad, *Oral History*, p. 322.
14. Solly Zuckerman, *Monkeys, Men and Missiles: An Autobiography 1946–88* (New York: W.W. Norton and Co., 1988), pp. 271–272.
15. Dirk U. Stikker, *Men of Responsibility* (New York: Harper and Row, Publishers, 1965), pp. 333–334. He wrote this just after the December 1960 meeting of the North Atlantic Council.
16. For a comparison of the various attempts at balancing these two roles, see Robert S. Jordan, ed., *Generals in International Politics: NATO's Supreme Allied Commander, Europe* (Lexington, KY: University Press of Kentucky, 1987).
17. Leon Sloss and Kemper Vest, *Nuclear Weapons and the Berlin Crisis*, Center for National Security Negotiations Occasional Paper, Monograph #2, Lessons from Nuclear History Project, April 1995, p. 6. See also the following unpublished draft papers by Michael Wheeler of the Center: "The Evolution of Harry Truman's and Dwight D. Eisenhower's Views on Nuclear Weapons as an Instrument of National Security Policy, 1945–1944" dtd 6/18/97; "Early U.S. Nuclear Doctrine and Command and Control" dtd 7/11/97; and "Nuclear Weapons and European Security: The Evolution of American Politico-Military Views, 1945–1954" dtd 6/27/97.
18. Norstad's path crossed MacArthur's in September 1950, when he was sent out to Tokyo to evaluate MacArthur's requests for more troops. He was then a Lt. General and Air Force Deputy Chief of Staff; with him was Lt. General Ridgway, the Army Deputy Chief of Staff. Averell Harriman joined the group after Norstad had "casually" invited him and Truman had agreed. (See Rudy Abramson, *Spanning the Century: The Life of*

W. *Averell Harriman, 1891–1986* (New York: William Morrow and Co., Inc., 1992), pp. 450–451.
19. Mark Perry, *Four Stars: The Inside Story of the Forty-Year Battle Between the Joint Chiefs of Staff and America's Civilian Leaders* (Boston: Houghton Mifflin Co., 1989), p. 120.
20. Norstad, *Oral History*, pp. 359–360.
21. Marc Trachtenberg, *History and Strategy* (Princeton: Princeton University Press, 1991), p. 167.

Appendix

1. *Newsweek*, dtd 1/63. He had received an honorary degree from Oxford.
2. This information was supplied by Professor John Hattendorf, who wrote a monograph on the history of the Chichele Chair. (See John B. Hattendorf, "The Study of War History at Oxford, 1862–1990," in John B. Hattendorf and Malcolm H. Murfett, eds., *The Limitations of Military Power: Essays Presented to Professor Norman Gibbs on His Eightieth Birthday* (London: Macmillan Press, 1990), pp. 3–61.
3. Norstad, *Oral History*, p. 559. His friend, Robert A. Lovett, had Norstad's various offers assessed to help Norstad evaluate better what his options were.
4. Ltr Houghton–Norstad, dtd 8/15/62.
5. "Gen. Norstad Tries His Hand at Corporate Strategy," *Forbes Magazine*, dtd 3/1/64.
6. *Time Magazine*, dtd 1/25/63.
7. *Toledo Blade* dtd 1/17/63. Owens-Corning had in November 1962 created a new Aerospace division, which was responsible for research and development, and marketing activities in specialized defense and space fields, with headquarters in New York City. This was a parallel operation to Norstad's, so that it remained true that Norstad was not engaged in activities with the government that bore directly on his military career. (*Toledo Blade*, dtd 11/2/62.) In 1966 the division was moved to Washington, D.C., headed by a Vice President, National Affairs. (*Toledo Blade*, dtd 7/22/66).
8. *Toledo Record*, dtd 1/25/67. Another vice president was Hal. M. Cranston, who unfortunately died in January 1967.
9. *Forbes Magazine* suggested why OCF was looking for new leadership:

> Of all the high-ranking military men who have gone on to head big business firms, probably none has had a more attractive opportunity than 56-year-old Lauris Norstad ... OCF is a growth company that has virtually stopped growing. Although during the last four years its sales have been advancing at an average annual rate of 6.5%, its earnings have gone nowhere. Over this period its operating income (before depreciation and income taxes) was actually down from $41.3 million to $26 million and earnings per share dropped from $2.43 to $1.86 ... Norstad's assignment: to help get Owens-Corning growing again ... Now, to grow appreciably, it must grab markets away from other materials. Fiber glass has certain advantages which should help it do so. It is

stronger than steel, lighter than cotton and flexible as silk. It won't burn and won't rot. But getting into new markets will be no easy task (*Forbes Market*, dtd 3/1/64).
10. *Toledo Blade* dtd 12/19/96. By then Norstad had become a director of McKennon and Robbins, Inc., and a Trustee of the Rand Corporation. In September 1965, the position of president of Owens-Corning Fiberglas, International was abolished, with Norstad's former responsibilities being assumed by Hal M. Cranston as a newly-created vice president of Owens-Corning International. As vice president of the international enterprise, Cranston continued Norstad's efforts at establishing and managing foreign subsidiaries and handling relations with foreign affiliates and licensees and export sales. (*Toledo Blade*, dtd 9/28/65).
11. *Forbes Magazine*, dtd 3/1/64. It was said in the corporation that Harold Boeschenstein liked very much the idea of recruiting someone like Norstad to come into the company, but like many "hands-on" corporate builders, he found it difficult in practice to let go the reins.
12. *Toledo Blade*, dtd 5/6/65.
13. *Forbes Magazine*, dtd 3/1/64.
14. *Toledo Blade*, dtd 2/1/66.
15. *Toledo Blade*, dtd 4/4/68. Norstad also presided over the move and consolidation of OCF's New York and Toledo corporate offices into Fiberglas Tower. The top nineteen floors were given over to the corporation. They were decorated,of course, with fiberglas draperies, fiberglas fabrics on the furniture, and fiberglas screen dividers in the open-bay work spaces. Fiberglas file cabinets and bookcases were placed around the desks, and the numerous plants were in fiber glass planters (*Toledo Blade*, dtd 5/17/70). The corporation was rightly proud of the building, the tallest at the time in Toledo. The corner offices, for the senior executives, were totally enclosed. Harold Boeschenstein had one of the corner offices on the top office floor, and Norstad another. On the very top of the building, the twenty-eighth storey, was the only sky-top restaurant in Toledo. As it was described: "... the restaurant has contemporary style, but unusual distinction — Fiberglas and fiberglas related products are used throughout, including chairs, dish carts, ceiling modules, and even window blinds. The latter represent the first new invention in the venetian blind field in over 50 years and soon are to be marketed nation-wide." (*Toledo Times*, dtd 1/19/71).
16. *Toledo Blade*, dtd 10/3/68.
17. Significant, also, was Norstad's emphasis on delegating downward to middle management. For example, at the April 1969 annual meeting, Norstad attributed the sharply rising sales and profits in part "from contributions by younger executives who have been given increasing responsibility and authority." (*Toledo Blade*, dtd 4/18/69).
18. I am grateful for the assistance of Dennison's University Archivist, Florence W. Hoffman, for providing this information.
19. *The Owens-Corning Lectures*, 1968–69 (Granville, Ohio: Dennison University, 1969). In keeping up his academic ties, recalling Winston Churchill's famous "Iron Curtain" speech, Norstad was especially gratified to receive an honorary degree of doctor of humane letters from Westminster College in Fulton, Missouri in 1967. He received a total of sixteen honorary degrees from such

universities as Oxford, Yale University, University of Toledo, Bowling Green State University, Defiance College, University of Maryland, and received decorations from ten foreign countries.
20. *Toledo Blade*, dtd 10/9/70.
21. William Boeschenstein succeeded John H. Thomas, who was elected Vice Chairman of the Board and Deputy Chief Executive Officer. Harold Boeschenstein was succeeded by John G. McLean, President of Continental Oil Company. John E. Bierwirth, who had been on the board for 22 years and had been elected as one of the initial group of outside directors, was succeeded by W. L. Hadley Griffin, President of Brown Shoe Company. Norstad commented: " ... the changes were made to strengthen the top management, to give recognition to the great contributions made to Owens-Corning by a group of younger officers, and to give increased authority and responsibility to the younger executives on whom the future of the business depends." (*Toledo Blade*, dtd 8/19/71).
22. Harold A. Boeschenstein died on October 23, 1972 at the age of 76, of a heart attack.
23. *Toledo Blade*, dtd 8/19/72.
24. *Toledo Blade*, dtd 1/7/73.
25. In 1978, William Boeschenstein somewhat reversed the decentralization trend by expanding in function and composition the "Office of Chief Executive" – formerly the Office of the President. Three executive vice presidents and four senior vice presidents were named. Richard Yudkin, who once worked at SHAPE headquarters, became Senior Vice President, Office of the Chief Executive. The three semi-autonomous group vice presidents were now made executive vice presidents in the Office. (*Toledo Blade*, dtd 10/20/78).
26. *Toledo Blade*, dtd 1/7/73.
27. *Toledo Blade*, dtd 1/7/73. At the time he retired Norstad was a director of United Air Lines and Continental Oil Company, among other corporations. He still retained his trustee's position of the RAND Corporation, and served on the President's General Advisory Committee on Arms Control and Disarmament.
28. Interview with *Dialog*, a Toledo magazine, undtd. Edward J Mikulenka III assisted in the preparation of this Appendix. I am grateful also for the cooperation of William Boeschenstein and Maj. Gen. USAF (Ret.) Richard Yudkin. Responsibility rests, of course, with the author.

Source Material

Selected Documentary and Reference Citations

Eisenhower Library (EL), Papers of Lauris Norstad (NP). (Cited also as DDEL).
Eisenhower Library (EL), Papers of Dwight D. Eisenhower (EP). (Cited also as DDEL).
Norstad's personal letters (NPL) concerning his appointment as SACEUR are deposited with the Papers of Lauris Norstad at the Eisenhower Library.
National Security Archive (NSA), The Berlin Crisis 1958-1962 (Berlin), Name Index: Norstad, Lauris (Norstad).
National Archives (NA), Records of the Department of State (State Dept.), Bureau of European Affairs (Eur. Aff.), Office of European Regional Affairs (Eur. Reg. Aff.), Political-Military Numerical Files (Pol-Mil. NF).
National Archives (NA), Records of the Department of State (State Dept.), Bureau of European Affairs (Eur. Aff.), Office of European Regional Affairs (Eur. Reg. Aff.), Records of NATO Advisor (NATO ad.).
National Archives (NA), Records of the Department of State (State Dept.), Bureau of European Affairs (Eur. Aff.), Office of Atlantic Political and Military Affairs (Atl. Pol-Mil. Aff.), Records Relating to NATO (NATO).
National Archives (NA), Records of the Joint Chiefs of Staff (JCS), Central Decimal File (CDF).
National Archives (NA), Records of the Joint Chiefs of Staff (JCS), Chairman File/General Twining (CF/GT).
NATO Official Communiques or Documents – North Atlantic Council (NAC) or Military Committee (MC).

Books

Abramson, Rudy, *Spanning the Century: The Life of W. Averell Harriman, 1891-1986* (New York: William Morrow and Co., Inc., 1992).
Acheson, Dean, *Present at the Creation: My Years in the State Department* (New York: W.W. Norton and Co., 1969).
Alperovitz, Gar, *The Decision to Use the Atomic Bomb* (New York: Vintage Books, 1996).
Alting von Geusau, Franz A.M., *Allies in a Turbulent World: Challenges to U.S. and Western European Cooperation* (Lexington, MA: Lexington Books, 1982).
Ambrose, Stephen E., *Eisenhower the President*, 2 Vols. (New York: Simon and Schuster, 1984).
Arnold, Henry H., *Global Mission* (New York: Harper and Brothers, Publishers, 1949).
Associated Press, *Addresses by Speakers*, 1960.
Backer, John H., *Winds of History: The German Years of Lucius DuBignon Clay* (New York: Van Nostrand Reinhold Co., 1983).

Baer, George W., *One Hundred Years of Sea Power: The U.S. Navy 1890–1990* (Stanford, CA: Stanford University Press, 1994).
Barlow, Jeffrey G., *Revolt of the Admirals: The Fight for Naval Aviation, 1945–1950* (Washington, D.C.: Naval Historical Center, Department of the Navy, 1994).
Barnet, Richard J., *The Alliance-America, Europe, Japan: Makers of the Postwar World* (New York: Simon and Schuster, 1983).
Beer, Francis A., *Integration and Disintegration in NATO* (Columbus, OH: Ohio State University Press, 1969).
Bischof, Gunter and Stephen E. Ambrose, eds., *Eisenhower: A Centenary Assessment* (Baton Rouge: Louisiana State University Press, 1995).
Bischof, Gunter and Robert L. Dupont, eds., *The Pacific War Revisited* (Baton Rouge: Louisiana State University Press, 1997).
Binder, L. James, *Lemnitzer: A Soldier for his Time* (London and Washington, D.C.: Brassey's, 1997)
Bland, Douglas L., *The Military Committee of the North Atlantic Alliance: A Study of Structure and Strategy* (Westport, CT: Praeger, 1991).
Bohlen, Charles E., *Witness to History, 1929–1969* (New York: W.W. Norton and Co., Inc. 1973).
Bowie, Robert and Richard H. Immerman, *Waging Peace: How Eisenhower Shaped an Enduring Cold War Strategy* (Oxford and New York: Oxford University Press, 1997).
Boyne, Walter J., *Beyond the Wild Blue: A History of the U.S. Air Force, 1947–1997* (New York: St. Martin's Press, 1998).
Bradley, Omar N., and Clay Blair, *A General's Life: An Autobiography by General of the Army Omar N. Bradley* (New York: Simon and Schuster, 1983).
Bradley, Omar N., *A Soldier's Story* (New York: Henry Holt and Co., 1951).
Brinkley, Douglas, *Dean Acheson: The Cold War Years, 1953–1971* (New Haven: Yale University Press, 1992).
Brodie, Bernard, *War and Politics* (New York: Macmillan Pub. Co., 1973).
Bundy, McGeorge, *Danger and Survival: Choices About the Bomb in the First Fifty Years* (New York: Vintage Books, 1988).
Buzan, Barry, ed., *The International Politics of Deterrence* (London: Frances Pinter, 1987).
Caraley, Demetrios, *The Politics of Unification* (New York: Columbia University Press, 1966).
Cardwell, Thomas A. III, *Command Structure for Theater Warfare, The Quest for Unity of Command* (Maxwell AFB, AL: Air University Press, September 1984).
Clay, Lucius D., *Decision in Germany* (New York: Doubleday and Co., Inc., 1950).
Clay, Lucius D., *The Papers of Lucius D. Clay: Germany, 1945–1949*, 2 Vols., ed. Jean Edward Smith (Bloomington, IN: Indiana University Press, 1974).
Coffey, Thomas M., *Decision over Schweinfurt: The U.S. 8th Air Force Battle for Daylight Bombing* (New York: David McKay Co., Inc., 1977).
Coffey, Thomas M., *Hap: The Story of the U.S. Air Force and the Man Who Built It, General Henry H. "Hap" Arnold* (New York: Viking Press, 1982).
Coffey, Thomas M., *Iron Eagle: The Turbulent Life of General Curtis LeMay* (New York: Crown Publishers, Inc., 1986).

Condit, Doris M., *The Test of War, 1950–1953, History of the Office of the Secretary of Defense*, Vol. II. (Washington, D.C.: Historical Office, Office of the Secretary of Defense, 1988).

Cook, Don, *Forging the Alliance: The Birth of the NATO Treaty and the Dramatic Transformation of U.S. Foreign Policy Between 1945 and 1950* (New York: Arbor House/William Morrow, 1989).

Copp, DeWitt S., *A Few Great Captains: The Men and Events That Shaped the Development of U.S. Air Power* (Garden City, NY: Doubleday and Company, Inc., 1980).

Copp, DeWitt S., *Forged in Fire: Strategy and Decisions in the Air War over Europe, 1940–1945* (Garden City, NY: Doubleday and Company, 1982 [for The Air Force Historical Foundation]).

Crane, Conrad C., *Bombs Cities, and Civilians: American Airpower Strategy in World War II* (Lawrence, KS: University Press of Kansas, 1993).

Craven, Wesley Frank, and James Lea Cate, *The Army Air Forces in World War II*, 7 Vols. (Chicago: University of Chicago Press, 1948–1958).

Crawley, Aidan, *De Gaulle* (Indianapolis, IN: The Bobbs-Merrill Co., Inc., 1969).

Cray, Ed, *General of the Army George C. Marshall: Soldier and Statesman* (New York: W.W. Norton and Co., 1990).

Davis, Richard G., *Carl A. Spaatz and the Air War in Europe* (Washington, D.C.: Smithsonian Institution Press, 1992).

Davis, Richard G., *HAP, Henry H. Arnold, Military Aviator* (Washington, D.C.: Air Force History and Museums Program, 1997).

De Gaulle, Charles, *Memoirs of Hope: Renewal and Endeavor*, trans. Terence Kilmartin (New York: Simon and Schuster, 1971).

Department of State, *Foreign Relations of the United States* (FRUS), 1952–1954, Vol II.

Divine, Robert A., *Eisenhower and the Cold War* (New York: Oxford University Press, 1981).

Divine, Robert A., *The Sputnik Challenge* (New York: Oxford University Press, 1993).

Dockrill, Saki, *Britain's Policy for West German Rearmament, 1950–1955* (New York: Cambridge University Press, 1991).

Dockrill, Saki, *Eisenhower's New-Look National Security Policy, 1953–61* (New York: St. Martin's Press, 1996).

D'Olier, Franklin, et al., *The United States Strategic Bombing Survey*, Summary Report, September 30, 1945 (Maxwell AFB, AL: Air University Press, October 1987).

Donovan, Robert J., *Eisenhower: The Inside Story* (New York: Harper and Bros., 1956).

Doolittle, James H. "Jimmy", and Caroll V. Glines, *I Could Never Be So Lucky Again: An Autobiography* (New York: Bantam Books, 1991).

Duke, Simon W. and Wolfgang Krieger, eds., *U.S. Military Forces in Europe: the Early Years 1945–1970* (Boulder, CO: Westview Press, 1993).

Dulles, Eleanor Lansing, *One Germany or Two: The Struggle at the Heart of Europe* (Stanford, CA: Hoover Institution Press, 1970).

Eisenhower, Dwight D., *Crusade in Europe* (Garden City, N.Y.: Doubleday and Company, 1948).

Eisenhower, Dwight D., *The White House Years: Mandate for Change, 1953–1956* (Garden City, NY: Doubleday and Co., Inc., 1963).

Eisenhower, Dwight D., *The White House Years: Waging Peace, 1956–1961* (Garden City NY: Doubleday and Co., Inc., 1965).
Epley, William W., ed., *International Cold War Military Records and History: Proceedings of the International Conference on Cold War Military Records and History Held in Washington, D.C. 21–26 March 1994* (Washington, D.C.: Office of the Secretary of Defense, 1996).
Etzold, Thomas and John Lewis Gaddis, eds., *Containment: Documents on American Policy and Strategy, 1945–1950* (New York: Columbia University Press, 1978).
Farago, Ladislas, *Patton: Ordeal and Triumph* (New York: Astor-Honor, Inc., 1964).
Ferrell, Robert H., ed., *The Eisenhower Diaries* (New York: W.W. Norton and Co., 1981).
Finletter, Thomas K., *Power and Policy: U.S. Foreign Policy and Military Power in the Hydrogen Age* (New York: Harcourt, Brace and Company, 1954).
Fisher, Nigel, *Macmillan: A Biography* (New York: St. Martin's Press, 1982).
Freedman, Julian, et al., *Alliance in International Politics* (Boston: Allyn and Bacon, 1970).
Friedmann, W., *The Allied Military Government of Germany* (London: Stevens and Sons, Ltd., 1947).
Friend, Julius, *Franco-German Relations, 1950–1990* (Westport, CT: Praeger, 1994).
Frisbee, John L., *Makers of the United States Air Force* (Washington, D.C.: Office of Air Force History, 1987).
Futrell, Robert Frank, *Ideas, Concepts, Doctrine: Basic thinking in the United States Air Force, 1907–1960* (Maxwell Air Force Base, AL: Air University Press, 1989).
Gaddis, John Lewis, *Strategies of Containment: A Critical Appraisal of Postwar American National Security Policy* (New York and Oxford: Oxford University Press, 1982).
Gaddis, John Lewis, *The United States and the End of the Cold War: Implications, Reconsiderations, Provocations* (New York: Oxford University Press, 1994).
Gaddis, John Lewis, *We Now Know: Rethinking Cold War History* (Oxford: Clarenden Press 1997).
Gaddis, John Lewis, Philip H. Gordon, Ernest R. May and Jonathan Rosenberg, *Cold War Statesmen Confront the Bomb: Nuclear Diplomocy since 1945* (Oxford and New York: Oxford University Press, 1999).
Gallois, General Pierre, *The Balance of Terror: Strategy for the Missile Age* (Boston: Houghton-Mifflin, 1961).
Gelb, Norman, *Desperate Venture* (New York: William Morrow and Co., 1992).
George, Alexander L. and Richard Smoke, *Deterrence in American Foreign Policy: Theory and Practice* (New York: Columbia University Press, 1974).
Goldberg, Alfred, ed., *A History of the United States Air Force, 1907–1957* (Princeton, NJ: D. Van Nostrand Co., Inc., 1957).
Golden, James, R., et al., *NATO at Forty: Change, Continuity, and Prospects* (Boulder, CO: Westview Press, 1989) – see especially chapter by General Andrew Goodpaster.
Gorn, Michael H., *Harnessing the Genie: Science and Technology Forecasting for the Air Force 1944–1986* (Washington, D.C.: Office of Air Force History, Air Staff Historical Study, 1988).
Graebner, Norman A., *The New Isolationism: A Study in Politics and Foreign Policy Since 1950* (New York: The Ronald Press Co., 1956).

Gropman, Alan, ed., *The Big "L": American Logistics in World War II* (Washington, D.C.: National Defense University Press, 1997).

Hamilton, Nigel, *Monty: Final Years of the Field-Marshal, 1944–1976* (New York: McGraw-Hill Book Co., 1987).

Hanreider, Wolfram F. *West German Foreign Policy, 1949–1963: International Pressure and Domestic Response* (Stanford, CA: Stanford University Press, 1967).

Hansell, Haywood S., Jr., *Air Plan That Defeated Hitler* (New York: Arno Press, 1980).

Hansell, Haywood S., Jr., *The Strategic Air War Against Germany and Japan: A Memoir* (Washington, D.C.: Office of Air Force History, USAF Warrior Studies, 1986).

Harmon, Christopher C., *"Are We Beasts?": Churchill and the Moral Question of World War II "Area Bombing"* (Newport, RI: Naval War College, The Newport Papers #1, December 1991).

Heidelmeyer, Wolfgang, and Guenter Hindrichs, *Documents on Berlin, 1943–1963* (Munich: R. Oldlenbourg Verlag, 1963).

Henderson, Sir Nicholas, *The Birth of NATO* (Boulder, CO: Westview Press, 1983).

Heuser, Beatrice and Robert O'Neill, eds., *Securing Peace in Europe, 1945–1962* (New York: St. Martin's Press, 1992).

Hill-Norton, Sir Peter, *No Soft Options: The Politico-Military Realities of NATO* (Montreal: McGill-Queen's University Press, 1978).

Hitchcock, William I, *France Restored: Cold War Diplomacy and the Quest for Leadership in Europe.*(Chapel Hill and London: The University of North Carolina Press, 1998).

Holley, I.B., Jr., *Ideas and Weapons* (Washington, D.C.: Office of Air Force History 1983).

Hoopes, Townsend, *The Devil and John Foster Dulles* (London: Andre Deutsch, Ltd., 1974).

Hoopes, Townsend, and Douglas Brinkley, *Driven Patriot: The Life and Times of James Forrestal* (New York: Alfred A. Knopf, 1992).

Horne, Alistair, *Macmillan 1894–1950* (London: Pan Books Ltd., 1988).

Horne, Alistair, with David Montgomery, *Monty: The Lonely Leader, 1944–1945* (New York: HarperCollins Publishers, 1996).

Hudson, G.F., *The Hard and Bitter Peace: World Politics Since 1945* (New York: Frederick A. Praeger, Publishers, 1967).

Hunter, Robert, *Security in Europe* (Bloomington, IN: Indiana University Press, 1969).

Hurley, Alfred F., *Billy Mitchell: Crusader for Air Power*, 2nd edn. (Bloomington, IN: Indiana University Press, 1975).

Immerman, Richard H., ed., *John Foster Dulles and the Diplomacy of the Cold War* (Princeton: Princeton University Press, 1990).

Immerman, Richard H., *John Foster Dulles: Piety, Pragmatism, and Power in U.S. Foreign Policy* (Wilmington, DL: SR Books, 1999).

Ireland, Timothy P., *Creating the Entangling Alliance: The Origins of the North Atlantic Treaty Organization* (Westport, CT: Greenwood Press, 1981).

Ismay, Hastings, Lord, *NATO The First Five Years 1949–1954* (Paris: NATO Information Services, 1954).

Ismay, Hastings, Lord, *The Memoirs of General Lord Ismay* (New York: The Viking Press, 1960).

Jackson, W.G.F., *The Battle for North Africa, 1940–1943* (New York: Mason/Charter, 1975).
Jordan, Ralph B., *Born to Fight: The Life of Admiral William Halsey* (Philadelphia: David McKay Co., 1946).
Jordan, Robert S., *The NATO International Staff/Secretariat, 1952–1957: A Study in International Administration* (London and New York: Oxford University Press, 1967).
Jordan, Robert S., *Political Leadership in NATO: A Study in Multinational Diplomacy* (Boulder, CO: Westview Press, 1979).
Jordan, Robert S., *Alliance Strategy and Navies: The Evolution and Scope of NATO's Maritime Dimension* (London: Pinter Publishers; New York: St. Martin's Press, 1990).
Jordan, Robert S., ed., *Generals in International Politics: NATO's Supreme Allied Commander, Europe* (Lexington, KY: The University Press of Kentucky, 1987).
Kaplan, Fred M., *The Wizards of Armageddon* (New York: Simon and Schuster, 1983).
Kaplan, Lawrence S., *A Community of Interests: NATO and the Military Assistance Program, 1948–1951* (Washington, D.C.: U.S. Government Printing Office, 1980).
Kaplan, Lawrence S., *NATO and the United States: The Enduring Alliance* (Boston: Twayne Publishers, 1988).
Kaplan, Lawrence S., *The Long Entanglement: NATO's First Fifty Years* (Westport, CT: Praeger Publishers, 1999).
Kaplan, Lawrence S. and Robert W. Clawson, *NATO After Thirty Years* (Wilmington, DE: Scholarly Resources, Inc., 1981).
Kaplan, Lawrence S., et al. *NATO After Forty Years* (Wilmington, DE: Scholarly Resources, Inc., 1990).
Keesing's Contemporary Archive, 1962.
Kenney, George C., *General Kenney Reports: A Personal History of the Pacific War* (Washington, D.C.: Office of Air Force History, USAF Warrior Studies, 1987).
Kerr, E. Bartlett, *Flames Over Tokyo: The U.S. Army Air Forces' Incendiary Campaign Against Japan, 1944–1945* (New York: Donald I. Fine, Inc., 1991).
Kinnard, Douglas, *The Secretary of Defense* (Lexington, KY: The University Press of Kentucky, 1980).
Kinnard, Douglas, *President Eisenhower and Strategy Management: A Study in Defense Politics* (Washington: Pergamon-Brasseys, 1989).
Koch, Scott A., ed., *Selected Estimates on the Soviet Union, 1950–1959* (Washington, D.C.: CIA History Staff, Center for the Study of Intelligence, Central Intelligence Agency, 1993).
Kohn, Richard H., and Joseph P. Harahan, *Strategic Air Warfare: An Interview with Generals Curtis E. LeMay, Leon W. Johnson, David A. Burchinal, and Jack J. Catton* (Washington, D.C.: Office of Air Force History, USAF Warrior Studies, 1988).
Korb, Lawrence J., *The Joint Chiefs of Staff: The First Twenty-five Years* (Bloomington, IN: Indiana University Press, 1976).
Lash, Joseph P., *Dag Hammarskjold: Custodian of the Brushfire Peace* (Garden City, NY: Doubleday and Co., Inc., 1961).

Legere, Lawrence J., Jr., *Unification of the Armed Forces* (Dissertation presented to Faculty of the Graduate School of Arts and Sciences, Harvard University, Unpub.).

LeMay, General Curtis E., with MacKinlay Kantor, *Mission with LeMay: My Story* (Garden City, NY: Doubleday and Co., Inc., 1965).

Liddell Hart, Basil, *The Liddell Hart Memoirs, 1895-1938* (New York: G.P. Putnam's Sons, 1965).

Lowenstein, Prince Hubertus and Volkmar von Zuhlsdorff, *NATO and the Defense of the West*, Edward Fitzgerald, transl. (New York: Frederick A. Praeger, 1960).

Maier, Charles and Gunter Bischof, eds., *The Marshall Plan and Germany: West German Development within the Framework of the European Recovery Program* (New York: St. Martin's Press, 1991).

Maloney, Sean M., *Securing Command of the Sea: NATO Naval Planning, 1948-1954* (Annapolis, MD: Naval Institute Press, 1995).

May, Ernest R., ed., *American Cold War Strategy: Interpreting NSC 68* (New York: Bedford Books of St. Martin's Press, 1993).

McCullough, David, *Truman* (New York: Simon and Schuster, 1992).

McNamara, Robert S., *The Essence of Security: Reflections in Office* (New York: Harper and Row, 1968).

Meilinger, Phillip S., *Hoyt S. Vandenberg: The Life of a General* (Bloomington, IN: Indiana University Press, 1989).

Meilinger, Phillip S., *American Airpower Biography: A Survey of the Field* (Maxwell AFB, AL: Air University Press, 1995).

Mets, David R., *Master of Airpower: General Carl A. Spaatz* (Novato, CA: Presidio Press, 1988).

Metz, Steven, *Eisenhower as Strategist: The Coherent Use of Military Power in War and Peace* (Carlisle Barracks, PA: Strategic Studies Institute, U.S. Army War College, February 1993).

Morris, Charles R., *Iron Destinies, Lost Opportunities: The Arms Race Between the U.S.A. and the U.S.S.R., 1945-1987* (New York: Harper and Row, Publishers, 1988).

Mortensen, Daniel R., *A Pattern for Joint Operations: World War II Close Air Support North Africa*, Historical Analysis Series (Washington, D.C.: Office of Air Force History and U.S. Army Center of Military History, 1987).

Murphy, Robert, *Diplomat Among Warriors* (Garden City, NY: Doubleday and Co., Inc., 1964).

Murray, Williamson, *Strategy for Defeat: The Luftwaffe 1933-1945* (Maxwell AFB, AL: Air University Press, 1983).

Newhouse, John, *War and Peace in the Nuclear Age* (New York: Alfred A. Knopf, 1989).

Ninkovich, Frank A., *Germany and the United States: The Transformation of the German Question Since 1945* (Boston: Twayne Publishers, 1988).

Nitze, Paul H. *From Hiroshima to Glasnost: At the Center of Decision, a Memoir* (New York: Grove Weidenfeld, 1989).

Nolan, Jane E., *Guardians of the Arsenal: The Politics of Nuclear Strategy* (New York: Basic Books, Inc., 1989).

Norton, Augustus Richard, et al., *NATO: A Bibliography and Resource Guide* (New York: Garland Publishing, Inc., 1985).

O'Connell, Robert L., *Of Arms and Men: A History of War, Weapons, and Aggression* (New York: Oxford University Press, 1989).
Oldfield, Barney, *Never a Shot in Anger* (Santa Barbara, CA: Capra Press, Inc., The Battle of Normandy Museum Edition, 1989).
Osgood, Robert E., *NATO: The Entangling Alliance* (Chicago: University of Chicago Press, 1962).
Osgood, Robert E., *The Case for the MLF: A Critical Evaluation* (Washington, D.C.: Washington Center for Foreign Policy Research, 1964).
Osgood, Robert E., *Alliances and American Foreign Policy* (Baltimore: The Johns Hopkins Press, 1968).
Overy, R.J., *The Air War, 1939–1945* (New York: Stein and Day, 1981).
Owens-Corning Lectures, 1968–69 (Granville, OH: Denision University, 1969).
Palmer, Michael A., *Origins of the Maritime Strategy: American Naval Strategy in the First Postwar Decade*, (Washington, D.C., Naval Historical Center, 1988).
Parker, R.A.C., *Struggle for Survival: The History of the Second World War* (New York: Oxford University Press, 1989).
Parton, James, *"Air Force Spoken Here" General Ira Eaker and the Command of the Air* (Bethesda, MD: Adler and Adler Publishers, 1986).
Paxton, Robert O., and Nicholas Wahl, eds., *De Gaulle and the United States: A Centennial Reappraisal* (Oxford: Berg Publishers, 1994).
Perry, Mark, *Four Stars: The Inside Story of the Forty-Year Battle Between the Joint Chiefs of Staff and America's Civilian Leaders* (Boston: Houghton Mifflin Co., 1989).
Pincher, Chapman, *Inside Story: A Documentary of the Pursuit of Power* (New York: Stein and Day, 1979).
Pfaltzgraff, Jr., and Uri Ra'anan, eds., *National Security Policy: the Decision-making Process* (New York: Archon Books, 1984).
Pogue, Forrest C., *George C. Marshall: Statesman* (New York: Viking, 1987).
Poole, Walter S., *The History of the Joint Chiefs of Staff, The Joint Chiefs of Staff and National Policy, vol. 4, 1950–1952* (Washington, D.C.: Historical Division, Joint Secretariat, Joint Chiefs of Staff, 1979).
Possony, Stefan T., *Strategic Air Power: The Pattern of Dynamic Security* (Washington, D.C.: Infantry Journal Press, 1949).
Prados, John, *Keepers of the Keys: A History of the National Security Council from Truman to Bush* (New York: William A. Morrow and Co., Inc. 1991).
Pusey, Merlo J., *Eisenhower The President* (New York: The Macmillan Co., 1956).
Putney, Diane T., ed., *ULTRA and the Army Air Forces in World War II: An Interview with Associate Justice of the U.S. Supreme Court Lewis F. Powell, Jr.* (Washington, D.C.: Office of Air Force History, USAF Warrior Studies, 1987).
Radford, Arthur W., *From Pearl Harbor to Vietnam: The Memoirs of Admiral Arthur W. Radford*, edited by Stephen Jurika, Jr. (Stanford, CA: Hoover Institution Press, 1980).
Rearden, Steven L., *The Formative Years: 1947–1950, Vol. I History of the Office of the Secretary of Defense* (Washington D.C.: Historical Office, Office of the Secretary of Defense, 1984).
Reeves, Richard, *President Kennedy: Profile of Power* (New York: Simon and Schuster, 1993).

Reynolds, Clark G., *Admiral John H. Towers: The Struggle for Naval Air Supremacy* (Annapolis, MD: Naval Institute Press, 1991).
Rhodes, Richard, *The Making of the Atomic Bomb* (New York: Simon and Schuster, 1986).
Rhodes, Richard, *Dark Sun: The Making of the Hydrogen Bomb* (New York: Simon and Schuster, 1995).
Richardson, James L., *Germany and the Atlantic Alliance* (Cambridge, MA: Harvard University Press, 1966).
Ridgway, Matthew B., *Soldier: the Memoirs of Matthew B. Ridgway*, as told to Harold H. Martin (New York: Harper and Bros., 1956).
Roman, Peter J., *Eisenhower and the Missile Gap* (Ithaca, NY: Cornell University Press, 1995).
Rosenberg, David Alan and Steven T. Ross, *America's Plans for War against the Soviet Union, 1945-1950* (New York: Garland Pub. Co., 1989).
Ross, Steven T., *American War Plans, 1945-1950* (New York: Garland Publishing Inc., 1988).
Rostow, Walt W., *The Diffusion of Power 1957-1972* (New York: Macmillan, 1972).
Ruffner, Kevin C., ed., *CORONA: America's First Satellite Program* (Washington, D.C.: CIA History Staff, Center for the Study of Intelligence, Central Intelligence Agency, 1995).
Schaffer, Ronald, *Wings of Judgment: American Bombing in World War II* (New York: Oxford University Press, 1985).
Schick, Jack M., *The Berlin Crisis, 1958-1962* (Philadelphia: University of Pennsylvania Press, 1971).
Schoenbaum, Thomas J., *Waging Peace and War: Dean Rusk in the Truman, Kennedy, and Johnson Years* (New York: Simon and Schuster, 1988).
Schratz, Paul, ed., *Evolution of the American Military Establishment Since World War II* (Lexington, VA: The George C. Marshall Research Foundation, 1978).
Schwartz, David N., *NATO's Nuclear Dilemmas* (Washington, D.C.: Brookings Institution, 1983).
Schwartz, Thomas Alan, *America's Germany: John J. McCloy and the Federal Republic of Germany* (Cambridge, MA: Harvard University Press, 1991).
Serfaty, Simon, *France, De Gaulle and Europe: The Policy of the Fourth and Fifth Republic Toward the Continent* (Baltimore: The Johns Hopkins Press, 1968).
Seton-Watson, Hugh, *Neither War Nor Peace: The Struggle for Power in the Postwar World* (New York: Frederick A. Praeger, Publishers, 1960).
Shapley, Deborah, *Promise and Power: The Life and Times of Robert McNamara* (Boston: Little, Brown and Co., 1993).
Sherry, Michael S., *Preparing for the Next War: American Plans for Postwar Defense, 1941-1945* (New Haven and London: Yale University Press, 1977).
Sherry, Michael S., *The Rise of American Air Power: The Creation of Armageddon* (New Haven and London: Yale University Press, 1987).
Sherwen, Nicholas, ed., *NATO's Anxious Birth: The Prophetic Vision of the 1940s* (London: C. Hurst and Co., 1985).
Sixsmith, E.K.G., *Eisenhower as Military Commander* (New York: Stein and Day, Publishers, 1983).

Slessor, Sir John, *The Central Blue, Recollections and Reflections* (London: Cassell and Co., Ltd., 1956).

Sloss, Leon and Kemper Vest, *Nuclear Weapons and the Berlin Crisis*, A Center for National Security Negotiations Occasional Paper, Monograph #2, April 1995.

Smith, Alice Kimball, *A Peril and A Hope: The Scientists' Movement in America; 1945–47* (Chicago: University of Chicago Press 1965).

Smith, Dale O., *Cradle of Valor: The Intimate Letters of a Plebe at West Point* (Chapel Hill, NC: Algonquin Books, 1988).

Smith, Dan, *Pressure: How America Runs NATO* (London: Bloomsbury Publishing, 1989).

Smith, Jean Edward, *The Defense of Berlin* (Baltimore: The Johns Hopkins Press, 1963).

Smith, Jean Edward, *Lucius D. Clay: An American Life* (New York: Henry Holt and Co., 1990).

Snyder, William P., *The Politics of British Defense Policy, 1945–1962* (Columbus, OH: Ohio State University Press, 1964).

Spaak, Paul-Henri, *The Continuing Battle: Memoirs of a European 1936–1966*, transl. Henry Fox (Boston: Little, Brown and Co., 1971).

Spangler, Stanley E., *Force and Accommodation in World Politics* (Maxwell AFB, AL: Air University Press, August 1991).

Spector, Ronald H., *Eagle Against the Sun: The American War with Japan* (New York: Vintage Books, 1985).

Speier, Hans, *Divided Berlin: The Anatomy of Soviet Political Blackmail* (New York: Frederick A. Praeger, 1960).

Stanley, Timothy, *NATO in Transition: The Future of the Atlantic Alliance* (New York: Frederick A. Praeger Publishers, 1965).

Steury, Donald P., comp., *Estimates on Soviet Military Power, 1954 to 1984* (Washington, D.C.: History Staff, Center for the Study of Intelligence, Central Intelligence Agency, December 1994).

Stikker, Dirk U., *Men of Responsibility: A Memoir* (New York: Harper and Row, Publishers, 1965).

Stoler, Mark A., *George C. Marshall: Soldier-Statesman of the American Century* (Boston: Twayne Publishers, 1989).

Stromseth, Jane E., *The Origins of Flexible Response: NATO's Debate over Strategy in the 1960s* (London: The Macmillan Press, 1988.).

Sulzberger, C.L., *A Long Row of Candles* (New York: Macmillan Publishing Company, 1969).

Sulzberger, C.L., *An Age of Mediocrity* (New York: Macmillan Publishing Company, 1973).

Sunderman, James F., ed., *World War II in the Air: The Pacific* (New York: Franklin Watts, Inc., 1962).

Talbot, Strobe, *The Master of the Game: Paul Nitze and the Nuclear Peace* (New York: Alfred A. Knopf, 1988).

Taylor, Maxwell D., *The Uncertain Trumpet* (New York: Harper and Brothers, 1960).

Thibault, George Edward, ed., *The Art and Practice of Military Strategy* (Washington, D.C.: National Defense University, 1984).

Thomas, Lowell, and Edward Jablonski, *Doolittle: A Biography* (Garden City, NY: Doubleday and Co, 1976).

Trachtenberg, Marc, *History and Strategy* (Princeton NJ: Princeton University Press, 1991).
Trachtenberg, Marc, *A Constructed Peace: The Making of the European Settlement, 1945–1963* (Princeton, N.J.: Princeton University Press, 1999).
Truman, Harry S., *Memoirs: Years of Trial and Hope* (Garden City, NY: Doubleday and Co Inc., 1956).
Truman, Harry S., *Public Papers of the President of the United States: Harry S. Truman, 1945* (Washington, D.C.: U.S. Government Printing Office, 1961).
Twining, Nathan F., *Neither Liberty Nor Safety: A Hard Look at U.S. Military Policy and Strategy* (New York: Holt, Rinehart and Winston, 1966).
Verrier, Anthony, *The Bomber Offensive* (London: Pan Books, Ltd., 1974).
Wampler, Robert A., *NATO Strategic Planning and Nuclear Weapons, 1950–1957*, Occasional paper 6, Nuclear History Program, Center for International Security Studies, School of Public Affairs, University of Maryland, 1990.
Wampler, Robert A., *Ambiguous Legacy: The United States, Great Britain and the Foundation of NATO Strategy, 1948–1957* (Dissertation presented to the Department of History, Harvard University, June 1991, unpub.).
Warner, Michael, ed., *The CIA under Harry Truman* (Washington, D.C.: CIA History Staff, Center for the Study of Intelligence, Central Intelligence Agency, 1994).
Watson, George M., Jr., *The Office of the Secretary of the Air Force, 1947–1965* (Washington, D.C.: Center for Air Force History, 1993).
Wiggershaus, Norbert and Roland G. Foerster, eds., *The Western Security Community, 1948–1950: Common Problems and Conflicting National Interests during the Foundation Phase of the North Atlantic Alliance* (Oxford: Berg Publishers, 1993).
Wenger, Andreas, *Living with Peril: Eisenhower, Kennedy, and Nuclear Weapons* (New York and Oxford: Rowman and Littlefield, 1997).
Wilkinson, Burke, *Night of the Short Knives*, A novel written about the Supreme Headquarters (New York: Charles Scribner's Sons, 1964).
Windsor, Philip, *City on Leave: A History of Berlin, 1945–1962* (New York: Frederick A. Praeger, 1963).
Wolfe, Robert, ed., *Americans as Proconsuls: United States Military Government in Germany and Japan, 1944–1952* (Carbondale, IL: Southern Illinois University Press, 1984).
Wolk, Herman S., *Planning and Organizing the Postwar Air Force, 1943–1947* (Washington, D.C.: Office of Air Force History, 1984).
Wolk, Herman S., *Toward Independence: The Emergence of the U.S. Air Force, 1945–1947* (Washington, D.C.: Air Force History and Museums Program, 1996).
Yergin, Daniel, *Shattered Peace: The Origins of the Cold War and the National Security State* (Boston: Houghton Mifflin Co., 1977).
Zachary, G. Pascal, *Endless Frontier: Vannevar Bush, Engineer of the American Century* (New York: The Free Press, 1997).
Ziegler, Philip, *Mountbatten* (New York: Alfred A. Knopf, 1985).
Zubok, Vladislav and Constantine Pleshakov, *Inside the Kremlin's Cold War: From Stalin to Khrushchev* (Cambridge, MA: Harvard University Press, 1996).
Zuckerman, Solly, *Nuclear Illusion and Reality* (New York: The Viking Press, 1982).
Zuckerman, Solly, *Monkeys, Men, and Missiles: An Autobiography 1946–1988* (New York: W.W. Norton and Co., 1988).

Articles

Bryan, J., III, "SHAPE and its Shapers," *National Review*, June 28, 1958.
Buffet, Cyril and Leopoldonuti (guest editors), "Dividing the Atom: Essarys on the History of nuclear sharing and nuclear Proliferation" *Storia Della Relazioni Internazionali, Special Issue*, Anno XIII/1998/1.
Buhite, Richard D. and Wm. Christopher Hamel, "War for Peace: The Question of an American Preventive War Against the Soviet Union, 1945–55," *Diplomatic History*, Vol. 14, No. 3 (1990).
Burr, William, "Avoiding the Slippery Slope: The Eisenhower Administration and the Berlin Crisis, November 1958–January 1959," *Diplomatic History*, Vol. 18, No. 2 (1994).
Coletta, Paolo E., "The Defense Unification Battle, 1947–1950: the Navy," *Prologue: The Journal of the National Archives*, Vol. 7, No. 1 (Spring 1974).
Combs, Jerald A., "The Compromise that Never Was: George Kennan, Paul Nitze, and the Issue of Conventional Deterrence in Europe, 1949–52," *Diplomatic History*, Vol. 15, No. 3 (1991).
Costigliola, Frank, "Kennedy, the European Allies, and the Failure to Consult," *Political Science Quarterly*, Vol. 110, No. 1 (1995).
Crowl, Philip A., "What Price Unity: the Defense Unification Battle, 1947–50," *Prologue: The Journal of the National Archives*, Vol. 7, No. 1 (Spring 1974).
Dockrill, Saki, "Eisenhower's New Look: A Maximum Deterrent at a Bearable Cost: A Reappraisal," Conference Paper, unpub.
Duchin, Brian R., "The 'Agonizing Reappraisal': Eisenhower, Dulles, and the European Defense Community," *Diplomatic History*, Vol. 16, No. 2 (1992).
Duffield, John S., "The Evolution of NATO's Strategy of Flexible Response: A Reinterpretation," *Security Studies*, Vol. 1, No. 1 (Autumn 1991)
Folly, Martin H., "Breaking the Vicious Circle: Britain, the United States, and the Genesis of the North Atlantic Treaty," *Diplomatic History*, Vol. 12, No. 1 (1988).
Furniss, Edgar S., Jr., "The French Military Position," unpub. Paper presented to a Study Group of the Council on Foreign Relations, March 1, 1958.
Gaddis, John Lewis, "Containment and the Logic of Strategy," *The National Interest*, No. 10 (Winter 1987/8).
Haynes, Richard F., "The Defense Unification Battle, 1947–1950: The Army," *Prologue: The Journal of the National Archives*, Vol. 7, No. 1 (Spring 1974).
Helmreich, Jonathan, "The United States and the Formation of EURATOM," *Diplomatic History*, Vol. 15, No. 3 (1991).
Hershberg, James G., "'Explosion in the Offing': German Rearmament and American Diplomacy, 1953–55," *Diplomatic History*, Vol. 16, No. 4 (1992).
Immerman, Richard H., "The United States and the Geneva Conference of 1954: A New Look," *Diplomatic History*, Vol. 14, No. 1 (1990).
Immerman, Richard H., "Confessions of an Eisenhower Revisionist: An Agonizing Reappraisal," *Diplomatic History*, Vol. 14, No. 3 (1990).
Jervis, Robert, "The Military History of the Cold War" (Review essay on McGeorge Bundy – *Danger and Survival*, Charles Morris – *Iron Destinies, Lost Opportunities*, John Newhouse – *War and Peace in the Nuclear Age*, Jane Nolan – *Guardians of the Arsenal*, Spencer Weart – *Nuclear Fear*), *Diplomatic History*, Vol. 15, No. 1 (1991).

Korb, Lawrence, "The Department of Defense: The First Half Century," in *U.S. National Security: Beyond the Cold War* (Carlisle, PA: U.S. Army War College, Strategic Studies Institute, 1997).

Mahan, Erin, "Kennedy and Eisenhower on Berlin and the Defense of Western Europe," *Miller Center Report*, Miller Center of Public Affairs, University of Virginia, vol. 15, No. 21 Summer 1999, pp. 25ff.

Mastny, Vojtech, "Stalin and the Militarization of the Cold War," *International Security*, Vol. 9, No. 3 (Winter 1984–85).

May, Ernest R., "The American Commitment to Germany, 1949–55," *Diplomatic History*, Vol. 13, No. 4 (1989).

Melissen, Jan, "Nuclearizing NATO, 1957–1959: the 'Anglo-Saxons', Nuclear Sharing and the Fourth Country Problem," *Review of International Studies*, Vol. 20, No. 3 (1994).

Melissen, Jan and Bert Zeeman, "Britain and Western Europe, 1945–1951: opportunities lost?" *International Affairs*, Vol. 60, No. 1 (Winter 1983–84).

Nelson, Anna Kaslen, "President Truman and the Evolution of the National Security Council," *Journal of American History*, 72 (September 1985).

Norris, Robert S., William M. Arkin and William Burr, "Where They Were: Between 1945 and 1977, the United States based thousands of nuclear weapons abroad," *The Bulletin of the Atomic Scientists*, Vol. 55, No. 6, November/December 1999, pp. 26–35.

Norstad, Lauris, "Defending Europe without France," (interview), reprinted from *Der Spiegel*, April 18, 1966, in *The Atlantic Community Quarterly* 4, no. 2 (Summer 1966).

Oldfield, Barney, "SHAPE, a Structure and a Sentiment," *NATO's Fifteen Nations*, Aug.–Sept. 1976.

Roman, Peter, "Curtis LeMay and the Origins of NATO Atomic Targeting," *Journal of Strategic Studies*, March 16, 1993.

Rosenberg, David Alan, "American Atomic Strategy and the Hydrogen Bomb Decision," *Journal of American History*, June 1979.

Rosenberg, David Alan, "The Origins of Overkill: Nuclear Weapons and American Strategy, 1945–1960," *International Security*, Spring 1983 (Vol. 7, No. 4).

Rosenberg, David Alan, "Origins of Overkill: Nuclear Weapons and American Strategy, 1945–1960," *International Security*, Vol. 7, No. 4 (Spring 1983).

Schwartz, Thomas Alan, "Lucius D. Clay: Reluctant Cold Warrior?" (Review of Jean Edward Smith), *Diplomatic History*, Vol. 16, No. 4 (1992).

Schwartz, Thomas Alan, "The United States and Germany after 1945: Alliances, Transnational Relations, and the Legacy of the Cold War," *Diplomatic History*, Vol. 19, No. 4 (1995).

Schwartz, Thomas Alan, "The Berlin Crisis and the Cold War," Feature Review, *Diplomatic History*, Vol. 21, No. 1 (1997).

Stabler, Elizabeth, "The MLF: Background and Analysis of Pros and Cons," *Congressional Record*, U.S. House of Representatives, January 5, 1965.

Warner, Geoffrey, "The Anglo-American Special Relationship," *Diplomatic History*, Vol. 13, No. 4 (1989).

Wheeler, Michael O., "Nuclear Weapons and European Security: The Evolution of American Politico-Military Views, 1945–1954," unpub. paper presented at the Nuclear History Project Study and Review Conference, Marburg, Germany, July, 1977.

Wolk, Herman S., "The Defense Unification Battle, 1947–1950: The Air Force," *Prologue: The Journal of the National Archives*, Vol. 7, No. 1 (Spring 1974), p. 232.

Documentary and Reference Collections

Air Force Historical Research Agency.
Air University Library.
Congressional Record.
Eisenhower Presidential Library (Eisenhower and Norstad Papers).
Hansard (House of Commons).
Library, U.S. Naval War College.
National Archives.
National Security Archive (The Berlin Crisis, 1958–1962).
Tilton Library, Tulane University.
University of Lancaster, U.K. (Clipping Files of the International Institute for Strategic Studies).
University of New Orleans, Earl K. Long Library.
Woodrow Wilson International Center for Scholars (Cold War International History Project)

Interviews (Note: Interviewees are not specifically cited in the text in order to respect confidentiality)

Boeschenstein, Jr., William W.
Gibson, Maj. Gen. USAF (Ret.) Kenneth.
Goodpaster, General, USA (Ret.) Andrew.
Hillenbrand, The Hon. Martin.
Jaffe, Kristin Norstad.
Jarvis, Dorothy (Mrs. Porter).
Martin, Lt. General, USAF (Ret.) Glen W.
Norstad, Isabelle Jenkins (Mrs. Lauris) – includes access to personal memorabilia, correspondence, etc.
Norstad, Isabelle Jenkins (taped interviews conducted by Axel C. F. Holm, Tubac, Arizona, October 4, 10, 16, 1995).
Norstad, Lauris, Oral History Interview, February 13–16 and October 22–25, 1979, Air Force Historical Research Agency, Maxwell AFB, AL.
Norstad, Lauris (taped Interviews with Professor Robert S. Jordan).
Oldfield, Col. Barney, USAF (Ret.).
Roberts, Sir Frank.
Scarbrough, Carl F.
Schuyler, General Cortlandt van Rennssaler.
Smart, General, USAF (Ret.) Jacob E.,.
Smart, General Jacob E., Oral History Interview, November 27–30, 1978, Air Force Historical Research Agency, Maxwell AFB, AL.

Vest, The Hon. George.
Wilkinson, The Hon. J. Burke.
Yudkin, Maj. Gen., USAF (Ret.) Richard A.
Zuckerman, Sir Solly (Lord).

Newspaper and Magazine Articles:

Air Force Times, July 15, 1952.
Air Power History, Special Edition, Fall 1997.
Chicago Tribune, July 20, 1952.
Cleveland Plain Dealer, May 28, 1972.
Continental Daily Mail, February 28, 1953.
Courrier de L'Quest Angers, July 9, 1952.
Daily Mail (London), December 11, 1952.
Daily Telegraph (London), December 11, 1952.
Department of State Bulletin, November 9, 1953.
Dialog, undated (A City of Toledo in-house journal).
Fiberglances (Owens-Corning Fiberglas in-house newsletter), January 1964.
Flight, January 16, 1953.
Forbes Magazine, March 1, 1964.
Jours de France, September 26, 1959.
Le Monde, July 20, 1962.
Life Magazine, November 1, 1948; October 5, 1959; September 8, 1961.
Newsweek, December 17, 1956; July, 1962; January 1963.
New York Times, August 17, 1962; August 31, 1945.
New York World-Telegram and Sun, April 21, 1956.
Paris Match, September 26, 1959.
Port of Toledo News, Issue No. 3, 1970.
Time Magazine, January 25, 1963.
Times (London), June 9, 1954.
Toledo Blade, (Specific issues are listed in the notes).
Toledo Industries, August 23, 1971.
Toledo Record, January 25, 1967.
Toledo Times, January 19, 1971.
U.S. News & World Report, April 13, 1959.
Wall Street Journal, August 23, 1971.
Allen, Robert S., "Bob Allen Reports," *New York Post*, July 18, 1952.
Baldwin, Hanson, *The New York Times*, July 25, 1962.
Beaton, Leonard, "NATO Strength Up by a Quarter," *The Guardian*, November 14, 1961.
Beal, Betty, "In Spite of All That Economy Talk, Paris is Still the World's Richest City," *The Sunday Star*, September 15, 1957.
Biddle, Margaret, "General Norstad: A Portrait of the Supreme Commander, Allied Powers in Europe," *Realities*, September 1956.
Cadett, Thomas, "General de Gaulle and Nato," *The Listener*, June 18, 1959.
Considine, Bob, "Loss by Early Retirement Snarls Choice of Air Force Chief," *Omaha World Herald*, March 31, 1953.
Cook, Don, "1953 is Pay-Off Year for NATO Air Planners," *New York Herald-Tribune*, March 15, 1953.

Cook, Don, "Norstad, Juin Given Broader Commands," *New York Herald-Tribune*, July 4, 1953.

Doty, Robert C., "McNamara Spurs NATO's Build-Up of Ground Units," *New York Times*, December 15, 1961.

Fleeson, Doris, "Norstad, Man of Many Talents," *Washington Evening Star*, March 25, 1959.

Herzog, Arthur, "A Visit with General Lauris Norstad: NATO's former Supreme Commander is now a corporation president," *Think Magazine*, March–April 1964.

Hudson, Harvey, "'Boy Wonder' General Fast Building European Air Defenses," *Port Arthur (Tex) News*, November 16, 1952.

Hultgren, Pat, "NATO Hostess in Paris: Entertaining on a Three Way Budget," *San Francisco Examiner*, January 24, 1958.

Lawrence, David, "Air Forces vs. Navy Enmity Seen Rising," *Washington Star*, March 22, 1946.

Lasky, Victor, "Norstad's Talk to GOP Group Expected to Stir Speculation," *Fort Worth Telegram*, May 25, 1963.

Norstad, Lauris, "NATO Strength and Spirit," *NATO Letter*, January 1960.

Rogers, Warren, Jr., "Norstad Quits as NATO Chief: Lemnitzer will Succeed Him," *New York Herald-Tribune*, July 20, 1962.

Taylor, Henry J., "Norstad's Fine Job", *Washington News*, April 24, 1962.

Van Zandt, Lydia, "Isabel [sic] Norstad Enjoys Official Busyness," *The Christian Science Monitor*, January 17, 1958.

Walker, Nadeane, "Mrs. Norstad Sponsors Project: Air Force Wives 'Adopt' Orphanage," *The Washington Post*, September 15, 1952.

Walker, Danton, "Broadway," *Boston Traveler*, November 1952.

Welles, Benjamin, "Norstad Discussed as NATO Air Chief," *The New York Times*, August 17, 1952.

Williams, Dick, "Philosophy, Sport, Politics; Gen. Norstad Runs Gamut," *Arizona Trails*, February 2, 1988.

Winchell, Walter, "The Washington Ticker," *The Washington Post*, August 2, 1952.

Bibliographic Note: General Norstad's Papers as SACEUR are deposited and placed in proper archival order in the Eisenhower Presidential Library. They are on microfilm at the National Archives and at the Air Force Historical Research Agency, Maxwell AFB, Alabama. Herewith is the official descriptions of the Papers as they had been assembled at SHAPE.

SHAPE, *A Memorandum for the Record*, dtd 10/29/62, \s\ Mark M. Boatner III, Lt. Col. USA, Secretariat, Project Officer.

The records marked "NORSTAD POLICY FILE" were assembled during the period June 1960 through October 1962 with a view to providing documentation of: General Norstad's personal influence on major NATO policy decisions during his tenure as SACEUR. This was done by screening the records of

SACEUR and INTAF. No material guidance was furnished as to what subjects General Norstad considered to be particularly important. Independently of the project that is the subject of this memo, OSACEUR administrative personnel screened their records and assembled a group of papers that will be stored with General Norstad's personal records. Independently of this project, also, a "Report of Stewardship" was prepared. The official SHAPE history also continues to be written by the SHAPE historian.

Since these projects were not coordinated and since they all bear on General Norstad's personal influence on major NATO policy decisions, the projects will have duplication on some topics and will complement each other on others.

The scope and organization of the NORSTAD POLICY FILE are explained in the General Index and the memorandum headed "Organization of Norstad Policy Files." Both papers are in a folder stamped "General Index." A "Special Index" has been compiled to help locate papers dealing with topics whose classification within the list of major subjects – that is, those listed in the General Index – is not apparent. Note that there is no completed index. To find a document it is necessary first to determine under which heading of the General Index it would most logically be filed. This subject file must then be searched. (Documents are filed in chronological order and are cross referenced to other subject files.) If the document does not fall under a heading of the General Index, the Special Index should be consulted.

It should also be noted that certain documents will be missing from the NORSTAD POLICY FILE. Reasons for this include: removal of the document from OSACEUR or INTAF files, records retired, document temporarily missing when the file was screened, document missing because it is in a special file to which the project officer was denied access, project officer failed to recognize the document as being pertinent, document never filed at SHAPE.

The file includes a large number of documents that furnish general or specific background on NATO policies, including policies on which General Norstad did not exert any personal influence. It was neither possible nor was it considered necessary to assemble all references cited in documents included in the NORSTAD POLICY FILE. Some cross-reference sheets from the INTAF files have been included to assist in securing from DOD and State Dept. archives certain documents that may later be wanted.

The NORSTAD POLICY FILE has been assembled without any exact knowledge of its intended use. It has been assembled on the understanding from OSACEUR that it will be kept in official custody, subject to US security regulations, and accessible only to General Norstad or individuals he personally designates [only until his death in 1988].

Index

Acheson, Dean, Secretary of State 42, 68, 168, 253, 263, 270, 279
Adams, Sherman 134
Adenauer, Chancellor Konrad xiii, 4, 118, 137, 219
   attitude to Berlin crisis 140, 142, 171
   and Berlin Wall 176
   discussion with Eisenhower on control and inspection regime 116–17
   and East-West disengagement 158, 159
   and GDR recognition 184
   and Kennedy 179
   Norstad's control and inspection system, disagreement with 199
   response to de Gaulle NATO nuclear proposals 123
   support for Norstad 12
   voice in NATO nuclear affairs 107
   see also Federal Republic of Germany (FRG)
"Ad Hoc" Committee for collaboration on UN Security Council functions 74
Air Corps (US) 14, 17
   Directorate of Management Control 19
   nature of, at start of war 19
   Tactical School 24
   ties between industry and 19
   see also Air Force
Air Force (US)
   Advisory Council 21–3
   creation of 61–3
   Flight Officer grade, establishment of 22
   functions and role of 61–3
   "Interim" (proposed) 48–9
   see also Army Air Force; Eighth Air Force; Royal Air Force (Britain); Third Air Force; Twelfth Air Force; Twentieth Air Force; US Air Force
air power doctrine, strategic 24–5, 45
Air Staff separate from Army 18
air superiority as first priority in Algeria 32
Alaskan Air Command 59, 70, 111
Allen, Robert S. 259
Allied Air Support Command 33
Allied Command Atlantic (ACLANT) 229, 231
Allied Command Europe (ACE) 106, 143, 144
Allied Control Council (ACC) (Berlin) 66
Allied Tactical Air Force (ATAF) 155
Alperovitz, Gar 248
Alsop, Joseph 58, 85
Alsop, Stewart 85
Ambrose, Stephen E. 261, 262, 270, 272, 273, 278
Ankenbrandt, Brigadier General Francis L. 64
armed forces
   structure of 62
   unifying 50–66
   see also Reorganization; US Armed Forces
Army Air Force (AAF) 23
   Air Defense Command (ADC) in 50
   Air Force Combat Command within, proposed 49
   Committee on Reorganization of 49

309

310 *Index*

Army Air Force *cont.*
  diversion of resources to independent 47–8
  organization of 46
  separation from army of 45–50
  strategic force in, proposed separation of 49
  Tactical Air Command in 50
  transition to peacetime force 49
Arnold, General Henry H. "Hap", Commanding General of AAF 3, 4, 14, 18, 23, 24, 27–8, 47, 214–15, 243, 249, 250, 271
  assent use of atomic bomb 40–1
  attitude to unification proposals 54, 63
  creation of personal Advisory Council by 21–3, 97, 215
  and formation of committee to assess implications of atomic bomb 44
  and formation of Eighth Air Force 26
  retirement of 41
  in separation of AAF from Army 45
  Twentieth Air Force under 38, 48
Atlantic Fleet 59
atomic bomb 19, 40
  authority to stockpile 84
  in Cold War strategy 91–5
  estimates of stockpile required 43–4
  likelihood of use of 74
  in NAC military plans 84
  secrets kept in American hands 90
  use on Hiroshima and Nagasaki 4
  as weapon of opportunity 26
  see also North Atlantic Treaty Organization; nuclear weapons
Atomic Energy Act (1954) 104, 109

Austin, Senator Warren R.
Austria 37

Backer, John H. 254, 271
Baer, George 77, 256
Baldwin, Hanson 57–8
Barlow, Jeffrey G. 255, 256, 257
Baruch, Bernard 97
Bay of Pigs 168
Beer, Francis A. 261
Belgium, contribution to NATO
Berlin
  access routes to 191
  Air Safety Center (BASC) 70, 139; action planned following Soviet withdrawal from 156
  Allies' wartime rights in 133
  control of 4
  and eventual German unity 138
  Tempelhof Air Drome 70
  "Trizonia", creation of, by US, Britain and France 67
  Western Air Traffic Controller in 156
Berlin Airlift (1948–9) 69–71, 143
  assessment of 71–2
  battle for unification of 45–72
  Blockade xii, 67–72
  Combined Airlift Task force 70
  contributions to 71
  currency reform as reason for 67, 71
  end to 71
  evacuation plans during 71
  events leading to final break with Soviet Union over 68–9
  and North Atlantic Treaty 72
  Operation Vittles 71
  possibilities of, assessed 69
  routes sealed off by Soviets during 67
  Soviet identification requirement for US personnel in 67

Index 311

as testing ground for West
  66–72
U.S. legal right to be in,
  disputed by Soviets during
  67
see also Federal Republic of
  Germany; German
  Democratic Republic;
  Germany
Berlin Ambassadorial Group
  guidance on command
  structure 162–3
Berlin Crisis (1958–9)
  "Agency principle" in avoiding
    direct confrontation over
    152
  and assignment of US forces to
    Norstad 143
  atomic weapons in, discussions
    on use of 155
  Berlin Airlift Plan,
    Quadripartite (QBAL)
    (LIVE OAK proposal)
    154, 157, 161, 162, 163;
    civilian 161, 162;
    garrison 161, 162;
    political nature of
    162; TRIPLE PLAY
    161, 162
  command and control in
    155–66
  contingency military planning
    for 141, 148–55, 161–2,
    169
  disengagement, East–West, and
    158–9
  East German refugees flow and
    134
  forces available to counter
    checkpoint incidents
    146
  garrison in city during 135
  and general hostilities, risk of
    157
  and IRBM deployment in FRG
    134
  Khrushchev demand for
    withdrawal of troops
    during 134

Khrushchev testing of Allied
  unity during 137
legal aspects of rights of access
  to 143
Lockheed Hercules dispatched
  along air corridor 147
"More Elaborate Military
  Measures" (LIVE OAK
  contingency planning
  document) 155, 161–2
NAC links to German
  reunification 141
"Occupying Powers" in, status
  of 148
options of Eisenhower
  Administration during
  135
origins of 133–41
posture of Western powers on,
  Norstad plans for 138–9
as potential flashpoint for
  nuclear war 136
probes in 163
responses to Agency Principle
  152–3
Soviet radar installations
  during 147
Soviets ban US military
  convoys (November 1958)
  136–7
Soviets hold convoy at
  Marienborn checkpoint
  (February 1959) 146
Tripartite convoys on
  autobahn (LIVE OAK
  proposal) 154
Western garrisons in,
  discussions on limitations
  on size of 154
Berlin Crisis (1961–2) 167–93
  airlift and land action 169
  and all-German problem 171
  and augmentation of garrison
    in 172–3: resistance
    expected to 175
  and Berlin Wall 172–81;
    crossing points 173:
    organizational and policy
    responses to 181–93

312 Index

Berlin Crisis (1961–2) *cont.*
 communications during   195
 contrasted with 1948 crisis
  177–8
 East German refugees and
  172
 election of Kennedy and
  change in policy   167–72
 harassment by Soviets,
  increasing   168–9
 Kennedy minimization of
  183
 Kruschev threatens restriction
  of air access   169
 limits to Norstad powers of
  retaliation   181
 and NATO cohesion   177
 nuclear weapons in   183,
  217
 operational command channels
  for   177–9, **178**
 proposals for harassment of
  Soviet cargo ships   205
 Soviet interference with Allied
  radar control   206
 Soviet loss of East Germany
  and   172
 Soviet restrictions on air travel
  in   203: motives for   206;
  Norstad response to
  204–5
 stoppage of inter-zonal trade as
  casus belli   192
Biddle, Margaret   262
Bildt, Carl   237
Blair, Clay   251, 253, 254, 256,
 260
Bland, Douglas L.   255, 259,
 260, 271
Blankenhorn, Ambassador
 Wilhelm   118, 171
Blue Streak program (Britain)
 112–13
Boatner, Brigadier General Brian
 L.   64
Boeschenstein, Harold   224,
 225, 226
Boeschenstein, William   225,
 226

Boeing
 B-29 Superfortress   26, 40, 41,
  48, 69, 78
 B-36, termination of
  construction of   78
 B-47s in Europe   184
 B-50 intercontinental bomber
  77
Bohlen, Charles E.   253, 254
bombing
 mass incendiary, of Tokyo
  40
 mass *versus* precision   25
 saturation *see* mass incendiary
 "strategic"   24, 45–6, 214
Bosnia, impact on SACEUR role
 232
Boyne, Walter J.   249, 250
Bradley, General Omar   67, 69,
 72, 251, 253, 254, 256, 257,
 260
Brandt, Willy   181
Brinkley, Douglas   251, 252,
 254, 270
Britain
 attitude to Berlin crisis   140,
  142–3
 B-29 bases in   69, 76, 77
 contribution to NATO   86
 cost of US air presence in
  Europe to   69
 defense of, in Soviet attack   75
 favoring disengagement
  schemes in Europe   117
 and NATO nuclear weapons
  103
 Norstad working with during
  World War II   xii
 nuclear weapons of   95:
  independent IRBM   113
 officers of, in USEUCOM   148
 views of Norstad role in Berlin
  crisis   163
 see also Royal Air Force
British Army of the Rhine (BAOR)
 156–7
British Fighter Command   131
BROILER   75, 76
Bryan III, J.   239

BULLMOOSE   76
Bundeswehr   142
   as heart of NATO shield   210
Bundy, McGeorge (Special Assistant for National Security Affairs)   201, *267*
Buzan, Barry   271

C-54 transport planes in Berlin airlift   70
Cabell, Charles Pearre   21, 23, 97
Cafritz, Gwen   58
Cairo-Suez, B-29 bases in   76
Canada
   contribution to NATO   86
   and LIVE OAK   150
Canberra bombers   106
Caniff, Milton   99
Cannon, General John K. "Uncle Joe"   28, 31, 71
Caribbean Air Command   59, 70
Carney, Admiral Robert B.   87
Casablanca Conference (1943)   35
Casablanca landings   32
Cate, James Lea   239, 242, 245, 247
Central Europe, Norstad plan for control and inspection regime in   116
Chennault, Claire   14
Chirac, President Jacques   231
CINCNELM   79
CINCEUR/SACEUR 958 Atomic Weapons Requirement Study   92
CINCUSAFE   79, 80–81
civilian casualties as inevitable consequence   25
Clarke, Lieutenant General Bruce C.   175, 194, 208
Clay, General Lucius D., US Military Governor (Berlin)   67, 68, 253
   appointment as Kennedy's Personal Representative in Berlin   177, 197
   in Berlin airlift   69–70
   and Berlin Wall   176, 177
   departure of   208
   Norstad's relations with   197, 207–8
   request for motor convoy to Steinstuecken   197–8
Coffey, Thomas M.   243
Cold War   73–99
   beginnings of   42
   differences in outlook on   77
   "High"   89
   see also Eisenhower; Norstad
Combined Airlift Task Force (CATF)   70
Commander-in-Chief, European Command (CINCEUR)   79
Commander-in-Chief, US Air Force, Europe (CINCUSAFE)
   Norstad appointed as   79
Commander-in-Chief, US Naval Forces, Eastern Atlantic and Mediterranean (CINCNELM)   79
Common Defense Act (1946)   54
Common Defense, Secretary of, proposal for   54
Conference on Security and Cooperation in Europe (CSCE)   230
Considine, Bob   260
containment, Truman's policy on   xii
Cook, Don   260, 261
Copp, DeWitt S.   251
Costigliola, Frank   239
Craig, Lieutenant General Howard A.   64, 78
Craven, Wesley Frank   239, 242, 245, 247
Craw, Colonel Demas   160
CROSSPIECE/GALLOPER (NATO MC/14)   77
Cuban Missile Crisis   4, 185, 217
Culton, Colonel Hugh G.   64
Czechoslovakia   159

314 *Index*

Davis, Richard G.   243, 248
Davison, Brigadier General F. Trubee   48
Dayton Accords   237
Debré, Prime Minister Michel   131
de Gaulle, President Charles   3, 4, 115–16, 219, 241, 267, 272, 278
  and Algerian insurrection   149
  Berlin crisis: attitude to   140; scepticism of UK/US constancy over Berlin   164–5
  and Berlin Wall   176
  and control of nuclear weapons extended to FRG   123
  creating dissension in NATO   127
  on credibility of US nuclear deterrent   116
  critical of US policies   142
  on "decoupling" of FRG from West   159
  derailing NATO tactical air defense plan   129
  and Eisenhower, meeting of   130
  Eisenhower view of   142
  and Kennedy on targets for nuclear weapons   122
  and Norstad   118–32, 218
  opposition to NATO arrangements for nuclear weapons veto   123
  refusal to allow stockpiling on French soil   125–6
  removal of part Mediterranean fleet from NATO   127–8, 131
  resisting emphasis on conventional weapons   8
  resisting integration of French forces into NATO   130
  as secondary figure   4
  three-power "Directorate" proposal of   122–3, 142
  view of Norstad   12
  and world-wide nuclear strategy co-ordination   122
  see also France
de Murville, Foreign Minister Couve   130, 164
de Staerke, André (Belgian Ambassador)   10, 268
deterrence, doctrine of   44
Devers, General Jacob L.   50
Dewoitine fighter planes (French)   30
Dillon, Under Secretary of State Douglas   164
D'Olier, Franklin   248
Doolittle, James H. "Jimmy"   14, 17, 27, 30, 31, 32, 35, 214
DOUBLEQUICK   75, 76
DOUBLESTAR   76
Douhet-Trenchard doctrine of strategic air power   218
Dowling, Ambassador Walter C.   197
Duke, Simon   269
Dulles, Secretary of State John Foster   4, 94, 104, 129, 133, 136–7, 140, 146, 164, 170

Eaker, Lieutenant General Ira C.   26, **37**, 45, 49
Eberstadt Report   51, 55
Eden Plan   134
Edwards, Lieutenant General Edward H.   **64**
Eighth Air Force Bomber Command   26–7, 28
Eisenhower, General Dwight D. "Ike"   xii, 3, 4, 27, 268, 270, 271, 272, 273, 274, 278
  as Army Chief of Staff   41–2, 47, 50
  on atomic weapons, use of   81, 88–9, 146, 220–1
  attitude on unification   54, 56, 61
  and the Cold War   84
  as Commander-in-Chief, Allied Forces   27, 34–5, **34**

Index   315

doctrine of massive retaliation   170
insists Berlin discussions include reunification of Germany   140
interest in Norstad's control and inspection regime   116
military leadership team of   87
"New Look" concept of   107
Open Skies proposal   117
response to Soviet aggression in Europe   208
response to Soviet provocation in Berlin crisis   136–7
as SACEUR   80
and separation of services   51–3
and TORCH operation   27, 28
willingness to negotiate Berlin status   164
withdrawal from public life   5
Eisenhower Administration "new look" of   84
Ely, General Paul   119, 149
Emergency War Plans (EWPs): DOUBLEQUICK   75; HALFMOON   75, 76; MAKEFAST   75; TROJAN   76
  Atomic Weapons Annex to   81
Epley, William W.   274
Europe
  contingency planning for   73–84
  danger of showing weakness in   168
European Advisory Commission agreement on rights of access to Berlin   143
European Allies' contribution to NATO goals   84
  see also Britain; Federal Republic of Germany; France
European Command   60, 79

European Defence Community
  attempts to found   xiii
  France turning down   219
European rearmament, costs of   84
European Security and Defence Identity (ESDI)   230, 231, 237
European Union (EU) Common Foreign and Security Policy (CFSP)   230

F-100 squadrons in Europe   184
Falconer, Group Captain C.L.   34
Far East Command   59, 85
Fascism   213
Federal Republic of Germany (FRG)
  as battlefield   202
  defensive line and   77
  and desire for independent nuclear capability   110, 126
  military buildup, encouragement for   168
  military contribution from   84
  in NATO   xiii; as second-class citizen in   109
  and NATO nuclear weapons   103, 114, 125
  nuclear weapons development with France and Italy   110–11
  sacrificed to Soviet military threats   159
  Socialist Party coalition with East Germany, fear of   164
  vulnerability to nuclear attack   5
  weapons made available to   108
  see also Adenauer
Field Manual   100–20; "Command and Employment of Air Power"   33

316 *Index*

Finletter, Ambassador Thomas 177, 196
"first strike" *see* deterrence
Fisher, Nigel 277, 278
flexible response, doctrine of 6, 13, 89, 167
Forrestal, James V., Secretary of the Navy 51, 55, 63, 69; Key West conference 72; Secretary of Defense 69
France
  agreement with Norstad on Berlin contingency planning 164
  aircraft stationed in FRG 131
  and Berlin crisis 150
  contribution to NATO 86
  difficulties of wartime role xii
  discussions on 121-2
  IRBMs in 111, 118-19; agreement on deployment of 120-1; failure of Dulles
  and NATO nuclear weapons 103, 126
  Norstad and 118-32
  nuclear capability 8, 95
  nuclear stockpiling in 177
  nuclear unilateralism of 105, 113, 121-2
  nuclear weapons development with FRG and Italy 110-11
  status of air defense forces of 131
  see also de Gaulle
Fredendall, Major General Lloyd 28, 32
Freedman, Julian 266
FREE STYLE Berlin contingency plan 169
Frisbee, John L. 242
Fulbright, Senator J. William 226
Fuller, General J.F.C. 25
Furniss, Professor Edgar S. 120, 267
Futrell, Robert Frank 244

Gallois, General Pierre 9, 266
Ganey, Major General Wiley D. 98
Gavin, Ambassador James 177, 222
Geneva Conference (1959) 164
German Democratic Republic (GDR)
  harassment by police of 139
  Khrushchev delays recognition of 140
  Khrushchev proposal for peace treaty with 133, 168, 171, 192
  reduction of forces in 159
  transfer of rights over Berlin access to 171
  West acquiescing in creation of 181
  West not recognizing official existence of 134
  West dealing with government of 139
Germany
  agreement with Norstad on Berlin contingency planning 164
  control of 4
  creation of West German government in, Soviet forestalling of 67
  Four-Power Conference proposal on 137-9
  partitioning of Germany, revaluation of mark in 67
  unification of 133-4
  see also Berlin; Federal Republic of Germany; German Democratic Republic
Gibbs, Professor Norman 224
Giles, Major General Barney M. "Bennie" 17, 18, 45-6
Goldberg, Alfred 253, 257, 258
Goodpaster, Andrew J. 257
Gorn, Michael H. 242
Great Britain *see* Britain
Greece 114, 125

Index 317

Gromyko, Andrei proposal on termination of Western rights in Berlin 164
Groves, Leslie R. 26
Gruenther, General Alfred A. 81, 87, 96, 261
on use of atomic weapons 91–4

Hagerty, James 136
HALFMOON 75, 76
Hansell, Jr., Haywood S. "Possum" 17, 38–9, 242, 244
Harmon, Christopher C. 248
Heidelmeyer, Wolfgang 270, 272, 273, 274
Henderson, Nicholas 254, 271
Herter Plan 208, 209
Herter, Under Secretary as Secretary of State Christian 163, 164, 208–9
Hill, Senator Joseph Lister
Hillenbrand, Martin 168
Hindrichs, Guenter 270, 272, 273, 274
Holm, Axel 240, 242
Home, Foreign Secretary Lord 206
HONEST JOHN missiles 108
Hoopes, Townsend 251, 252, 254
Horne, Alistair 277
Houghton, Ambassador Amory 137–8, 224
Humphrey, Group Captain R.H. 35
Hungary 37
Hunter, Ambassador Robert 212, 228–38
Hutchinson, Major General Donald W. 98

ideological warfare 213
Implementation Force (IFOR) NATO 231
Intercontinental Ballistic Missiles (ICBMs) 107–8, 167
Intermediate Range Ballistic Missiles (IRBMs)
  agreement on deployment of, in France 120–1
  as "holding operation" 108
  in NATO 104; distribution of 111; and effect of advent of ICBMs 167
  "second generation" solid-propellant 111–12
  under control of SACEUR 107
International News Service (INS) 71
Ireland, Timothy P. 257
Ismay, General Lord Hastings, NATO Secretary-General 23, 83, 244
Italy, nuclear weapons development with France and FRG 110–11

JACK PINE Tripartite plan Rules of Engagement 179
Japan, air war against 4
Jessup, Philip, Deputy U.S. Representative 69
Johnson, Helen K., Norstad letter to 15
Johnson, Louis, Secretary of Defense 73
Johnson, Vice President Lyndon B. discussions on Berlin Wall 176–7
Joint Chiefs of Staff (US) (JCS) 6, 7, 59, 60
  and Berlin Blockade 67–8, 72
  and Berlin crisis (1958–59) 139, 147
  categories of steps to be taken in Berlin crisis 141
  guidelines (NSC 162/2) on economic and military strengths 90
  planning activities of, by Arnold's Advisory Council 22
  and use of atomic weapons 74

318 *Index*

Joint Outline War Plan BROILER 75
Joint Staff Planners (JSP) 73
Joint Strategic Plans Group (JSPG) 75
Joint Strategic Capabilities Plan (US) 92
Joint Strategic Survey Committee (JSSC) 73–4
Joint War Plans Committee (JWPC) 73, 75
Jones, Major General Junius W. 64
Jordan, Ralph B. 252
Jordan, Robert S. 241, 244, 256, 257, 259, 260, 261, 268, 271, 273
Jours de France 96
Juin, Marshal Alphonse 89
JUPITER liquid-fuelled missiles 111

Kaplan, Lawrence S. 239, 256
Kennedy Administration
 "controlled partial mobilization" of 171
 and doctrine of flexible response 6, 13
 favouring conventional weapons 170
 Norstad differences with 9, 129
 position paper "US Policy on Military Actions in a Berlin Conflict" 201
Kennedy, President John F.
 and Adenauer, tensions between 179, 210
 authorization of Norstad's action on Soviet air travel restrictions 204
 bypassing Norstad's Berlin crisis communication structure 177
 committed to nuclear weapons to hold Berlin 184
 complementing Norstad on handling of Soviet air restrictions 205
 disagreements with Norstad 198–202; on extent of authority 196–8; on primacy of NATO/US command 199
 election of 5
 emphasis on conventional forces 184
 final audience with Norstad 10
 and JCS, distrust of 170
 military advice from civilian colleagues of 170
 minimizing Berlin crisis 183
 on Norstad–Clay tension 207–8
 response to Norstad resignation 10–11
 restricting Norstad to military matters 196
 and retirement of Norstad 6
 support for "flexible response" 209
 taking Norstad "out of the loop" 195
 ten questions to military and intelligence advisors 185–6; Norstad's reply 186–8; concerted reply 189–90
 valuing Washington-Bonn axis over Washington-London 210
Kenney, George C. 14, 50, 247
Khrushchev, Nikita
 attempts to change status of Berlin xiii, 165
 delays recognition of GDR 140
 on NATO IRBM agreements 114
 proposed peace treaty with GDR 133, 168, 171
 proposes West Berlin becomes "free city" 140
 see also Soviet Union
Kinnard, Douglas 239, 257, 259
King, Admiral Ernest Jr 51

Knerr, Major General Hugh J. 64
Kohler, Foy (Assistant Secretary of State for European Regional Affairs) 168
Korean War xii
  costs of 84
  effect on NATO 80
Kosovo
  air operation 233
  impact on SACEUR role 232
Krieger, Wolfgang 260, 269
Krock, Arthur 58, 85
Kuter, Lieutenant General Laurence 23, 45, 214

Lash, Joseph P. 272
Lasky, Victor 241
Lawrence, David 58, 252
Leach, W. Barton 19
Leahy, Admiral William 51
LeMay, General Curtis E. "Curt" 4, 17, 18, 23, 24, 39, 40, 41, 78, 244
  as Air force Chief of Staff 85
  in Berlin airlift 69
  as Deputy Chief of Air Staff for Research and Development 44, 75
  and low-altitude fire-bombing of Tokyo 26
  "retardation operations" 81–2
Lemnitzer, General Lyman L. 7, 11, 170, 172, 195, 221
Life magazine 78
Lightner, Allan, detained at Berlin checkpoint 192
Lillienthal, David E. 65
"Lisbon goals" (NAC military plan) 84
LIVE OAK 160
  contact with FRG 157
  establishment of 149
  and NATO 179, 182
  response to Soviet ground provocation of 170
  structure of 150–1, **150**

terms of reference of 150–1
Tripartite Ambassadorial Group in **150**, 151
Lloyd, Foreign Secretary Selwyn 149, 159
Lockheed Hercules 147
Lovett, Robert A., Secretary of Defense 83

MacArthur, General Douglas xiii, 3, 4, 221
MacGregor, Air Commodore H.D. 37
Macmillan, Prime Minister Harold 6–7, 143, 149, 159, 164
MAKEFAST 75
Malik, Jacob, Soviet representative to UN 71
Maloney, Sean M. 256, 257, 274, 275
Manhattan Project 44
Marine Corps 51, 55, 61
Marshall Plan 228
Mastny, Vojtech 253
MATADOR missiles 108
May, Ernest R. 256
McDonald, Major General George C. 64
McKee, Brigadier General William F. 64
McMahon Act (1946) 104
McNamara, Robert S. (Secretary of Defense) 5, 6–7, 8, 220, 239, 278, 282, 283
  Athens speech (May 1962) 7–8
  comments on "SACEUR's instructions" 200
  encouragement of Allied conventional build-up 8, 201
  meeting with Norstad at SHAPE 171
  referring to Norstad's "health problems" 9
  revising Berlin Contingency plans 170

McNamara *cont.*
  revising Norstad's terms of reference   179
  taking Norstad "out of the loop"   195
  visit to Norstad to discuss Kennedy policy paper   201
  see also Pentagon
Mediterranean Air Command   37
Mediterranean Allied Air Forces (MAAF)   35–7, **37**
medium-range ballistic missiles (MRBMs)   5, 170–1, 197, 218
Meilinger, Phillip S.   241, 244, 245, 246, 248, 254
Mesta, Pearl   58
Mets, David R.   242, 246, 249
Metz, Steven   250
Military Air Transport Service (MATS)   70
military profession, requirements of   xi
Minimum Forces Study (Norstad)   95
Mitchell, Brigadier General Billy   14
Moffat, Colonel Reuben C.   47
morality, military, and technology   24
Mortensen, Daniel R.   245, 246, 247, 260
Mountbatten, Lord Louis   11
Murphy, Robert   245

National Defense, Department of, recommended by Truman   53, 55
National Defense, Secretary of   60
National Security Act (1947) (S.758)   17, 61
National Security Action Memorandum (NSAM) 109   184, 198, 211
  Norstad's refusal to adopt   211–12

National Security Council (NSC) (US)   70
National Socialism   213
Navy opposition to unification of armed forces   51, 54, 57, 58–9
Netherlands
  agreement on IRBM   114
  contribution to NATO   86
Newhouse, John   244, 257
New York Herald-Tribune   58
New York Times   53, 57–8, 85
Night of the Short Knives   99
NIKE missiles   108
Nimitz, Admiral Chester W., Chief of Naval Operations   51, 56
Nitze, Paul H.   261
Norstad, General Lauris
  abilities of   97–9
  as Acting Vice Chief of Staff   78
  advice from, in England, to Isabelle   27
  as agent of governments   219
  in Air Corps   17, 214
  as Air Deputy   90–1, 96
  as Air Force Chief of staff   85, 87, 215
  in Air Force Combat Command Headquarters   18
  Air Force plan, preparation of   48
  Allies' confidence in, during Berlin crisis   135
  at All Souls College, Oxford   224
  antipathy to within AAF   64
  Army Air Force objectives, formulation of   49
  aspirations of, and international political system   4
  assessment of Soviet strength by   74, 95
  as Assistant Chief of Air Staff for Plans   41, 46, **46**, 74
  as aviator   xi–xii

background 214
before World War II xi-xii
belief in massive air power 41, 43-4
belief in nuclear weapons xii, 11
belief in representing NATO member states to Washington 11
and Berlin Airlift 68
and Berlin contingency planning 141-2, 161
and Berlin crisis 134-5, 164-5, 175-6, 190-2, **191**; disagreements with US policy on 198-202; increasing difficulty of obtaining agreement in 193; response to Soviet restrictions on air travel during 203; restriction of authority in 197-8
Berlin Tripartite arrangements, as overall commander of 156
Berlin wall, reaction to 177
bombers, love of 35
Brigadier General, promotion to 36
brothers of 15
Camp Funston, contact with soldiers at 16
as cavalry second lieutenant 14
character of 39, 85, 129, 149
Clay relations with General Lucius D. 197
and Cold War "grand strategy" 73-99
as Commander-in-Chief, Allied Air Forces, Central Europe (CINCAAFCE) 81, 82, 86
as Commander-in-Chief, US Air Force, Europe (CINCUSAFE) 79, 81, 85-6
contacts with family 14-15

control and inspection system for Central Europe of 117, 127, 159, 199
coordinated planning attempts in Berlin crisis 141-7
corporate career of 224-7
defining role in war 18
on de Gaulle antipathy to "Anglo-Saxon" powers 124
as Deputy Chief of Staff for Operations in USAF HQ 64, **64**, 73
diplomatic roles of 218
as Director of Plans and Operations for War Department General Staff 56
on East-West disengagement during Berlin crisis 158
Eighth Air Force Bomber Command in England, assigned to 26-7
as Eisenhower *protégé* 11, 50, 216, 219-20
father of 15, 16
forces assigned to, as SACEUR in peacetime 143-4
foundations of career of 13-20, 213ff
as four-star general 86
France, de Gaulle and 118-32
friendship with Vandenberg 28
German military buildup, differences with Kennedy over 168
gold medal award by US Senate 13
grandfather of 16
heart attack of 7
and ideological warfare 213-14
Isabelle Jenkins, meets 16
Jewell, Iowa, family in 16
joins General Arnold's Advisory Council 21-3

322 Index

Norstad cont.
Kennedy Administration, disagreements with 9, 89, 218
Kennedy restricting powers of 195–6
Kennedy's attempt to retire 6
Kennedy's ten questions, answers to 186–8
landing at Oran (North Africa) 30
leadership of 216–22
letter of resignation of 10
Lieutenant General, promotion 62, 78
Life cover story on 78–9
and LIVE OAK 149–61, 220
as MAAF Director of Operations and Intelligence 36
Major General, promoted to 42
mandate as SACEUR 144, 221
Manhattan, Kansas, staying with father in 16
as man of his generation 213–16
marriage of 16
McNamara: differences with 189; meeting with, at SHAPE 171
meetings with McNamara (June 1962) 8, 9–10
military command channels established by 194
Mitchel Field, Long Island, assignment to 16–17
Mountbatten view of 11
and National Security Act (1947) 17, 61, 216
as NATO commander first 199
NATO Emergency Defense Plan (EDP) of 212
NATO as "fourth nuclear power", attempt to establish 110–18
on NATO IRBMs 108
and NATO nuclear tactical capability 89
and NATO policies, disagreements over 209
and NATO Secretary-General 95–6
and NATO stockpiling arrangements 126
on negotiation 218–19
in North Africa 27–38
in Northwest African Air Forces (NAAF) 34, **34**
as "nuclear SACEUR" 96, 213, 217–18
obligations to European allies 8–9, 221
in *Oral History Interview* 239, 240, 241, 242, 243, 244, 245, 246, 247, 248, 249, 250, 251, 252, 253, 271
organizing post-war Air Force 17
origins 14
at Owens-Corning Fiberglas Corporation 224: achievements at 225–6, 227; as Chairman of Board 225; as President 224–5; as President of OCF International 224; retirement from 226
"pause" concept of 208
Pearl Harbor commemoration attack, proposal for 40
personality of 215
physical characteristics of 4, 39
in planning and operation in North Africa and Pacific 21–44
"Plans" 208, 218, 220
political influence in Washington 8
and politics of command 215
popularity with NATO 212
at Potsdam Conference 66
promotion, early, and retirement at early age 87
promotion to full General 79
public attitudes to, in Europe **174**

Red Wing, family in 14, 15
  relationship with death in
    formative years of service
    23
  riding and fencing 16
  as SACEUR 5, 6, 96–9,
    103–213, 220
  "SACEUR's instructions to
    SHAPE planners" 200
  Schofield Barracks, Hawaii,
    stationed at 16
  self-appraisal of 99
  as servant of government and
    NAC 4
  SHAPE, appointment to
    89–90, 90
  SHAPE study by 211
  and Admiral Forrest Sherman,
    collaboration with 42,
    65
  social activities and contacts of
    7, 58
  as symbol of commitment of
    US air power to Europe
    81
  as "thinker" rather than "doer"
    215
  "three hats" of 160
  ties forged during and after war
    23
  in Toledo 225
  and TORCH landings 29
  as Twelfth Air Force Assistant
    Chief of Staff for Plans and
    Operations 28
  as Twentieth Air Force Chief of
    Staff 38–44
  as USCINCEUR 5, 6, 144–5,
    145, 220
  views on prospect of
    conventional forces defeat
    or nuclear exchange 202
  at West Point 14
  and work on unification
    of armed services
    54–63
  see also SACEUR
Norstad, Isabelle 7, 27, 58, 160
Norstad, Kristin 160

North Africa 21, 27–38
  landing 28
North Atlantic Council (NAC)
  107, 125, 127, 144, 219, 236,
  237
  adoption of MC/41 on "long
    haul" 91
  agreement to European military
    plan 84
  and Bosnia 235
  control of SACEUR 83, 233,
    235
North Atlantic Council (NATO),
  Military Committee 107
North Atlantic Treaty
  Organization (NATO)
  ACE forces assigned to 143
  aims of 228
  Air Force units assigned to
    143
  air power of 86
  atomic stockpiling in 95,
    104–6, 177: objection to
    106–7, 119, 131
  Atomic Strike Plan 127
  atomic weapons introduced
    into 94, 103–10
  Berlin Airlift 72
  Berlin crisis and cohesion of
    177
  compared to EDC xiii
  conventional defense shield
    107
  conventional forces and US
    abandonment of Europe
    197, 202
  delivery systems with atomic
    warheads 157–8
  Eisenhower and 3, 84, 127
  Emergency Defense Plan
    (Norstad) 212
  Executive Committee proposal
    for control of IRBMs 115
  exercises CHECKMATE and
    CHECKMATE II 176
  as "fourth nuclear power"
    110–18
  Heads of Government meeting
    105

NATO cont.
  institutional strength of 229
  IRBM agreement 114–15
  leadership challenges of future 228–38
  and LIVE OAK 179, 182
  MC/48 as strategic statement of 94
  MC/70 on use of conventional forces 170, 189–90, 202
  multilateral force (MLF) proposal (Herter Plan) 208–9
  new doctrine for 208–12, 237–8
  and Norstad, trust in 199
  nuclear weapons in 88, 103–10; and conventional weapons imbalance 104; costs of 112–13; Norstad plan for control of 116; unilateral or multilateral 103–4, 112, 119; US assistance and NATO control of 112; US control of warheads for 109, 118, 210
  Parliamentarians' Conference (1959) 115
  political reassurance provided by 73
  readiness of air power in 87–8
  Seven-Power Ambassadors' Committee in formulation of 72
  unification of air forces in 83, 86
  US commitment and leadership to 229–30
  see also SACEUR, role of
Northeast Command 59
Northwest African Air Forces (NAAF) 34, **34**
see also Northwest African Coastal Air Force; Northwest African Strategic Air Force
Northwest African Coastal Air Force (NACAF) 35

Northwest African Strategic Air Force (NASAF) 35
  targets after North African Campaign 36
nuclear submarine technology, France wanting to share US 129
nuclear war 5
  avoiding, by miscalculation 202
  in Central Europe 6
  as mutual suicide 43
nuclear weapons xii
  in Berlin crisis 183, 211
  command and control of 217
  credibility of NATO's 7–8
  Eisenhower on 88, 146–7
  location of 106
  movement of 106
  mutual destruction in use of 5
  in NATO 88–9, 103, 132
  as only true deterrent 6
  parity of US and USSR in 134
  public information on 114
  as regional deterrent 5–6
  tactical: Kennedy view of 13, 89; Norstad's search for 89
  threat of, shared by European Allies 5
  use against the Soviet Union 4, 134
  US reluctance to use in defense of Europe 12
  see also atomic weapons; Cuban Missile Crisis; Intercontinental Ballistic Missiles; Intermediate Range Ballistic Missiles; North Atlantic Treaty Organization; nuclear war

O'Connell, Robert L. 239
Oder–Niesse line 171
OFFTACKLE 76–7

Index 325

Okinawa
  B-29 bases in 76
  IRBMs in 111
Open Skies proposal (Eisenhower) 117
operational analysis in Air Force 19
operations research *see* operational analysis
Operation TORCH xii, 27ff
Operation Vittles (Berlin Airlift) 69–71
Oran (North Africa) landings 30–2
"Ostpolitik" foreign policy (Brandt) 181
Overy, R.J. 247
Owens-Corning Fiberglas Corporation (OCF) 224–7, 289, 290

Pacific 21
Pacific Command 59
Palmer, Michael A. 251
Pantelleria, Island of 36
Paris *Communiqué* following Berlin airlift 143
Paris Conference (1960) 165
Partnership for Peace, (NATO) 236
Partnership Coordination cell (PCC) 236
Partridge, Major General Earle E. 64
Patterson, Robert P., Secretary of War 42, 50, 63
Patton, Jr., Major General George S. 28, 32
Pearl Harbor xi, 18, 53
Pedlow, Gregory W. 257, 260, 274
Pentagon
  McNamara bringing to heel 220
  riding roughshod over military community 196
Perry, Mark 240
PINCHER operation 74, 76

Pleshakov, Constantine 272, 278
Poland 37, 159
POLARIS missiles 112, 113; submarines 208, 286
Potsdam Conference 40, 58, 66
Power, General Thomas 40
Prados, John 258
Putney, Diane T. 246
Pyrenees 75

Quadripartite Powers
  and Berlin crisis 179
  differences of approach between 179–80
Quarles, Donald, Deputy Secretary of Defense 97–8, 111, 113
Queseda, Lieutenant General Elwood A. "Pete" 17, 18, 23, 50, 57, 78

Rabinowitch, Eugene 43
Radford, Vice Admiral Arthur W. 54, 55, 63, 92–3
Rae, Bruce 248
Rapacki Plan 134
Rawlings, Lieutenant General Edwin W. 64, 78
Realities 96
Rearden, Steven L. 253
Reid, Whitelaw 58
Reorganization, JCS Special Committee on (Richardson Committee) 51
Rhodes, Richard 244, 249
Richardson, Brigadier General William L. 64
Richardson, James L. 264
Ridgway, General Matthew B. as SACEUR/USCINCEUR 84, 89
Roberts, Sir Frank 149
Roman, Peter J. 256
Ross, Steven T. 256
Royal Air Force (RAF) 68
Rusk, Dean (Secretary of State) 8, 200, 226, 284
  Berlin Task Force of 168
  visit to Norstad to discuss Kennedy policy paper 201

326 Index

SACEUR
  as American 230–1
  Bosnia, impact on role of
    231–2, 234–5
  differences in role in post-Cold
    War era 231
  ESDI, SHAPE and 237
  Kosovo and role of 234
  and NATO Secretary-General
    236
  and nuclear weapons policy
    233
  as operational commander
    232
  and political leadership
    233–4
  as reassurance for Allies 233
  role of 228–38
  similarities during and after
    Cold War 228–9
  see also NATO; Norstad
Sardinia 36
Schaffer, Ronald 244, 248
Schick, Jack M. 270, 274, 276
Schratz, Paul 252
Seafires 30
Senate Military Affairs
  Committee 51, 53, 60
SHAEF 76
SHAPE see Supreme
  Headquarters Allied Powers,
  Europe
Shapley, Deborah 240
Sherman, Vice Admiral Forrest G.
  42, 56, 63, 215
Sherry, Michael S. 214, 244, 249
Sicily 36
Sixsmith, E.K.G. 246
Slessor, Air Marshal Sir John C.
  37, 79
Sloss, Leon 264
Smart, General Jacob E. 22, 243,
  246
Smith, Alice Kimball 249
Smith, Jean Edward 254, 272,
  274
Smith, Perry M. 243
Snyder, William P. 265
Soapes, Dr Thomas 240

Soviet Union
  assessments of strength of 74
  authorizing GDR to function as
    Soviet agents (Agency
    Principle) 152
  deterring aggression of 228
  IRBM targets in 111
  nuclear capability of 107, 190
  peace treaty with GDR 192
  protest on NATO IRBM
    agreements 114
  weakness in withstanding
    strategic attack xii
  see also Khrushchev
Spaak, Paul-Henri (NATO
  Secretary-General) 4, 116,
  118, 127, 134–5, 218, 219,
  267, 268, 271
Spaatz, General Carl A. "Tooey",
  Air Force Chief of Staff 4,
  14, 17–18, 23, 26, 32–3, **34**,
  35, 43, 44, 47, 49, 63–64, 69
  as AAF Chief of Staff 50, **64**
Spaatz Board 44
Spector, Ronald H. 247
SPEEDWAY 76
Spitfires 29
Sputnik 5, 107, 217
Stabilization Force (SFOR) NATO
  231
Stabler, Elizabeth 263
Staercke, Ambassador André de
  118
Stalin, Joseph 228
Stanley, Timothy 258
STATE SCARLET 155
Stikker, Dirk, NATO
  Secretary-General 10, 11,
  118, 183, 209–10, 219
Strategic Air Command (SAC) 4,
  48, 60
  Coordination with SACEUR
    81–2, 86
  Operation Plan (OPLAN 14–47)
    75
Strategic Bombing Survey (SBS)
  40, 43
Strategic Reserve Army Corps
  (STRAC) 189

Index 327

Stratemeyer, Lieutenant General George E. 50
Strauss, Minister of Defense Franz-Joseph 168, 267
Stromseth, Jane E. 241
Sulzberger, C.L. "Punch" 85
Sunderman, James F. 248
"Support Aviation" concept 33
Supreme Allied Commander, Europe (SACEUR) 5, 80
  control by NAC 83
  see also EWP; Norstad
Supreme Headquarters Allied Powers, Europe (SHAPE) 56, 80, 128, 196, 236, 237
  battlefield nuclear weapons discussions at 104
  planning cell, tripartite politico-military (LIVE OAK), at 148–9
  role in Berlin crisis 145
  rumours of Norstad leaving 7
Symington, Stuart, Assistant Secretary for War 50, 55, 57
Syrett, David 246

Tactical Air Command 70
Taylor, General Maxwell D. 9, 11, 208, 221, 270
  appointment as chairman of Joint Chiefs of Staff 12
  comments on Norstad memo of 16 November 200–1
  as military advisor to Kennedy 170
Taylor, Henry J. 6
technology, military, testing of 24–5
Tedder, Air Chief Marshal Sir Arthur 34–5, **36**, **37**
Third Air Force 81
Thomas, Senator Elbert D. 54
Thompson, Ambassador Llewelyn 168, 192
Thurston, Ray 10
Time Magazine 224
TORCH, Operation 27
  air support for 28–9
  Central Task Force (landing at Oran) 28, 29–33, **30**
  Western Task Force (invading Morocco) 28
Trachtenberg, Marc 259, 262, 263, 274
TRADE WIND Berlin contingency plan 169
Tripartite Chiefs of Staff (Berlin) 157
TRIPLE PLAY PLANS 157
TROJAN 76
Truman, Margaret 40–1
Truman, President Harry S. xii, 40, 42, 251, 253, 254, 261
  on atomic weapons 91
  and Berlin blockade 67, 70
  hope for international control of atomic weapons 74
  support for unified Services 53–4, 59
  on US commitment toward Europe 80
Tunner, Major General William H. 70
Turkey
  IRBMs in 111, 125
  Soviet Union threat to 42
Twelfth Air Force 27, 28, 81
  Air Support Command 28
  Bomber Command 28
  command structure 28–9, **29**
  Fighter Command 28
  formation of 28
  "strategic elements" of, definition of 28
Twentieth Air Force
  314th Wing of 40
  Bomber Command 38, 48
  Norstad as Chief of Staff of 38
Twenty First Air Force
  Bomber Command 41
Twining, General Nathan Farraghut "Nate", Chairman of JCS 17–18, 87, 98, 196

Ultra intercepts 35
Uncertain Trumpet, The (Taylor) 170

unification bill for armed forces 50–66
  commands created in 59–60
  legislation approved for 61
  proposals sent to Truman 60–1
Unified Command Plan, approval of 60
United Kingdom *see* Britain
United Nations 71, 74
United Nations Protection Force (UNPROFOR), dependence on US of 230
United States
  air power in, interwar debate over 14
  air presence Europe, cost of 69
  armed forces: equipment of 14; size of 14
  Armed Forces, structure of 66
  Atomic Energy Act (1954) 104, 109
  commitment toward Europe 80
  elections (1952) 86
  and international Communist threat 90–1
  leadership transfer from military to civilian channels 235–6
  Mutual Security Act (1954) 120
  nuclear policy of 104
  power, diminished specialness of 232–3
  reliance on nuclear power 91
  troop levels in Europe 171
United States Air Force 3, 23
  in Berlin airlift 80
  estimates of required size 78
  Europe (USAFE) 80
  Headquarters structure 64
  lobbying with Congress 78
  units assigned to NATO 143
USCINCEUR 5
  see also Norstad

US Commander Berlin (USCOB) as single commander 194–5
US European Command (USEUCOM) 83
  establishment of 148–9
  Joint Capabilities Plan I-55 92
US News and World Report 58

V-2 rockets 26
Vandenberg, General Hoyt S. "Van", Air Force Chief of Staff 4, 14, 17–18, 23, 24, 28, 39, 64, 70, 78, 87
Vandenberg, Jr., Major-General Hoyt S. 28, 30, 35
van den Perre, Roger 224
van Rennssaler Schuyler, General Cortlandt 10
V-bombers 106
Vest, Kemper 264
"V-J Plan" 48
von Geusau, Franz A.M. Alting 241
VOPOS (GDR police) 193

Wallace Clark management consultancy 19
Wampler, Robert A. 258, 259, 261
warfare as honorable profession 26
Warsaw Pact xi, xiii, 104, 228
Washington News 6
Washington, Treaty of 232
Watkinson, Harold, British Minister of Defence 209
Watson, Major General Albert T. 175, 194, 197
weapons as ninety-nine per cent of victory 25
Welles, Benjamin 260
Westendorp, Carlos 237
Western European Union 230
Western Mediterranean (MEDOC) 129
  Norstad proposal for two commands in 129

Western Union Chiefs of Staff 76
Western Union Defense Organization 76
West Germany *see* Federal Republic of Germany
Weyland, General Otto P. **64**, 85–6
White, General Thomas D. "Tommy" 12, 17, 18, 87
Whitney, Mrs Cornelius Vanderbilt 58

Wilkinson, Burke 99
Wilt, Alan F. 246
Winchell, Walter 85

Yergin, Daniel 274
Yugoslavia 37

Zachary, G. Pascal 242
Ziegler, Philip 241
Zubok, Vladislav 272, 278
Zuckerman, Sir Solly (later Lord) 42, 43, 44, 249